Norman Jewison

A DIRECTOR'S LIFE

Norman Jewison

A DIRECTOR'S LIFE

IRA WELLS

sh.
SUTHERLAND
HOUSE
TORONTO, 2021

Sutherland House
416 Moore Ave., Suite 205
Toronto, ON M4G 1C9

Sutherland House and logo are registered
trademarks of The Sutherland House Inc.

First edition, May 2021

If you are interested in inviting one of our authors to a live event or
media appearance, please contact publicity@sutherlandhousebooks.com
and visit our website at sutherlandhousebooks.com for more
information about our authors and their schedules.

Manufactured in Canada
Cover designed by Lena Yang
Book composed by Karl Hunt
Cover photo courtesy Alamy
Leonard Cohen lyrics courtesy Hal Leonard Music
Bob Dylan lyrics courtesy Universal Music Group

Special thanks to the Norman Jewison Papers collection in the
Wisconsin Center for Film and Theater Research at the
Wisconsin Historical Society for photo permissions

Library and Archives Canada Cataloguing in Publication
Title: Norman Jewison : a director's life / Ira Wells.
Names: Wells, Ira, 1981- author.
Description: Includes bibliographical references and index.
Identifiers: Canadiana 20210124652 | ISBN 9781989555385 (hardcover)
Subjects: LCSH: Jewison, Norman, 1926- |
LCSH: Motion picture producers and directors—Canada—
Biography. | LCSH: Motion picture industry—United States—
History—20th century. | LCGFT: Biographies.
Classification: LCC PN1998.3.J49 W45 2021 |
DDC 791.4302/33092—dc23

ISBN 978-1-989555-38-5

For Michael Kovrig

I'm sentimental, if you know what I mean,
I love the country but I can't stand the scene.
– Leonard Cohen, *Democracy*

Contents

The Dance

T HE 71ST ACADEMY AWARDS CEREMONY took place at the Dorothy Chandler Pavilion on March 21, 1999. Viewers tuned in to see if the evening would belong to John Madden's *Shakespeare in Love* or Steven Spielberg's *Saving Private Ryan*. The next day, the papers declared that it belonged to the actor Roberto Benigni, who crawled over the seats and avowed his wish to "lie down in the firmament and make love to everybody." But for seven minutes, it belonged to Norman Jewison.

Now nearly 74-years-old, Jewison had been nominated for Best Director four times over a span of three decades. He would finally deliver his first Oscar speech as recipient of the Irving G. Thalberg lifetime achievement award. Jewison had always wanted big audiences for his work, and it didn't get any bigger than this: 80-million viewers saw a montage covering his greatest hits, *In the Heat of the Night, Fiddler on the Roof, Jesus Christ Superstar, The Thomas Crown Affair,* and *Moonstruck,* scenes that reminded them of why Jewison was entering a pantheon of Thalberg winners that included Walt Disney, Cecil B. DeMille, and (Jewison's hero) William Wyler. When the showreel ended, the assembled Hollywood royalty rose for an ovation, and conductor Bill Conti's orchestra burst into strains of "If I Were a Rich Man." That was Jewison's cue. He entered, dancing.

Each of Jewison's films had begun with a "dance." That was what he called the pitch, the moment when he would walk into a room and sell his idea to those who controlled the money. Audiences never saw it, but Jewison considered it the most important moment in the history of every movie. "It's part enthusiasm, part confidence in yourself," he said, "but you have to have a salesman's mentality to walk into an office of real tight-assed business people experienced in absolute corporate thinking, and you have to sell them. It's called doing your dance." Every director did it in his own way: some insisted on being at home; others could do it in an office or restaurant, but everyone did it. Coppola, Spielberg, Fellini, all "terrific salesmen," Jewison said. "Hitchcock manipulated studio people beautifully. He created an aura about himself that was just superb, I mean he played a character."[1]

Jewison, too, was a born salesman, and his ability to excite executives about his ideas was one of the keys to the stunning longevity of his career. That career began in Toronto in 1952, where he worked as a floor director on the first English-language television broadcast in Canada. He directed episodes of Canada's first television series, *The Big Revue*, and honed his craft writing and directing hundreds of hours of live television. By 1958, he was based in New York, where he revived *Your Hit Parade* for CBS and directed television specials for Harry Belafonte, Danny Kaye, and Judy Garland. At the invitation of Tony Curtis, Jewison made the leap to Hollywood for *40 Pounds of Trouble* in 1962. In 1968, his *In the Heat of the Night* beat out three epochal films—*The Graduate*, *Bonnie and Clyde*, and *Guess Who's Coming to Dinner*—to win Best Picture.[2] All told, his twenty-four motion pictures amassed a total of forty-six Academy Award nominations over four decades. *The Hurricane* was the last major Hollywood release of the century, and *The Statement* followed in 2003. Jewison's career in show business spanned the entire second half of the twentieth century, from the America of Harry S. Truman to that of George W. Bush.

The danger of a bird's-eye appreciation of Jewison's career is that the whole thing seems to take on an air of inevitability, as though he were somehow fated to direct two dozen films. But trace the career as it unfolded through the daily grind of letters, memos, meetings, minor misunderstandings and major conflicts, and you realize that it could have ended almost anywhere. Some of the films he failed to make, such as *The Confessions of Nat Turner*, left a deeper imprint than some he did. Precarity was the default condition for those working in an "art form locked up in an industry," as Jewison once put it. His twenty-four films could just as easily have been a dozen, or three, or none. The director's story is all the more meaningful when considered not in the epic sweep of decades but in the granular passage of moments, decisions that could have gone either way, human transactions influenced by individual temperaments and moods and blood sugar levels, pharmaceuticals consumed or sleep lost.

* * *

"Success or failure isn't the point in commercial Hollywood movie making," Paul Rosenfield declared in the *Los Angeles Times* in 1985, "the point is to stay in the game. And Jewison, at 58, not only has staying power, he's once again got timing."[3] Up for Best Picture for *A Soldier's Story* that year, Jewison was already considered an almost mythic veteran of the industry. And yet, improbably, Jewison would direct another nine films over the following two decades: nearly as many films in his proverbial golden years as Quentin Tarantino planned to direct in his lifetime.

Despite the geniality of his public presence, Jewison's ability to stay in the game was partly due to a private toughness. Burt Reynolds once called Jewison "the nicest director, maybe, in the history of Hollywood," before conceding, "But 'nice' doesn't explain anything about that career, does it? He must be able to kick the shit out of people in meetings."[4]

He may have been a "tough motherfucker," as fellow director Bruce McDonald remembered, but Jewison's career longevity was also the product of adaptability, a capacity for self-reinvention. He weathered epochal paradigm shifts in the film industry that swallowed the careers of all but a few contemporaries. His journey began at the end of the Studio System's "Golden Age" at Universal Pictures, with satiric Doris Day and Rock Hudson comedies that are more thoughtful than anyone remembers. He emerged among the most successful directors of the New Hollywood with *The Russians Are Coming, In the Heat of the Night,* and *The Thomas Crown Affair.* By the late-1960s, journalists were calling him "Hollywood's Hottest Director." Rocked by the assassination of Bobby Kennedy in 1968, and wanting his children to grow up far from Hollywood's influence, Jewison started a new life in London, working out of the UK's Pinewood Studios. During the gritty, auteur-driven American cinema of the 1970s, he returned to his musical roots, exploring tradition in *Fiddler on the Roof* and filming the world's first rock opera, *Jesus Christ Superstar.* By the early 1980s, with the age of the blockbuster and rise of the Hollywood conglomerate, Jewison again reinvented himself as a mid-budget, prestige filmmaker, the consummate "actor's director," to whom the stars would turn when they wanted to play against type. When Hollywood stopped financing mid-budget, adult-oriented films in the late 1990s, betting the house on blockbuster franchises, Jewison briefly persevered in the world of indie financing, with funding (and artistic priorities) split between multiple small companies. Those were some of the hardest dances of all.

At certain moments of his career, such as when he produced the Academy Awards in 1980, Jewison seemed like the consummate Hollywood insider. Yet he always felt that he was an outsider. ("Relentless Renegade" was the subtitle of a fifteen-film, six-day Lincoln Center retrospective in 2016.) His politics didn't always help. There was a period where "he was not very popular" in industry circles, acknowledges Larry Auerbach, Jewison's agent. Part of it was "an ability to be brash and outspoken," part of it was "running off to England and making speeches about this country."[5]

"People tell me he's controversial," Jennifer Jewison said of her father, "that he's a black sheep. He doesn't do sci-fi when sci-fi is popular, he doesn't do animation, he doesn't do all these things that are trendy."[6] Jewison had been conscious of a growing aesthetic gulf between himself and the industry since 1972, when *Fiddler and the Roof* lost Best Picture to *The French Connection*. "It surprised Norman when *The French Connection* won," said Michael Barker, co-President of Sony Pictures Classics. "It told him there was a change. He sees those gritty movies, and he doesn't want to make *The French Connection*. He wants to make *Rollerball*, which is a violent movie, but it's very different than *The French Connection*."[7]

Jewison's ambivalence to Hollywood came across when he told the writer Joe Eszterhas why he'd bought an ocean-facing property in Malibu. "You know why I like to sit here by the beach?" he asked, turning his back on LA "So I don't have to look at those motherfuckers back there," he said, gesturing toward Hollywood.[8]

* * *

People sometimes mistook Jewison's endurance as a measure of his power within the industry. Yet the director was keenly aware of the limits of his power. He could never initiate his own projects without the green lights from studio heads, with whom he often had deeply adversarial relationships. "I'd be fighting for money," Jewison recalled, "I'd be fighting for more shooting time, for more sets to be built which they didn't want to build. I'd be fighting to shoot on location, fighting for scenes I wanted, scenes that perhaps weren't written." It was "a constant struggle" with the studio's production head.[9]

The studios and executives changed, but the struggle for resources to execute his vision remained constant throughout his career. Perhaps over all else, this is what I discovered in the years of archival research that went into this book. The image that emerges from the thousands of pages of letters, contracts, memos, production schedules, casting notes, draft screenplays, and countless other documents is of a director fighting for every frame of his vision. No sooner had he finished his "dance" with executives than a whole series of other dances began: dances with agents, actors, production members, exhibitors, reporters. The director's life involved ceaseless struggle to get his cinematic vision out of his head and onto the screen. He was gut-wrenchingly aware of moments that fell short, scenes that didn't live up to their imaginative potential. "I don't think there ever was a film I made that wasn't less than I wanted it to be," he once said. "It was all supposed to be wonderful. All supposed to be grand. The images in my mind . . ."[10]

Over time, Jewison grew adept in the arts of leveraging the power he had. Unlike his former partner Hal Ashby, Jewison could control his anti-establishment impulses and knew how to speak to executives. He also spoke the language of movie stars, and knew the importance of keeping them on his side.

"If the stars are not in your corner, then you're weaker," he said. "Once you are established, and have the aura of a George Stevens or a

Frank Capra, you can perhaps manipulate certain stars a little bit easier by reminding them that they were there because they were chosen." Critics often associate the work of a film director with images, a certain visual signature. But much of a director's work lies in maneuvering other professionals into alignment with his creative vision. By necessity, there was always "a great deal of manipulation going on," Jewison said.[11] One of his great strengths was his ability to read, and control, very powerful people—including megalomaniacal stars who were often barely in control of themselves.

"The first thing each filmmaker does is play a character—a persona who creates confidence in the film they want to make."[12] He was talking about "the dance," but Jewison would also play different characters on set, according to the needs of his actors. A nurturing father figure, a wise older brother, an old fling—Jewison would become what his actors needed him to be. In the press, Jewison started off playing the hyperactive boy genius ("puckish," "impish," and "elfin" were reporters' adjectives of choice in those early years), and graduated, by the century's end, to an avuncular gadfly. (Only rarely, such as when one reporter noted Jewison's capacity to "freeze you with thirty seconds of breathtaking silence" if displeased by a question, did you glimpse the concealed edge of his personality.)

What those versions of Jewison fail to convey is the searing intensity of his artistic desire. "When I become involved with something, I go to bed with it," Jewison said in 1970. "It means more to me than anything in the world. Anything. When I commit myself to something, I want to commit my mind and my body and my spirit and every ounce of energy and effort I have to make it successful, to make it work. To make it somehow materialize into something that's beautiful and good and moving."[13]

Jewison always expected that the dance would get easier as he got older. He believed that after all the years of success, the films brought in on time and on budget, that he would finally have earned enough industry clout to call his own shots. But the dance only got harder as the years went by. Those close to Jewison couldn't help but notice his exasperation. "I see it a lot when he tries to sell a picture," Jennifer Jewison said. "I see that he has this wonderful idea, and it's meaningful to him, and he thinks it will be meaningful to everyone else. That's a real insecurity for him, that he's constantly slapped back, after all these years." In the mid-1980s, Jewison was heavily invested in re-making *The Man Who Could Work Miracles*, a film he'd loved since seeing it at the Beach Theatre in Toronto in 1937. He'd invested perhaps a year in preparing the script, and Richard Pryor signed on to star. Then came the rejection, first from Columbia, then from every other studio in town. "This system can be very destructive to the strong creative artists," Jewison mused around this time:

> I think it was very destructive for Orson Welles. I think it was very destructive for William Faulkner and F. Scott Fitzgerald and for many, many filmmakers. I think it's very destructive for me at times. When I become depressed and disillusioned and forsaken and nobody believes in you anymore . . . you take it personally. They don't believe your dream, you weren't successful in your dance. Well that can be kind of devastating, because that means you couldn't pull it off, you weren't clever enough. Sometimes people don't get over things like that.[14]

* * *

Jewison's capacity for disillusionment was the flip-side of his vaulting idealism. When he was working in television in the 1950s and early 60s, on those pioneering specials with Harry Belafonte and Judy Garland, he believed TV was the most important medium of communication devised in human history. In the 1960s, when he was among the first wave of directors to pry creative control from the studios, Jewison often spoke with ecstatic reverence about the power of film. He had come to artistic maturity at a time when a director could speak in unembarrassed tones about the meaning and social importance of his art. Many of Jewison's films, from *Jesus Christ Superstar* to . . . *And Justice for All* to *The Hurricane*, tell the story of embattled idealists in ways that resonate with their creator.

Yet critics struggled to find a distinctive through-line uniting movies as diverse as *The Cincinnati Kid*, *Rollerball*, *Agnes of God*, and *Moonstruck*. In their very diversity, however, these films reveal something of the director's restlessness and insatiable yearning for experience. He repeatedly pulled the plug on his life to start over—moving to New York, Los Angeles, London, and back again to split his time between his rural Ontario farm and Malibu. He was never happy in one place, personally or artistically, and his filmography reflects his restiveness and ambition. Jewison was a cinematic voluptuary who reinvented himself with the times but who never went with the flow. He never directed a sequel. He would have hung up his director's cap before directing a Marvel film, and would have hated the idea of film as "content."

Norman Jewison lived an improbably fascinating life. That life did not begin in a place of privilege, and his very name fated him to identify with history's victims. He befriended and worked for Bobby Kennedy, marched in Martin Luther King Jr.'s funeral procession, exchanged letters with Israeli Prime Minister Golda Meir, stayed in Bill Clinton's White House. His films were lauded and condemned not just by critics but by politicians and religious authorities the world over. *Jesus Christ Superstar* elicited responses from the Vatican and the Knesset; a review of *The Russians Are Coming* was entered into the US Congressional Record. His films tell the story of postwar America from the 1960s to the dawn of the twenty-first century. They also tell a more personal story of the director's commitment to Civil Rights, his political outrage, religious curiosity, sexual abandon, and artistic yearning. And they tell the story of Hollywood itself, charting the zenith and decline of the last Golden Age of American film.

Above all, they reveal the story of a survivor, a model for creative people everywhere who must fight to keep their candles burning.

CHAPTER 1

"Dying Was the Highlight of My Repertoire"

"NO JEWS, N******, OR DOGS."

The sign was posted at Kew Beach, a five-minute' walk from Norman Jewison's childhood home in the Beach district of Toronto.[1] He passed it countless times during his childhood, on summer days spent swimming and canoeing in Lake Ontario, among families whose day at the beach was not to be spoiled by the sight of a Black person or Jew. He had seen similar signs barring Jews from the nearby Balmy Beach Canoe Club, but paid them little mind. They were a feature of the environment into which he was born, as real and unremarkable as the algae and dead alewife fish that occasionally washed ashore. Still, while many of Jewison's boyhood memories took place in the shadow of that sign, much of his professional life was defined in passionate opposition to everything for which it stood. The future director of *In the Heat of the Night* and *Fiddler on the Roof* would even grow up to become a dog person.

Norman Jewison was born on July 21, 1926, in his grandmother's house on 63 Lee Avenue, not far from where he would grow up. The Beach was a rough, working-class neighborhood in the eastern reaches of Toronto. Most of its residents, as Jewison would recall, relied upon government "relief" during the Great Depression. Horses were still common on the roads of a city that awaited the arrival of traffic lights. Six-hundred-thousand people lived in Canada's largest city, 85 per cent of them white Protestants of British extraction. The churches held two services each Sunday, and Blue laws ensured that people could do little else on the Sabbath.[2]

Two of those white Protestants were Norman's parents, Joseph and Dorothy Jewison, who ran a dry goods store at the corner of Kippendavie and Queen Street East. Joseph Jewison made a specialty in women's undergarments and was known as the "Beaches corsetiere." Norman and his older sister Betty grew up in a small apartment above their parents' store, which also housed a post office. The Jewison kids were expected to help in the family business, and Norman soon discovered a natural flair for salesmanship—not that business was booming during those lean years. Each December, brother and sister sold Christmas trees on the street corner. Norman was sworn in as postmaster when he was sixteen, and tended the store when his parents were out. "It got pretty funny sometimes," he recalled, "when I ended up waiting on women who would come in to buy corsets and brassieres!"[3]

Hollywood screenwriters could not have scripted a more distinctively Canadian meet-cute for Jewison's parents, who met while tobogganing in Toronto's Riverdale Park. Dorothy Jewison (nee Weaver) was born in Wells, Somerset, and immigrated to Canada from England in 1905 at the age of nine. Joseph Jewison, known as Percival Innes Jewison before changing his name, hailed from Millbrook, Ontario.[4]

Norman's great-grandfather emigrated from Yorkshire, England to a Protestant settlement near Cork in Southern Ireland, where he married a squire's daughter, flew off to the colonies, and pioneered a farm on Rice Lake in south-eastern Ontario.[5] His father's family was a "rather joyless lot" of teetotaling Calvinists, remembers Norman, although he also grew to admire their unyielding work ethic and integrity. He would often unspool a bit of family lore about his great-grandfather delivering his yearly harvest of wheat to the Port Hope granary. "When he pulled up after a two-day journey, the mill owner would ask how much grain was in the wagon. Great-grandfather would tell him there were so many tons and the miller would always say, 'Okay, dump it in because it's Joseph Jewison, and we don't have to weigh his wheat.'"[6]

Norman would always think of the Jewisons as "farm people." After two decades in New York, Los Angeles, and London, he bought a farm near Caledon, Ontario in 1978, where he would spend much of the next forty years. Having only ever lived in big cities, he thought of the farm as a return to roots.

Norman progressed from Kew Beach Public School to Malvern Collegiate, where he was a few years ahead of Glenn Gould. One of the most formative influences on his education was Bertha Jewison, an unmarried aunt who cultivated in her nephew a love for literature, music, and poetry. Norman spent his early summers at Aunt Bea's cottage on Lake Simcoe, where he also acquired a lifelong love of nature (two of his later production companies would be called Simcoe and Algonquin Productions). By six, Bertha had Norman reading Macaulay's *History of England* and reciting Psalms from memory. This was followed by a steady diet of Charles Dickens and Sir Walter Scott. Aunt Bea paid for lessons at the Royal Conservatory of Music, where Norman studied piano and musical theory, and forced him to memorize poetry. "She would *pound* it into me," he remembered.[7]

Norman soon discovered a fondness for the spotlight. His mother had a carnival game, knock-down-the-bottle, three balls for a nickel, that she toured around the fall fairs of Uxbridge, Markham, and other small Ontario towns. Norman's job was to serve as the carnival barker, which he executed with relish.[8] By seven, he was a familiar sight in lodge halls across the Beaches, where he regaled audiences with the "strange things done in the midnight sun / By the men who moil for gold." Audiences found something amusing, even faintly freaky, about the boy's dramatic rendition of Robert W. Service's lurid rhymes. "He had a wonderful memory. He could recite poems and remember stories so well," recalled Betty Robertson, his sister. "He's a good storyteller. Always was."[9]

He was also an enterprising kid who could always find a way to scrape together a few cents during the Great Depression. Sometimes he walked horses around Woodbine racetrack; sometimes he charged for his amateur theatrics. Jewison recalled going to the Allen and Beach theatres in East Toronto, where admission was ten cents or a jar of food (destined not for any foodbank but for the mouths of hungry employees). He would then charge neighborhood kids two cents apiece to watch his re-creations of the films. "I used to do all the sound effects," he recalled. "I guess I started telling stories that way." The invariable highlight of the show were the elaborate death scenes: "dying," as he would later write, "was the highlight of my repertoire."

To the chagrin of family members, Norman's death scenes were not reserved for his paying audience. "Every night Norman decided that he knew a new way of killing himself," Betty recalled decades later, with a residue of sisterly disdain. "Every night, at dinner table, he would do this: 'I found a new way to die! Watch, watch!'"[10] He would grab his chest, pop his eyes, gasp, lurch from his chair, and expire.

* * *

What with the carnival barking, poetry recitals, and his thousand ways to die, Jewison seemed destined for the stage. At Malvern Collegiate, he wrote and directed school musicals. "We used to write original songs for them," he recalled, and "they were quite successful."[11] He performed scat songs in Cabbagetown for anyone who would listen. While his mother nurtured his performative nature, his father was skeptical that Norman's theatrics would lead anywhere productive. "I don't think any family in those days supported the idea that someone wanted to be an actor," Norman recalled. "My dad just wanted me to get a job."[12] He would later describe his parents as "very real. They brought me down to earth. There was no false praise in our family." He would always remember how, after the premiere of *In the Heat of the Night*, his mother hugged Sidney Poitier and "told him that he was a good boy and did his lines well."[13]

Even after he'd begun his ascent in show business, Norman was aware of the faint praise emanating from Queen and Kippendavie. Once, after his first special with Harry Belafonte had aired on American television, the *Toronto Star* sent a reporter to interview Norman's father about his accomplishment. The reporter asked if he'd seen it and, as Norman recalled, Joseph answered, "Yeah, by God, I saw it . . . you mean with that Black fella on it, Belafonte!" But what had he thought of his son's work? "Well, I thought it was alright, you know. To tell you the truth, he didn't do any songs I know. He didn't do 'Take Me Out to the Ballgame,' or a real toe-tapper like that. But yeah, I liked it."[14]

Norman's piercing desire for parental approval led to what he would later call "one of the most traumatic moments of my life." Joseph and Dorothy came to visit him in California in 1962, for a special advance screening of *40 Pounds of Trouble*, his first picture. According to Norman, they could barely wrap their minds around the fact that their son had made a movie, and had only the vaguest idea of what he had been doing in Hollywood. Prior to the screening, Norman's wife, Dixie, prepared an elaborate roast pork dinner—she spent an afternoon finding a Los Angeles butcher who left the skin on the pork for crackling, the way Joseph liked it at home. Norman had arranged a studio limo to take them to the screening after dinner. It was his parents' first time in a limousine and Norman wanted them to be impressed with their bigshot Hollywood son. The armed guard waved them through at the Universal studio gate, and they seated themselves in the empty screening room. Norman's father wondered why they were all alone in the theatre. Then, with exquisite pomposity, and to his eternal embarrassment, Norman looked up at the projectionist's booth and said, "Okay, roll 'em." ("I really did. I was that corny. I was trying to impress my parents and wanted that pat on the head.")[15]

The lights went down, the curtain parted, and Norman's parents gazed upon their son's handiwork. Joseph leaned over to ask if there was a newsreel. Norman explained that there was not, that this was the movie. For the next 100-or-so minutes, his parents sat in silence. *40 Pounds of Trouble* was supposed to be an uproarious comedy, with wild, Keystone Cop style humour, but Joseph and Dorothy Jewison might have been in church. "Not a laugh, not a snicker, not a peep out of them at all," Norman remembered. "No reaction." Finally, the lights came up. "My heart was in my mouth," he recalled. He looked at his parents, yearning for affirmation. Then his mother burped a deep, aromatic burp. She thumped her chest and said, "Gosh, it must have been the roast pork."

"Well, I thought it was very good," Joseph announced. "I especially liked the part when the little girl cried. How did you make her cry?"

"I told her some terrible things, Dad. Let's go."

The limo took them home. "I was never more totally defeated in my life to that point because I felt that they didn't understand," Norman said. Only later would he realize how nervous his parents were, how alien the whole thing must have been. Back in Toronto, his mother dragged everyone she knew to the film and gave newspaper interviews about how wonderful it was. "But they couldn't tell me, because we are a very uptight, Canadian, bourgeois Victorian family that found it hard to express our feelings to each other.

"But God, I'll never forget that night."[16]

* * *

For children growing up in Canada during the Great Depression, "film director" was not high on the list of viable occupations. Movies might as well have come from Mars. Jewison's parents rarely took him to the cinema. His father's idea of a good time was an afternoon at the "Hipp"—Shea's Hippodrome, the vast, 2700-seat vaudeville theatre located at Terauley (now Bay) and Queen. Before it was demolished to make way for Toronto's new City Hall, the Renaissance-style Hippodrome was one of the great vaudeville venues in North America (a Wurlitzer organ, orchestra pit, a dozen opera boxes, and ornate plaster moldings on the 'electrified' ceiling), attracting once-famous acts like Kip and Kippy, the Karnos Comedy Company, and Jack Benny.[17] Coin-operated candy dispensers built into each seat meant that kids could indulge without even visiting the lobby.[18] Jewison always remembered seeing Jimmy Durante, one of the world's great vaudeville stars, famous for his song: "Ink, a dink a dink, a dink a doo, a dink a dee / Oh what a tune for croonin' / Ink, a dink a dink, a dink a doo, dink a dee / It's got the whole world swoonin.'" Durante had little Norman swoonin.' "I had a love affair with Jimmy Durante," he said. "I thought he was great."[19]

But Jewison also loved his afternoons in the Beach theatre which consisted of two movies, the news, and a cartoon, lasting from 2:00 p.m. to 5:30 p.m. "I was influenced by all kinds of movies when I was a kid," he recalled. One of his favourites was *Gunga Din*, the 1939 George Stevens movie based on the Rudyard Kipling poem. He was very fond of Laurel and Hardy, and of Mack Sennett's Keystone Cops. "I loved that kind of slapstick, staged humour, and visual jokes," he said.[20] Jewison would always remember what it felt like to emerge from the theatre, squinting as his eyes adjusted to the late-afternoon sun.[21]

Perhaps the film that left the deepest imprint on his youth was Alexander Korda's 1937 *The Man Who Could Work Miracles*, a comic Faust tale in which celestial beings bestow God-like abilities upon an ordinary shopkeeper to see how humans would cope with such power. Based on H.G. Wells's 1898 short story (Wells also co-wrote the screenplay), with its mild socialist critique of the English elite, *Miracles* may have crystalized in Jewison's youthful imagination a connection between the cinema and an ability to change the world. "I saw [*Miracles*] when I was ten years old in the east end of Toronto and I never forgot it for the rest of my life," he recalled.[22] The fantasy of playing God, changing the world for the better—it seized his imagination, and the idea that films *themselves* were magic, that movies could bring miraculous change in the world, would become an *idée fixe* for Jewison, although he would also fight against it at various points in his long career.

A desire to remake the world was palpable in 1930s Toronto. Jewison remembered "communist meetings by the boardwalk, near the lake, on hot summer evenings with the moths swarming around the streetlights and young men making passionate speeches about the threat of fascism and the Spanish Civil War."[23] Meanwhile, members of what the papers called the "swastika movement" were engaging in their own, equally passionate demonstrations in support of fascism and Hitler.

One summer night, three weeks after Jewison's seventh birthday, tensions erupted after a Willowvale Park baseball game between Harbord Playground (with mostly Jewish and Italian players) and a team sponsored by St. Peter's Catholic Church. After the final out, someone unfurled a large white blanket emblazoned with a swastika. The field had been surrounded by the "Pit Gang," several hundred youths "openly flourishing pieces of metal pipe, chains, wired broom handles, and even rockers from chairs," as the *Toronto Star* described the group.[24] Cries of "Heil Hitler!" pierced the air. The ensuing riot, ostensibly over possession of the swastika flag, attracted as many as 10,000 Torontonians and "soon developed in violence and intensity of racial feeling into one of the worst free-for-alls ever seen in the city," the paper reported the following day.

"Heads were opened, eyes blackened and bodies thumped and battered as literally dozens of persons, young and old, many of them non-combatant spectators, were injured more or less seriously by a variety of ugly weapons."[25] The following night, members of the Pit Gang reconvened in the park for an encore; rather than dispersing the "hoodlum street gang," police positioned on Harbord street warned Jews to keep their distance. Eventually, the gang began roaming the streets in search of Jews, where they surrounded a twenty-two-year-old medical student named Louis Sugarman, "pummeling him with their fists and inflicting acute damage on his head with a heavy iron pipe."[26] Witnesses claimed that police efforts to pursue the perpetrators was lackadaisical. After Toronto Mayor Walter Stewart banned citizens from flaunting the swastika, reporters uncovered that "scores of Toronto constables today carry swastikas around on their keyrings" and that the emblem was stamped on locker keys at a police motorcycle depot. Asked if Toronto police would stop carrying the swastika keychains, the Deputy Police Chief replied, "I hardly think we'll go that far, except under orders."[27]

Anti-Semitism was woven into the social fabric of a city in which Jews were banned from hotels and beaches and blocked from entering the professions. Two major publications, *The Telegram* and *Saturday Night*, were openly prejudiced against Jews.[28] And Toronto's anti-Semitism was a physical reality for a boy named Jewison in the 1930s. Norman remembers being called "Jewy" and "Jew-boy" from the age of three or four. He befriended Jewish kids in the neighbourhood—everyone thought he was Jewish, anyway, and there was safety in numbers, although they were still beaten up from time to time. Jewison's best friend in these years was a Jewish kid named Sidney, whose parents ran a dry-cleaning store. Jewison would join the family for Sabbath dinner on Friday nights, borrowing Sidney's spare yarmulke. One night, he mispronounced a Yiddish word and outed himself as an "Anglo." "I wasn't invited back to Sabbath dinner anymore," Jewison remembers. "Embraced by the family because of my name, then rejected from the Christian community because of my name, then rejected from the Jewish community when they found out I was Christian."[29]

"The whole thing of carrying this name that starts out with the letters J-E-W—it affected me deeply," Jewison later said. Even as an adult, he couldn't get into a Scarsdale golf club. "One thing that really sets me off is any kind of racial prejudice or intolerance," he said. "I am deeply offended by that."[30] Others of Jewison's generation would arrive at anti-racist attitudes by way of education. Jewison's anti-racism, no less than his affinity for poetry, was pounded into him by experience.

Jewison would always remember his first visit to the United States. At eight, his parents took him to view the Niagara Falls from the American side of the border. His most vivid memory of the excursion was not the six million cubic feet of water plummeting over the falls each minute, but the fact that American police officers wore guns. "I went up to one and asked if I could touch it," Jewison later recalled.[31] It was his first glimmer of awareness of the cultural differences that existed between the two countries in which Jewison would spend most of his life.

Those differences became more obvious to Jewison, who had done a stint in the Canadian Navy after high school, while travelling through the American South in 1945. The war over, he had been ordered to take his sixty leave days and demobilize. While in Memphis, Tennessee, and still in his Navy uniform, he boarded a bus and flopped down in the back. "You tryin' to be smart, sailor," the driver yelled. Jewison was nonplussed. "Can't you read the fucking sign?" hollered the driver. Jewison looked up to see a crude sign hanging from a wire: "Colored people in the rear."[32] While there is no verifying whether Jewison grabbed his bag and removed himself from the bus, as he claims, his experience of what he often called "apartheid" in the American South left a lasting impression. He would often cite this moment as an origin of *In the Heat of the Night*.

* * *

In the fall of 1947, Jewison first ascended the steps of Victoria College in the University of Toronto, where he had enrolled as an undergraduate. With its vaulting red turrets and spires, Romanesque arches, and fantastical gargoyles peering down from their hidden recesses, "Old Vic" was a fitting intellectual home for Professor Northrop Frye, whose *Fearful Symmetry*, published the year Jewison arrived, redefined the study of William Blake. (By the time Jewison was installed as Victoria's Chancellor in 2004, Frye's name would adorn a building of its own). In Burwash dining hall, Queen Victoria's Royal Standard, which draped her coffin in 1901, was displayed on a wall above High Table, where the professors had lunch. The atmosphere at Vic may have been redolent with scholarly tradition, but the 1940s campus could also be a raucous place. Residents of the all-male "Gate House" were known for their rugged hazing rituals, boisterous caroling, and "incessant pounding" of their table in Burwash. Keith Davey, one of Jewison's friends (and a future Canadian Senator), once contracted an airplane to fly over the campus and drop leaflets on students, encouraging them to attend a campus event; an unopened bundle of leaflets nearly crushed passers-by.[33]

Jewison's experience in the Navy's entertainment unit had nourished his love of the stage. His fleeting interest in becoming a journalist (preferably in some far-flung, war-shattered region) was overtaken by a desire to become an actor. While an undergraduate at Vic, he also discovered the joy of directing other performers. He became involved with the "Vic Bob," a major social event and theatrical extravaganza ("apples and cider, song and skit, violin and cheers") which in those days served to initiate new students and nurture a "friendly antagonism" between the first- and second-year classes. Despite the "tendency for college shows to be quite lusty when the moderating influence of girls is absent," a writer for *Acta Victoriana*, the College's longstanding journal, praised a "diversified and highly imaginative" performance "built around the showmanship of Norm Jewison, one of Vic's finest entertainers."[34] Stages around the University of Toronto (including the 1949 *All Varsity Revue*, which he directed and co-wrote) provided important early experiences in writing, staging, and working with actors—a toolkit from which the director of *Fiddler on the Roof* and *Jesus Christ Superstar* would continue to draw.

If Victoria College was where Jewison acquired his first experiences as a director, it was also where, over cups of Murray's coffee and plates of shepherd's pie at Burwash Hall, Jewison acquired certain artistic values, ideas about art's reason for being, which would inform the rest of his life. Three decades later, in conversation with a Soviet writer, Jewison would mention "an old teacher who used to say that art educates us in specific ways and leads us in specific directions."[35] The "old teacher" was Northrop Frye, and the "education" was eventually distilled in *The Educated Imagination* (1962), in which Frye tried to articulate, for a lay audience, the value of creative expression. Frye claimed there were three "levels of the mind," each with its own distinctive kind of language: first was the ordinary language of self-expression; second was the more technical language of science, law, religion, and the professions. But what most interested Frye, and what he impressed upon his students, was the value of "imaginative" language used "not to describe nature, but to show you a world completely absorbed and possessed by the human mind." The imagination involved "the power of constructing possible models of human experience," Frye wrote. It was our capacity to compare how our world functions, what we literally do in this life, with what we "can imagine being done."[36]

At the time, of course, Jewison's great aspiration was to amuse university students with slapstick song-and-dance numbers. If he also impressed Inge Hansen, the Scandinavian brunette with whom he'd fallen in love at the U of T, so much the better. In truth, Jewison would never fully outgrow the populist sensibilities he picked up in the vaudeville halls and honed in his early musical comedies. But Frye's ideal of the educated imagination provided Jewison with an aspirational model of the artistic vocation. As a mature filmmaker, Jewison would often emphasize the primacy of the "idea" behind his films, that any film worthy of the medium needed a *raison d'être*. For Jewison, that *raison* resided precisely in the "power of constructing possible models of human experience"—in revealing the discrepancy between the world as it is and how we can imagine it.

In 1950, what Jewison wanted to imagine was a job, something besides waiting tables or driving a Diamond cab, which he did briefly after graduation. Despite his passion for performing, his skills as an actor were not in high demand. Working as a hotel waiter one summer, he finagled a part as a railroad worker fleeing marauding Indians in a western called *Canadian Pacific*; try as he might, he never could spot himself in the finished picture. In a final attempt to jumpstart his acting career, he hitch-hiked to Hollywood and tried to connect with the few actors and film professionals he knew. Within a week, he had exhausted both his industry leads and his meagre funds. He checked out of his flea-bag hotel in Santa Monica and tried to sleep on the beach near the Pier, but it was too cold. He eventually retreated to an apartment lobby, partially concealed beneath a stairwell. It was there, huddled beneath a Mexican shawl he'd bought his mother, that Jewison knew that he would never "make it" as an actor in Hollywood. He started hitch-hiking home the next day.[37]

Back with his parents on Queen Street and chastened by his Hollywood rejection, Norman was increasingly vulnerable to his father's admonitions to get a proper job. He reluctantly applied for a junior Foreign Affairs role, a tentative step toward a career as a bureaucrat. At the same time, however, an alternate gateway to show business presented itself. Like many young Canadians in 1950, Norman was enamored with the emerging medium of television. He'd sit for hours in the Silver Rail Tavern on Yonge Street, watching the fuzzy black-and-white image broadcast from Buffalo. Now, he discovered, the Canadian Broadcasting Corporation intended to establish a television network of its own.[38]

Television was coming to Canada, and Jewison was determined to become part of it.

CHAPTER 2

The Pixie of Jarvis Street

CANADIAN TELEVISION WENT LIVE AT 7:15 P.M. on September 8, 1952. The first televised image broadcast from CBC-TV's Toronto studios was an upside-down, left-to-right CBC identification logo.

Jewison, who was working as a floor director on opening night, recalls the feeling of "total chaos" in the Jarvis street studio. "Live TV was an adrenaline rush like nothing you could imagine," he said. The studio floor was a welter of activity: Jewison remembers the "stage manager, floor director, and people pulling cables and cameras around. Maybe twenty-five people tied together by headphones, trying not to bump into each other. Backstage, writers are cutting things, last minute. Your orchestra leader is working on arrangements until air time. Actors are throwing up." Then you're live, and anything can happen.[1]

In 1951, Jewison had met with Stuart Griffiths, the twenty-nine-year-old head of CBC English language television in Toronto. With the network's studios still in the early stages of construction, Griffiths advised Jewison to seek out any television experience he could get, so he set his sights on the BBC. In London, Jewison appealed to the Canadian television personality Bernard Braden, host of the BBC's *Bedtime with Braden*, and ended up working as Braden's stand-in during rehearsals for thirteen weeks. He also pitched in as a writer.[2] Mostly, he kept his eyes open, absorbing technical knowledge about TV production. To pay rent for his modest boardinghouse room in Notting Hill, he babysat for his future CBC colleague Don Harron, and acted in small roles here and there, although acting wasn't as lucrative as babysitting. Jewison's highlight upon the British stage was "as the ass-end of a cow in a third-rate British panto production of *Aladdin* at the Woolwich Armoury theatre." London also provided Jewison with a taste of real poverty: a personal low-point arrived when he found himself shoplifting a turnip.[3] It came as a relief when Stuart Griffiths invited Jewison to join a new trainee program in CBC's television division. He became one of the original 296 employees of the corporation's English-language television division. As the CBC Radio personality Peter Gzowski later recalled, they would hire anyone with glasses.[4]

With the CBC's television studio still under construction, the trainees congregated for a crash-course in TV production in nearby Quonset huts. The CBC partnered with broadcast pioneer Sylvester Weaver (Sigourney Weaver's father would become President of NBC the following year), who dispatched advisors to help train the upstart Canadians. On January 15, 1952, Jewison scrawled notes on the "History of Television," covering innovations from the invention of the electroscope in 1753 and the microphone in 1829 to the discovery of the cathode ray in 1859. The next day, Jewison wrote "T.V. Technical Philosophy" at the top of a piece of standard binder paper and drew a simple diagram illustrating televisual transmission, from a photo-sensitive tube with silver globules in the image orthicon through a path of electrons to coils in a receiver tube within the viewer's television set. "When light strikes, photo-cathode converts light to electric impulses which by means of the image focus and image accelerator are shot back to the target," Jewison wrote in his notes.[5]

Later sessions introduced trainees to "TV-Video Tools": cameras (mountings, lenses, cranes), monitors (master, preview, floor), projection equipment, lighting equipment, switching equipment. Jewison let it all soak in, learning about depth of field, defocusing, reversal composition. Another consultant taught trainees about the various positions and functions within a television studio (audio operator, video operator, tech producer, and so on; the studio director, soon to be Jewison's role, was "responsible for all people in studio.") Trainees were introduced to the different genres of TV "presentation": news, drama, variety, dancing, opera, puppets. They got deeper into photography ("the diameter of the lens divided into the focal length gives aperture," Jewison put down in his notes), learned the basic principles of composition and design, and learned to avoid or work around the technological limitations of the medium: spurious visual effects (halo, ghost, clouding, streaking), limited detail resolution and luminance transfer distortion (which could cause the normal contrast range of 20:1 to increase or decrease). Particular care was given to the intricacies of lighting, the "chief objective" of which was to "reproduce the human form with beauty and dramatic effect, particularly that portion which is not clothed," according to one training document.

Jewison's copious notes reveal the enormous effort required of the trainees simply to get a handle on the technical execution of televisual transmission, prior to any consideration of what was televised.[6] A safety document reminded trainees that "a lens will not bounce," and that they should not attempt to repair microphones or lights: "Remember, you'll be dead a long time." Given the technical complexities, and the general inexperience of all involved, mishaps were inevitable.

"The things I saw!" Jewison would later marvel. "Directors losing their cool, screaming like lunatics. Sets collapsing. People falling down. Cameras getting lost. But when it worked, the high was incredible."[7]

Meanwhile, when he wasn't learning about spotlights and lenses and image orthicon tubes, Jewison had pursued the life of a twenty-five-year-old bachelor in Toronto. And he had met Dixie.

* * *

The daughter of a well-to-do stockbroker, Margaret Ann ("Dixie") Dixon drove a yellow convertible and seemed to exist on a different and higher plane than Norman. Indeed, her large brown eyes were often looking down at him from billboards around Toronto, where she was the face of "Black Cat" cigarettes. History differs on whether Norman and Dixie met at a party (Jewison's version) or on a blind date before he left for England (as their daughter Jennifer Jewison recalls). But there was little disagreement on how Dixie felt toward her suitor.

"Mom couldn't stand Dad," Jennifer said. Four years younger than Norman, Dixie "was like this little princess, you know," who had grown up in relative luxury and affluence. Norm Jewison, meanwhile, was an artsy scamp then making his living writing dialogue for a cantankerous bald puppet named Uncle Chichimus. "He was scuzzy, you know," said Jennifer. Her mother always emphasized "how scuzzy he was. He was wearing sandals and he had a beard and he had beads and was all dirty, you know, he was an artist. He wasn't a businessman like her daddy. Of course, *her* mom was just outraged . . . apparently, she didn't really accept him until after her first grandchild."[8] Jennifer's vision of a sandaled, bearded Jewison doesn't align with the clean-shaven man in the suit and tie who appears in all the photos from this period. But while the beads and sandals wouldn't arrive until the mid-1960s, Jennifer's recollection reveals how her father was perceived by his future in-laws.

At the CBC, meanwhile, Jewison was learning his craft on *The Big Revue*, the network's flagship variety show. Filmed in CBC's Studio A on a budget of $6,000 per week, any given episode featured an assortment of jugglers, fiddlers, dancers, and sketch comics.[9] The show was not always the most finely wrought urn of entertainment. Once, a performer in a bird costume began her musical number carrying two pigeons, who promptly filled her hands with shit on live television. Then there was an awkward segment in which a hypnotist reduced the host into a semi-conscious, blubbering mass (Parliament banned hypnotists from the airwaves that year, perhaps fearing mass mind control).[10] Still, interest in the hour-long variety format was immense—8,000 Canadians auditioned to sing or dance for television in 1957—and Jewison soon made a name for himself in the area of sketch comedy.[11] His occasionally biting sense of humour also attracted attention. A magazine profile later described a rehearsal in which "a well-known actor complained to Jewison that the television crew was not according him his due respect. The young director grabbed a studio microphone and boomed, 'Let's show a little respect for what's-his-name!'"[12]

In July 1953, Dixie overcame whatever dreams she may have had of landing a doctor or businessman and married the director of a puppet show. (To be fair, Uncle Chichimus had evolved a topical and surreal sense of humour as the episodes went on. Jewison was amazed by what a puppet could get away with saying on TV.) Norman and Dixie settled into a house on Bingham Avenue in the Beaches. Their first son, Kevin, arrived in 1956. Michael followed in 1958. Lullabies, first words, bedroom doors left open just a crack. The routines of early marriage and childrearing offered a vision of an entire life that could unfold on leafy Beach avenues, within a one-mile radius of where they had grown up.

Inside the yellow brick CBC-Television studio, the "Pixie of Jarvis Street," as one journalist had dubbed Jewison, continued to thrive. *The Big Revue* and Uncle Chichimus led to *Jazz with Jackson*, *Wayne and Shuster*, and the *Barris Beat*, which Jewison considered "one of the most sophisticated Canadian shows." As the episodes and years ticked by, his interest migrated from sketch comedy to music. His ability to read music, all those hours at the piano at the insistence of Aunt Bea, gave him a leg up other directors, because he could plan the movement of images in unison with the music. Over time, however, Jewison started to butt heads with CBC brass over creative control. At one point, after he felt that the CBC hadn't sufficiently backed him in a conflict with General Electric, the sponsor of *Sunday Night Showtime*, Jewison resigned as director-producer. He couldn't stand creative interference.

Then, one day in 1958, a performer who had appeared in Jewison's shows presented a reel of her clips to an agent at William Morris in New York. As the film unspooled, the agent found himself less interested in the performer than in what was happening behind the scenes. Who directed this stuff?[13]

Larry Auerbach, who was to become Jewison's agent at William Morris, encouraged Norman to send him a clip reel of his own. That reel found its way to Michael Dann, the powerful head of east-coast programming at CBS. When Dann asked what Jewison did, Auerbach answered, "Well, he does everything . . . he choreographs, he designs, directs, produces."

Dann showed Jewison's reel to Bob Banner, a top variety producer in the United States, who assured him that the work was the product of a genuine talent. "Well that is all I had to hear because he was in Toronto and had a lot of talent," Dann said, "that was just great for me. I knew he would come cheap."[14] They arranged for Jewison to fly to New York for an interview.

Dann would become an influential executive responsible for bringing the *Mary Tyler Moore Show*, the Smothers Brothers, and *60 Minutes* to the airwaves. Already, he was a force in the industry. He took an immediate dislike to Jewison. "The kid walked into my office in sneakers. In denims. And Norman looked very young for his age," Dann said.

"I'm very impressed by your work," the executive said.

"You like it, huh," Jewison replied, in what Dann remembers as his "little pixie voice."

Dann was flummoxed. "No 'thank you' or anything else," he recalled. "I said, 'how would you like to work in New York?' He said something like, 'what's so great about New York?' I knew right away that I was dealing with a pretty fresh kid. I didn't like him. I was about to give this guy a big opportunity at that big time and he was saying, 'so what.'"[15]

In Auerbach's telling of these events, Jewison merely expressed some "trepidation" about moving to New York. He knew that Dixie was unenthusiastic about uprooting their comfortable life in Toronto and abandoning those visions of all that might unfold on leafy Beach avenues. But Jewison's clashes with CBC execs were getting worse. "By 1958, when I was doing *The Barris Beat*, I felt there was no leadership at the top of the CBC," he said. "The executives were afraid of anything that smacked of good showmanship or theatricality. And I'd gotten to the point where I didn't even really care."[16] No one would begrudge his showmanship at CBS, where his work would find a bigger audience and he would earn more money. He also appreciated that Americans regarded show business with a certain respect. Canadians loved their TV, but they also loved to peer down their noses at those who produced it.

Dann offered him $175 per week. Jewison haggled him up to $300, and signed the deal.

Larry Auerbach's next "assignment" was to find the Jewisons somewhere to live within their price range. They would ultimately settle on a two-bedroom apartment near Van Cortland Park, in the northern reaches of the Bronx. From the CBS studios, Jewison would take the D train as far north as it went, then a bus—more than an hour's journey. They signed a one-year lease, rented furniture, and squashed the cockroaches. Norman, who worked late most nights, was almost never home. Dixie, pregnant with their third child, almost never left the apartment. He was so engrossed in his own work that he barely noticed how difficult things were at home.

For Auerbach, one matter remained before getting his client on track for a successful career in New York: the matter of the J-E-W in Jewison. Norman recalls his shock when, on an early trip to New York, Auerbach asked, "Have you ever thought of changing your name? Jewison sounds a little too Jewish."

"I looked at him and said, 'Larry, you're Jewish.'" Even decades after the fact, Jewison's eyes still grew wide with incredulity.[17]

* * *

Jewison's assignment at CBS was to rejuvenate *Your Hit Parade*, which staged performances of the week's top ten songs. The problem with the show was baked into its format. As hit songs stuck around for week after week, they became increasingly hard to stage in new ways. Perry Lafferty, an expert in the variety form, was brought in as a producer and given a clean slate. Next came Jewison, as director. Within three weeks, Lafferty and Jewison created what Dann later described as "perhaps the greatest creative team in the history of the variety show . . . and they did *Hit Parade*, as tough as it was, so beautifully, so magnificently . . . they were all young kids, and they worked and killed themselves."[18]

Auerbach remembers Jewison's work on *Your Hit Parade* in more measured terms. "He did a nice job. You know, the show was the show, whatever it was." Everyone agreed that Jewison's real advance came with the program he directed next. Jewison's work on the *Andy Williams Show*, Dann said, was "extraordinarily good . . . one of the best variety shows." Designer Mike Smith, who worked with Jewison on *Andy Williams*, described it as a "turning point" in their lives.[19] It was on *Andy Williams*, Auerbach said, that Jewison started to make "a considerable impression in this country with his ability."[20]

Jewison stood out from other directors in two respects. "He understood, or had a good feel for, lighting," Auerbach recalled, "and he excited his crews." Auerbach remembers how, in the days of live television, directors would speak to their performers over a microphone. Jewison "would get close to his microphone and direct a move, and he would talk to the talent in such a way it was like they were having a sexual affair. I mean he would make love to them over the mic to coax them, get them into the feeling, the movement. It was marvelous chemistry."[21]

"I think the greatest gift that he had at the beginning was his beguiling personality, to cajole people to do exactly what he wanted," Dann said.[22]

He could also be extraordinarily stubborn when it came to his creative integrity. Unlike most directors, Jewison refused to direct the commercials interspersed throughout his live TV broadcasts. "I believed deeply that it was somehow demeaning to take a great medium of communication and spend so much time on something as uninvolving as Ronny Reagan talking about a G.E. refrigerator," he said later.[23]

Auerbach remembers a blow-up on *The Big Party*, Jewison's assignment after *Andy Williams*. At the time, *The Big Party* was a "big to do," Auerbach said, with high-profile stars including Rock Hudson. Almost immediately, however, Jewison began to feel that Revlon, the show's sponsor, had become accustomed to an undo level of artistic influence on the show. Jewison would not be dictated to by sponsors. "It got so uncomfortable that after two shows, he left the show, without a job," Auerbach remembers. Jewison may have suspected that the show was doomed to fail for other reasons, but Auerbach was astonished that his client, with two small kids at home and a third on the way, would walk away from work with nothing else lined up.[24]

For Dann, Jewison's tenacity was tinged with arrogance, as though he didn't take his colleagues seriously. "He didn't take *me* seriously," Dann said. "Norman was always brash, cocky, ready to fight the system—whatever system it was," said Auerbach. "Maybe it was because he was poor as a kid. I really don't know where it came from." Dann remembers that Jewison would "walk into the office and treat me like the office boy, simply because he refused to show any deference to me—and he shouldn't have shown any deference to me—but he wanted to make sure I knew it." Dann may have been the first executive that Jewison didn't afford the customary respect, but he was far from the last.[25]

* * *

Jewison's television career took another evolutionary step forward with a series of hour-long "specials" devoted to a single performer. The first, *Tonight with Belafonte*, which aired December 10, 1959, was also the first American television special dedicated to a Black performer.[26]

Harry Belafonte was at the height of his popularity. Following the release of his breakthrough album *Calypso* in 1956, Belafonte had sold out clubs and arenas, toured Europe, and played Carnegie Hall. The TV special was an opportunity to connect with Americans in their own homes. Belafonte wanted not only to introduce viewers to a greater range of African American music with nuance and sensitivity, but also to situate that music within an intergenerational frame of family and community. The special was not business as usual, and Belafonte wanted to signal his revolutionary intent through the very look of the show.

"We had a meeting at Belafonte's house where he gave a half-hour speech on how 'I don't want scenery, I don't want any of that,'" remembers designer Gary Smith. The performer was objecting to the usual pretty curtains and drapes then favoured on television stages. "Scenery," he said, "is also a big length of rusty chain, it's a piece of rag that's hanging with barbed wire behind it" to delineate a jail.[27]

Smith remembers *Tonight with Belafonte* as "one of the most artistic" hours of television ever produced. Beginning with the nineteenth-century folk song "Shenandoah," *Tonight with Belafonte* presented a striking array of African American creative expression. Together with the singer Odetta, twelve dancers, and a twenty-six-voice chorus, the performer sang songs from the chain gang, spirituals, love songs, and playful nonsense lyrics. Between numbers, the program cut to images of Black portraits, faces upturned in spiritual anguish or ecstasy. One of Jewison's favourite moments featured Belafonte on a playground, singing Leadbelly's nonsense lyric "Mo Yet" to an interracial group of children. This was followed by "Hole in the Bucket" with Odetta (which would reach the Billboard charts the following year). The contrasting moods of solemnity and mischievousness, the power of the Belafonte chorus, the spare, expressionistic staging—*Tonight with Belafonte* was stirring television. "All of the numbers were executed with talent and imagination," claimed the *New York Times*.[28] Even though (Jewison later claimed) twenty of CBS's southern affiliates refused to broadcast the show, Belafonte won an Emmy for Outstanding Performance in a Variety or Musical Program.[29]

Perhaps the clearest assessment of the show's significance came from the Black press. "For the first time, a Negro was the production company head, as well as the star performer, in a televised spectacular seen in millions of homes," wrote A. S. "Doc" Young in the Los Angeles *Sentinel*. The show's treatment of racial harmony "was not blatant integration, as if somebody wanted to brag about the mere association of Negroes and Caucasians; it was as natural as a morning's sunrise."[30]

In seven years, Jewison had gone from CBC trainee, learning the most basic mechanics of televisual transmission, to directing Harry Belafonte in one of the most culturally momentous hours of American television. Most thrilling, for Jewison, was how the Belafonte special had brought his creative energies into alignment with a larger social purpose. *Tonight with Belafonte* had transcended the variety format to become a socially conscious form of art. Asked on a 1960 youth-oriented TV program about how to prepare for a career in television, Jewison reminded viewers that "television is not a single field"—it included skills from theatre, radio, and film—adding, "I don't think television is a goal in itself."[31]

Belafonte would later call *Tonight with Belafonte* "the happiest experience I've had in television. It was unique for me because of Normy's ability to adapt himself to the world of Negro art. It was amazing how he knew, better than anyone, how to light that beautiful Black face of Odetta's, how he'd ask about the meaning and submeaning and sub-submeaning of the words of the songs."[32]

"I've met very few people who have his kind of passion," Belafonte said, "where it's just in every aspect of his life."[33]

* * *

Jewison would always remember that the linoleum floor felt strangely cool beneath his cheek.

All the anxiety leading up to a live television special, the weeks of tireless preparation, breaking down the scenes, the meetings, rehearsals, the potential for career-ending calamity, combined with the climactic release of energy after a successful completion of the live TV high-wire act—it wiped him out. He was more than just exhausted, or empty. He was filled with loss, suddenly brimming with existential pointlessness. It was live TV, and everything that he had created was gone. The post-partum desolation had visited him occasionally since his CBC days, and would haunt him even after the completion of film projects in later years. For decades, interviewers would rhapsodize about Jewison's almost superhuman energy, but they didn't see him in a project's aftermath. They did not see him on the kitchen floor.[34]

Dixie had come to expect these episodes. "I would lie down on the cold linoleum floor of the kitchen and Dixie somehow knew that was the sign. I would just lie prostrate, and she would step over me and act as if I wasn't there. She'd say, 'Oh, don't worry, Daddy's just experiencing some disillusionment at the moment.' She never really faced it, and not facing it was of course the best thing she could do. I would eventually get up off the kitchen floor and go about my business."[35]

The business was increasingly based out of Los Angeles, which didn't make life any easier for Dixie, who remained with the Kevin, Michael, and Jennifer in New York. A few years before, Dixie had enjoyed a flourishing artistic life of her own. She loved to paint, and had trained at the Ontario College of Art. Now, her artistic aspirations (along with her modelling) had been put on hold to help advance Norman's career. Dixie "could have continued her art work," according to Jennifer, "but she kept moving everywhere . . . her life just kept changing."[36]

A newspaper profile would later describe Dixie a "typical Canadian homemaker" who loves "cooking, entertaining, caring for her house and children."[37] The description is at odds with the determined, no-bullshit woman recalled by those closest to her. "She's strong—oh, man," Jennifer said. "I think that's what dad loves about her. You can't get anything past her." She had refined tastes, but she would also trek through Algonquin Park with her husband and never complain about the deer flies and mosquitoes. Norman once glowingly boasted that she could "portage a mean canoe or more than her own weight in gear."[38]

Dixie was also more intimately involved in her husband's career moves than may have been apparent from the outside, counselling him to take the most ambitious path. Still, despite the pivotal role she played in partnership with her husband, and her acceptance of that role, his more frequent, extended absences had begun to take their toll. When Norman left, a consciousness of her own deepening discontent descended upon her.

After *Tonight with Belafonte*, Norman had his pick of musical specials. He did one with Danny Kaye, one with Pat Boone, another with Belafonte. Despite the rapid upward trajectory of his career, he was already wearying of the hour-long special format. In 1960, he ventured into dramatic territory with an episode of *Diagnosis Unknown*, a medical drama, which offered the additional novelty of shooting on film, outdoors. ("Here we were, dragging these fucking eight machines with miles of cable through the sand dunes," he marvelled, reflecting on the experience. "I mean it was ridiculous.")[39] His episode of *Diagnosis Unknown* featured Jackie Gleason, then one of TV's biggest stars. "He's very quick, almost too quick, and rather impatient with other people who can't stay with him. I didn't think he was exceptionally hard to handle," Jewison said at the time through a sly smile. Already, his métier was knowing how to "handle" stars.[40]

That reputation may have secured his involvement in a television special for Judy Garland. She had already weathered innumerable downfalls and comebacks in her long career in show business. Only four years Jewison's senior, Garland had starred in films he might have seen as a child in the 1930s. Her 1954 remake of *A Star is Born* marked one career revival; a 1961 concert at Carnegie Hall marked another. By the time of Jewison's television special in 1962, Garland had not appeared on television for six years. She was thirty-nine-years-old.

Jewison adored Garland as a performer, although he also understood her personal complexities. "No matter how difficult things got for her, with her husband and her family and her problems and her health and addictions, there was a personal courage about her that I admired," Jewison said. "It's hard for me to describe. I wasn't in love with her. I mean, I was her director. She trusted me. And sometimes I think I was the only person to tell her the truth, not lie to her."[41] He felt a profound personal responsibility to ensure that the special was a success. Gary Smith remembers long evenings of "drinking and reminiscing and bullshitting, and holding hands, and very little planning of the show, I've got to tell you that. She wanted company. She was an insomniac."[42]

Unconvinced that Garland could carry the program on her own, CBS arranged to have contributions from Frank Sinatra and Dean Martin. It fell to Jewison to convince Sinatra that he should rehearse (which he did). Tony Curtis made an appearance during one rehearsal, and took note of the kid director buzzing around set. The show itself, like the Belafonte special before it, would be spare, lean, and focused on the music. Gary Smith remembers coming up with an idea for a "wall of light bulbs— those big R-40 type light bulbs" that spelled Judy's name. Things were coming together, but they were running perilously short of time. Smith remembers that it all weighed heavily on Jewison: "The pressure, with Judy, and Sinatra, and Dean Martin . . ."[43]

Before anyone was ready, it was show time. The *Judy Garland Special* broadcast from NBC's Studio Four in Burbank at 9 p.m. on Sunday, February 25. Garland, in a coruscating sequined blouse, sashayed through lively renditions of "You Made Me Love You," "Swannee," and "I Can't Give You Anything but Love." According to Smith, Jewison had never rehearsed the final segment, a thirteen-minute "mini-concert" in which Garland belted out a medley of her most beloved tunes. The director mostly kept Garland in full-shot, centred in the frame, tracking as she pranced and shimmied laterally, reserving close-ups for Garland's blasting crescendos. All of it was improvised. "We just ran out of time and Norman had to wing it. No director likes to do that on television," Smith said, "but watching Norman handle that trio, and those people. It's a live situation . . . [and] that was all basically one take, that last concert segment . . . it was quite frantic."[44]

Frantic or not, the evening went down as a triumph. "Miss Garland's program, thanks to Norman Jewison and Kay Thompson, was sublimely content to let Miss Garland and her colleagues speak for themselves," noted the *New York Times*. "Judy Garland held television in the palm of her hand last night . . . It was the spell that the occasional performer can weave in his or her own way and everyone, without knowing precisely why, is glad to savor."[45] Four Emmy nominations followed, including "The Program of the Year." A star was reborn.

* * *

Within three years of his arrival in New York City, Jewison had become the highest paid TV director in North America.[46] He'd worked with Richard Burton, Julie Andrews, and Maurice Chevalier on *The Broadway of Lerner and Loewe*. He'd done *The Fabulous Fifties* with Rex Harrison,

Henry Fonda, and others. He'd even done a TV special with Jimmy ("Inka Dinka Doo") Durante, his childhood idol. But some of that post-program "disillusionment" was now starting to take up permanent residence in his mind. What was all this work *for*? Would he just go on directing Pat Boone specials for the rest of his life? At the same time, he felt that television itself was becoming an appendage of the advertising agencies. Was he an artist who engaged in the imaginative education of others, or a corporate shill who sold Revlon lipstick?

Jewison set out to devise new television ideas, programs that would allow for more intellectual depth. One was called "Focus," a variety show dedicated to current affairs rather than light entertainment, which took inspiration from magazines like *Time* and *The New Yorker*. (Jewison appears to have been anticipating *60 Minutes*, which launched in 1968). Another concept was "Words & Music: U.S.A.," a television special about poetry in America, "from nursery rhymes and greeting cards to beloved folksongs and blues . . . from Ogden Nash to Carl Sandburg . . . from rock n'roll to our national anthem."[47] Neither idea went anywhere.

With three children under the age of six, the domestic pressures were increasingly demanding, and Norman was less present than ever. While he had been supporting Judy Garland, Dixie had been supporting him, maintaining the home life that provided structure and sanity. Eventually, the situation became untenable for her. Norman remembers how once, after what might have been months of consecutive work on alternating coasts, he considered taking on a project called "The Gershwin Years." He tried to sell Dixie on the idea—imagine Gene Kelly dancing 'American in Paris' on the banks of the East River!—when she finally drew the line. "You go ahead and do it," she said. "Why not do 'em all, why don't you just never stop. Of course, *I* won't be here. The kids and I will be back in Toronto, but you go ahead and do 'The Gershwin Years.' You do em' all, Norman."

"And then I realized I'd been away from her for so long," he said, "and been working on the West coast, and I was never at home . . . and that's when I realized that my marriage was in trouble. So I didn't do 'The Gershwin Years.' I put Dixie in the car—it was February, it was so cold—so we drove to the Florida Keys, in search of sun . . . and I tried to patch up my estrangement from my wife and family, and I think that was all a part of this disillusionment.

"Not knowing where you're going can become very troubling."[48]

CHAPTER 3

The Sunshine Kid

NORMAN JEWISON DIRECTED HIS FIRST SCENE for a motion picture on April 19, 1962, on a Universal soundstage in San Fernando Valley, California. He'd decided to ease into the production with something simple, a straightforward expository scene in which veteran comedian, Larry Storch, would pick up the phone and speak to his boss. Still, he was so nervous that he forgot to say "action" after the clapboard snapped down for take one.[1]

Perhaps some part of Jewison's mind was still amazed to find himself on set at all. Little more than a decade earlier, he had been driving the night shift for Diamond Taxi in Toronto. Only months earlier, he had felt increasingly caged by the conventions of live television. Today, he was embarking upon a major Hollywood motion picture, directing one of the biggest stars in the world.

That star, Tony Curtis, had seen something promising in Jewison during rehearsals of the Judy Garland Special. They were less than a year apart in age, but Jewison was conscious of the chasm of power and prestige that separated him from the Oscar and Golden Globe-nominated star of *The Defiant Ones*, *Some Like It Hot* (the funniest American film ever made, according to an American Film Institute survey) and *Spartacus*. By 1962, Curtis was the face of his own production company, Curtis Enterprises, and Jewison had been handed directorial duties on the first property it developed.

That property was *40 Pounds of Trouble*, already the second remake of a 1934 Shirley Temple comedy called *Little Miss Marker*. Curtis played Steve McCluskey, a womanizing Nevada casino manager suddenly responsible for a five-year-old girl. Jewison bore no pretensions about the aesthetic importance of this venture, which he referred to at the time as a "strictly commercial Hollywood comedy."[2] Nor did he harbour any illusions about why he'd been chosen as director. Curtis was used to the likes of Stanley Kubrick, Stanley Kramer, and Billy Wilder, but now, as the head of his own production company, he needed someone talented and cheap who would not become a rival for power over the picture.

Curtis and the producer Stanley Margulies invited Jewison to a meeting in LA and asked if he was interested in making a movie. Jewison frankly reminded them that he "had never exposed a foot of film."[3] But Jewison's television experience was a selling point. A decade later, Hollywood producers would turn to the film schools for invigorating new talent. In the early 1960s, that talent came from television: Sidney Lumet, John Frankenheimer, George Roy Hill, and Arthur Penn were just a few film directors graduating from TV.

If only the script had been more promising.

"So I read the screenplay," Jewison recalled, "and the only thing that excited me was one paragraph which said 'Tony Curtis takes the child to Disneyland and a chase ensues . . . and I said, oh God! I could do a Mack Sennett chase!" He adored Sennett's Keystone Cops, always had. Jewison campaigned for three days of filming in the Magic Kingdom, but the producers were skeptical. "Don't you realize how great this could be, how much fun we could have!" he implored. In the end, "they added three days to the schedule, if I would write the chase sequence."[4]

There was no mistaking who was really in charge on set, and it wasn't the director. Curtis delivered a gentle ribbing on Jewison's first day: he may look like your paper boy, but he really is the director.[5] Jewison's TV experience didn't mean much to the veteran Universal crew, nor had it given him a comprehensive technical grasp of film production. He decided to play up his inexperience: it would keep expectations low, and allow the crew to feel like generous mentors.

Jewison didn't regard *40 Pounds* as marking a permanent career transition. He and Dixie rented a furnished place in Los Angeles and kept their belongings in storage, half-expecting they would end up back in New York. Jewison's mind was already drifting back to television. Days into filming, Jewison sent Harry Belafonte a letter proposing that they collaborate on another television special in the fall of 1962. "Of course, you can't afford me now," Jewison joked, "but then, you never could."[6]

* * *

It should have been a thrilling time to work at Universal. While Jewison was learning the ropes on *40 Pounds*, the adjacent soundstages played host to Alfred Hitchcock (filming *The Birds*), Marlon Brando (*The Ugly American*), and Stanley Kramer (*It's a Mad, Mad, Mad, Mad World*). On lunch break at the Universal commissary, Jewison may have rubbed shoulders with Spencer Tracy, Janet Leigh, Sid Caesar, and Carl Reiner.[7] Yet in letters to friends back home, Jewison sounds more concerned with missing the opening of trout season in Algonquin Park than with fraternizing with Hollywood royalty. Part of the problem was that he felt no pride of ownership over *40 Pounds*. Then there was the fact that the daily grind of filmmaking could be downright boring. Far from the break-neck pace of live television, he spent much of his day on set waiting for various crew members to complete their set-ups. His mind wandered amid the tedium. "I bet [your] farm is beautiful now that spring is here," he fantasized in a letter to his old CBC friend Wally Koster, "and I would give anything to be able to spend a few days there this time of year."[8]

On set, he milked his "inexperience" for all it was worth. His diminutive physical frame, boyish smile, and innocent eyes put everyone at ease. Reporters had already identified Jewison's charm as his greatest asset: one described it as "compounded of truly monumental self-confidence and equally great friendliness which, in combination, enable him to handle performers with exceptional ease."[9] The kid who looked like your paperboy soon inspired the loyalty of the veteran crew. ("The beret, the German accent, and the riding crop all worked," he joked to Belafonte.)[10] Never a morning person, Jewison was slow to adjust to the early start times required on film production; midway through the shoot, he sent a note apologizing to Suzanne Pleshette, Curtis's love interest in the film, "for being surly every morning, but it's something that's been going on for about thirty-five years and it's going to be rather difficult to change."[11] Overall, he was forced to admit that the shoot was proceeding "amazingly well."

Jewison had found his groove by the time the production moved to Anaheim. The Keystone Cops-inspired chase through Disneyland's exteriors allowed the director to romp through the history of American cinema. We see cowboys battling Indians, a parody of a car chase (on Disney's Autopia ride, where Curtis and the pursuing detective ride shotgun with children "driving" the cars at low speeds), and characters racing alongside steam engines, through faux desert landscapes, and across rickety bridges. Critics would complain that the Disneyland scenes in *40 Pounds* amounted to the crassest form of product placement; for Jewison, they were the most artful part of the film.

Filming in the Magic Kingdom presented some prickly logistical challenges. The production, consisting of more than a hundred studio technicians, a massive camera crane, power trucks and trailers, shot during regular hours, alongside thousands of tourists. California law required children to attend school while on movie locations: the Disneyland Little Theatre was therefore converted into an open-air school, where nearly a hundred children were subjected to the cruel and unusual punishment of attending school while at Disneyland.[12] Walt wanted Jewison to keep a low profile, but, as the film's Press Book noted, the production inevitably became one of the park's attractions: crew carrying microphone booms and brilliant reflectors trailed the actors, attracting crowds. Some young women suddenly forgot about Mickey Mouse and vamped for the camera, hoping to be discovered. Movie fans shoved their autograph books in front of anyone who might "be somebody." One strapping utility man provided at least fifty autographs before the location wrapped.[13]

Of the picture's many challenges, the greatest for Jewison turned out to be the eponymous forty pounds of trouble, played by Claire Wilcox. With three young children at home, Jewison thought he knew how to deal with kids, but child actors came with unique complications. Because Wilcox couldn't read, Jewison had to give her line readings. "She is extremely retentive," he said at the time, "but when you tell her what to say and do, you'd better be right the first time. Because that's the only way she'll do it, even if you decide to change."[14] Then there was the fact that Wilcox could not bring herself to cry on cue. With the clock ticking, Jewison decided upon a truly desperate measure. As the camera rolled, he informed the young actress that her dog had died.[15] The precious tears immortalized on film,

Jewison told Claire the truth, and her involuntary experience with Method acting was over.

In addition to a crash course on dealing with child actors, *40 Pounds* provided Jewison with a life-changing gift. Alice Lee Boatwright, or "Boaty" as she is universally known, was a casting director for Universal, where she had recently cast the three child actors in *To Kill a Mockingbird*. From the moment Jewison entered the Universal office, "I just adored him," she said. "He was funny and cute and smart and we hit it off from the first day we met. We liked each other and he liked the things I liked, which were theatre and films, and we became instant friends." Jewison was captivated by her vivacity, her Southern accent, her outrageous sense of humour. They developed a close friendship, seeing one another when business allowed, exchanging long letters when it didn't.[16]

* * *

By the time *40 Pounds* wrapped on June 16, Jewison, who had gone months without working the previous year, found himself with more offers than he could entertain. His deal with Tony Curtis called for two more films with Curtis Enterprises. Universal wanted to lock him into a multi-picture deal. Producer Martin Ransohoff came calling with a property entitled "The Wheelerdealers," while Columbia Pictures offered him something called "Three on a Couch." There were plans for additional TV specials featuring Garland and Belafonte. Most enticingly, Meredith Willson, composer of *The Music Man*, floated the possibility of a Broadway collaboration. They met over the summer but Jewison was frankly "doubtful of landing a Broadway show of this size."[17] The project he ultimately settled on was *The Thrill of it All*, a Doris Day vehicle produced by Ross Hunter. For Jewison, the glossy romantic comedy was scarcely more interesting than *40 Pounds*. But Doris Day was one of the most successful female stars of the era, and the script allowed for a withering satire of television commercials, which he loathed.

By now, Norman's professional centre of gravity had shifted decisively to the west coast, and the Jewisons were ready to put down roots. Dixie didn't push for anything extravagant—"She'd live in a room," Norman said around this time—but his earning power had increased, and it was time to give up the furnished rental in the valley. In January 1963, Norman and Dixie took possession of 313 North Barrington Drive, a Brentwood ranch house. Jewison would later complain about "trying to fix up the house with what little money we have left after buying it."[18] But they loved the half-acre yard, plenty of room for gardening and for the kids to romp around, even if Norman found it hard to accept the move as permanent. In letters, he described it as "our home for the next three or four years."[19]

Around the same time, Jewison was discovering that some of the most important work in film occurs after the shoot has wrapped. In live television, he had effectively served as his own editor, selecting camera angles in real time and actively "performing along with the cast," as he once said. Post-production on *40 Pounds* revealed to Jewison the extent to which the editor was responsible for shaping the finished product. At the time, the studio's editors answered to producers, not to directors.[20]

The national press preview of *40 Pounds* took place on January 19, 1963, at Harrah's Tahoe, the location of Curtis's resort in the film. Reporters were treated to a tramway ride and lunch at Heavenly Valley, cocktails with Tony Curtis and the cast, dinner in the opulent 750-seat South Shore room before, finally, the lights were dimmed for the first important public film screening of Jewison's life. For the rest of his career, he would find these first screenings gut-wrenching. He paced the hallways before it began, anxious about things he could no longer control.[21]

Jewison was often dismissive of *40 Pounds of Trouble*. In one surprisingly frank assessment shortly after the film's release, he called it "just an above average comedy." Critics mostly agreed, characterizing *40 Pounds* as a perfunctory exercise. Few were as cantankerous as the *New York Times*'s Bosley Crowther, who bemoaned the "slapdash and witless script" full of "laboured humour." Considering that the rookie director was "straight from television," sneered Crowther, "it's no wonder that it has a video look." But if *40 Pounds* was not the triumph Jewison may have wanted for his debut, neither was it the abject failure he feared. Looking back, Tony Curtis said that *40 Pounds* "didn't affect my career much one way or the other." It would have a mostly positive effect on Jewison's.

Over the last few months, Jewison had been working intensively with screenwriter Carl Reiner on revisions for *The Thrill of it All*. Budgeted at $5.5-million, *Thrill* was in a different league than *40 Pounds*, and came with increased pressure. Filming began at Revue Studio in New York on October 16, 1962, months before *40 Pounds* was released. "Maybe I'm trying to get in as many movie jobs as possible before my pictures are shown and I have to head back to Canada," the director joked to a reporter.

Jewison again deployed his persona of the novice director to great effect. "Normy has a knack for establishing rapport with the most pampered of prima donnas," said producer Ross Hunter. "They see this precocious boy, who looks as though he just delivered the coffee. He seems so puckish and sweet and defenceless . . . He also radiates enthusiasm and makes each one of them feel their acting is the greatest thing since sliced bread." Hunter went on to dub Jewison the "Sunshine Kid."[22]

Still, Jewison's passion for *The Thrill of it All* was dampened by the fact that it was not really "his" movie. As far as Universal was concerned, *Thrill* was a Doris Day film, with Jewison once again serving as artistic chaperone.

By 1962, Day had been a marquee star for more than a decade, and her public image had undergone multiple evolutions. From early genre work on *Romance on the High Seas* (1948) and *Calamity Jane* (1953), Day had branched into dramatic fare including Alfred Hitchcock's *The Man Who Knew Too Much*, opposite Jimmy Stewart. By the end of the fifties, Day, who had toured with all-male bands from the age of seventeen and was twice-married by twenty, was typecast in wholesome, all-American "forty-year-old virgin" roles, in stark contrast to the openly seductive images of Ava Gardner, Lana Turner, or Marylin Monroe. As humourist Al Capp wrote in a cutting profile of the star, "Compounded of the wishful thinking of middle-aged matrons, movie moguls' wild dreams of avarice, and the frustrated nightmares of every red-blooded American matinee idol, that professionally gelid miss, Doris Day, has become the hottest property in Hollywood."[23]

Day, Jewison quickly ascertained, needed to feel like a serious artist. "I got close to her," he remembered, "because I treated her as a talented actress and not a star." Jewison admired Day, although he worried she was being manipulated by those near to her. He was also unsettled by the star's habit of scrutinizing her appearance in the rushes. Jewison tried to cure her fixation with a bit of reverse psychology. "'Doris,' I said, 'look at the rushes if you feel that insecure about them—go on, *look*. Of course . . . it's never happened to me before . . . not with Judy or Belafonte or Gleason or Julie Andrews . . . but if you must, you must.'" However temporarily, the star found she could do without the daily affirmation of the rushes.[24]

Jewison got along well with Day, who he called "a joy to work with," although, he added somewhat ominously, she "does a lot of crying."[25] For her part, Day later called *Thrill* her favourite film. Jewison's energy stayed with her for decades. "I just remember his twinkly eyes, his marvellous smile, and his warmth and genuine qualities," Day said of him. "I liked him because he really is a gentle man, and yet strong at the same time. He isn't a screamer. He is quiet and makes his point with great authority—and you really have to run the ship, I'll tell you that."[26]

* * *

Day's vast appeal came from an ability to appear glamorous and ordinary at the same time. Jewison and Carl Reiner built Day's formula for success into the plot of *Thrill*, in which an "average American housewife" is discovered and offered a job as a TV pitch-woman. Still nurturing his grudge with Revlon, Jewison portrayed television advertising as an orgy of stupidity beholden to every facile fad and passing trend. When Day spectacularly flubs her lines on live TV, the creatives first laugh hysterically at her unspeakable folly and then, realizing that their boss had *liked* the performance, praise the authenticity of her work. The more bumbling and maladroit Day's efforts at selling "Happy" brand soap, the more she is seen to approximate a real housewife, and the "better" her performance.

Jewison had fun with these scenes of advertising farce, although beneath them lay a real contempt for the industry. "I am very proud," he would later reflect, "and I know this sounds pompous and childish and insolent and cavalier, but I am proud I have never shot a TV commercial. There has to be one thing you don't sell out on, there has to be one fucking thing that stops you from becoming a total whore."[27]

The notion that advertisers exerted an unhealthy influence over production decisions was axiomatic among industry creatives, but Jewison took an extreme view. Advertisements, he believed, represented the debasement of a great human achievement. He considered television "the most powerful medium of communication which mankind and the world has ever known." As a director, he found it "totally demeaning to get excited about a refrigerator or selling underarm deodorant . . . drawing upon that for my inspiration as a director."[28] The intensity of Jewison's contempt for TV advertisements stemmed from his understanding of creativity. He believed that the Platonic ideal of the creative concept lived inside the director's imagination: before set designers or lighting technicians or actors plied their trades, the idea was alive in the director's mind. The success of an idea came directly from the director's ability to believe in it with total commitment. Jewison's own capacity for excitement was, at a visceral level, the wellspring of his directorial power.

Everyone in Jewison's orbit recognized his irrepressible exuberance. Midway through a routine 1963 interview, a journalist remarked that "Mr. Jewison's enthusiasm had reached such a point" that he nearly knocked over a table. On set, his energy had "an almost hypnotic effect" on the cast and crew, according to his former secretary Barbara Geist. During rehearsals, she said, he played every part in the script "with such delight and love that everyone connected with the show would get wildly excited."[29]

It was a habit that would persist throughout his career. Decades later, Jewison invited Bruce McDonald to his office over lunch to discuss the script for *Dance Me Outside*, which McDonald was directing. Jewison was producing the film, a coming of age story set on a First Nations reserve in Northern Ontario. "We sat down at his table," McDonald remembers, "and he started to read. And he played all the parts and read every word. And it was like—I couldn't believe it. I'd never been to a meeting like this." It was like a full-cast read-through of a screenplay where Jewison was the entire cast. "I just watched him perform the movie for me at the table, and once in a while he'd have a bite of his tuna sandwich . . . it was sort of jaw-dropping."[30]

* * *

Jewison's protest against the advertising business wasn't the only subtext carried by this apparently slight Hollywood rom-com. In 1963, Betty Friedan published *The Feminine Mystique*, a landmark of second-wave feminism in which she identified an unnamed problem. "As she made the beds, shopped for groceries, matched slipcover material, ate peanut butter sandwiches with her children, chauffeured Cub Scouts and Brownies, lay beside her husband at night—she was afraid to ask even of herself the silent question—'Is this all?'"[31]

Is this all? The title of Jewison's film provided an ironic reformulation of Friedan's question. In exposing the "mystique of feminine fulfillment," Friedan reports on an epidemic of existential uncertainty that had gripped legions of American housewives, women who, the culture told them, "had it all," and yet whose profound lack of fulfillment and self-knowledge had resulted in tears, tranquilizers, rage, and nervous breakdowns. "The only way for a woman, as for a man, to find herself," Friedan wrote, "is by creative work of her own."

As *Thrill* opens, Doris Day's Beverly Boyer betrays no sense of this alienation: she seems too consumed with domestic drudgery (including the bottling of home-made ketchup) for such thoughts. But the offer of a job as a TV pitch-woman awakens her latent feelings of independence, which soon sparks marital strife. James Garner's Dr. Boyer is not the sort of man who will tolerate a working wife. ("Why is Daddy yelling at Mommy?" one of their children ask. "Because he doesn't want her to be a TV star," answers the other.) Yet the issue for Garner's character is not the nature of Day's work, but the very fact of it: "There is no *reason* for you to work," he blasts her in a heated moment. "You have the PTA! You have your bottled ketchup!"

While Jewison drew a sharp line between his Universal products and those over which he had creative control, *The Thrill of it All* was perhaps more socially engaged than its director recognized. In retrospect, *Thrill* offers a surprisingly direct comedic counterpart to the polemics of second-wave feminists like Friedan and Gloria Steinem, who were steering postwar American gender politics in a more liberal direction.

"Whatever happened to my rights as a woman!" Day yells at Garner.

"I'll tell you what," he shouts back, "they grew and they grew until they suffocated my rights as a man! Whoever said that all men are created equal didn't anticipate a woman earning $100,000 a year!"

When Garner's character threatens to move out until she gives up her career, she hands him his suitcase and ushers him out of the house.

* * *

As *The Thrill of it All* wrapped in December 1962, Jewison was feeling, as he confessed to Boaty, "tired and depressed."[32] This post-project ennui was the usual byproduct of his restless temperament and ambition, the fact that the next big thing couldn't come along fast enough. He had been working continuously since March, and his interest in the Universal projects was waning. He had left television because he felt that the medium's creative potential was increasingly subservient to commercial interests. Having made two pictures within the studio system, he found that the situation in movies wasn't much different. Universal had simply offered him a place on the assembly line. "The idea of making twenty films annually, announced a year in advance and without twenty story properties that have a reason for being, appalls me," he wrote in 1962. A "movie should never be made unless it has a *raison d'être*."

Jewison was aware that his own films did not satisfy his aesthetic criterion. They had helped launch his career, but what did he intend to do with that career? Make more Hollywood baubles for Ross Hunter?

Jewison was valued as a studio technician, but in no sense was he an auteur. He could vent his spleen by satirizing television commercials within his films, but *The Thrill of it All* was itself largely a commercial for a product called Doris Day. He concealed his anxieties from collaborators, of course, but those closest to him understood the depth of his dissatisfaction.

"I think you should get out of Hollywood for a while and do a play," Boaty implored him, "or go to England or Canada and do TV or films. Maybe I make it sound too simple (when I do realize that it isn't that simple) but I wish you'd stop doing work that 1) You aren't happy doing; 2) Doesn't deserve your talent or effort; 3) Is done only for the money or the option . . . No one ever asked you to get rich . . . and I still don't think it means a damn to you."[33]

Jewison had already come to the same conclusion and, however improbably, fate cooperated. Meredith Willson called to deliver news that Jewison had assumed was almost impossible. He was headed to Broadway.

* * *

Where motion pictures had offered an escape from television, Broadway now offered an escape from motion pictures. Jewison began spending weekends with Meredith Willson at his house in Bel Air, writing and rewriting the book for *Here's Love*, the musical that would begin rehearsals in the new year.

Meanwhile, with Christmas approaching, Jewison was wearying of Tinsel Town. Compared to previous Christmases in New York and Toronto, the scattered, metallic wreaths on Ventura Boulevard were pathetic. One late-November morning, he took his sons to the Santa Claus parade. "No fairy tale floats, no red and green, no clowns," he reported to Boaty. "Gene Autry and an old hooker dressed up as Cinderella. It was really the saddest comment yet. Kevin and Michael didn't recognize anybody except Santa Claus, and he was a skinny one out of central casting."[34] Boaty wrote back, teasing him with images of Christmas in New York, the white and blue trees on Park Avenue, the "mass of gold" which was the tree in Rockefeller Plaza, decorations at Saks. "Have the happiest Christmas, dear boy," she wrote him. "One of the nicest things that happened to me in '62 was meeting you."[35]

At thirty-seven, little more than a decade since he began at the CBC, Jewison's Broadway debut felt like yet another career rebirth. *Here's Love* rekindled a youthful enthusiasm for the theatre, for childhood dreams that pre-dated his interest in TV and movies. The intervening projects might have seemed like steps in a journey destined to bring him back to the stage. The director of the Vic Bob now had his own Broadway musical.

Here's Love had an impressive pedigree. After decades of scoring films for Charlie Chaplin and William Wyler, two of Jewison's idols, Meredith Willson had made his Broadway debut with *The Music Man*, which ran for 1,375 performances. *Here's Love*, about a young girl convinced that the Macy's Santa Claus is the authentic Kris Kringle, was an adaptation of another hit, *Miracle on 34th Street*. All signs pointed to a major success, and Jewison launched himself into the production, conceiving elaborate song-and-dance numbers alongside choreographer Michael Kidd and producer Stuart Ostrow. Willson's script had required some serious attention. In one early run-through, the first act alone had run over two hours. But the work seemed to be paying off. "We have made tremendous changes and Meredith is a dream to work with," Jewison wrote that April.[36]

He felt optimistic about the show heading into a final stretch of run-throughs before opening in Detroit. He characterized his relationship with

Willson as "exceptional," and believed that, despite their many (amicably resolved) disagreements, he and Ostrow were also on solid ground. Then, one Wednesday afternoon in late July, the cast of *Here's Love* stumbled badly in a run-through. "It was extremely hot in the theatre and obviously everyone was a little tired," Jewison remembered. An intense, two-hour meeting followed between the director, Willson, and Ostrow. "Ostrow expressed great pleasure at the results of the meeting and Meredith and I walked up the street arm-in-arm," Jewison said. After the next morning's rehearsals, Phyllis Rabb of William Morris arrived to tell Jewison that he had been fired. Stu Ostrow was taking over as director.[37]

Jewison was stunned. Willson had never said anything about being displeased with his direction. The cast seemed equally shocked. Jewison's agent Larry Auerbach warned him over the phone not to leave the theatre; if he did, they might accuse him of quitting and cancel his contract. Finally, Ostrow arrived to face Jewison in person and informed him that the production would be better off without his services. Jewison proceeded directly to Willson's hotel room to vent his frustration. Willson told him that, "unlike a film where the author is rather unimportant after the script, in a play the author is wholly important," and he had decided to give the play to Ostrow.

"I realize now," Jewison later wrote to his lawyer, "that Meredith must be treated as a star and must come before the stars of the play, or indeed the play itself."[38]

Jewison believed his firing was the result of momentary panic after a bad run-through, but that was little consolation. After eight months of work, from casting and set design to costumes, to say nothing of his countless hours working on the book with Willson, he had been sacked four rehearsals from the finish line. Jewison's name was scrubbed from all production materials, his contract cancelled. In the arbitration that followed, Willson and Ostrow claimed that he had barred them from rehearsals, made numerous unauthorized script changes (Jewison countered that perhaps twenty-five lines in the 2.5-hour play were altered), and that some sort of physical altercation had taken place in which Jewison had "removed Willson's hand from his shoulder."[39] ("Since Meredith embraced me roughly twenty times a day it is impossible for me to remember every withdrawing from him," Jewison told his lawyer.)[40] He fought the decision at every step, eventually winning a percentage of the gross box office receipts in a settlement. The affair dragged on for months.

The firing re-awakened feelings of rejection he had experienced as a young actor—the sleepless night under the stairwell, and the pilfered turnip in London. For years, he had been steadily building a reputation on personal confidence and competence. His firing left a terrible gash in that identity, a defect that could not be undone. Cast members thought he'd been set up to fail. "Losing you was a great and serious loss to the cast and the play and one from which it has never recovered," wrote star Craig Stevens.[41]

"Poor Norman," wrote Laurence Naismith, who played Kris Kringle. "You fell into a pool with two man eaters, from which there was no escape."[42]

CHAPTER 4

"I Want It to Be Funny"

B Y THE SPRING OF 1963, just months after the release of his first picture, Jewison was already receiving letters from fans asking how to "make it" in Hollywood. While he would receive countless such letters over the course of his career, and personally answer a surprising number of them, one early reply stands out for its candour. "When you choose as a career an art form, one must also accept the cold fact that there are no rules or place where one can easily find acceptance," Jewison counselled in April 1963. He warned that "Hollywood is an extremely difficult place to break into. Most of the studios are overstaffed and lack projects." True to form, however, he concluded on a more optimistic note. "The only realistic advice that I can give you is that if you write, act, direct anything at anytime, anywhere . . . I am sure your talent, desire and burning ambition will carry you the rest of the way."[1]

The recipient of those words was one Ralph Sarson, a down-on-his-luck twenty-something living at the YMCA in Hamilton, Ontario. Jewison probably felt that a few words from a Hollywood director would mean something to a kid like Ralph. But there is also a sense in which Jewison may have been addressing himself. Yes, he had "made it" in Hollywood, hence the letters asking how others could do the same. But if Hollywood was a difficult place to "break into," it was turning into an even more challenging place in which to survive. According to film historian Tino Balio, the total number of moviegoers had dropped 73.4 per cent between 1946 and 1962. The major studios had drastically cut their releases, from an average of 450 to 240 a year, over the same period.[2] "If you look at the statistics in the industry, you will find that the middle sixties were the nadir of the film business in terms of [box office] admissions," according to Columbia executive Gordon Stulberg.[3] Studios were hiring production staff on shorter-term contracts or laying them off entirely. That Jewison could rise within this declining industry was testament to his reputation for competence and capacity to deliver. But the "cold fact" was that he was not working as the artist he imagined himself to be. Instead, he was living according to some version of the advice he provided Ralph: just keep working, direct anything at any time, even, God forbid, another Doris Day comedy, and your burning ambition will carry you the rest of the way.

And work he did. Little more than a year after his letter to Ralph, Jewison had completed three motion pictures, eight episodes of *The Judy Garland Show*, and had seen the Broadway musical *Here's Love* through to its final stages of production. Yet only the Hollywood work had been an unqualified commercial success. *40 Pounds of Trouble* and *The Thrill of It All* had led to *Send Me No Flowers*, "another innocuous, commercial comedy starring Miss Doris Day," as he described it to a friend at the time. With that one in the works, Universal wasted no time in exercising its option, putting Jewison to work on *The Art of Love*, which he characterized as "another improbable, impossible, but elegant-looking Ross Hunter picture."[4]

Most improbable of all was that Jewison found himself enjoying work on *The Art of Love*, particularly because Hunter mostly left him alone. The Carl Reiner screenplay, about an artist who decides to fake his own death to increase the value of his paintings, offered just the sort of off-kilter, high-concept lunacy that tickled Jewison. Universal saw the film as another slick, made-to-order romantic comedy starring Dick Van Dyke (fresh from the enormously successful *Mary Poppins*) and the German actress Elke Sommer, but Jewison felt optimistic about the picture. *The Art of Love* seemed like a step up from his previous fare, although it still wasn't "his" film in any meaningful sense.

In the summer of 1964, creative satisfaction still eluding him, Jewison took his family on a late summer vacation on Balboa Island, an ocean resort south of Los Angeles. He had been an avid outdoorsman his whole life, and nurtured a love of outdoor sports in his family, but watching his children learn how to surf proved to be a "hair-raising" experience. "When you see an eight-year-old disappear in the foam of a six-foot breaker for about thirty or forty seconds, it's a little disconcerting," he wrote to friends back in Canada, "but they all seem to enjoy the battering, and surfing is one of the big pastimes in California." Jewison enjoyed sailing and (ever mindful of the bottom line) agonized over whether he should buy a boat big enough for the whole family. In the end, he borrowed an "ancient, creaking old sloop" from an actor friend.[5]

Back on Barrington Avenue in September, with Michael and Kevin in class and Jennifer starting nursery school, the house was quiet, and Jewison felt the old sense of ennui lingering with the late summer heat. It was time to get back to work, but there was no work to get back to. His immediate artistic fate was in the hands of Tony Curtis, who had until the end of October to exercise his option and put him to work on whatever vapid romantic comedy the actor was doing next. The prospect of doing his fifth consecutive rom-com was enough to make Jewison feel slightly dead inside.

So he busied himself with movie properties, combing through the various novels, scripts, and treatments that had come his way. When he was working concertedly, he could review as many as twenty-eight potential properties in a month. While most players in the industry farmed this grunt work out to assistants, Jewison believed that others couldn't "see" a film the way he could[6] and insisted upon doing it himself. But in his current listless mood, with the hours crawling by, he often found himself grubbing around in the garden, tending to the begonias, gladiolus, and what remained of the Lilies of the Nile. "If it wasn't for some of my plants dying off," he complained to the producer Stanley Margulies, "one wouldn't even be conscious of the passage of time. More and more out here I feel I am in some sort of suspended animation. Just one big blue sky and eternal sunshine."[7]

With the 100-degree temperatures lasting into October, Jewison yearned for Ontario's autumn colours, for the smell of frost in the air. He thought about taking a jet to Winnipeg and stealing up to James Bay for goose season, but worried that he had taken too many holidays already. He thought maybe he and Dixie should have another baby, yet suspected Dixie would rather have a horse.[8]

Mostly, though, he thought about *Russians.*

* * *

The Toronto press would occasionally dispatch reporters to check on Jewison's progress in Hollywood. While the official purpose of these visits—there would be dozens over the years—was to trumpet Jewison's conquest of the film industry, their unofficial purpose, at least at first, was to scrutinize the director for any incipient symptoms of Americanization. So, when the Toronto *Star Weekly* sent reporter Frank Rasky to tour 313 Barrington Avenue one August afternoon, Jewison made a point of showing off his Inuit carvings, and the Union Jack and new Canadian maple leaf flag that festooned the walls of his children's bedrooms. Rasky didn't fail to note the "opulence" of the $125,000, two-acre "mansion" in Brentwood, and reported that Jewison was "in danger of falling into a mink-lined rut." The director may have scoffed at the insinuation of extravagance—Dixie ferried the children around in an unpretentious Ford Falcon station wagon—but there was no denying the "rut" part.

"I'm so afraid that the Hollywood life will eat me up," he confessed. "I'm afraid I'll wind up doing nothing but slick, innocuous, we're-off-to-the-seashore, happy-holiday comedies. From now on, I only want to do what I really *want* to do."[9]

But what did he want to do? Who *was* Norman Jewison, and what sort of director did he imagine himself to be?

To answer that question, he would need a property. In February 1963, *The New York Times* reported that Jewison had an option out on a novel called *The International* by Alfred Munk. "It has to do with unions and is a struggle between the young and the old," he explained. "I have Robert Mitchum in mind, but Orson Welles would be good too."[10] *The International* went nowhere, but Jewison soon discovered a novel that would change the course of his career.

When it came out in the summer of 1961, Nathaniel Benchley's *The Off-Islanders* had been received as lively beach reading: "A mixture of comedy, farce and melodrama with a pinch of satire for seasoning," is how the *New York Times* described it. Jewison didn't care about the work's literary quality; what grabbed him about *The Off-Islanders* was its inciting incident: after running aground on a sandbar off the Nantucket coast, Russian submarine officers attempt to steal a boat to dislodge their vessel, causing the insular natives to presume that their piddly island is ground zero of a Russian invasion and World War Three.

Jewison gushed over the filmic possibilities. In the islanders' misunderstanding, he saw an opportunity for the zany, madcap humour that had become his specialty. More importantly, he imagined a film that could speak directly to the times. Here was a film with a reason for being, one that gave *him* a reason for being. The prospect was enough to animate him physically. "Norman flailed his arms about excitedly" while describing the idea to Rasky, the *Star* reporter. "I'd like to call the picture *The Russians Are Coming! The Russians Are Coming!*" Jewison yelled. "I'd splash those stark words on billboards all over the world. Imagine the impact it would make. It'll be funny, and yet make an important and significant comment."[11]

Jewison bought the rights to Benchley's novel in the fall of 1963. "Now all I have to do," he joked to his old CBS pal Jerry Leider, who had recommended the novel, "is find someone who will give me about a million dollars to make it, someone who will give me a submarine, someone who will write it, a big Hollywood star to play in it and a new lens for my Brownie."[12]

Jewison stood no chance of making the film under his deal with Universal, where he was strictly a hired gun. As a studio director, he "was allowed a certain number of weeks of preparation, a certain number of weeks for shooting, and the right to make the first cut. After that it was goodbye. It became the studio's picture afterwards," remembers Patrick J. Palmer, Jewison's long-time production partner. "The studio did all the post-production work, graded the final answer print and the soundtrack. The studio also did the titles. The studio earlier had examined the script to determine if a scene were to be shot on location, on the back lot, or if a process shot were to be used instead.* The studio did all the casting. During shooting, the studio looked at the dailies before the director did."[13]

By the mid-1960s, however, Jewison could detect hints of change in the air. The mythic version of Hollywood's liberation, as etched into popular culture by Peter Biskind in *Easy Riders, Raging Bulls*, is that the startling success of *Bonnie and Clyde* (1967) and *Easy Rider* (1969) emancipated Hollywood directors from their studio shackles. But by 1965, Jewison had already declared, "There's a new freedom in Hollywood." The immediate source of that freedom, for Jewison, was the Mirisch Corporation, a rising independent production outfit. The Mirisches had enshrined greater directorial freedom as part of their ethos, and they were on a hot streak: before Jewison approached them with *The Off-Islanders*, they were coming off a run that included *Some Like It Hot* (1959), *The Apartment, The Magnificent Seven* (1960), *West Side Story* (1961), *The Great Escape* (1963), and *The Pink Panther* (1963). "Any outfit that attracts such men as John Sturges and Billy Wilder," Jewison said at the time, "has a lot in its favour."[14]

The Mirisch Corporation was run by three brothers: Harold (b. 1907), the president, was the relationship guy; Marvin (b.1918) negotiated deals and oversaw legal and accounting; and Walter (b. 1921) was most directly involved with development and production.[15] The Mirisches knew as well as anyone that stars were the key to box-office success. But while Hollywood consensus held that stars (and their agents) were attracted to properties, the Mirisches were ahead of the curve in understanding

---

* The "answer print" is the first print made from camera negatives, normally requiring colour correction in preparation for the "release print." In "process shots," actors were filmed in front of a pre-filmed background rear-projection screen. Process shots were commonly used in driving scenes.

stars' attraction to top directors. "We obviously tried to develop material," said Walter Mirisch, "but at the same time we continued to develop the relationships with the directors. The actor works on a picture for twelve or fourteen weeks and then he wants to start work again. As a rule, he's not a person who wants to sit in an office and work with a writer and develop a screenplay."[16] To secure top-flight directors, the Mirisches offered generous contracts for multiple-picture deals that were non-exclusive: directors could work for other studios as well, which, given the tight strictures of the studio era, seemed an especially attractive proposition. There was nothing to lose by signing with the Miriches. The brothers worked with low overhead, operating out of an office on the Goldwyn lot that was "a far cry from the grandeur of Beverly Hills," according to Balio, the film historian. A 1964 *Variety* article quoted by Balio says that "98 per cent of all costs of a [Mirisch] picture will be seen on screen."[17]

It helped that Jewison genuinely liked Walter Mirisch, particularly in comparison to Edward Muhl, the long-time vice-president of production at Universal. "God, Boaty," Jewison wrote to Boatwright after dinner with Walter Mirisch one evening, "what a difference between Mirisch and Muhl . . . Walter is a well-read, cultivated, sensitive man, and at this point anyway, seems so understanding and easy to work with that I really am looking forward to the Mirisch association. It is absolutely a directors' group. They seem to only be interested in the property and the director first, then everything else follows."[18]

Jewison agreed to a two-picture deal with the Mirisch Company, the precise terms of which would be established after they knew more about the fate of his existing options with Curtis and Universal. Mirisch offered script approval, which was a big deal to Jewison. They also cut a check for ten-thousand dollars to acquire the rights to *The Off-Islanders*, on the understanding that this would be the first of the two pictures (Benchley later picked up another \$1,000 to extend the option on *The Off-Islanders* for another year).[19]

Of course, there could be no film without a script, which meant that in the interminable summer of 1964, as Jewison tended to the dying flowers in his garden, his hopes for the future hung on a man named Rose.

* * *

Jewison had never met the reclusive screenwriter William Rose; almost no one in Hollywood had. His work was widely recognized—the screenplays for *Genevieve* (1953) and *The Ladykillers* (1955) had earned Oscar nominations—but the man himself was an enigma.

Rose's own story was stranger than fiction. Born in Jefferson City, Missouri, in 1914, he briefly attended Columbia University before dropping out to fight for Finland after the Soviet invasion of 1939. (The United States didn't enter the war in Europe until 1944.) Rose later volunteered with the Canadian Black Watch and was stationed in the United Kingdom. After the war, he toiled as a screenwriter in England for more than a decade before wearying of his adopted country and moving with his wife, Tania, to the Channel Island of Jersey, where he cultivated the role of recluse. He could be a prickly personality (the widow of one collaborator described him as an alcoholic egotist) and Jewison would discover the perils of working with the volatile screenwriter.[20] But Rose was also, in Jewison's view, "one of the best screenwriters in the world." He sent Benchley's novel to Jersey, along with a letter describing his intentions.

"I want to make a film about the Cold War, about the absurdity of international conflict," Jewison wrote. He imagined a political satire fueled by the intense paranoia that, Jewison felt, had unhinged the political class. Above all, Jewison told Rose, "I want it to be funny."[21] Jewison sent the material via Mike Zimring, Rose's agent, and waited for a reply. He would later learn that Rose was "intimidated by the transatlantic telephone."

On January 28, 1964, the reply arrived. "Feel novel much underdeveloped with several serious problems," Rose wrote. "But unquestionably potentially marvelous picture . . . Also welcome opportunity to work with Norman Jewison."

These few lines came as a relief for the director. But Rose wasn't kidding about the "serious problems" with Benchley's novel. He followed his telegram with a letter in which he bemoaned the "wobbly" structure, the complete absence of anything resembling a climax, and the fact that "none of the characters is really allowed to develop into a major character (who's the hero, for God's sake)." Most grievously, Benchley devolves into portraying the Russians as "traditional stage villains."

Still, Rose affirmed that "the basic idea is great." He loved the "general atmosphere of idiotic incompetence on both sides, all the stupid bickering and so on." Rose thought it possible to reconstruct the novel into a more coherent treatment in six weeks, and produce a good first draft in as little as three months, by May 1964.* But first, he wanted to ensure that he and Jewison were in synch about what they hoped to accomplish.[22]

They agreed to meet in Paris on April 4, 1964. Rose prepared for the conversation by typing up thirty-four pages of notes on Benchley's novel which, upon second reading, yielded fresh concerns. "I read the first sixty pages or so with delight and the beginnings of enchantment," Rose told Jewison,

---

* A "treatment" is a condensed version of the entire story written in prose. Most screenwriters won't move to the screenplay stage without a sound treatment.

because Benchley had established the whole [Russian] crew as a hapless, hopelessly incompetent, nervous, bumbling, backbiting, querulously ineffectual assortment of lackbrains, zanies and dunderheads . . . Then, suddenly (and presumably because Benchley got out of the wrong side of the bed), a big tough Russian is pleasurably beating poor Olin Leveridge to unconscious pulp . . . and another (this one sex-starved) Russian is trying to strip poor Alice's clothes off with a big menacing Russian knife. Well, my stomach turned over all right, and Benchley's dad* (God rest his delightful soul) turned over in his grave.[23]

To Rose, Benchley's erratic portrayal of the Russians was symptomatic of a deeper confusion over what his book was about. Sure, the idea was engrossing: a scenario that brought the world's rival superpowers into immediate, unintentional, face-to-face conflict. But the author himself seemed to have no point of view. That was fine, but Rose wanted to be clear on one thing. "Do we want to make an important movie," he asked, "even though it may be somewhat difficult, or is this merely another routine assignment?" It was an honest question. The material could have gone either way.

For Jewison, *The Off-Islanders* represented an escape from the "routine assignments" that had thus far consumed his entire film career. He was just idealistic enough to think that, done properly, their version of *The Off-Islanders* might even do some good in the world. While slightly less sanguine about the power of film, Rose, too, wanted to write a movie they could be proud of. But their self-conscious commitment to making

---

* Benchley's father was the esteemed *New Yorker* and *Vanity Fair* humourist Robert Benchley. Nathaniel's son, Peter, wrote the novel *Jaws*.

an "important" film would drastically increase the difficulty of the task ahead.

* * *

Jewison had always imagined Jack Lemmon, who had recently starred in *The Apartment*, in the film's leading role. The problem, as Rose was quick to observe, was that there was no leading role for Lemmon to play. Jewison's first inclination was that if they combined two of Benchley's characters they might have a protagonist worthy of Lemmon. But Rose was in favour of ditching Benchley's characters altogether for a new protagonist made to order for Lemmon. What sort of protagonist would that be? Faced with this question, and throughout the entire writing process, Rose found himself paralyzed by options. Lemmon's character could be a doctor or lawyer or clergyman, or he could be on the island to recuperate from some illness or nervous breakdown, or he could represent a real-estate development company sent to buy property, or be a travelling salesman, or a former advertising executive who ran off to do something creative. Rose didn't know what direction to take, but told Jewison, "the day I can't come up with a script with a hero that has Jack Lemmon on his knees begging to play the part for nothing is the day I hang up this typewriter and retire from the game."[24]

Rose had an easier time identifying the problems with Benchley's novel than with coming up with workable solutions. He conjured a wild subplot in which the islanders lured the Russian captain ashore and took a compromising photograph as *kompromat*, which they threaten to send to Moscow unless he left peacefully. Rose thought it would be hilarious to include a sequence where Island spinsters do their make-up in preparation for the sex-starved Russian sailors, then become enraged when they are rescued and "haven't a hope in hell of being raped now."[25]

Rose was grasping. As he admitted to Jewison, "the biggest trouble here is that the possibilities are literally limitless." Even Rose's proposed title of the film, "The Day We Licked the Russians," suggests that he hadn't really understood Jewison's unifying vision. Eventually, he arrived at a few concrete ideas about structure: a forty-five minute first act to establish characters and lead up to the discovery that the Russians aren't really invading; a thirty-five minute second act, where the embarrassed islanders try to kill the Russians, and a twenty-minute third act, full of peace and understanding and all that "crap." Rose wanted to avoid an endless succession of time-wasting "treatments" until they had established the story. After that, he would start scripting.[26]

Jewison was still feeling invigorated about the project. Rose had a reputation for being difficult, but the director left their Paris meeting with a better understanding of how to manage him. As always, Jewison would play a character: that of a naïve, provincial, patriotic Canadian (Rose liked to condescend to Canadians, who he felt mistreated him during his time with the Black Watch). Rose may have been a neurotic Missourian, but Jewison would address him as the phlegmatic British county squire he imagined himself to be. It was a schtick, designed to make Rose feel secure enough to write. Still, Rose's baroque correspondence with Jewison fell into a pattern of inflated progress reports punctuated by long silences.

More than a month after their meeting in Paris, Rose had finally arrived at a sketchy idea of their protagonist: the last of the Island summer tourists, married with at least one child, stressed with work, "and then this day comes along and he's up to his distracted ass in a lunatic miniature war."[27] Jewison was fine with all this, although part of him must have wondered what Rose had been doing since their meeting. Lacking anything more substantive to say, he urged Rose to write scenes that took place indoors. "[A]t the moment we have to shoot everything outside and it's a little difficult due to weather," Jewison wrote, "and besides, I get terribly sunburned."[28]

By June 1964, well past Rose's original delivery date, Jewison hadn't seen so much as a treatment. He busied himself with other projects, including filming of *The Art of Love* through most of the summer. He had to tread lightly around Rose; too much pressure could cause a man of his temperament to snap. Still, Jewison found it hard not to worry.

Jewison's mood was not improved by the fact that Boaty Boatwright had moved to England earlier that year. The pair exchanged letters throughout the 1960s, confiding aspirations, gossiping about show-business colleagues, cataloguing the cultural touchstones of that convulsive decade. Boaty saw the Beatles at Carnegie Hall and was thoroughly unimpressed. "I can only describe that event as mass hysteria," she told Jewison. "At one point in the evening, Mike Nichols turned to me and said, 'I'm so embarrassed to be here,' which sums them up beautifully."[29]

Their correspondence was often wild.

You are a mean, lying, conniving, hateful son of a bitch!!! I will never call you again . . . or write you a letter! All the way from home from Cleveland I kept thinking how nice it would be to have a letter from you to make me laugh when I got home last night. You never wrote me a letter . . . because you don't know how to write – script or type – and you can't spell my name . . . or yours! I have already told Santa Claus to fill your stocking with switches and pictures of [*Here's Love* producer] Stu Ostrow . . . and Rock Hudson's nightgown! So there. You really are terrible. My address is 400 East 55 St. My home phone is TE-8-1973. Please lose both of them. Farewell, mean bad boy.[30]

But sincerity was never far from the surface. Three days after the assassination of John F. Kennedy, Boaty sent Jewison an emotional letter: "You were the first person I thought of on Friday when I heard the tragic news—and you were the only person I felt I could talk to then . . . There are so many things I'm grateful for . . . especially the reassurance I get from you as a devoted friend. I hope I shall always make you proud of me—and happy too."[31]

With Boaty across the Atlantic, Jewison took longer to respond to her letters. She noticed, and he tried to smooth things over. "I don't feel we have really lost touch with each other," he wrote, "I think it is because it has been so long since we have been able to sit down and really communicate. Since I don't express myself as well as you do on paper, you often misconstrue some of the things I do say."[32]

Jewison must have envied Boaty's freedom. Bored of the American scene, she had picked up and moved to swinging London at age twenty-nine. He was tied to Los Angeles, tied to his contract with Universal, tied to his wife and three children, a 115-pound white German Shephard, and a six-toed turtle named Fred. "Outside of the turtle dying this morning, life goes on in its rather dull, suburban, Brentwood way," was how he characterized his home life in this period.[33] Boaty was young and free in a way that Norman had never been young and free, and now she was an ocean away. He encouraged friends visiting the UK to meet with her and send him their impressions. "Have managed to see the dear girl on several brief but pleasant occasions and there is no question about it—she is every bit as much a phenomenon as Niagara Falls, and possessed of equal energy," wrote the producer Stanley Margulies. "It really would have been perfect if both of you could have been here."[34]

With the days crawling by, and still nothing from Rose, the burst of excitement that had followed their meeting had mutated into a sense of nervous dread. What if Rose couldn't crack the screenplay? Everyone agreed that the basic idea was great, but what if Rose, the "best screenwriter in the world," couldn't convert that idea into something fit for film? Where would Jewison be then? He had to confront the possibility that his dream project, and the career he had envisioned, might never get off the ground.

Then, on June 3, 1964, a telegram arrived.

> Sudden unexpected and unbelievable breakthrough last night.
>
> Turned all keys at once. Middle and end all solved and unified whole story now absolutely credible but incredibly funny and tremendously moving. Not just best story I've ever written but genuinely valuable. You and Mirisches and audiences will flip because this thing certainly biggest hit in years. Will write explaining at great length but ecstatically happy for both of us so please forgive Hollywood hyperbole.[35]

"Hollywood hyperbole" was classic Rose. The euphoric quality of the letter, the heap of adjectives ("incredibly" "tremendously" "ecstatically") is at least partly symptomatic of a defensive writer trying to justify his tardiness. But his final two words offered an escape hatch. Distancing himself from such "Hollywood hyperbole," Rose implied that he was only ironically participating in the tawdry enterprise of commercial filmmaking. Jewison understood that this was part of their game: "God, what enthusiasm," he replied. "Little do we know what enthusiasm, passion, and excitement lies beneath the tweedy coat of a rather thoughtful, taciturn Jerseyman."[36]

* * *

Rose finally had the ending they needed. After his months-long dry spell ("We had a lot of problems, buying a new house, one thing and another," he'd blithered at one point) Rose confessed that he had "spent almost two months wrestling with one Goddamned problem." He needed a convincing way of turning the islanders and invaders into allies without devolving into moralistic speeches. "If *only* there were some way of playing the whole story for *real*," he wrote, "some way of getting the Russians and the Americans to the point at which they are *really going to start killing each other*, and then at the very last moment some way of working some incredible switch." But what could motivate such a radical reversal?

On June 2, Rose was discussing the problem with his wife, "repeating for the hundredth time that it was beyond the realm of possibility when (for no reason I can understand) I suddenly finally saw how simply and easily the whole thing could be done—and done in a single minute, in one single scene." The dam had burst: "[I]n eighteen years of scribbling movies I've never had such a piece of luck as I've had on this thing now."[37]

Rose's ending, which Jewison would film almost exactly as Rose outlined it in his letter, hinges upon an insight that audiences care more about an individual child than about the prospect of global annihilation. The Soviet sub, now dislodged from the sandbar, sails into the town's harbour. The Russian Captain trains the submarine's guns at the town and threatens to blow it off the map. The Islanders won't back down. "It's the Cuban confrontation in miniature," Rose explains, and "it seems absolutely inevitable that all hell—and real hell—is going to break loose in the next ten seconds."

Just as the standoff reaches almost unbearable tension, a six-year-old boy slips from a nearby belfry, slides down the roof, catches his belt loop, and hangs there—suspended fifty feet above the ground. "And in an instant," Rose wrote, "the war is forgotten." The Russian shore party forms a human ladder to rescue the boy. The islanders repay them by providing an escort out to sea, protecting the sub from incoming fighter jets. A recognition of their shared humanity brings the Cold War powers back to their senses.

"Louis B. Mayer used to say that a picture was no good unless the audience went away with a warm feeling inside," Rose wrote, "and I reckon that the average American audience will leave our theatre with a warm feeling that will persist right up till the next time they encounter some Negro boy trying to buy a hamburger or something really outrageous like that."[38]

Jewison was elated. "Ecstatic about ending," he dashed off in a Telegram. "Always in love with the brotherhood concept and islanders coming to aid of Russians saving child give it raison d'être and full dramatic meaning. I have goosepimples. You're brilliant."[39]

Over the next month, however, Rose exhibited more signs of stress. Jewison began to worry that their extensive correspondence about the screenplay had become a way for Rose to avoid writing it. At one point, Rose suggested, in all seriousness, that Jewison could simply use their letters to convince Jack Lemmon to sign on. But Jewison needed his screenwriter to write a screenplay, not letters. Rose suggested a first draft by October. Jewison replied that if they wanted a Lemmon or Dick Van Dyke on board for a spring shoot, they'd need a script by September 1.

By August, the triumphant adjectives had vanished from Rose's prose: he was starting to squirm. He expended great verbal energy bitching about Benchley's novel and the remaining story problems. "I don't think it's because I'm old and fat and burnt-out, I think that making something as good as this thing *can* be is just a very tricky business." Jewison's nationality heightened Rose's sense of persecution. "It's a hell of a thing, after all these years," he moaned, "to have any sudden pressure put on me by a Goddamned Canadian, I can tell you. The Canadians pushed me around, and deliberately, for five and a half years. If Mackenzie King turned over in his sleep for God's sake they'd put a forty-pound pack on my back and make me walk for three days and three nights."[40]

By August 9, Rose was on the brink. Jewison's proposed deadline, which inadvertently coincided with the writer's forty-sixth birthday, had triggered intimations of mortality. He was emotional and drinking heavily. In one exquisitely neurotic missive, he proposed wild comic ideas for the film, including a giant swarm of bees that suddenly appears and starts stinging everyone on both sides. When Jewison protested that insects are hard to film, Rose replied: "As for the bees, you idiot, the funny thing is that you wouldn't see them."

Rose did propose one idea Jewison loved: an extended comic sequence involving the town drunk trying to catch his horse, which would give the film its unforgettable final shot. For the most part, however, Rose wallowed in indecision, oppressed by the "the hundreds or possibly thousands of notions which I've been trying to juggle." He knew the script would work eventually. But:

> whether I'm going to be able to tie up enough half-baked notions
> and hopefully optimistic notions that may or may not work when
> it comes to scripting to convince somebody as intelligent as D.
> Van D. that he should play a part that doesn't exist in N. F'ing
> Benchley's half-arsed lying excuse for a novel—and—AND—
> perform that little trick by the first of September is a point that
> can only be described, on this sunny ninth of August, as moot.
> You hear? You apprehend my meaning? I said moot. Moot, moot,
> MOOT!

Jewison was already in a foul mood before reading those words. He had returned from a pleasant jaunt to Montreal for a National Film Board symposium on the future of Canadian film, where he had caught up with old CBC pals. But re-entry into the daily domestic grind had been painful. That morning, Jewison's dog had put a "hole" in the family cat. Four of his tomatoes had been ruined by snails, which was irritating. And he had suddenly inherited responsibility for dressing his younger son Kevin as a pirate before a 9 a.m. appointment. Now Rose was openly flirting with quitting the whole project.

Jewison chose to take it well. Anything was better than silence. He reasoned that Rose's contortions were evidence that the project had gotten under his skin. "I'm just drunk enough this evening to abandon my customary almost-British reserve to make a personal statement," Rose had written. "I like you. Personally, I mean. I don't have any feeling about you professionally speaking, for the simple reason that I've never seen a movie that you made."

Fair enough, Jewison may have felt. He didn't care much for his own professional output to that point. But if that was going to change, he would need to coax a screenplay out of Rose in one way or another. He wrote:

> I know you're the most important screenwriter on Jersey, or at least in St. Brelade; I know you're extremely temperamental; I know you were bitterly mistreated by Canadians since the war and have harboured a grudge ever since; I know Nathaniel Benchley is a f'ing bad novelist; I even know that you can't get a treatment ready by the first of September. In spite of all that, and the fact that you're much older than I, I still love you. I don't know why, but I even have implicit faith that you'll write the screenplay.

Who knows, maybe it'll even be good! You did write other good scripts when you were younger . . .

Please don't worry about tying up all the ideas and half-baked notions, etc. etc. into a tidy package by the first day of September. The second of September would do just as well unless, of course, you really are too old and fat and too rich to care at all.

"Seriously speaking," he added, "the important thing is that we make a good film." He advised Rose not to worry about the Mirisch brothers, United Artists, or contracts—the "Canadian flash," as he called himself, would "handle all that stuff."

By now, *The Art of Love* had completed post-production; Jewison screened it for producer Ross Hunter on September 2.[41] Jewison had hoped to proceed straight to *Russians*, but Rose had fallen further behind. On September 15, their much-extended due date, Jewison received not the treatment, but a one-line telegram: "Substantial treatment developing well but cannot deliver for three or four days stall for me if necessary."[42]

On November 18, Rose sent a long letter explaining why he wasn't going to begin writing the screenplay until he had solved some basic "constructional" problems. "[E]ven though you may be alarmed at the news that there's no actual script yet," Rose wrote, "I'm encouraged."[43]

Nearly eight months and over one hundred pages of correspondence after their dinner in Paris, Rose had not written one word of the screenplay. When agent Stan Kamen wrote to Jewison about a troubled production that required a new director, Jewison did not hesitate. For months, he had hoped that his next project would be *The Russians Are Coming*. Now, thanks to some racy footage coming out of New Orleans, he would take over the reins on *The Cincinnati Kid*.

* * *

"First thing almost everybody notices about Norman Jewison is his enthusiasm," the reporter David Cobb observed in December 1964. "Not merely enthusiasm, but a habit of getting his way, via persuasion and a certain ruthless tact, with tricky stars."[44]

"Enthusiasm" is a word that often found its way into press accounts of Jewison. "Ruthless" far less so, and yet Cobb landed on that word for a reason.

The interior of Jewison's office on the Goldwyn lot, which had once been Samuel Goldwyn's private dining room, now looked more like an apartment. He paced the lush piling of the wall-to-wall carpet, talking to Cobb while gathering papers for a trip to New York.[45] He was preparing to meet with Martin Ransohoff, the *Cincinnati Kid* producer who had acquired a reputation as "an aggressive wheeler-dealer" in the industry.[46] Between phone calls, Jewison told the story of how he had come to be the film's director.[47]

On December 4, Sam Peckinpah, who was directing the film on location in New Orleans, sent home the scheduled cast members and proceeded to shoot an improvised nude scene. When a studio official reportedly asked Peckinpah if the nude scene was for the "European version," Peckinpah replied that it was "for my own version." On Monday morning, Ransohoff announced that Peckinpah had been replaced, and that the production would pause for a week while Jewison studied the script.[48] Jewison's deal was for $125,000 against 10 per cent of Ransohoff's gross in his co-production with MGM.[49]

The interview with Cobb was interrupted by another telephone call. "It's Eddie," said Nadine Phinney, the director's assistant. "Eddie" turned out to be the actor Edward G. Robinson, whose 1930s gangster pictures

Jewison had seen as a kid. Robinson was alarmed by the fact that his role was shrinking in the rewrites. (Robinson himself had replaced Spencer Tracy on the production two weeks prior.)[50] Cobb scribbled notes as Jewison offered "ten minutes of brilliantly courteous explanation" about why he'd cut scenes of Robinson's character waxing poetic about his glory days as a gambler.[51] "Only a has-been reminisces," Jewison exclaimed. "You're the king. You come into this picture like Lucifer, on a cloud of steam."[52]

With Robinson appeased, Jewison returned his attention to Cobb, explaining that the film would do for poker what *The Hustler* did for pool. Jewison's vision had necessitated not only script revisions but also stylistic updates. He'd spent three hours that day going over costume changes for Steve McQueen's character. Increasingly excited during the interview, Jewison was now jumping and punching the air to punctuate his points. "Oh yeah, things are really starting to crackle!" he enthused about the script revisions. "Oh the whole thing is crisper, tighter, more believable. Oh God, yeah!"[53]

Jewison was unapologetic about taking over from Peckinpah. In his memoir, he repeats the story that Peckinpah went rogue, turning in material that would have earned the film an "X" rating, adding that he was "a hard drinker and a loose cannon."[54] Peckinpah put a slightly different spin on the situation in a 1972 *Playboy* interview:

> Marty Ransohoff fired me from *The Cincinnati Kid* after only four days. He gave a story out to the trades that I was vulgarizing the picture by injecting a nude scene into it. There was a scene in a hotel room between Rip Torn and this girl who was playing a dreary little hooker. Well, we worked on it and the scene got sadder and sadder. It just happened that the girl turned out to

be naked under her coat. It was only one element in a much bigger scene. But I learned one thing about Marty: He had a tremendous hatred of real talent.[55]

"It was nearly four years before I worked again," Peckinpah added. "I got by on moonlighting, borrowed money, and an occasional script. I couldn't get people on the phone or get through a studio gate. I was out."

Given that Jewison had been replaced on *Here's Love* little over a year before, he would have been conscious of the ethical dimensions of his decision. "Jewison takes 'Kid' from Sam Peckinpah," ran the headline in *Variety*, as though he'd stolen another director's baby. The move revealed a certain ruthless pragmatism underlying Jewison's idealism. One journalist would later describe the "iron will and awesome drive" masked behind Jewison's "boyish face and disarmingly garrulous manner."

"He looks like a nice gentle kid," warned one associate in this period, "but don't cross him—he fights like a tiger."[56]

* * *

Just as Jewison was getting into *The Cincinnati Kid*, Rose reared up in a state of panic. Finally scripting *Russians*, at a pace of four or five pages a day, he was still nominally trying to meet a deadline of Christmas 1964. But the writing was not going well. In fact, Rose described it as "increasingly nightmarish." The "lunatic" deadline was approaching so fast that Rose was "beginning to write without thinking." He imagined Jack Lemmon reading a hastily cobbled-together draft and rejecting it out of hand. Therefore, he implored Jewison, it is "in everybody's best interests—the Mirisch Company's, Lemmon's, yours, mine, and everybody's—to ease off the intense pressure," and allow him to submit *half* of the screenplay by Christmas. "Couldn't you talk to Jack himself, and put all this to him?" Rose begged. "Can't you do something? And doesn't it make sense to try? Please consider talking to Mike [Zimring], the Mirisches and Jack about it."[57]

We don't know the exact terms in which Jewison rejected Rose's proposition, although we do know the end result: Rose submitted a complete first draft on December 23, 1964. Jewison and Rose won a $500-dollar wager with Harold Mirisch, who had bet that the screenwriter couldn't deliver.[58] With Jewison now at work on *The Cincinnati Kid*, Rose would have until the following April to turn around his second draft.

If life had been moving slowly for Jewison in the autumn of 1964, the pace was frenetic by December. After reading the screenplay for *The Cincinnati Kid*, which had already undergone multiple drafts at the hands of high-profile writers Paddy Chayefsky, Charles Eastman, and Ring Lardner Jr., Jewison decided to overhaul the whole thing.[59] He cancelled the family ski trip and spent the next three weeks holed up in his MGM office with Terry Southern, intensively rewriting "every page" under "tremendous pressure."[60] (Southern stuck around to rewrite scenes on the fly during production). It was the first time in his career that Jewison had this much creative control of a film, and he was going to use it. His contract guaranteed the first three cuts of the picture. He would oversee the dubbing and stay involved with every aspect of the film "right to the bitter end."[61]

One thing Jewison could not control was the cast, which was set. Steve McQueen, flying high off the success of *The Great Escape*, would play the titular "Kid," a cocksure, Depression-era card shark out for Lancey "the Man" Howard, played by Robinson. The Kid's desire to beat the Man honestly is complicated by Slade (Rip Torn), a Southern grandee who blackmails the dealer Shooter (Karl Malden) to ensure that the Man loses.

Ann-Margret would play the dealer's duplicitous wife (a classic early scene shows her filing pieces of a jig-saw puzzle to make them fit) with Tuesday Weld as Christian, the Kid's wholesome, cornfed girlfriend.

Jewison began principal photography in New Orleans that January, committed to the idea that the film should be infused with a sense of place. While on location, he sat for an interview with a nineteen-year-old freelancer from *Cinema Magazine*. Feeling positive about his new associations with Ransohoff and the Mirisches, he used the interview to fight back against "the whole theory that producers are really interfering, meddlesome, unartistic, cigar-smoking businessmen, who are only concerned with gross receipts." That was "a lot of nonsense," he said, insisting that many producers "are terribly creative."

The young interviewer then asked about technical aspects of the medium. Jewison agreed that editing was important, but added, "I'm not the kind of director that shoots a scene from every conceivable angle and then makes up his mind about interpretation of pauses and staging and so on, in the editing room."

Jewison left an impression on the cub reporter, one Curtis Lee Hanson, whose own films would include *L.A. Confidential* (1997), *Wonder Boys* (2000), and *8 Mile* (2002), and whose gambling picture *Lucky You* (2007) would elicit direct critical comparisons with *The Cincinnati Kid*.[62]

* * *

If Jewison had earned a reputation as a director who could manage difficult stars, Steve McQueen was the quintessential difficult star known for challenging directors. The specific challenges he posed, a neediness and tendency to manipulate, came from a seemingly bottomless reservoir of insecurity.

McQueen's impoverished childhood had included spells in a travelling carnival and time on the streets. His mother had so many husbands she'd lost count. His grandmother, with whom he lived for a time, was institutionalized for insanity.[63] His formal schooling ended in grade nine, after which he worked on oil rigs, as a lumberjack, construction worker, and towel boy at a brothel. Poverty had left a deep imprint. Later in life, according to biographer Penina Spiegel, McQueen would "go to a restaurant and order two of everything: two steaks, two baked potatoes, two salads," fearing that the restaurant would run out of food.[64] Jewison would become intimate with McQueen's fears and appetites over the course of the two films they would make together. In December 1964, however, he had only a vague sense that McQueen could be a handful. He asked Stan Kamen, an agent they shared at William Morris, to set up a meeting.

Jewison spent an evening with McQueen, playing pool and talking about the film.[65] McQueen opened up to Jewison about his past and experiences in film. Jewison understood that McQueen responded best to older, fatherly directors, something he couldn't provide at thirty-eight. So Jewison devised a new role to play. "Look on me as your older brother who went to college and who will always protect you. I'll always look out for you and serve your interests. I'll do everything in my power to make you wonderful in this film."[66] Jewison thought he had McQueen's number, and they seemed to get along.

On set, however, McQueen could be exasperating. Steve "wasn't what you'd call a giving man. Frankly, he was a cheapskate," Jewison reflected on McQueen's acting style. "McQueen had this habit of looking down at the floor between setups, so no one could take their cue from him. Then, promptly on *Action*, he'd come up, shoulders rising, with that open-eyed animal expression—a readiness to please and also, if necessary, to maul you."[67]

McQueen was a cheapskate in more ways than one. "When Steve left the set at night he'd always hit up me or one of the crew for five bucks 'gas money,' which we never saw again," Jewison recalled. McQueen would then peel off in his Jaguar, Ferrari, or Porsche.[68]

"I can't honestly say that he was the most difficult person I've ever worked with because the rewards were so great," Jewison would later reflect. "But of all the actors I've worked with, Steve was the most alone."[69]

* * *

While on location in New Orleans, Jewison decided to film a sequence involving a Dixieland brass band playing a funeral march, which he felt would root the film in a more authentic feeling of place. The scene wasn't in the script, but it felt right for the film.

Martin Ransohoff, reviewing the rushes back in LA, was apoplectic. Hadn't he just fired a director for filming scenes that weren't in the script? He sent notice to Jewison, telling him to pack up the location shoot and return to Los Angeles immediately. Jewison thought about it. Steeped in the gambling ethos of *The Cincinnati Kid*, he knew that if he overplayed his hand, he was likely to end up like the Kid, losing his first dramatic picture. Someone would replace him, just as he had replaced Peckinpah. But he also knew that if he ever wanted to become the kind of film director he imagined himself to be, he would have to fight for his vision. He sent a telegram to Ransohoff:

At present time half day behind schedule. Fully understand and sympathize with your budget position but since I'm not responsible for any overages at this time it is unfair to exert this pressure upon me. If weather holds will do my best to complete location shooting by Saturday night. However if necessary must remain until scheduled scenes are completed. Expect your continued support and confidence.[70]

Jewison finished location shooting in New Orleans, as planned. Yet tensions with Ransohoff only intensified after the production moved to the MGM lot, where the producer was known to make sudden appearances. "Whenever Ransohoff walked on the stage, I'd walk off," Jewison recalled. "One time I ran round the corner and hid in a prop elevator we were using in this particular scene. It was a fake elevator. All it did was sit there . . . I crouched inside for about ten minutes, holding my breath every time I heard Ransohoff's voice asking where I was." McQueen finally told Jewison he was safe to come out.[71]

Even his relationship with the film's editor, Hal Ashby, who would become one of his closest friends, strained under the pressure of those early days. While dedicated to both the director and project, Ashby was accustomed to a certain level of freedom as a creative professional. During his work directing live television, however, Jewison had acquired a tic of snapping his fingers where he sensed there should be a cut. After three days of Jewison snapping his fingers in the dailies, Hal pre-empted Norman by snapping his own fingers. They laughed it off, but Jewison didn't snap his fingers in the dailies again.[72]

The long hours, harried pre-production, and unwanted attention from the "front office" were all starting to take a toll. "God, Norman, where did you get those bags under your eyes?" Boaty asked. By the time he wrote Boaty a Valentine's letter it was February 17. "The picture is coming slowly and hard," he wrote, "and I have absolutely no idea how good it is. I alternate from moments of great elation to deep despair. I'm very tired and am now feeling the pressure of the lack of preparation. Another problem is that I have shot too far out of sequence and I'm afraid of the ending, which, of course, has already been shot."[73]

That final poker sequence presented an unusual technical conundrum: with characters seated around a circular table, Jewison would have to work carefully with Ashby to ensure that characters weren't facing the same direction when speaking to one another in close-ups. He also worried that a card game was not a sufficient dramatic climax for a motion picture. In the westerns, poker was always the prelude to the gunfight. Here, it had to *be* the gunfight.

"I realized that the only way a card game was going to work," Jewison remembered, "was that you had to get involved in the people." He evoked his characters' psychological traits through concrete details: the ritualistic way in which McQueen packs his suitcase ("like a bullfighter," Jewison said) or his habit of smelling the cellophane on a new deck of cards to ensure it hadn't been opened. Jewison had McQueen and company use real money in the poker sequences: he believed that actors handled actual dollar bills differently than fake money, that you could see it in their performance. Jewison kept McQueen and Robinson apart, shooting their scenes separately until they met in the climactic card scene.[74] The Oedipal tension of the film, in which the ambitious Kid tries to take out the aging champion, found a parallel in the real lives of his actors: Edward G. Robinson (b. 1893) was one of the leading actors of Hollywood's Golden Age, starring in *Little Caesar* (1931) and *Double Indemnity* (1944). McQueen (b.1930) was on his way to becoming the iconic male star of the 1960s counterculture—brooding, monosyllabic, and oozing existential hipness.

With the film's climax, Jewison set out to film the most intense, if not longest, poker scene yet committed to celluloid. The game is no-limit five-card stud: players receive four "up" cards and one concealed card. As the pressure mounts, the supporting players fold one by one, leaving only the

Kid and the Man. After a montage in which the Kid appears to win several hands, the final hand is dealt, in which the Kid ends up with an aces over full house. "I've got him!" the Kid says in a voice-over, "I've got the Man!" The Man turns over a Jack of Diamonds, beating the Kid with a straight flush.

For decades, poker experts have debated that final hand.[75] According to one authority, "the chances that *both* of these hands will appear in one deal of two-handed five-card stud have been calculated at a laughable 332,220,508,619:1—or well over 300 *billion*:1 against. If these two played fifty hands of stud an hour, eight hours a day, five days a week, the situation should arise about once every 443 years."[76]

Well, Jewison had wanted a dramatic ending. *The Cincinnati Kid* was "not really about stud poker," he would always contend. "Cards are merely the weapons."[77]

Certain aspects of the film were decidedly of the moment. A wandering interlude, in which Christian takes the Kid to meet her parents on their idyllic farm, reveals the influence of the French New Wave in its disregard for plot ("All of us have been influenced a lot by Truffaut, by *Jules et Jim*" Jewison said at the time).[78] The climactic game, with perspiring actors shot in extreme close-up, also upsets the usual narrative expectations. After his defeat, the Kid stumbles out into the alley and loses his last coin to a shoeshine boy, a final humiliation. Even the film's muted use of colour, "a kind of natural monochromatic effect," as Jewison described it, seemed a repudiation of the bubblegum palette of the director's Doris Day films.[79]

Yet these avant-garde gestures are contained within a largely conventional package: stereotypical characters acting out an archetypal plot, told in a film language that was cool and contemporary but not radical or alienating. If *The Cincinnati Kid* was a kind of bridge between the old Hollywood (of Robinson, Karl Malden, Joan Blondell) and the new (Ashby, Southern, McQueen), Jewison's own cinematic sensibilities lay somewhere in between.

CHAPTER 5

Fourteen Weeks

J EWISON SPENT MUCH OF THE FINAL PUSH on *The Cincinnati Kid* in a literal haze produced by the kerosene incinerated to produce the smoky atmosphere on set. He was juggling three different film projects, each with its unique problems. Universal had recently conducted a test screening of *The Art of Love*, and the news wasn't encouraging. "There just have to be further cuts in the first twenty minutes of the picture," he wrote Boaty. "Why we ever left the Ethel Merman song in, I'll never know." Hoping the poor results were just a regional aberration, or one ill-tempered audience, he asked producer Ross Hunter to set up a second preview in another area.[1]

The Cincinnati Kid was scheduled to wrap on March 12, 1965. Jewison anticipated a "tremendous amount of editing" on the picture. More dispiriting was the fact that his creative control of the film had turned out to be more limited than he had hoped. Martin Ransohoff could force significant changes. The ending was especially contentious. In Jewison's finale, the camera froze on McQueen's face after his final loss for ten seconds, an eternity in film time, before the credits rolled. Ransohoff didn't care for this arty flourish. He wanted a more upbeat ending that reunited McQueen with Tuesday Weld. "I have been fighting for my cut on the picture for the past two months," Jewison wrote to his former CBC collaborator Alex Barris. Ransohoff "is a strong personality," he added, "and I hope that what emerges in the end is not vitiated too much."[2]

Meanwhile, the Mirisches were growing increasingly nervous about the state of *Russians*. William Rose, for his part, was no longer concerned. "[I]t's the best script I've ever read," boasted the screenwriter, who had been a blubbering wreck mere months before. "It's got the construction of Hitchcock at his best (of which there isn't very much) and it's got all that warm sentiment of Capra at his best (of which there was too much) . . . the whole business of the escort and the brotherhood crap is simply unbelievably effective and good." Jewison loved the "brotherhood crap," but there was still too much screenplay: without major cuts, *Russians* would be three hours long. Rather than slashing whole scenes, Rose proposed a general compression, making two-minute scenes of three-minute scenes, and sixty-second scenes of ninety-second scenes. He assumed that Jewison, "an old television hack," would understand that approach.[3]

Rose's jab was a sign of the times. By 1965, the entertainment press often grouped Jewison with John Frankenheimer, George Roy Hill, Arthur Hiller, and others as a "new generation" of director who had graduated from television. This new "breed," while in some ways more autonomous than their studio-era predecessors, were beholden to familiar anxieties. "There is an appalling fear among younger directors, myself included, about the possibility of making a movie that will not be profitable," John Frankenheimer said. "It is this sense of fear that inhibits real experimentation with new techniques . . . Nothing can kill a career faster than an 'arty' reputation."[4]

Jewison didn't want an "arty" reputation, but he did want more artistic freedom than he was given on *The Cincinnati Kid*. In the weeks that followed, as Jewison undertook the final, intensive rewrites on *The Russians Are Coming*, the first film he would produce as well direct, his decisions would reveal an awareness of his paradoxical position: an artist who could not afford to appear "arty," who was nevertheless determined to push beyond the formulaic boundaries of standard Hollywood product.

"I tell you, Bill, this picture will be more than just another Hollywood comedy. It's got to be more," he wrote to Rose. "The opportunities are so rare. We will only come upon a situation or idea like this *once*."[5]

* * *

While the script for *Russians* was taking more filmable shape at last, the cast was up in the air. Jewison, for the first time, found himself responsible for attracting talent to the property; his previous five films had all been "packaged" by producers and agents. He hit an immediate roadblock with their male lead. Jack Lemmon, for whom the role had been tailored, was unavailable. Jewison tried to look on the bright side: "With Lemmon, Garner, Van Dyke, Hudson, or any of these Hollywood stars, our realism is vitiated," he pointed out to Rose. With a script that could easily tip into farce, a base level of realism was crucial to unlocking the piece's full emotional potential. When he found that most Russian-speaking actors in America were over the age of forty-five, he entered negotiations with the US State Department in hopes of employing Russian actors for the submarine crew. "Since I don't feel a contemporary submarine crew should be made up of fatties in their late middle-age," Jewison said, "we have been trying to obtain visas for some talented young Slavic types in Europe."[6]

Secure in his conviction that *Russians* could deliver an impactful message about transcending political difference, Jewison could seem remarkably cavalier about the political consequences of appearing sympathetic to communism at the height of the Cold War. William Rose was under no such illusion. "All the Communists in the world can get lost or just drop dead as far as I'm concerned," Rose said, adding, "I don't want even a controversial picture." He deliberately crafted a screenplay that "would offend nobody this side of the John Birch Society."[7]

It wasn't long before Jewison's attempt to cast actual Russians caused an uproar. "We have had an influx of British actors lately," the talent agent Jerry Rosen wrote in a letter published in *Variety*, "but now, to bring in communists to replace our own actors is ludicrous."

Rosen was just getting warmed up:

> Norman Jewison, a neophyte director out of live TV with high-handed methods and small knowledge of the wealth of fine actors we have here, should be stopped before our money comes back to us in the form of bullets! If Mr. Jewison, who loves publicity so much, would give the agents a character breakdown on the roles he needs filled, I guarantee the parts would be set to his satisfaction from our own American actors.

Rosen called on the Screen Actors Guild, the United States Department of Labor, and the local Department of Employment to "take a stand against his brand of directorial tyranny."[8] Rose's hopes for an uncontroversial picture had vanished even before the production had been cast. The news was all over town. "If I had known then the trouble I would cause when I handed you [*The Off-Islanders*]," Jerry Lieder wrote Jewison the following week, "I would have slit my wrists!"[9]

The Mirisch brothers, operating as independent producers for United Artists, weren't worried by the rumours that Jewison was a closet pinko. In fact, they were more focused on locking him in for his next picture. By May, all signs were pointing toward *How to Succeed in Business Without Really Trying*, based on the 1962 Pulitzer and Tony Award winning Broadway production. The project was a natural fit for a director with roots in musical comedy and Broadway experience. The Mirisches offered $175,000 plus 10 per cent of the profits for a sixteen-week shoot, in addition to office space, a personal assistant, bankrolling his secretary, and billing as "A Norman Jewison Production." Jewison's William Morris agents countered with *How to Succeed* as a part of a four-picture deal over six years, calling for $175,000 plus 25 per cent of the profits for the first two, and $200,000 plus 33.3 per cent of the profits on the last two.[10]

It was shaping up to be a great deal for Jewison, with more money and more freedom. But it was also highly theoretical: Jewison wouldn't begin filming his first film under the Mirisch banner for another few months. Meanwhile, he was "bouncing between MGM and Goldwyn like a rubber ball," trying to persuade Marty Ransohoff not to slash up *The Cincinnati Kid*, while at the same time trying to keep Harold Mirisch calm about casting *Russians*.

Despite what Jewison had said to Rose about wanting to cast unknown actors for realism's sake, the Miriches and United Artists wanted a star for Whittaker, the American lead. Jewison had repeatedly struck out. As he reported to Rose, "Van Dyke wasn't available. Johnny Carson wasn't available. Merv Griffin wasn't available. Dick Crenna wasn't available. Bob Redford felt the part was too straight, as did Alan Arkin."

Jewison offered the primary Russian role to Peter Ustinov: "I can think of no one better on the English or Russian stage for Rozanov than Mr.

Ustinov." Whether or not the actor appreciated being addressed in the third person, he declined the role.[11]

Jewison wanted Elaine May for Mrs. Whitaker, but felt he couldn't offer her the part until the male lead was locked in. The idea of casting Russian actors as the submarine crew was scuttled by the Russian Central Committee, although Jewison hadn't given up on finding some Polish or Czech actors who spoke Russian. "If I sound a little depressed, don't be alarmed," Jewison told Rose.[12] The script, he said, "is the star of the picture."[13]

In truth, the script still needed a serious polish. Rose had submitted what he called an "incomparably better" second draft, and collected his second installment of $50,000. While Rose had now fulfilled his obligations for the picture, he remained available for rewrites. Jewison still worried about length. A reading of the latest draft clocked in at two hours and forty-seven minutes. By "the time one adds stretch for business, dissolves, etc., we probably have a film closer to three hours, which just horrifies the Messrs. Krim, Picker, Mirisch, et al," Jewison wrote, referring to United Artists executives Arthur B. Krim and David Picker. To reduce costs of location shooting, Jewison scouted a small harbour near Fort Bragg in northern California, which could pass for New England. It "hasn't changed in eighty years," he said, "and has a feeling of the east coast." Still, when below the line estimates came in at over two million dollars, Jewison felt increased pressure to cut the script.*

Rose was alarmed at Jewison's psychological state. "I worry sometimes (seriously) about the goddamn pace you seem to have to go at these days,"

---

* In film budgeting, "above the line" refers to line items for the principal creators (producers, director, actors) while "below the line" includes line items for every other distinct aspect of the production: all credited functions, from designers to hair stylists to caterers, plus taxes, insurance, and so on. Film budgets once separated these two categories of expense as "above" and "below" a literal line.

he wrote. "Don't trust Ransohoff; and, incidentally, don't trust anybody else, either."

As for cuts, it was predictable that a screenwriter would want to preserve his precious words from the philistines in the front office, who presumably lacked the appropriate respect for his work. Rose, however, made just the opposite argument: the problem was that the screenplay was being treated with *too much* respect. "Trust me," he wrote, "two hours and forty-seven minutes my bloody British arse."

> When we read through the script I was several times really shaken by the ponderous reading you tended to give the majority of those scenes. Lad, take this in. You were reading everything . . . with a slow, careful, full-value kind of get-all-the-content reverence for the material that simply horrified me. Christ, it was like Eugene O'Neill, with overtones of Kafka.
>
> Get it into your head that the script is a lot of crap . . . Lickety-split, goddammit, the thing has to go like a proper farce, and the values thing that you respect and admire in it be thrown away as if it never mattered for an instant. Otherwise you're dead. All that Kameradschaft-Brotherhood stuff can only be convincing by implication, only by throwing it away, not by dwelling on it or pointing it up or waving it like the Maple Leaf Forever . . . You may be making a great farce, you may be making a farce with the most important values ever built into any motion picture, you may have the United Nations Award in your outhouse already, but I will say and say again that you are still making a farce.

Rose assumed that Jewison wouldn't listen. "The trouble with your generation is that all you nouvelle vague guys think you know everything.

You sit there in Brentwood, cut off, so provincial that people in Toronto would laugh at you, with no idea at all of what's really happening in the world."[14] Rose may have been theatrically phlegmatic, but he had correctly sensed that Jewison's idealistic instincts, if left unchecked, could manifest a moralizing tone that was anathema to the picture's madcap humour. Rose may have saved the picture by reminding Jewison that his script was to be treated as a load of "crap."

* * *

The day after Jewison received Rose's letter, *The Art of Love* began its theatrical run. On the surface, it was more of the same, another opulent Ross Hunter production for Universal on which he was merely a hired gun. Yet Jewison had long felt there was something special about this one. "*Art of Love* is different," he wrote Stanley Margulies. "I think it has more style than anything I've done since *40 Pounds of Trouble*. It's very plotty, but rather warm and delightful in spots."[15] The Carl Reiner screenplay centred on an American odd couple in Paris: Paul (Dick Van Dyke), a devoted artist who can't sell a painting, and Casey (James Garner), a dissolute, womanizing writer who can't sell a story. Most of the script involved screwball antics stemming from Paul's fake suicide (to increase the value of his paintings); after Paul discovers that Casey has been seducing his fiancé, he begins feeding the Paris police clues to frame Casey for what is now his "murder." Most of the film is played for broad, slapstick comedy in the spirit of *The Pink Panther*.

On first blush, the nonstop lunacy of *Art of Love* would seem infertile ground for any sort of aesthetic statement. But Paul's artistic frustration dramatized Jewison's own exasperation with his studio products in 1964. "Artists of the world," read Paul's suicide note/manifesto, "in the age of

the Zorgases"—Zorgas was the name of Paul's mercenary art dealer—
"we are no longer permitted to live for art. I therefore undertake the
ultimate rebellion: to die for art."

Zorgas was not a straightforward stand-in for Ross Hunter or any other
executive, but the dynamic between artist and commercial gatekeeper was
familiar. Jewison needed no reminder that his artistic fate was governed by
business-minded philistines. He also knew as well as John Frankenheimer
that nothing was more lethal for a Hollywood director than an "arty"
reputation.

Jewison was proud of what he had been able to accomplish within
the Universal template. He thought it was a slick, stylish, even sexy film
and, most importantly, he found it hilarious. He'd learned a thing or
two over the years about what worked and what didn't. He'd suffered
his share of setbacks, but this was a commercial vehicle written by a
proven collaborator and featuring some of the most bankable stars in
the business. If Jewison had a wheelhouse in 1964, *The Art of Love* was
in it.

Critics excoriated the film. They hated the continuous absurdity
and manic pace: "The picture looks like one that kept changing as each
member of the company suggested some new cute bit," *Variety* claimed,
calling the final product a "garbled mixture of coquettish comedy" that
"never once settles down to a consistent point of view."[16] Others would
call *The Art of Love* a "tasteless film" that was "bloated with lunacy." Its
"few good ideas are soon flogged to death."[17] Most devastatingly, they
hated it for being generic. Universal "is still grinding them out from the
same old mold," began the *New York Times* review. The film may have had
the lavish accoutrement typical of Ross Hunter productions—the Cartier
jewels, the A-list actors, and, in this case, the exotic location—but *The Art
of Love* "is straight from the assembly line."[18]

If anything, critics in 1965 were lenient. The characters portrayed by Elke Sommer (Nikki) and Angie Dickinson (Laurie) in *The Art of Love* were embarrassingly facile, lacking any sense of psychological interiority or even personality. In scene after scene, Sommer grovels before Van Dyke, begging him to paint her in the nude, marry her, or simply "bother" her. No amount of rejection or abuse will slake her desire. Dickinson's character, meanwhile, exists as a narrative prop, someone to be hoodwinked by the rascals. One running gag finds Dickinson fainting in every scene in which she appears, literally overwhelmed by her own stupidity. Jewison would later attribute the film's failure to a plot hole, a screenplay that asked audiences to accept the proposition that artworks automatically increase in value when the artist dies. The more likely explanation was a screenplay that failed to treat the female half of its cast as human beings.

The Art of Love became the thirty-first highest-grossing film of 1965, an amazing feat given the star power of Van Dyke and Garner. It was Jewison's first flop, and he took it personally. "I was getting very depressed," he remembered. "After *The Art of Love*, I thought my career was over. I said, 'I'm just going to sit here at this studio, and if they force me to do films I don't want to do, then I'll just sit at home.'"[19]

* * *

"(I Can't Get No) Satisfaction" topped the charts four straight weeks in the summer of 1965, and Jewison could relate. While artistic satisfaction remained elusive, he had been in Hollywood long enough to have become a minor celebrity in his own right. "Our home in Brentwood has become as popular a stopping point as the Canadian Consulate," he told the columnist Alex Barris.[20] It wasn't just Canadians. The Jewison home had become a point of interest for all manner of celebrity-obsessed tourists, to the mild consternation of neighbours. "The neighbourhood deeply appreciates the true class your presence gives," a dentist by the name of Dr. Robert C. Reed wrote to Jewison,

> however there is a fundamental problem to be solved. It has been noted of late that the goddamned tour bus is now stopping in front of your house. I don't mind the tourists basking in your glory, but upon stopping all the heads pop out of the windows, and great quantities of hay, straw, and similar material fall to the street and cause an unsightly mess. I offer no solution to this problem. Perhaps this can be referred to one of [President] Johnson's new bureaus.[21]

Jewison was preparing to leave for his Fort Bragg location to film *Russians*, but couldn't leave a message like this unanswered. "[Y]ou must understand that this is the price one must pay when living close to some of the more famous film luminaries," he joked. "I'll instruct the tour bus to stop at least six feet south of your property line, but I wish you would hurry up with that goddamned construction because it really gives the area the feeling of a new tract development."[22]

Casting problems plagued *Russians* almost until the film began to roll and, once again, he had Jack Lemmon to thank. After declining the male lead, Lemmon had a hand in robbing the film of its female lead: Felicia Farr, the actor's wife, bowed out at the eleventh hour due to pregnancy. Jewison scrambled to replace Farr with Eva Marie Saint, who had performed opposite Marlon Brando in *On the Waterfront*.

As Jewison was patching up his cast, production crews began literally patching together the submarine that would feature prominently in the film. Jewison had secured cooperation from the US Department of

Defense (which provided information on Russian Navy uniforms) and the Air Force, which agreed to provide McDonnell F-101 Voodoo jets for the film's finale. But his luck had run out with the Navy: under no circumstances, officials made clear, would a US naval unit be dressed up to look like a Russian submarine. Instead, the production would retrofit a Unifoam and plywood replica built to represent a Japanese submarine in *Morituri*, a recent World War II film. The 165-foot-long replica, cut into ten pieces and then reassembled in Noyo Bay, cost $18,000 to move, more than the $12,000 it had cost to lease.[23] It took special effects supervisor Danny Hays and his crew two weeks to assemble the vessel, which involved filling it with seventeen tons of Styrofoam.[24]

In September 1965, Jewison flew from LA to Fort Bragg, a lumber and fishing community of some 4,000 residents located 130 miles north of San Francisco. Jewison had the actors for one week of rehearsals before beginning his shoot. It was his sixth film, the first he would produce as well as direct, and shepherd through the entire production cycle. Now thirty-nine years old, his brown hair streaked with grey, Jewison was no longer the cherubic boy wonder who went to Disneyland with Tony Curtis. Wrinkles branched out from the corners of his ever-squinting eyes. He had grown a beard. One observer called it "Chekhovian," although it made him look more like a 1960s revolutionary. Perhaps he'd simply stopped shaving to save time. He had to be on location by 5 a.m. to make the most of the light. [25]

Watching the sun break through the early morning California mist, aqueous light shimmering in the harbour, Jewison felt invigorated. Whatever the failure of *The Art of Love*, this was his opportunity to get his career back on track. Two years had passed since he first read Benchley's *The Off-Islanders*—two years of writing, revising, pushing, worrying, dreaming. Now, on location, the autumn breeze sweeping off the Pacific, it was real. He had fourteen weeks to make it all pay off.

* * *

Jewison cupped his fingers around the flame as he lit a cigar and surveyed the Mendocino coast. It was the most beautiful part of the country he'd ever seen. He liked hunting and had brought his guns on location, but the quail and deer around his rental house were so abundant he felt there wasn't any sport in it.[26] From some angles, the area didn't resemble Cape Cod as much as he had hoped, but the imported New England outriggers, maple trees, and lobster traps would help. Crews were erecting a pre-revolutionary town hall, and several of the buildings along Fort Bragg's colourful main street had been given flat-front, shingled facades in the Cape Cod style.[27] Still, Jewison wouldn't know definitively how well Noyo Harbour could pass for New England until he'd seen it dressed up on film.

Rehearsals quickly revealed the benefits of a cast that wasn't dominated by one big star. Alan Arkin, who had acquired some Russian and grown a thick black moustache for the role of Lt. Rozanov, leader of the Russian landing party, was a generous presence, a far cry from McQueen. Arkin's contract called for $75,000 plus a $500 living allowance for twelve weeks in his first film role: he had come via Broadway, where he had recently played the role of David Kolowitz (a fictionalized Carl Reiner) in Reiner's semi-autobiographical play, *Enter Laughing*. Reiner was paid $150,000 to play Whitaker, the bumbling pater familias, with Eva Marie Saint (paid $5,000 per week plus living accommodations and meals for her children) as his wife and the brains of the operation.[28] Brian Keith would snarl and smirk his way through the role of the crusty police chief. Theodore Bikel (co-founder of the Newport Folk Festival, where Bob Dylan had "plugged in" just weeks before) brought a whiff of genuine socialism to the part of the Russian Captain, while the gifted comic actors Ben Blue, Paul Ford, Tessie O'Shea rounded out the ensemble.

Jewison encouraged his cast to ad-lib and experiment with Rose's script, which he treated as a living document: "It grows and develops, takes a turn here, a thrust there. It's breathing. It's fresh."[29] Sometimes, he kept rolling after the end of a scene, just to see what happened. Arkin, a veteran of New York's Second City improvisation troupe, would ad-lib until told to stop. "In my zeal I just kept going until I heard him say 'cut,'" he said.[30]

As ever, Jewison's boyish enthusiasm set the tone. One observer called him a "constant-talking, always-moving bundle of atomic energy."[31] The actors found his vitality infectious. "After you're with him for a while, you realize that this enthusiasm is for real," Eva Marie Saint said at the time. "He's actually delighted with everything and everyone. He even makes you love everything."[32]

Nadine Phinney, Jewison's secretary since 1962 and now his executive assistant, thought "it took him time to adjust," to the new role of producer. "But he got help from all departments. He wasn't afraid to ask."[33]

She added: "No one just works for him. He lets you work with him. He makes you a part of everything he does."[34]

That spirit of collaboration extended to include the entire community of Fort Bragg. Jewison made the unusual decision to make the daily rushes a public event. In the evenings, cast and crew would gather with townspeople in Fort Bragg's State Theatre, a musty, defunct movie house, to review the previous day's shooting. "People would show up with their dogs, their babies, their grandparents, the halt and the lame," remembers Arkin, "and every couple of weeks Jewison would have to stand up in his seat and yell to the assembled town, 'People, I'm going to have to ask you to leave your babies and dogs at home, because we can't hear the soundtrack!'"[35] Hollywood veterans were nonplussed: "It's unheard of to permit outsiders at rushes," said a Mirisch Company public-relations staffer.[36] But Jewison saw the delight the townspeople took in seeing their community on the big screen, and thought the gesture would make them more responsive to his direction in the panic scenes requiring hordes of extras.[37]

Meanwhile, Jewison was discovering the vicissitudes of outdoor filming. One day in early October the crew set up a straightforward shot of Ben Blue on his horse only to have the fog roll in. Jewison had a back-up plan and rushed to set up another shot that could be done in flat light. Before he could roll, the sun came out and over-exposed the shot. Back to Blue and his horse.

Weather problems notwithstanding, the first month of filming went smoothly. The Mirisches were turning out to be a director's dream. "There is a lack of pressure on the film like nothing I have ever felt," he wrote to Stanley Margulies, "and sometimes I even miss it. No one to fight with and no one to complain about. We are a completely independent company and function much like a freelance organization . . . I've never heard a word from United Artists since shooting began."[38]

In truth, United Artists was not as disinterested as it may have appeared. "They could not spend anything without our approval," said Arthur B. Krim, the longstanding UA chairman said of the production. He considered the Mirisch Company to be "like our west coast office or subsidiary." By the mid-1960s, UA had as many as fifty independent producers under contract. Many of these relationships were fruitless, but the Mirisches, as film historian Tino Balio writes, "delivered an incredible sixty-seven pictures in eighteen years."[39] They "gave autonomy to a lot of their own people," Krim recalled, "always with our blessing. Everything with the Mirisches was done with the closest of contact and we had great respect for what they were doing and therefore there was a minimum of controversy."[40] After his infuriating experience with Ransohoff,

Jewison thrived under the free-range production mentality embraced by UA-Mirisch.

Jewison was grinding his way through the production schedule. Dixie flew up for a brief visit: it "was nice to see someone in high heels," Jewison said. He was generally pleased with the performances, and particularly with Brian Keith, Jonathan Winters, and Paul Ford. "Alan Arkin still feels a little strange in the medium," he confided, "but I think he will become an American Peter Sellers if he chooses his properties well." Nearing the half-way point, the production was on track. "We've actually been very lucky so far," he reported.[41]

Then it started to rain.

* * *

The production lost one day of shooting, then two. Expected seasonal drizzle had turned into extended, torrential downpours. In periods when the rain subsided, a thick shroud of fog remained to spoil any shooting. On one sunny morning, the crew began setting up a shot and then had to retreat due to a sudden hailstorm. At one point, weather prevented them from shooting outdoors for two straight weeks. Jewison was feeling increasingly powerless and frustrated. As time slipped by, he felt his future hanging in the balance of this fourteen-week shoot.

There was a related problem, something Jewison wouldn't have anticipated until he confronted it. It had to do with the energy of his cast. Because they had been cooped up in motel rooms for hours on end, it was often difficult for Jewison to re-ignite the sense of urgency when they finally did catch a few hours of sunlight. Boosting the *esprit de corps* became a top priority. He organized games of charades and a Scrabble tournament, with a prize that would catch any actor's attention: an extra close-up. He made a point of walking around the location with a beaming smile on his face at all times. The unwavering optimism rubbed off on the cast. "When fog closed in on us and stayed for three days," Reiner recalled, "Norman just grinned. When the rain started, he broke out into a broad smile. Adversity seems to agree with him. How can you help but be cheered by a fellow like that?"[42]

If Jewison's jubilance was initially forced, the reviews of *The Cincinnati Kid*, which had opened in Los Angeles on November 5, gave him reason to smile. The critical reception could not have been more different from that of *The Art of Love* five months earlier. Almost every reviewer would note the similarity to *The Hustler*, the 1961 Paul Newman movie that stages a similar showdown between young and old. But the consensus was that *The Cincinnati Kid* was something special.

"A superb picture, one of the year's best," declared James Powers in the *Hollywood Reporter*, adding that "Norman Jewison's direction stamps him unmistakably as an important movie director, daring, imaginative, assured."

The Independent Film Journal called the film "Cinematic art of the highest order for the sophisticated set," and speculated that it was headed for Oscars.

"Norman Jewison is at his directorial best in building a beautiful series of preliminary climaxes to the ultimate grand hand," wrote Judith Crist in the *New York Herald Tribune*. (Jewison confessed that he found it "rather astonishing" that Crist had liked the picture.)[43]

In *Life*, Richard Schickel lauded Jewison's eye for detail, for capturing the "atmosphere, traditions, rituals, lore and language" of poker, as well as for "his sensitivity to the character of others in almost the manner of a psychological novel."

The Cincinnati Kid was in some respects an unusual picture. The narrative structure, turning on the question of man's fate in the universe, is as broadly allegorical as a medieval morality play, yet the film's visual style, its sombre use of colour and attentiveness to the details of poker, registered as "realistic" to many viewers. It was a strange mix, but it worked for audiences, and the critical response validated Jewison's technical *savoir faire*: he'd proven that a card game could be as dramatic as a gunfight or a boxing match.

Jewison wasn't wholly satisfied by the picture: "It ended up being a little slicker than I had wanted it to be," he confessed in a letter to his friend Didi Daniels Peters.[44] MGM had insisted upon a more upbeat ending, in which the Kid reunites with his girlfriend, for the European release—a perverse decision, in Jewison's view, given that "at both previews more than 70 per cent of the cards revealed that audiences found the ending to be the most unique aspect of the film," Jewison wrote.[45] He fired off a telegram stating that "I personally am violently opposed to such reconstruction and am shocked that the foreign sales division of any studio has final judgment on an artistic level."[46] Regardless, the film did what the trade papers invariably described as "boffo" box office as it opened around the country.[47]

While *The Cincinnati Kid* was a major success, Jewison worried about the extent to which it was perceived as "his" success. While some reviews singled out Jewison for praise, others reserved their hosannas for the producer: "Martin Ransohoff has constructed a taut, well-turned-out production in his latest bid to come up with something off the beaten path," wrote *Variety*, reflecting the Studio Era attitude that the producer is the primary author of a film, not its director.

This rankled Jewison for numerous reasons, not least that Ransohoff had often fought him tooth and nail on creative decisions and was now butchering the European ending. While Jewison had mostly kind remarks for Ransohoff in the press, he tasked his public relations firm, I.C.P.R., with ensuring that the public understood that the director, not the producer, was responsible for the film's success. "Norman, let me assure you again that we are doing everything humanly possible to establish the fact that you directed this enormously successful motion picture," wrote David Foster of I.C.P.R. "Everybody I have talked to in the business is keenly aware that you directed the movie, and, furthermore, they are keenly aware of the brilliant job you did."[48]

* * *

Filming on *Russians* picked up as the weather improved in November. Optimism prevailed among the cast and crew: "Most of his performers feel they have an extra special picture," noted one visitor to the set. But the isolation and duration of the shoot were beginning to take a personal toll.

"This location has been extremely long," Jewison wrote on November 30, "and in spite of the fact that it's probably the nicest part of the country I've yet found, I'm now anxious to get home."[49]

When it became apparent that he was not going to be finished by Thanksgiving, as initially planned, Dixie packed up Kevin, Michael, and Jennifer and joined him in Fort Bragg for the weekend. He loved messing around with the kids. "Norman doesn't have to pretend to be a pal to the children," Dixie said. "He's actually one of them. He enjoys what they're doing as much as he enjoys what he is doing."

Reiner said something similar in explaining why Jewison was a good director for a comedian. "He laughs at all your jokes. He's a beautiful audience because, like a child, he's ready to believe in you. He has a child's joy of life."[50]

One benefit of the foul weather was that Jewison had time to ponder his next project. While *How to Succeed At Business* was still officially next on the docket, Jewison was devoting more thought and energy to something completely different. That August, the agent Dorothy Cohen had sent Harold Mirisch a treatment for a western, something with a "sense of bigness and class," called *The Wind on Fire*. Written by the veteran scribe Harry Kleiner, based on his own free-verse poem, the treatment promised a sprawling epic set in nineteenth-century Mexico. It opened in a courtroom, where an American named Corey is found not guilty of murdering the son of Don Albanez, a local bigwig. Albanez refuses to accept the verdict, and informs the jurors that they have thirty days to execute Corey themselves. After initially rejecting Albanez's demand, each juror capitulates in turn when Albanez threatens to expose their misdeeds and ruin them in various ways, setting the stage for a sweeping chase through the desert, with the jurors hunting down their innocent prey.

The treatment lacked polish, but Jewison found the idea captivating. It was a total departure from anything he'd done, an opportunity for exciting visual storytelling. Jewison could imagine shooting the film in Spain or Italy, where Clint Eastwood had recently made *A Fistful of Dollars* (1964). The idea of escaping the Hollywood hustle had already taken root in his consciousness, if only as fantasy. Indeed, what he loved most about Fort Bragg was its remoteness. "The salmon and steelhead are running in the rivers, the pines smell as strong and the one thing we don't have is smog. Hollywood, New York and the business seem so far away," he wrote the *New York Times* reporter Peter Bart late in the shoot. "Maybe I'll never come back!"[51]

In early November, Kleiner joined Jewison in Fort Bragg for three intensive writing days on the western, now called *The Judgment of Corey*. Jewison wanted to lighten the first half of the script, to contrast with the grim second half. He also encouraged Kleiner to conduct further research to establish the particulars of the Mexican setting. Mostly, however, Jewison was concerned with the script's length, which was on track to exceed 180 pages. As a screenwriter, Kleiner was in some ways the mirror opposite of William Rose. Kleiner lacked Rose's self-consciousness, and had no trouble turning out pages.[52] But where Rose had encouraged Jewison to use the screenplay as dispensable raw material, Kleiner treated his own words with reverence. He staunchly opposed any major cuts: the thematic weight of the material justified the length, he felt. If the film proved too long for one sitting, Kleiner was in favour of adding an intermission (a non-starter for Jewison). He'd even written lyrics for a love song for the heroine to sing at key points throughout the film: "With every breath I draw / I love you more and more," it began, "Leave me never oh leave me never / Heart of me forever."[53] Kleiner's letters to Jewison could be as mannered as his dialogue. "With both hands dipped in the blood of the Muse," he wrote, "I remain your sincere scribe." Jewison managed to hack forty pages from the screenplay before Kleiner had left Fort Bragg.[54]

By the end of the location, physical exhaustion had become an almost material presence in Jewison's life. He tried to maintain his usual atomic energy levels on set, but Nadine Phinney could see cracks in the performance. "Norman is tiring," she wrote to Hal Ashby, the film's editor. "It's not been an easy one."[55] Often, Jewison would review scripts or other properties in the evenings, but these days he was finding it too difficult to concentrate. "This is probably the most physically difficult picture I've ever done," he confessed, "and I'm beginning to get weary." He was bored with Fort Bragg. For fun, the townspeople would walk down to the water at night to watch Alan Arkin wash his dirty laundry.[56]

The final stretch on location was full of trivial annoyances. Earlier in the shoot, Jewison had used the actor John Phillip Law's dog in a scene. At the time, Jewison thought it fitting to make a "token adjustment" to

Law's salary based on the location payment for animals, which was ten dollars per day. In mid-November, long after the scene had been shot, a letter arrived from Law's agent negotiating a higher fee for the animal. If Law felt that his dog deserved a princely sum, he should had said so before shooting, Jewison insisted to Mike Rosenfeld, Law's agent. "On top of this, since when have you started representing animals?"[57] Jewison was exasperated. Did Stanley Kubrick spend his days haggling with agents over canine performers?

Jewison was spent, but it no longer mattered. By the first week of December, his fourteen weeks were up, and he had done what he needed to do. The location wrapped, and the first "Norman Jewison Production" was in the can.

CHAPTER 6

To Russia With Love

AFTER THE GRUELING LOCATION SHOOT in northern California, the dawn of 1966 brought the return of something like domestic normalcy for Jewison. The kids were back at school after a family ski trip over Christmas. Dixie, who was learning to ski and "getting pretty good," in her husband's estimation, had recently gotten a pixie haircut and to him looked "like a child bride again."[1]

The Jewisons had now been in their Brentwood home for three years. The addition of Georgia, the kids' beloved nanny, had eased Dixie's workload. She had started playing tennis, popular among their social set, and had taken to "rushing in and out of Schwab's like a native," Jewison observed, referring to the famous Sunset Boulevard pharmacy where the stars filled their prescriptions.[2] Dixie had become increasingly involved with charity work, often alongside other industry wives. She would later co-found Neighbors of Watts, a community organization that supported childcare services for low-income families in south-east Los Angeles.

Kevin, Michael, and Jennifer (turning ten, eight, and six, respectively) were growing up to look "exactly like their father," according to one observer.[3] They were California kids, tanned, fashionably dressed, hip to the current slang. Kevin composed the following for his father's birthday:

Dear Daddy

Birthdays are a wonderful occasion because they give us a chance to tell certain people how much we relay [sic] love them, and how much we appreciate all the things they do for us. This is why I want your Birthday to be the grooviest, happiest birthday of all time.

Lots of love, Kevin[4]

As Jennifer recalls, Kevin was "sort of the loner" of the family, "you know, the confident one . . . like Mr. Macho." Michael was particularly attached to Dixie, and Jennifer was closest with Norman. Their childhoods were largely insulated from exposure to Hollywood; certainly, they didn't think of their father as anything special. "His big thing in our family," as Jennifer recalled, was "don't sit and watch eight hours of television. Read a book, go out and play in a tree, mow the lawn, go for a walk, do something." Friends would always comment on how well adjusted the Jewison children were, which was largely true, although Dixie and Norman worried about Michael's occasionally explosive temper.[5]

Never a devotee of the LA scene, Norman had recently dragged himself out to some "groovy Hollywood parties." At a "very dull" opening for singer Barbara McNair, he made small talk with the director Arthur Penn with whom he would compete for the Best Director Oscar in 1968. He marveled at some of the more outlandish characters on the party circuit, including "some cat with a monocle."[6] While he could play the bon vivant, he mostly steered clear of whatever Caligulan pleasures were to be derived in LA nightlife around this time, as did most other industry professionals. Joan Didion, who wrote for and about Hollywood, insisted that the community was as "intricate, rigid, and deceptive in its mores as any devised on this continent," and that the real industry players upheld a highly conservative if unofficial code of social and sexual conduct. Didion estimated "the average daily narcotic intake" of young Hollywood at "one glass of a three-dollar Mondavi white and two marijuana cigarettes shared by six people," and described "a community whose notable excesses include virtually none of the flesh or spirit . . . flirtations between men and women, like drinks after dinner, remain largely the luxury of character actors out from New York, one-shot writers, reviewers being courted by Industry people, and others who do not understand the *mise* of the local *scène*."[7]

Jewison drank scotch and admired women—"you know how I am about mammary glands," he winked to a friend—but exhibited the same "tropism toward survival" that Didion noted as characteristic of his *milieu*.[8] He was happiest in the garden, which he weeded and watered each morning before work. Neighbours, who fussed over their fancy purple fuchsias and orchids, sneered at his "plebeian" tastes, appalled that "Jewison has turned over about $50,000 worth of backyard to growing such prosaic items as radishes and corn."[9] He shrugged off the scorn; in fact, he took distinct pride from getting three ears of corn per stalk. He grew decorative flowers as well, but primarily used his garden to cultivate a more substantial crop, plants that had a reason for being: a practice that mirrored his attitudes about cinematic creativity.

* * *

Russians would open on May 25, 1966, at three theatres in New York: the Murrayhill and Translux on the east side, and the Astor on Broadway.[10] But there was a mountain of post-production work to scale before then. Most urgently, he needed to find scenes to trim, after a rough cut turned out to be twenty minutes too long.[11] Thankfully, he could once again count on the expertise and devotion of Hal Ashby in the editing room.

Ashby had apprenticed under Robert Swink, William Wyler's editor, who educated him on everything from the technical methodology of film editing to a broader philosophy of film. Ashby developed his own intuitive approach. "Once the film is in hand," he said, "forget about the script, throw away all of the so-called rules, and don't try to second-guess the director. Just look at the film and let it guide you. It will turn you on all by itself, and you'll have more ideas on ways to cut it than you would ever dream possible."[12] Ashby quickly earned a reputation as an obsessive in the cutting room. "He wouldn't go home for a week," remembers Marvin Mirisch. "He would sleep on the floor of the editing room, smoking pot or whatever. His lifestyle was not the most . . . it wasn't a good recommendation, put it that way."[13]

Jewison grew increasingly close with Ashby and would later describe them as "brothers," but he was careful to give Hal the space he needed to work. Ashby couldn't operate with a director standing over his shoulder, and anyway Jewison soon learned that he could trust Hal. While Ashby was cutting *Russians*, Jewison was working with screenwriter Harry Kleiner to reduce the length of the script for *The Judgment of Corey*. "Although I have been cutting madly," Jewison wrote the literary agent Herb Jaffe, "it's still long and we must find further deletions."[14] By the third week of March, Kleiner turned in a final draft of the screenplay incorporating Jewison's requested changes, and was paid $37,500 for the job.[15]

That month, the United States government announced the expansion of military forces in Vietnam. There had been 23,500 combat troops in the country at the end of 1965. By the end of 1966, there would be more than 400,000. Anti-war demonstrations were ramping up across the US. America's Cold War with Russia may have been the stuff of farce for Jewison, but there was nothing funny about Vietnam. Vietnam was napalm and Agent Orange. It was images of American youth bandaged and shattered in foreign muck, and gaunt Vietnamese faces frozen in portraits of pain. Vietnam was Norman Morrison, the thirty-two-year-old Quaker and father of three who burnt himself to ash in front of the Pentagon.

Jewison opposed the war, although he kept his political views hidden in his friendly working relationship with the US Air Force. "By the time you get this note you'll either be deep in the jungles of Vietnam or out on a golf course somewhere with Bob Hope," Jewison joked in a thank-you letter to Colonel Sherwood Mark, who had arranged for the McDonnell F-101 Voodoo jets—used heavily as reconnaissance aircraft in Vietnam—for the finale of *Russians*.[16] Colonel Mark had gone so far as to shoot some cockpit footage of his pilots at the Oxnard air field for Jewison to use in the film. He promised to invite Mark to a screening "so you can see how good your boys look in action."[17] Jewison knew the real jets would lend the picture a sense of authenticity, and would do whatever it took to get them, even if that meant striking an obsequious posture *vis-à-vis* the American war machine.

* * *

Around this time, Jewison became intrigued by a property called *In the Heat of the Night*, based on a novel of the same name by John Ball. The previous summer, agent Martin Baum had brought the book to Walter Mirisch as a possible vehicle for Sidney Poitier.[18] Ball's plot follows Virgil Tibbs, a Black homicide detective from Pasadena, who investigates the murder of a symphony conductor in the small town of Wells, South Carolina. Mirisch read the book and "found it wanting in many ways," but sensed great cinematic potential in the relationship between the sophisticated Black detective and the boorish sheriff, Bill Gillespie. Mirisch had met Poitier years earlier and had been on the lookout for something they might do together. The Mirisch Company optioned the book and commissioned a screenplay.[19]

Meanwhile, with *Russians* in the final stages of post-production, the Mirisches were ready to offer Jewison a longer-term deal. On April 5, 1966, William Morris agents Joe Schoenfeld and Leonard Hirshan opened negotiations with Walter and Marvin Mirisch. Everyone was in favour of tearing up Jewison's existing contract in the hopes of firming up a new three-picture "Joint Venture." Schoenfeld proposed that Jewison receive $200,000 plus 30 per cent of the profits for the first picture, and $300,000 for the second and third films, plus 33 per cent of the profit or 20 per cent of the gross, whichever was higher. The Mirisches, who had already indicated they'd be more comfortable paying $150,000, $275,000, and $300,000 for each of the three films, said that they'd consider it. They agreed to all of the editing provisions Jewison requested, as well as complete control of the screenplay once principal photography had started, as long as his decisions didn't impact the budget.[20]

Yet nobody knew what the first film of Jewison's new contract would be—not even Jewison.

"It was carefully stated that Norman will be going to Hong Kong in a couple of weeks to meet with Steve McQueen to get his answer with regard to the western," wrote Leonard Hirshan in a memo to the

William Morris office, where the "western" was *Judgment of Corey*. "Should McQueen's answer be affirmative and the date pinpointed interfere with *In the Heat of the Night*, then Jewison would have to forego *In the Heat of the Night*."[21]

McQueen arrived at Kai Tak airport in Hong Kong with Neile Adams and their two children on March 22, 1966, having just completed a "very trying" location shoot in Taiwan. *The Sand Pebbles*, directed by Robert Wise and co-starring nineteen-year-old Candice Bergen as McQueen's love interest, would eventually earn the actor his only Academy Award nomination. But in the spring of 1966, McQueen was feeling the effects of the bruising location. Scheduled for twelve weeks, the shoot had lasted more than seven months. "There were problems with snakes, disease, drinking water, bribes, and student riots," according to one of McQueen's biographers.[22] "Anything I ever did wrong," McQueen later said, "I paid for in Taiwan."[23] McQueen trusted Jewison and wanted to work with him again. But Jewison was asking him to commit to another foreign-filmed epic at the worst possible time.

McQueen passed on *Judgment of Corey*, and Jewison became the director of *In the Heat of the Night*.

* * *

After a false start with the television writer Robert Alan Aurthur, the screenplay for *In the Heat of the Night* went to Stirling Silliphant, another television scribe who had penned episodes of *Alfred Hitchcock Presents*, *Perry Mason*, and *Route 66* (which he had created). Silliphant's stature in the world of television was suggested by the title of a 1963 *Time* profile: "The Fingers of God." Said director Sidney Pollack: "He could write on a plane, in a waiting room, on napkins, and he didn't know where it came from. He was a very mystical guy, and he thought his own talent was mystical."[24]

While Jewison had dealt with tricky writers in the past, Silliphant posed unique challenges. He was prolific, busy, and incredibly successful. Jewison sensed that if Silliphant understood the true scope of the script revision that lay ahead, he would not respond well. So the director took a different approach. "[Jewison] called me and said, 'Stirling, in all the years'—which at this point hadn't been too many—'I've been in the business, I have never read a first draft which is so brilliant. I want you to know that I'm not going to change a word. I'm shooting it precisely as it is.'" Silliphant had been around long enough to know that directors don't shoot first-draft screenplays. He nevertheless set up a lunch with Jewison.

"I'm troubled by your easy acceptance of the script," Silliphant remembered telling Jewison. "What I'd like is to go over it page by page."

"It really isn't necessary, Stirling," Jewison replied, "but since you insist . . ."

Jewison removed the screenplay from his capacious leather bag. Silliphant couldn't help but notice that it was "bristling" with paper clips.

"What are all those clips, Norman? Are those places you're troubled by the material?"

"No, no," he replied, "those are just places I've made notes to myself. Let me just check."

He flipped to the first page, and said, "Well, I do have a slight problem on this page."

Months later, Silliphant realized that Jewison had guided him through a substantial overhaul.

"I have to tell you few directors have that panache, that sensitivity," Silliphant says. "He handled me beautifully."[25]

* * *

In early April, Boaty wrote her "Dear Sweet Boy" to tell Jewison that she was getting married to the agent Terence Baker. She envisioned a proper Southern affair—wedding in the Baptist Church, breakfast at the Country Club—to take place in Reidsville, North Carolina. Gore Vidal and superagent Sue Mengers (with whom Boaty had shared a "swinging" trip through the Greek islands on Gore's boat in the summer of 1964) were on the guest list.[26] "You, of course, I have for some time now considered to be my most special and dearest friend," she wrote Jewison, "and it would me us so happy to have you with us on that very happy day."

Boaty asked Jewison to let her know if Dixie might come, in which case she'd write a "'proper' personal note inviting you both.'"

"I do miss you," she said, "and often wish I could reach for the phone and have one of our long chats. Everything is beautiful these days, and I'm happy and very much in love."[27]

Jewison promised he would try to make it, although he was heavily involved in planning the promotional tour for *The Russians Are Coming*. The Washington leg of the trip was turning out to be a grand affair, and Jewison was as giddy as any bride-to-be. "It's really so exiting, Boaty," he enthused. "We have a screening in Washington, a black-tie sit-down dinner for fifty with H. Humphrey as guest of honour and we really have a turnout."

In addition to Vice-President Humphrey, confirmed guests included Jack Valenti, who had just resigned as Special Assistant to Lyndon B. Johnson to assume the presidency of the Motion Picture Association of America, Supreme Court Justice William O. Douglas, broadcaster David Brinkley, the ambassadors of France, Argentina, and Belgium, and an assortment of senators.[28] Valenti had offered to give the Jewisons a tour of the White House. It was all slightly surreal. A few months back, William Rose had made an absurd joke about Jewison hanging the United Nations Award in his outhouse. It seemed less absurd now that publicists were arranging an invitational screening at the United Nations, where it would be the first film ever screened in the Dag Hammarskjöld Library.[29] Of course, whether audiences would actually *like* the film was still anyone's guess.

Jewison and Alan Arkin began their promotional tour in the second week of May. After a strong start in New York, the crowds were smaller than anticipated in some peripheral markets. Audiences in Dallas responded with comments like, "We don't think it's funny. What's funny about the Russians?" and "Is it another one of them message pictures?"[30]

While Jewison had enjoyed working with his ensemble cast, he was now receiving an education on the challenges of promoting a film without a bankable star. In reflection, he was forced to admit that "no one is particularly interested in meeting Alan Arkin and Norman Jewison unless they have seen the film. This particular fact was proven in almost every case."[31]

Washington, however, was a different story. The gala evening, which included cocktails and a formal dinner before a screening of *Russians* at the MPAA headquarters, had been arranged by Arthur B. Krim, the president of United Artists and finance chairman for the Democratic National Committee, and Paul G. Hoffman, an automobile executive who had overseen implementation of the Marshall Plan. Jewison had never been in such proximity to power. The Ambassador of Belgium carried on a good-natured argument with Baroness Louis Scheyven on the benefits of comedy over tragedy (ambassadors can't cry in public, he explained). Dixie wore a Grecian-style, one-shoulder dress in rose from Sak's, only to find that Krim's wife had arrived wearing the same dress in green.

("Embarrassed to go to a party and find another woman wearing your dress? Do you panic, blush, and hurry home?" opened the resulting story in the next morning's society pages.)[32]

Jewison, always apprehensive before screenings of his films, was particularly anxious as the lights dimmed for this premiere of *Russians*. He was proud of his work, but had not forgotten that two studios had passed on the film for reasons of political sensitivity. America's schoolchildren were still performing "duck and cover" exercises in preparation for a Soviet nuclear attack. Even if the film-going public was ready for a Cold War farce, there was no guarantee that its national representatives would be prepared to laugh along with a film depicting Americans as paranoid rubes.

"Vice President Humphrey laughed until the tears rolled down his cheeks," Jewison told a reporter following the event. The evening was a triumph. "We showed it to people in the United States Information Agency and our culture advisors and we showed it to the Russians. They all liked it."[33]

In truth, reaction to a separate screening at the Russian Embassy was measured. Jewison went so far as to re-dub one line of the film after the event—changing "Russians are taught to hate Americans" to "Russians are taught to mistrust Americans." Soviet officials who had seen the film remained skeptical about the welcome it would receive behind the Iron Curtain.[34]

No such ambivalence, however, marked the film's reception among American audiences in Washington. On May 25, 1966, the *Washington Daily News* took the unusual measure of devoting its editorial page to the film. *Russians* wouldn't open in Washington for another month, yet the breathless editorial writers felt it their "bounden duty to warn our warn readers that, if they see it, they may never be quite the same again." The editorial compared the film to the best Charlie Chaplin comedies ("when, wildly shaken by laughter, one is suddenly made deeply aware that man, however simple, is a glowing and glorious creature") and suggested that it may receive consideration for the Nobel Peace Prize. Jewison's film "is bound to have a profound effect on millions of Americans who see it" and may have already "achieved what the world's diplomats have thus far failed to do."

Later that day, Ernest Gruening, the seventy-nine-year-old senator from Alaska, made a speech from the Senate floor lauding *Russians* as "one of the most amusing and entertaining films that I have known" which "implies a profound and salutary lesson." Gruening moved that the *Daily News* editorial be printed in the Congressional Record for May 25, 1966,[35] and it was.

* * *

After the tour had ended and he was "back again in the Hollywood smog," Jewison was elated at the film's Washington reception and early box-office performance in New York, where it was setting house records. "We're riding pretty high," Nadine Phinney wrote to a friend in Fort Bragg. "We got only sensational reviews in all the New York papers—outright raves, every one of them, and without exception, they make Alan Arkin an overnight star."[36]

The New York Times admired both the film's political message ("Russians and Americans are basically human beings and, therefore, share basic human qualities") and the fact "not one whit of this lesson is accomplished by preaching, but rather by a hilarious troupe of actors telling a hilarious tale in a hilarious way."[37] *The Hollywood Reporter* called it "the most hilarious picture of the year,"[38] while the *Boston Globe* predicted that *Russians* would "be the funniest and most successful entertainment of 1966."[39]

In the weeks ahead, critics would cool to *Russians*. Brendan Gill recoiled from Jewison's populist farce in *The New Yorker*, sneering that the "heavy-handed" director had "permitted nearly every moment to become twice as brightly coloured, twice as noisy, and twice as frantic as it needed to be." *Time* likewise bemoaned Jewison's "ding-dong farce," his reliance upon "a corps of hard-sell comedians to transform the townsfolk into strident cartoons," and *Newsweek* bemoaned the "intrusive metaphor" in the Cuban Missile Crisis-inspired finale that "plays crudely on the hopes of an audience to see the real cold war turn out to be a joke."

The Russians Are Coming was not a film for the high-minded *cineaste* of the mid-1960s. It was not an intellectual argument for *détente*, nor was it even faintly interested in political theory. (The word "communism" is not mentioned in the script.) Stylistically, the film could not have been more out of sync with the self-consciously hip, black-and-white noodlings of the French New Wave, all the rage at the art houses. ("When was the last time you saw a play in black and white," Jewison once cawed to a journalist.) As far as William Rose was concerned, "ding-dong farce" was exactly what they were aiming for all along. The frenetic visual idiom harkened back to earlier moments in Jewison's work (especially the Disneyland sequence in *40 Pounds of Trouble* and the third act chase in *The Art of Love*) as well as classics of the genre (Chaplin's *The Great Dictator* or the Marx Brothers' *Duck Soup*). The film's message, salutary if not exactly profound, was "that Russians were human beings, pretty much like us," as Arkin put it. "It sounds inane now, but at that moment in our history the Soviet Union was so demonized that making a movie that challenged that view was actually a pretty courageous thing to do."[40]

So generous was the film in its portrayal of Russians that some viewers assumed it was Soviet propaganda. "Since the nineteen-thirties I have heard that the Commies were trying to brainwash the movie industry but

never saw more concrete evidence until I saw *The Russians Are Coming*,"
one John W. Davidson of Boston wrote to Jewison. "I'm wondering
how much the Russian government paid toward making the picture."[41]
(Perhaps equally inevitable is the contemporary academic view that
Jewison's *ersatz* radicalism reinforces the capitalist assumptions of postwar
Hollywood.)[42]

The real "message" of *Russians*, conveyed in its rollicking style, was that
slapstick cinema revealed an underlying humanity that cut across political
and economic boundaries. Hence Jewison's decision to show the film's
dailies to the townspeople of Fort Bragg, who also filled in the margins
of the film as extras, and whose untutored, spontaneous responses to the
film-in-progress rubbed off on the sensibility of the finished product. The
film's comic zest has less to do with political sermonizing than with the
visual humour of which Jewison was fond: a plump Tessie O'Shea hopping
around and "squashing" the gagged Carl Reiner; an ancient townswoman
bound and hung up on the wall while still seated in her chair ("What are
you doing up there on the wall, Murial?," asks her doddering husband). It
may have been coarse for the refined critical palate, but audiences found
it hilarious. One early reviewer noted that "the dialogue is occasionally
smothered by screams of merriment from the audience; the laughter is
full-bellied and spontaneous."

But while it was succeeding for American audiences, the success of
Russians was as yet only partial. For it to be complete, Jewison knew that
Russians would have to work for Russians.

* * *

By early June 1966, it had become clear that Jewison, the Mirisches, and
UA had a *bona fide* hit on their hands. "Russians Coming Strong," "Russians

Smash Record," "Russians, Figuratively And Literally, Dominate 1ˢᵗ-Run Broadway Boxoffice," read the trade paper headlines.

The film grossed $1,246,795 nineteen days into its New York run, breaking all United Artists Premiere Showcase records except those of the James Bond films.[43] "Hollywood is so excited over the picture that you'd think everyone in this town had had part of it," wrote Nadine Phinney at the time. She'd been working to arrange overflowing special screenings each night for two weeks, "and still the requests keep coming in from all the Hollywood bigshots, asking to be invited."[44] Kirk Douglas took out a newspaper ad to praise the film: "All of us in Hollywood should be very grateful for the understanding, warmth, and laughter that this picture brings to the world."[45] UA's marketing team had printed bright *"The Russians Are Coming!"* stickers that were starting to appear all over town. Jewison suggested sending them to colleges and high schools "because the kids are getting quite a kick out of the thought-provoking title."[46]

By mid-June, Jewison was promoting the release of *Russians* in Los Angeles—rolling around town in his white E-type 4.2L Jaguar convertible, the Stones' "Paint it Black" on the radio, stopping in for live TV interviews with the likes of Wayne Thomas on KHJ TV on Melrose Avenue, and Paul Condylis on KABC on South La Cienga.[47] He turned the famous Jewison charm on full blast, smiling wide enough to make his eyes disappear behind his cheeks. A journalist at the time described him as a "Thirty-nine-year-old teddy-bear of a wonder boy," who leaps to his feet and "paces around, playing all his characters."[48]

There was much to be excited about. *Russians* was starting to gain an international profile. Jewison's goal of showing the film behind the Iron Curtain suddenly seemed within reach, when *Russians* was selected as the official American entry for the Karlovy Vary Film Festival in Czechoslovakia. Czech programmers, however, afraid of Russian disapproval, quickly vetoed the choice. The Americans boycotted the festival in retaliation. "It's too bad that politicians and international relations have to fuck up the arts," Jewison moaned to Boaty at the time.[49] Shortly thereafter, he learned that *Russians* had been selected to screen out of competition on opening night at the Berlin Film Festival.

On June 24, 1966, *The Russians Are Coming* would open Berlin's 16th Inernationalen Filmfestspiele. Some German officials worried that the title was too provocative. "It was feared," one German reporter wrote at the time, "that some confused fellow-citizen could take the title seriously, could panic and commit suicide."[50] Officials proposed "Tovarisch Rozanov Discovers America" as an alternative. While Jewison admitted that it was "tricky" to have the title *The Russians Are Coming! The Russians Are Coming!* "plastered all over the big cinema billboards in West Berlin," he was not about to bowdlerize his title. Mayor Willy Brandt eventually intervened on Jewison's behalf and the title was permitted to stand.[51]

West Berlin's Congress Hall was a soaring steel and concrete structure gifted by the Americans for the 1957 World Exhibition. Jewison found the venue "large and cold" for a film screening, but it was situated only a few hundred metres from the Berlin Wall, which felt symbolically appropriate. In his opening remarks, Brandt, who would ascend to the German Chancellorship in 1969 and be named *Time*'s "Man of the Year" in 1970, called for films from the Eastern bloc to be shown at the festival in the future. From his seat in the seventh row, Jewison sensed that the 1,200 West Berliners in the audience were in the mood for *rapprochement*. When the director appeared on stage after the screening, dapper in a white suit with a checkered ascot, "Jewison received deafening applause lasting several minutes" according to the following day's news reports.[52] Jewison was then chauffeured to a reception held by Brandt at Charlottenburg, the seventeenth-century rococo palace.

At 11:00 a.m. the next morning, with the nine-hour time difference and previous night's champagne not doing him any favours, Jewison left his room at the Berlin Hilton for a press junket with German film critics. They were struck by the energy of what one described as "a small, gay man: you would never think that he is forty already." In fact, Jewison was still a few weeks shy of that milestone, though middle-age was evidently on his mind. "I've lived half my life already," he said, after one journalist criticized the love plot between an American girl and Russian sailor. "I'm not naïve in concerns of war or concerns of love. Nobody will suppose that I take the sunny East-West beach romance as any kind of solution of the problem."

Overall, German critics admired that "the Americans" were willing to joke about themselves in a film that struck them as free of propaganda. "It's full of little and big truths and wisdoms," one wrote, "its people are marked with understanding and love."[53]

London was next. Fifteen years earlier, an English reporter made a point of reminding him, Jewison had been "starving in Bayswater."[54] Now, he would join forty members of parliament for a private screening of *Russians*. The lawmakers "howled with laughter throughout the showing," according to reports.[55]

The participation of William Rose, writer of much-beloved Ealing comedies, predisposed English critics in the film's favour: one affirmed that the true setting of the film was not America but "Ealingland," populated as it was by "dotty old postmistresses, picturesque village drunks, deaf grandfathers, monster children, and fresh-faced boys and girls to provide a touch of wholesale romance."[56]

Jewison was glad to be back in his favourite city, although he was shocked by London's transformation over the past decade, and particularly the appearance of "that whole playboy, gambling scene which really kind of depressed me . . . Las Vegas just doesn't belong on the banks of the Thames," he wrote Boaty, and "this frantic attempt to avoid the devaluation of the pound" seems like the "final twitchings of a corpse rather than any real renaissance or progress."

Jewison would have enjoyed another day or two in London, especially as Boaty had promised to introduce him to Harold Pinter.[57] But another opportunity had arisen. A print of *Russians* had made its way to Moscow where, apparently, the film had been warmly received by authorities. United Artists suddenly felt that Jewison's dream of distributing *Russians* in Russia was within reach. He dropped everything and flew from London to Moscow.[58]

Jewison made the trip with Ilya Lopert, a Russian-speaking UA publicity man in Paris, and Arnold Picker, the vice president of UA and a top Democratic fundraiser later revealed as Richard Nixon's number-one enemy on his 1971 list of targets. The trio touched down in Moscow in early July. Lopert had arranged for rooms in the Hotel Ukraina, then the largest hotel in Europe, and warned Jewison that anything said on the premises could be recorded. Two private screenings followed in the days ahead: one for the Soviet Film Export group, the other for the Union of Soviet Filmworkers, with many top Russian directors, writers, and critics in attendance. Accounts differ as to how many Muscovites attended these screening: Jewison remembers an immense movie palace, bigger than the Radio City Music Hall in New York, "jammed with over 2,000 Russians," listening to an interpreter provide a simultaneous translation over the PA system. A contemporary news report claims that about 300 Russians saw the film. Regardless of the size of the audience, everyone agreed that the ending of the film brought a mixture of tears and applause from the Moscow audience.[59]

Communist critics welcomed *Russians* as an encouraging, if flawed, film. Writing in the Prague literary magazine *Literární noviny*, Jiri Hochman praised the film as an "excellent" advance over Hollywood's previous depictions of diabolical Russians—particularly that "masterpiece of very dirty fraud-propaganda," *The Manchurian Candidate*—and admired that Jewison paid a minimal tax to the American "religion" of anti-communism. Vladimir Pozner, of the Soviet Novosti Press Agency, observed that Alan Arkin's comic exaggeration of Rozanov's poor English wouldn't play well for Russian audiences. But Pozner confirmed that the film's broad physical comedy had Russian audiences in hysterics, and that Russian audiences were in complete sympathy with the film's plea for brotherhood. After the Soviet Filmworkers screening, Pozner said, one reputed art critic had declared that the film's finale "will go down in cinematographic history as something on par with the Odessa steps sequence in *The Battleship Potemkin*."

During the long trip home, Jewison contended with mixed feelings. For a brief moment, inside that Moscow theatre, Russians had felt the same fraternal communion that he had seen in audiences across America. As he wrote Boaty: "When the lights went up, there were so many tear-filled eyes that I was absolutely overwhelmed." But Soviet authorities had definitively declined a Russian distribution deal. Jewison had imagined the film playing to audiences all over the USSR—audiences composed not only of party officials and filmmakers but of regular people, the kind of people who saw the film emerge in dailies in Fort Bragg. That dream died in Moscow.

"I will never be truly contented until this film is shown publicly behind the Iron Curtain," Jewison wrote that July. "[I]f it wasn't for Vietnam and the strained international scene," he felt, things could have been different.[60]

If Jewison needed any reminder of the depth of political animus between the two superpowers, it came when he arrived in New York.

In making his last-minute plans to fly to Moscow from London, he'd failed to obtain clearance from American immigration. The US border agents now confiscated his visa, took his fingerprints, and forwarded the case to the FBI. To the director of *The Russians Are Coming*, the whole episode felt like an absurd dénouement. "After all my efforts at improving Russian-American understanding, the g- d- Yanks won't take me back," he complained.[61] "I am moving ahead with a new film based on my experiences, called CANADIANS GO HOME."[62]

* * *

A few months before, agent John Flaxman sent Jewison an original screenplay called *The Crown Caper*. Written by a Boston lawyer named Alan R. Trustman, the script was an underdeveloped romantic thriller in the vein of *Charade*, the 1963 chase movie with Cary Grant and Audrey Hepburn. Flaxman knew of Jewison's interest in topical social issues. "One of the most intriguing unanswered questions of our times," Flaxman bloviated in his letter, "is whether the 'moral man' must fight the 'immoral man' by moral means or will he perish if he does not use immoral methods himself." What that had to do with *The Crown Caper* was anyone's guess, but the concept intrigued Jewison. He could see Julie Christie and Sean Connery in the main roles, although Flaxman had proposed—inevitably, it must have seemed—that "Jack Lemmon would be ideal for the role of Thomas Crown."[63]

There were more immediate casting problems to deal with. George C. Scott, who Jewison and Walter Mirisch agreed would be perfect for the role of Gillespie in *In the Heat of the Night*, had committed to star in William Rose's next project, *Flim-Flam Man*. Rod Steiger was their second choice. Burly, imposing, yet also sensitive, Steiger—who had studied under Lee Strasberg and was closely associated with Method acting—did not present like a typical Hollywood star, and in many ways he wasn't. He could play the tough guy (as, say, Brando's brother in *On the Waterfront*) but he spoke with a baroque, almost poetic, flourish. By the time he met Jewison, Steiger was married to the English actress Claire Bloom (Blanche DuBois in *A Streetcar Named Desire*, and future wife of Philip Roth), and had recently starred as Komarovsky in *Doctor Zhivago*. He signed on to *In the Heat of the Night* for $150,000. Poitier's deal, meanwhile, called for $200,000 plus 20 per cent of the profits.[64]

Jewison had a cast, a script, and an early September start date. Now all he needed was a location. As far as United Artists was concerned, there should have been no location shoot at all. "From the outset, we understood that we were dealing with a piece of material that might not be shown in the South," remembers Walter Mirisch. "There might be picketing or disturbances that could result in violence or, at the least, have our play dates canceled."[65] *In the Heat of the Night* would get made for what Mirisch euphemistically called the "disciplined price" of $2 million. Jewison, however, insisted that a Hollywood soundstage was not conducive to the sweltering feel of this picture. He kept looking for the right location.

"I am having problems in finding a southern town which will have us on Sidney Poitier's terms," he wrote Boaty that July, "which are really our terms also. Tomorrow I leave for Missouri as that area seems to be a little more liberal than southern Tennessee."[66]

So began a mid-summer odyssey to find a town that could stand in for Mississippi, the setting of *In the Heat of the Night*. "I set out by car on a search that stretched from California to Kentucky," Jewison recalled. Of all the small towns he visited—Jewison later guessed he'd seen upwards of two hundred—something about Sparta, Illinois, stood out. "Of course, you know where that is," he'd say with a wry smile. "It's right there between Baldwin and Percy and not far from Pinckneyville."

What he liked most about Sparta was that it felt frozen in time. The railroad station hadn't been renovated in decades, and the police department and funeral home had a southern feel. It was also close enough to St. Louis that they could fly the dailies out for processing by jet.[67]

Jewison did what he could to stay informed about *Russians*'s international box office during his never-ending tour of small-town diners and train stations. Despite various offers of assistance, his visa situation remained unresolved. "If I do have to leave the country," he wrote to Arnold Picker, "do you think we could shoot *In the Heat of the Night* around Leningrad?"[68]

Driving hundreds of miles around middle America provided ample opportunity for the director to reflect. It had been a year of extremes: days in Fort Bragg when it felt like the rain wouldn't end; nights of extravagance in Washington and Berlin and Moscow. Boaty was now married and living thousands of miles away. Yet, improbably, their brief time together in London had revealed how their relationship would evolve. "We both adore having you and Dixie here," Boaty wrote that August.

> The other thing that makes me terribly happy is that Terence, who knows how dear you are to me, feels the same way about you too. You are just a very important part of my life, and I have so much to be grateful to you for. Knowing you, and sharing so much with you, has made me far better and stronger for Terence. That may sound a bit dramatic but I'm sure you understand. I am sure I'm probably the luckiest girl in the world now, and my life has truly taken on a new and complete meaning. I'm glad we got to have a little time alone together to talk to each other . . . as next to Terence, I guess there is no one else who I worry more about, or care more about, or want as much for as I do you.[69]

The waning days of the summer of 1966 found Jewison doing much the same thing as he had been doing in the summer of 1965: preparing to shoot a film in some miniscule American town that time had all but forgot. His budget on *Heat* was small—about half of what it had been for *Russians*. But despite the small towns and smaller budget, *In the Heat of the Night* was another big step toward the socially meaningful cinema he wanted to make. The journalists used to ask him what a "Norman Jewison Film" would look like. Now they knew.

CHAPTER 7

The First Black Detective

ON OCTOBER 21, 1966, Jewison wrote a letter to the Los Angeles Bureau of Adoptions to provide his "unqualified recommendation" to Hal and Shirley Ashby as prospective parents.[1] Jewison had known Ashby for four years and they had grown steadily closer as friends and co-creators. Jewison was famously collaborative, but his relationship with Ashby was unique. They shared an anti-war, anti-establishment political sensibility and a conviction that motion pictures could serve a higher purpose than commerce. In other ways, however, they were an odd couple.

"Hal is about as far away from Norman in personality" as one could be, said David Picker, former CEO of United Artists. Ashby was the freewheeling, younger creative who dabbled in LSD and worked obsessively in the editing room for days on end, while Jewison was the family man, trusted by suits to manage budgets and schedules. "I cannot think of anybody who, working on the same films, brought such different personal attitudes towards them," Picker said.[2]

There had been a time when Jewison believed that nobody else could "see" a picture the way he could, but by 1966, he and Ashby were one of the great creative teams in Hollywood. Ashby not only shaped Jewison's footage, determining the pace and visual grammar of the film, he also played a role in many of the creative decisions through production. Jewison nurtured Ashby's growth, giving him an associate producer credit on *In the Heat of the Night*.

At the same time, Jewison knew Ashby's capacity for personal chaos— Shirley was his fourth wife—although he may have felt that Ashby would thrive under more domestic responsibility, as he had with increased creative responsibility. Hal and Shirley already had one daughter, Carrie, who, as Jewison wrote to the adoption agency, "is being brought up in an atmosphere of love and security. We have three children of our own, and have found Hal and Shirley as interested in their personalities, development and welfare as we are."[3] The following spring, the couple would adopt a toddler named Steven.[4] Their marriage dissolved shortly thereafter.

* * *

Heat's sixty-person production crew descended upon the Augustine Motor Lodge in Belleville, Illinois, on September 19, 1966. Jewison rented a house nearby, where Dixie and the kids could visit. Ashby remained in Los Angeles, feeling he could assess film more objectively if he hadn't seen the effort of creating it. Sidney Poitier, who arrived the following week, remembers his first impressions of Jewison. "I was surprised at the youth of the man. He was quite young and quite boyish in appearance," Poitier recalls. "Norman had, and I think still has, a kind of mischievous smile . . . there's just a little bit more going on underneath than you can read in that smile."[5]

It was past 8:00 p.m. on a rainy Monday in late September when Jewison called "action" on the opening shots of *In the Heat of the Night*. He was filming in Compton's Diner, a roadside greasy spoon outside Belleville, illuminated by a neon sign that said: "EAT." Warren Oates, in costume as officer Sam Wood, exchanged a few words with the proprietor, plonked a coin down on the counter, and sauntered out, screen door clapping shut behind him. "Cut!" Jewison yelled. A crew member with a walkie-talkie called a nearby highway patrolman, who released the traffic that had lined up for twenty minutes on the adjacent Illinois 400 highway.[6]

Jewison, sucking on a cigar, worried that the lighting was off. "That baby spot is too bright," he said, pointing to one light. "He'll burn up in that." Someone from wardrobe decided that Oates's shirt was too nicely ironed and set about wrinkling it and spraying fresh perspiration on the actor. Jewison had a word with actor Anthony James, the counterman, who turns out to be the murderer in the film, although none of the characters knew it yet. "You're not to show any hostility here," Jewison warned, acting the scene out for James—something he never would have done for Steiger or Poitier. "All right, let's do it again," Jewison said, and Oates assumed his position on the counter. Traffic stopped, film rolled. The scene played out again, with no discernible difference to the untrained eye. "Good," said Jewison. "Print it."[7]

Inevitably, the production made quite a splash in Sparta, where the local newspaper contributed breathless reporting on the film's progress. "Children, young adults, grandmas, grandpas" all stood "transfixed" as crews repainted signs and repurposed various locations around town, including "Pig Alley" and "Baue's Garage south of town," the paper noted.[8] "We were the biggest thing," remembered cinematographer Haskell Wexler. "Their life was pretty mundane, pretty boring. When we came it was like the carnival coming."[9] The unit production manager hired a Sparta real estate agent to liaise with the locals. One morning, after calling for extras on the local radio station, 250 people lined up outside his office doors.[10]

"It's exciting to watch and see what's going on," said Carri St. James, an extra.

"It beats cleaning house," explained another. "We are having a ball and earning $1.50 an hour—plus we get to eat lunch." (The production had brought its own chef and cooking facilities from Hollywood. A typical evening meal included sirloin steak, baked potatoes, asparagus tops and hot rolls.)

When school let out at 3:30 p.m., local kids tried to get in on the action. Jewison mostly ran an open set, as he had done in Fort Bragg. The occasional misunderstanding was inevitable. Once, a mustachioed location scout walked into a Sparta bank, turned to his companion with a briefcase, and said, "Yeah, this looks good." A clerk assumed she was being robbed and called the police.[11]

Aside from the plummeting temperatures—as the days got colder, Jewison had actors put ice in their mouths before a take to prevent their breath from registering on film—Sparta was a serviceable substitute for Mississippi.[12] But Jewison also knew that to capture the authentic flavour of the South, he needed the cotton fields and Southern mansions, and a hint of "that rarified, white, established political ambience."[13] Sidney Poitier, however, would not be persuaded to shoot south of the Mason-Dixon line.

Poitier recalls that Jewison's direction took some getting used to.

I had been exposed to a few directors by then in my life, and I found him—his style—unsettling a little bit in that he was so . . . casual, so subtle. He created an atmosphere that allowed me something that I had not had before—a freedom to create, and if I was wrong he would tell me I was wrong in very gentle terms, so I was not afraid to be wrong; I was not afraid to try, but

at the same time it gave me more freedom and more room than
I ever had before been accustomed to.[14]

"All the other guys," Poitier added, referring to the directors he'd worked
with, "would tell you what to do and how to do it." Jewison "gave
instructions, and he gave you direction, but he also encouraged you to
reassociate and play your own instincts."

The film's emotional nucleus was the relationship between Poitier's
Tibbs and Steiger's Gillespie. The two actors were not exactly fast friends.
"I don't think Sidney knew what to make of Steiger," Jewison remembers.
"I think there was this kind of tension between them—which I encouraged,
because I felt that it was healthy as far as their performances went."[15]

In some ways, their off-screen differences were as pronounced as
those between their characters. Poitier was a disciplined early riser on a
strict diet of brown rice. ("Your body is a high-grade machine," he said.
"You wouldn't put cheap oil in a Cadillac, even though a Cadillac can be
replaced.") Steiger, trying to pack on as much weight as possible for the
role, stayed up until all hours eating greasy food in the hotel bar. "I'm on
a new diet," he joked at the time, "the high carbohydrate diet. I hear it
works."

Steiger seemed to contain multitudes. Lounging in the hotel bar, dressed
in a nondescript polo shirt and slacks, he looked more like a tourist than
a movie star. He seemed perfectly suited to portray the Southern sheriff
in *Heat*, but then he'd seemed equally suited as a Russian lawyer opposite
Julie Christie in *Dr. Zhivago*. His real aspiration, he claimed, was to play
Ernest Hemingway or Edgar Allan Poe. In conversation, Steiger had a
penchant for sweeping social denunciation: the subjects of his Jeremiads
included contemporary actors, the movie industry, and the country itself.
"America has become adolescent," he declaimed from his barstool. "We're

bowing to that mob—never before in history has a country allowed itself to be governed by the fads and fashions of its youth." A waiter then arrived to deliver what one onlooker described as "a mammoth pizza loaded down with mushrooms." Steiger's eyes widened. "Look at that," he said, struggling to extricate a slice from a molten web of cheese, "I'm in trouble again."[16]

* * *

"On your feet, boy." In the first scene featuring Hollywood's first Black detective, Virgil Tibbs is arrested on suspicion of murder. One moment he had been sitting in the Sparta train station, flipping through a magazine, dapper in a well-tailored suit; the next, Warren Oates has his gun out and Poitier's hands are up against the wall for a body search. Poitier's performance is defined by silence and restraint. Only his eyes are alive, conveying the inner humiliation of the moment. Jewison wanted his audience to feel the full force of that humiliation.[17]

Yet neither Jewison nor the film's white audience could feel exactly what Poitier had felt when, twenty-five years earlier, he had inadvertently hitched a ride with white policemen. "They marched me into an alley, these cops," Poitier later remembered. "They said to me, 'Walk, and if you turn around we shoot you.' And I walked, and they stayed behind me in that patrol car, with the gun pointed at my head . . . for more than twenty blocks, until they got tired of the fun." The feeling of being mistreated at the hands of white police was no feat of imagination for Poitier.

"Sweet Jesus," he said, "such memories."[18]

By 1966, the Bahamian immigrant who had been taunted by Miami police had become one of the most marketable movie stars in the world. Yet in many ways Poitier remained hostage to racist expectations. The dynamic between *Heat*'s stars was layered with irony: on the surface, Poitier was obviously the locus of power on set. Steiger had replaced George C. Scott in the role of Gillespie; if need be, Steiger could have been replaced in turn. But Poitier was irreplaceable. He made more money than his white co-star, and had a hand in shaping the script. The very prospect of Poitier's appearance in the film had been heralded by the press as an historic occurrence: "The screen is about to have what is believed to be its first Negro detective hero," the *New York Times* had reported in June.[19]

Yet despite the trappings of power, Poitier felt increasingly confined by his on-screen persona. The die had been cast by his first film performance, in Joseph L. Mankiewicz's *No Way Out* (1950), where Poitier played a doctor tasked with saving a white racist. While his subsequent characters varied in some obvious respects—he played an escaped convict on the lam with Tony Curtis in *The Defiant Ones* (1958), a disabled beggar in *Porgy and Bess* (1959), an itinerant worker devoted to helping nuns in *Lilies of the Field* (1963), the love interest of a blind white girl in *A Patch of Blue* (1965)—Poitier remained the healer, tasked with soothing the nation's racial wounds. His character, invariably defined by decency, nobility, and graciousness, was programmed to appeal to the sensibilities of a white movie-going audience and provide an occasion for catharsis.

Hollywood loved Poitier: his Oscar-winning stardom was living proof that the industry was on the progressive side of history. But Poitier was less enamored with Hollywood. It wasn't just the unwavering moral rectitude of his performances that bothered him. As virtually the sole representative of his race on screen, even Poitier agreed that he shouldn't play villains. What gnawed at Poitier was that his roles were so hygienically asexual, so "neutered" (as he said) in the writing process, "which is easy, right? You put him in a shirt and a tie and give him a white-collar job; you make him very bright and very capable at his job, then you can eliminate the core of the man: his sexuality. His sexuality is neutralized in the writing. But it's not intentional; it's institutional. To think of the American Negro male in romantic social-sexual circumstances is difficult, you know?"[20]

Poitier's neutered professional roles were created in direct opposition to, and therefore defined by, the racist myth of predatory African American male sexuality. Yet Poitier did not see his participation in the industry as a capitulation to institutional racism. "It's a choice," he said, "a clear choice. I would not have it so, and if the fabric of society were different I would scream to high heaven to play villains and to deal with different images of Negro life that would be more dimensional. But I'll be damned if I do that at this stage of the game. Not when there is only one Negro actor working in films with any degree of consistency, when there are thousands of actors in films, you follow?"[21]

* * *

It was early October, and Jewison was rehearsing in the Sparta Equipment Co., a walk-and-talk scene in which the town's mayor warns Steiger that he'll be out of a job if he doesn't find the killer before Tibbs. Steiger, dressed in his blue police uniform, black boots, and yellow-tinted sunglasses, conveyed his character's thought process through the rhythms of his gum chewing. Jewison had managed Steiger with a light touch. "You didn't realize what he was up to half the time," Steiger recalled. "He's always in command, but you never get a feeling that you are being commanded. He'd take you aside and say, 'I think you can do one better,' or 'I think it was a little too much, can you bring it down a little?' But there was no great discussion of method or intellectual bullshit. Norman doesn't tolerate things like that. It's much appreciated by actors of experience."[22]

While Jewison rehearsed with the actors, grip crews began setting up lights and laying down wooden track: the camera would be mounted on a base with wheels and manually pulled alongside the actors.[23] Jewison, sliding into a chair made of polished saddle leather, hoped to wrap by 3 p.m. The Los Angeles Dodgers were playing in the World Series, and the LA crew had a tendency to wander off at game time. While his cameramen and actors threw a football back and forth across Route 4, waiting for the set-up to be completed, he wondered how he should respond to Ashby.[24]

On October 5, Ashby had sent Jewison what he described as "the ramblings of a very very angry young punk":

Norman, since I talked to you this afternoon, I've become so goddamned furious, frustrated from anger I don't know what to do except sit here at this typewriter and rant and rave and hope I can cope with everything without blowing my cool completely.

To think Walter would put this kind of pressure on you is beyond the realm of my comprehension. It is so dumb; so stupid; so far out ridiculous I could cry. I guess *Russians* wasn't enough to prove you are an honourable and respectful man. I swear to Christ what do you have to do. When I look at our dailies, and see the extra quality—I'm talking about those values which cannot be evaluated—and then I hear what you told me today I feel like I'm going kill crazy . . .

If there is anyone you want me to kick in the shins or bite, please, please let me know.

Love,

me

oxoxoxoxoxoxoxoxoxoxoxoxoxo[25]

The hyperbole was partly just Ashby's style. But while Jewison shared (and to some extent nurtured) Ashby's distrust of "the man," he also knew how to take budgetary pressure in stride. Walter Mirisch had his eye on the bottom line, which was not surprising. For his part, Mirisch remembers a "constant struggle" over the budget of the film. "I felt the obligation of my commitment to United Artists strongly and tried as hard as I could to adhere to it," Mirisch said.[26] Ashby, however, was so earnest about their artistic integrity that the mere mention of budgetary constraints could provoke a rhetorical aneurysm.

Budgetary pressures notwithstanding, the creative forces behind *Heat* had hit their stride. Cinematographer Haskell Wexler came from the documentary world, and had since worked with Irvin Kershner, Elia Kazan and, most recently, Mike Nichols on *Who's Afraid of Virginia Woolf?* Wexler, who wore a wool hunting cap and always seemed to be gnawing on a pipe, brought a documentarian's visual sensibility to the material. Where Jewison's early films had popped with colour, Wexler conjured a darker, grainier world in *Heat*. In fact, it was Wexler's first colour film, but Jewison found him to be a wellspring of creative ideas. Just as important, they were affordable creative ideas. To achieve the film's distinctive opening—what appear to be abstract balloons of light slowly coalescing into a train's light—Wexler had bought a window screen from the hardware store and placed it over the lens to prevent it from focusing. In other scenes, Wexler experimented with telephoto lenses and small 35mm handheld cameras (rare in those days) for filming in cars and other confined spaces, which gave parts of the film a gritty, *cinéma verité* feel. One day, while filming actor Scott Wilson being chased, Wexler heard a freight train in the distance. "I said, 'Norman, let's go!' It was a freebie." They timed the shot to begin with the arrival of the train, then filmed Wilson's character darting across the tracks. "We didn't have any money to hold trains up," Jewison remembers, "so we waited until the train came and then shot the scene."[27]

Wexler's daughter, Katharine, just out of college, accompanied him on set and worked alongside Meta Rebner, the film's script supervisor and former mistress (or "Hollywood wife") of William Faulkner. Jewison had enlisted Rebner, a petite, soft-spoken Mississippian, to police the accents of his performers and alert him if anything felt inauthentic. As script supervisor, Rebner would sit on a nearby camp stool, matching the action with the script and tracking continuity. "Rod Steiger called one day and asked if he should shave for a scene," Rebner remembers. "I had to see what time of day the scene was depicting to know if he should shave."[28]

* * *

"In movies," Rod Steiger said, "the only thing that gives you time to rehearse is bad weather." The weather was terrible on the night they were scheduled to shoot the film's pivotal scene: an intimate, emotionally revealing moment between Steiger and Poitier in Gillespie's house. A torrential rainstorm hammered down on the house's tin roof; filming was out of the question.

"Norman and I and Sidney sat in the car across the street from the little house and kind of improvised and carried on and rewrote it a little bit," Steiger recalls. What emerged was a classic western campfire scene, the two taciturn gunfighters lost in their reflections, atmosphere loosened by the bottle of bourbon on the table. For Steiger, Gillespie's defining feature wasn't racism but solitude: his character was a "lonely, unhappy human being. He's got this empty house, no love in his life but a sense of pride and duty and belongs to nobody." In that sense, Steiger sensed a familiarity between Gillespie and Tibbs. "They had a lot in common in a strange way. They were both brave, they were honourable, they both did their duty. They both didn't talk about themselves very much; that's why the scene in the house works—all of a sudden they are talking."[29]

Poitier remembers Steiger as highly unpredictable. "He would always find the offbeat, unusual way to express the moment. He underplays where other people would be coming on strong; he would suddenly explode when you would think there was no reason for it, but then you would see it on film and it works a treat. He has an instinct for that—playing against the role."[30]

"Rod allows himself to get so vulnerable," Jewison says of the scene, "and then the moment he gets the tiniest bit of pity from an African American, he gets angry."[31]

Jewison had secured another powerhouse performer in Lee Grant, who played the murder victim's wife. "It was a great coup for me to talk her into being in this film," Jewison said. Grant was nominated for an Academy Award for her debut film, William Wyler's *The Detectives* (1951). Shortly thereafter, Grant was called to testify against her husband, the writer Arnold Manoff, before the House Un-American Activities Committee. She refused and spent the next twelve years professionally blacklisted.

To Jewison, Lee Grant was a survivor. At forty, Grant brought to *Heat* the idealism and gravitas that she had earned through her years in the wilderness. And her off-screen trials were inspirational to the creative minds behind *Heat*. "The commitment to social change was the motivating factor of practically everyone on that film," remembers Wexler. "We wanted the film to make money, but we also wanted to prove that human values can supersede bigotry. In a way, we felt as though it was a patriotic film."

* * *

Nobody remembers exactly how Jewison talked Sidney Poitier into shooting in the South. (Jewison "is very wily," said Steiger. "He's a wily fox. I mean that in the nicest way.") Poitier wasn't happy about it, but Jewison promised that the crew, which included "some big guys," would ensure his safety. In the end, he agreed to one week of filming in Dyersburg, Tennessee, where Tibbs would confront Endicott on his cotton plantation.

They checked into the Holiday Inn, the only hotel in Dyersburg, Jewison said, that accepted Black people. While in Sparta, the production had confronted racism through a dramatic lens; in Tennessee, they confronted it in the flesh. "[T]he moment they found out the movie was about a Black detective and they saw Sidney Poitier in an expensive suit . . . it upset people," Jewison remembers. "There were pickup trucks circling the hotel at night, people getting drunk, driving into the courtyard, that kind of thing."[32] Steiger remembers that he and Poitier kept their adjoining hotel room door open and that Poitier slept with a gun under his pillow. "I remember one incident in a restaurant where they were not very happy to see us eating together, a white man and a Black man," Steiger recalls. "They didn't dare, thank God, go too far, but the least one could say was that the service was belligerent."[33]

Legal segregation ended with President Johnson's Civil Rights Act of 1964 and Voting Rights Act of 1965, but in practice much of the United States remained a segregated country. On November 9, 1966, Jewison awoke in Dyersburg to peruse the results of the previous day's US midterm elections. Headlines across the country focused on Ronald Reagan's defeat of the Democratic incumbent in the California gubernatorial election. Less widely reported on was the victory of Edward Brooke, a Republican from Massachusetts, who became the first ever African American popularly elected to the Senate.

If there is a single moment in 1960s American film that captures the disillusionment and anger over the pace of social change—and a moment that differentiates Virgil Tibbs from Sidney Poitier's other stoic professionals, aligning him with an angrier phase of the Civil Rights movement—it arrives in Sidney Poitier's famous slap of Endicott, the wealthy industrialist. Echoing the paternalistic social Darwinism of some prominent postwar social policy minds, Endicott compares "the Negro" to delicate, epiphytic orchids that must be nurtured and nourished by their gardeners. But when Endicott realizes that the detectives have arrived to question him for murder, he slaps Tibbs like an insolent child. Without hesitation, Poitier's right hand flashes up and belts Endicott across the side of the face. It was an iconic moment of 1960s popular culture: a slap announcing that, from now on, the dignity of Black Americans was backed with physical force. Looking back, Poitier said it was easy for viewers to forget how radical *Heat* really was. This was a picture filmed "in a country where they lynched Black people in the South," at a time when "people were being dragged from lunch counters in St. Louis and were beaten outside because they wanted a hamburger in a restaurant." *In the Heat of the Night*, Poitier says, was "so fucking revolutionary we don't realize it now."[34]

* * *

"The shooting of many films is accompanied with a great deal of Sturm und Drang," Walter Mirisch observes. *In the Heat of the Night* was "not one of those."[35]

With the Mirisch Company's usual sound stages occupied, the final stretch of shooting took place in a small, east Hollywood rental studio called the Producers.[36] By early December, Jewison was "almost a total basket case, mentally and physically," as he said at the time. He estimated that he had been working fifteen or sixteen hours per day for the last three months.[37]

No sooner had the film wrapped than Jewison set off for New Haven to address an audience at the Yale School of Drama. The tight scheduling had left him almost no time to collect his thoughts. Even at the best of times, Jewison was more comfortable engaging in dialogue than giving speeches. Still, Jewison's address at Yale that frigid December evening provided a distillation of his philosophy of filmmaking in 1966.

After opening with a few predictable jokes about confusing Yale with Harvard, Jewison offered an analysis of film's competing interests as art, entertainment, and business. He established his hipster-intellectual *bona fides* for the university crowd, citing figures like Andy Warhol and Marshall McLuhan. But in contrast to those who had made film suddenly "fashionable" in certain circles, Jewison defended the idea of cinema as entertainment. Jewison's "entertainment" included Shakespeare, Henry Fielding, and Charles Dickens, narrative artists who balanced artistic ideals with the commercial necessity of captivating audiences. Some "fashionable" filmmakers sneered at popular acceptance: Truffaut supposedly claimed that "too many people" went to see *The 400 Blows*. "Yet it is difficult for us to find a truly significant piece of film art that has not captured the imagination of the cinema-goer," Jewison argued.

He repeated for his Yale crowd what was by now a personal credo: film needed to entertain, and it needed a *raison d'être*. Yet while filmmakers' primary consideration ought to be communication with their audience, they also needed to recognize that the top priority of the distributor, exhibitor, and financier would always be profit. The alternative, a state-sponsored, European-style model of film culture, might allow for more daring modes of expression (and Jewison conceded that, partly due to lower production costs, the purely "artistic" director probably had an easier time of it in the United Kingdom, France, and Italy). "But whether film is controlled by the state or by the distributors or major studios," Jewison warned, "the individual filmmaker will have to continually fight for his freedom of expression and resist the attempts at conformity. For once you move out of the documentary and information field, state control can be just as great an evil as control by the banks."

Jewison wasn't sure his pragmatic message would fly with college students in 1966. In fact, he feared a "vicious" response. But while the mood on many college campuses was growing restive, Jewison enjoyed a collegial reception among the Yale crowd. "Throw in a large measure of empathy and liking for you," his host wrote after the fact, "and it's kind of hard to bare your fangs at a nice, groovy stranger."[38]

Work on *In the Heat of the Night*, meanwhile, had not stopped—it had only changed. Ashby was compulsively working and re-working material in the editing room. Quincy Jones was writing songs and supervising the soundtrack. Jewison called for "an authentic, southern, funky mood"; he wanted the sound of "sweat-soaked cotton fields of Tennessee," and of "the small forgotten towns of the rural south." Jones enlisted his friend Ray Charles to sing the film's title track, "a slice of real, rural backwoods gospel," as one critic would call it, with lyrics from Alan and Marilyn Bergman.[39] Ambient music, the jukeboxes and transistor radios playing the Lewis and Clark Expedition, Glen Campbell, and Gil Bernal, added sonic texture. Rahsaan Roland Kirk, a blind flautist from Chicago, layered an ethereal, unsettling dimension to the film's sound. "I need his anger, man," Jones said, "and his loneliness."[40]

* * *

Back at 313 Barrington, Kevin, Michael, and Jennifer were excited for Christmas. Jewison, never enthusiastic about the juxtaposition of palm trees and Christmas decorations, arranged for a family ski trip to Sun Valley, Idaho.

Conventional wisdom held that, by 1966, Aspen had been overrun by hippies and ski bums ("the drug situation is out of control," according to one observer), while Sun Valley attracted wealthy, health-conscious Californians. There was almost never a line for the chairlifts. The likes of Jimmy Stewart, Gregory Peck, James Garner, and their wives provided fodder for the society pages of the newspapers: "Even the Sun Valley divorces are fun," chimed the *New York Times*. Steve McQueen would shout down photographers who tried to shoot his awkward skiing.

The Sun Valley social set prided themselves on the informality of their nightly parties: while the women wore the latest pant suits and furs, the men made a point of wearing sport jackets—*not* tuxedos—to dinner. Some of them did, however, wear cashmere long johns.[41]

Jewison was part of the scene. Michael and Kevin were strong skiers and competitive in the races. On December 23, however, eight-year-old Michael lost an edge in a downhill race and took a bad fall, breaking his leg. He was not the only casualty on the slopes that day: shortly before the chairlifts closed at 3:30 p.m., Joseph Kennedy, Senator Robert Kennedy's fourteen-year-old son, fractured his foot while skiing Warm Springs International on the back side of Mt. Baldy.[42] Jewison met Bobby Kennedy in the Sun Valley hospital waiting room; they commiserated while their sons were fitted with casts.

Kennedy invited the Jewisons to a New Year's Eve gathering that he and Ethel were hosting at their lodge. Jewison remembers that Jim Whittaker, the first American to reach the summit of Mt. Everest, climbed the fifty-foot riverstone fireplace in the living room of the Kennedy's A-frame.[43]

Jewison talked with the senator for New York, and told him that he'd just completed a picture about a Black detective who investigates a murder in a southern town. Kennedy, a major civil rights advocate, was taken by the idea. Jewison's recollection of what Kennedy said next became an oft-repeated anecdote in the decades to come. "The time is right for a movie like this," Bobby Kennedy said. "Timing is everything in politics, in art, and in life itself."

Michael's injury aside, Christmas with the family was restorative. Jewison sometimes felt that the film business was in competition with family life. Yet in some ways, Jewison's experience as a father may have dovetailed with his work as a director. Reflecting upon his experience with Jewison in *Heat*, Rod Steiger observed, "A director is really a gifted father to a large family . . . either he has a gift for knowing people, and taking care of them and keeping them together, or he can forget about all the theories, and shots, lighting and all the technical stuff altogether. Norman has that gift."[44]

CHAPTER 8

The Juice

I N EARLY 1967, Norman Jewison invited dozens of friends and industry acquaintances to a Russian-themed cocktail party at his home. *The Russians Are Coming* had just been nominated for three Golden Globes, including Best Picture and Best Actor (musical or comedy) and Best Screenplay.[1] Industry players mingled in the Jewisons' cavernous thirty-by-fifty-foot family room, a dramatic space with exposed brick walls, red wood ceiling beams, and concrete floor tinted with green wax, all lit by gothic candles set in wrought-iron fixtures. By now, Dixie was an experienced hand at hosting these lavish soirees. Julie Andrews, Mike Nichols, Terry Southern, James Garner, and Steve McQueen had been dinner guests. A sit-down dinner party for sixty people was no longer intimidating: it was just a matter of hiring the right help. "I have a marvelous caterer who helps with everything—menu, linens, table settings—and my own florist who knows what I like," Dixie said at the time.[2]

The Jewisons had been on Barrington Avenue for nearly five years, and Dixie had adapted to Hollywood life. She had picked up some of the habits of her social milieu, learning to play tennis and piano, while continuing to paint. The proximity to fame had not gone to her head. "She was a mom, you know," remembers Jennifer Jewison, "she made horrible lunches and all that kind of stuff."

"She woke up with us, sent us off to school, she brushed our hair, she pulled out what we were to wear for the day, you know; we got the hair brush if we did something really bad," Jennifer said. While the kids attended private school in Los Angeles and were brought up in comparatively luxurious circumstances, their parents made a point of not showering them with gifts. "We had to work for things," Jennifer remembers. "We weren't brought up on the idea of 'well, you get your Porsche for graduation.' There were no material objects at all." A Jewison kid who aced a test or did something special was awarded the El Clubbo cup. "We had this little ceremony and everything" where the honoured child was presented with the red and white striped cup, which they got to drink from for the rest of the month. "If you did something really bad," Jennifer remembers, "there was another cup."[3]

"Everything was discussed" at the Jewison dinner table, says Jennifer. If Norman was in town, the family waited for his return before sitting down for dinner, even if it was 8 p.m. "Drink times at the house, it was always when Dad came home and we were watching TV or doing our homework, and you'd always come down and see Mom and Dad huddled in a conversation, you always saw them communicating. It was always, 'So how was your day at work?' And they'd honestly sit down [and talk about it], and it wasn't like, 'Oh, it was fine, how was your day?' They always talked about it over drinks. Mom was really involved even though she wasn't in the light; they always had this little thing going that they'd really discuss things. And I think that helped Kevin, Michael, and I really sort of figure ourselves out."[4]

Norman and Dixie kept any marital tensions out of the children's sight. "I never, ever heard them fight," Jennifer says. "You know, you'd catch them making out in the kitchen, all that kind of stuff and kissing . . . we'd see all that part of it, but we never really saw the other side of it, the arguments or whatever they might have had."[5]

Family friends were aware of Norman and Dixie's efforts to shield their children from the excesses of 1960s Hollywood. "I think they could have grown up on the moon," Marilyn Bergman, songwriter and family friend, says of the Jewison children. "I think Norman and Dixie came from a very . . . structured kind of upbringing. Certainly not anything like where they ended up spending their lives, and I think they have very strong family values and very strong work ethics, and a sense of what is appropriate, and what is inappropriate. I remember always being very aware that Norman is swimming against the tide here . . . They were careful, always, about any feeling of excess or what was inappropriate."[6]

* * *

Representatives of excess were not hard to find in early 1967, with Steve McQueen lobbying Jewison to star in *The Crown Caper* (a film that was, in a sense, *about* the excess and spiritual emptiness of the moment). Jewison had heard about McQueen's drunken fistfights on location for *The Sand Pebbles*. He'd probably also heard the more salacious rumours about McQueen's drug use and sexual escapades. McQueen had been an insecure and volatile presence on the set of *The Cincinnati Kid*, and didn't seem to be mellowing with age.

McQueen was an awkward fit for Thomas Crown. In Alan Trustman's script, Crown was a debonair Harvard alumnus, equally at home on the polo field or sipping scotch with other Boston Brahmins. Sure, he was a bank robber, but those robberies were intellectual exercises, feats of engineering. McQueen, by contrast, spoke and often looked like a grease monkey. Thomas Crown's patrician dialogue might sound downright silly as mumbled by McQueen. Still, Jewison had to let him down easy; he still hoped to do *Judgment of Corey* with McQueen when their schedules allowed.

My dear Steve:

I called you but you're off chasing Indians again.

So far, the pressure from United Artists and Mirisch is to cast CROWN CAPER according to the script and avoid any major changes or conception. I'll call you upon your return.

Your deal with Warner's sounds very exciting, and you've got a good man in Bob Relyea. I envy you.[7]

The last three words would, Jewison hoped, appease the demon of McQueen's ego.

Unfortunately, the project he hoped to do with McQueen was plagued with its own problems. Jewison and Walter Mirisch had requested feedback on the *Judgment of Corey* screenplay from two trusted friends. The first was James Ruffin Webb, a veteran scribe of Hollywood westerns and Mirisch associate, who would eventually write the sequel to *In the Heat of the Night*. "The chief trouble with *Judgment of Corey*," Webb wrote, "is that I don't believe it." The set-up was far-fetched, the characters were inconsistent, and the protagonist, a shell of a character who "has no part at all," overcomes the villains due to "sheer luck."[8]

United Artists executive David Picker was equally unimpressed. "I know I don't like the script," Picker wrote, and "I think it will take an experienced screenwriter to do a complete rewrite, rather than just a few changes (the kind of second guesses we executives love to throw around)."[9] Jewison was prepared to fight for projects he wanted to make, but was starting to feel that *Judgment of Corey* wasn't worth it. Trade reports continued to list *Corey* as "upcoming" for Jewison, sometimes with McQueen's name attached. But Jewison stopped talking about it, and his epic western gradually faded from view.

* * *

Jewison's top choice for Thomas Crown had always been Sean Connery. He even had a way in: Connery was represented by (and had been discovered by) London theatrical agent Richard Hatton, business partner of Terence Baker, Boaty Boatwright's husband. "I have spoken with Sean about it several times and of course have asked him to get on with reading" the *Crown* script, Hatton wrote to Jewison. But Connery, who had just finished another arduous outing as James Bond on *You Only Live Twice*, was less than enthused about reading a script with the word "caper" in the title.

"He has been absolutely adamant with me that until he has had a holiday, he is not going to react to any of the scripts we have currently got on hand," Hatton said, emphasizing that Connery "really does need the holiday." The agent said that his client would bring Jewison's script with him to the Bahamas, "but frankly I am not at all certain that he will read it."[10] Hatton hoped to be able to respond to Jewison in three weeks.

Three weeks later, Jewison learned that Connery had extended his stay in the Bahamas and that "we are not yet sure when he will return."[11]

McQueen, meanwhile, was intensifying his campaign. Jewison remained unenthusiastic. "Steve had never played a part that required him to wear a tie," Jewison recalled. Eventually, however, he acquiesced to a meeting.

McQueen drove over to Jewison's house one afternoon, where the director explained why the part just didn't fit his image. "What's going to happen when you have to look people in the eye?" Jewison asked him. "Thomas Crown doesn't look at his feet. He doesn't scuff his shoes. He doesn't pull at the brim of his hat and squint," he continued, rattling off a few of McQueen's favourite acting tics. "He looks people in the eye . . . and lies."[12]

Jewison and McQueen spoke for nearly three hours in Norman's sprawling garden. Curiously, as Steve continued pressing his case, his confidence only increased, and Jewison gradually began to see how it could work. "The more he talked," Jewison recalled, "the more I saw him as Thomas Crown."[13] Jewison also knew how hard it could be for an independent producer to secure a star of McQueen's stature, and how dispiriting it had been to promote *Russians* without a bankable star. High-profile casting was even more crucial in this case, because *The Crown Caper* was built around the personality of the male lead. The film simply would not be made without an A-list star in the title role.

Besides, Jewison rationalized, he'd already worked with McQueen once, and made it work. How much worse could it get?

* * *

McQueen may have seemed desperate to play Crown, but he wasn't about to give Jewison a break for his services. His deal called for $750,000 cash, nearly double what Poitier and Steiger had earned together on *Heat*, plus 15 per cent of the gross receipts after break-even, for twelve weeks of the actor's time, plus four free weeks. The deal also stipulated that McQueen's star billing would be "equal in all respects to the title of the picture, and no other members of the cast may receive credit on the same line with Mr. McQueen."[14] Then there were the fringe benefits: $1,000 per week in expenses while outside Los Angeles, plus first-class transportation for himself, his wife, two children, and a nurse to the shooting location, plus a chauffeured limousine to and from airports, plus a car and driver while on location and another car (sans driver) for his use in LA. McQueen was explicitly entitled to the "best" dressing room while on location, which was to be furnished with a set of barbells (200 lbs) and a set of dumb bells (80 lbs). The Mirisches were on the hook for McQueen's secretary's salary, plus her transportation and lodging; for shipping his motorcycle to the location; for providing a still photographer if he wanted one; and for shipping McQueen's camper to the location and back. Those details in place, Jewison could again look forward to the experience of working with Steve McQueen.[15]

Jewison knew that the script had to be tailored to his star. Many of Crown's lines were condensed, or cut entirely. "It's thin on dialogue, but big with image" was how Jewison framed the revised draft when sending it to his lead, concerned with how McQueen would react to Crown's vanishing lines.[16]

Jewison, Hal Ashby, and a variety of agents then turned to casting "the girl," as they invariably referred to the part of Vicki Anderson, the female lead. An early favourite was Anouk Aimée. Her recent credits, including Federico Fellini's *8½* and *La Dolce Vita*, suggested the European air of art-house sophistication with which Jewison hoped to infuse *Crown*. Catherine Deneuve (who had starred in Roman Polanski's *Repulsion*) and Joanna Pettet (from *Casino Royale*) were also in the mix.[17]

Around the same time, Jewison flew to Boston for an intensive writing session with Alan Trustman. On his last several pictures, Jewison had worked with some of the most respected screenwriters in the industry, including Carl Reiner, Terry Southern, William Rose, and Stirling Silliphant. Trustman, by contrast, was a rookie: a thirty-seven-year-old Boston lawyer who didn't know how to format a screenplay. "We always capitalize each character upon its first appearance in the script," explained Nadine Phinney, who tutored Trustman while re-typing the script in a conventional format. Phinney went over the formal conventions of screenwriting, patiently describing when a screenplay needed to indicate "Dissolves" (to indicate the passage of time in an otherwise continuous scene) and "Inserts" (to pick up important close-ups that might be impossible to shoot within the body of a scene). She also combined paragraphs in the script to make it appear shorter. "Mr. Jewison is always fighting the front office about the length of his scripts," Phinney confided to Trustman, "so we do anything and everything we can to make sure we don't repeat unnecessarily, take too much space, indent too much, etc. It is our own personal piece of chicanery against the front office."[18]

Boston in January was grey and depressing. Trustman had taken Jewison for a walk to scout locations along the Boston side of the Charles River, looking back over the bleak industrial area of Cambridge and MIT. The leaden city appeared to be covered with "grit and slime."[19] The script was in awful shape. Trustman's prose was snappy and economical, but his dialogue was flat and the characters all sounded the same. Back in Los Angeles, Jewison undertook his own rewrites, continuing to shape the title role for McQueen. Possibly at his star's insistence, he inserted a scene on the beach in which Crown tore around on a dune buggy.

Trustman found it preposterous. "A dune buggy! What is he, some kind of flit? Or is Stevo determined to stay on his motorcycle, and if he can't have it, a dune buggy is next best?" It was out of character for Crown, Trustman stormed: "Damn it. You must know it is."

Trustman also balked at Jewison's decision to cut his opening scene, in which Crown recruits one of the bank robbers. Jewison's instinct was to open with the robbery. Trustman, however, had shown the script to several friends over Christmas who had specifically praised the scene for its suspenseful introduction of Crown's character.[20] Trustman did his own rewrites and put the scene back in.

* * *

Toward the end of February, the Academy announced the Oscar nominations for 1966. *The Russians Are Coming* picked up nominations for Best Picture, Best Adapted Screenplay, and Best Actor for Alan Arkin. While Jewison was disappointed to miss out on a director nomination, the Best Picture nomination was a triumph in itself, and Hollywood took note. The producer Stanley Margulies congratulated him in typically droll fashion.

> Dear Norman,
>
> On behalf of all our comrades—Lenin, Stalin, Khrushchev, and Kosygin—congratulations on the well-deserved Academy nominations. Truly the film has done more for our country than anything since borscht.
>
> And we promise a trip to Siberia to the idiots who failed to acknowledge your contribution as Best Director.
>
> As ever,
>
> Stan[21]

The 1967 Academy Awards, hosted by Bob Hope, took place on April 10 at the Santa Monica Civic Auditorium. *The Russians Are Coming* was shut out by *A Man for All Seasons*, which took Best Picture, Best Actor (Paul Scofield), and Best Adapted Screenplay (Robert Bolt, adapted from his own play), among its six Oscars.

A Best Picture nomination was a boon to any filmmaker's career, but it came with a downside: Jewison was now targeted by an endless procession of agents who came knocking about opportunities for actors they represented. Agent Tom Korman was pressuring him to use Rip Torn or Julie Harris in *Thomas Crown*.[22] Richard Gregson was pushing his client (and later wife) Natalie Wood as Vicki Anderson opposite McQueen. "Honestly, Richard, I feel the part is just not for her," Jewison told him. "I think she's a shade young, and perhaps too warm a personality."[23] Jewison hated rejecting actors—certain casting decisions would cause him considerable turmoil over the years—but his success had ensured that it was something he would have to do with greater frequency.

In the spring of 1967, what Jewison needed most was the right actress for the role of Vicki. A March 17 memo from casting director Lynn Stalmaster listed five actresses under consideration: Sharon Acker, Samantha Eggar, Suzanne Pleshette, Romy Schneider, and Faye Dunaway. For the role of Eddie, the detective tracking McQueen, Stalmaster recommended Burt Reynolds, Richard Crenna, Robert Redford, and Robert Forster.[24]

Meanwhile, Jewison had held four or five heated meetings with McQueen and Ashby about the script. Jewison agreed to restore Trustman's opening "recruitment" scene, but in return he wanted more detail and realism woven in throughout the screenplay. It wasn't even clear what Thomas Crown did for a living: how was he supposed to have made his millions? (Whatever his line of work, Jewison wanted Crown's office to be outfitted with one of those "new GE computers" to indicate he was on the cutting edge.) Jewison worried that Vicki was "a little too bitchy, too smartass, too flip, too one-dimensional. She must have some depth and true intelligence, and also an air of mystery."

Jewison scolded Trustman for soliciting feedback from random friends, a rookie move. "My God, you'll be getting like Jule Styne next, asking the caretaker of the theatre what he thought about the big number. Seriously, I would rather you not show the script around, because of the great danger of plagiarism and talk."[25]

Weeks away from their start date, *The Crown Caper* still didn't have a female lead. Nadine Phinney sent Trustman a frank assessment of the state of the production. "We have no girl. We have no Rolls," Phinney said, referring to Crown's car. On the plus side, "we've hired a tailor for Steve whom he likes, and who will not allow him any of his wild ideas for clothes that will be 'in' five years from now."[26]

Around this time, Jewison received an unexpected breakthrough on "the girl." Brigitte Bardot was an international icon in 1967: her image combined the sophistication of the French New Wave with an air of sexual abandon. "Seen from behind, her slender, muscular, dancer's body is almost androgynous. Femininity triumphs in her bosom," Simone de Beauvoir rhapsodized in "The Lolita Syndrome," her essay on Bardot. "She goes about barefoot, she turns up her nose at elegant clothes, jewels, girdles, perfumes, make-up, as all artifice. Yet her walk is lascivious and a saint would sell his soul to the devil merely to watch her dance."[27]

Bardot didn't make American films: she'd starred in just one, a forgettable James Stewart comedy called *Dear Brigitte*. Now, however improbably, "B.B." was interested in *The Crown Caper*. In fact, while Bardot was already booked that August, she indicated that she would postpone that film if she liked Jewison's script. There was just one caveat: her role must be "as important as Steve's."[28] Jewison wasted no time in dashing off a response:

I believe Brigitte part more important than Steve's.

McQueen / Bardot combination will be marvelous. Sending script.[29]

"I see this picture as a love story played against a suspense background," Jewison followed up in a letter to Olga Horstig, Bardot's agent. "It is a romantic thriller between two unique and intelligent characters. It is a sophisticated, high-style film which I will shoot principally on location in Boston."[30] Jewison offered to fly to Paris to sell the film to Bardot.

Meanwhile, the director reassembled his team. Cinematographer Haskell Wexler was back; his stark, unflattering close-ups of Richard Burton and Elizabeth Taylor on *Who's Afraid of Virginia Woolf?* had recently earned him an Academy Award. (Wexler's job, as he bluntly put it, was to make Elizabeth Taylor look ugly.) Hal Ashby returned as editor and all-purpose associate producer. "It was a total trip, and I really felt as if I were giving as much to the film as possible, without actually being the director," Ashby said. "It was the most productive relationship imaginable."[31] Jewison remained an enthusiastic collaborator and was rarely concerned with being the lone "author" of his films—unless executives tried to usurp credit, in which cases he could get fiercely defensive.

With the clock ticking, and still no word from Bardot, Jewison decided to engage his friend Ilya Lopert, the Paris-based United Artists fixer, to see what he could do. "Must make decision soon," Jewison wrote. "Need reaction pronto. See if you can find out anything."[32]

Jewison was about to receive another surprise, this one courtesy of Haskell Wexler. Like Ashby, Wexler did not hold conventional Hollywood filmmaking in high esteem. He'd cut his teeth on independent documentaries like *The Bus*, which captured footage of a coach full of Civil Rights activists en route to Martin Luther King Jr.'s epochal March on Washington in 1963. Wexler often derided Hollywood product as manufactured fantasy, and attacked the industry's practice of "put[ting] labels on people; so-and-so is an editor, so-and-so is a cameraman." Said Wexler: "I stick my nose in everywhere." He had contributed to the script of *In the Heat of the Night*, which he deemed "mediocre"—"a fake sociological script, with little understanding of today's South." Jewison, he said, "encouraged me to contribute what I could to the script. The Sidney Poitier character, he was just a plain smart-ass—unsympathetic, one-dimensional Mr. Negro. It's like having a flag; if you like the flag then you salute it. Well, that's not drama."[33] If Wexler thought the script to *Heat* was bad, the screenplay for *Crown* was incomparably worse. Rather than tinkering around the margins, Wexler decided to rewrite the whole thing from scratch.

That April, Wexler unveiled the fruit of his labour: "The Name of the Game," an entirely new screenplay, co-written with Michael Butler, based on Alan Trustman's "The Crown Caper." The seventy-two-page script retained the general bank heist premise, but departed in tone and style from Trustman's original. In Wexler's version, Crown did voice imitations of famous performers (Jimmy Stewart, Humphrey Bogart, Bing Crosby, and so on) to disguise himself in his capers. "When Crown does his TV-video tape impression, he should mess his blond hair, wrap a sheet around his middle, and imitate Phyllis Diller," Wexler wrote in a note accompanying the new script. "It will bring us close to high camp . . . wild, wild!"[34]

Thankfully, Wexler agreed to remain with the production, for $2,000 per week, even after his screenplay was declined. Jewison was grateful to have Wexler back as cinematographer, but his contributions had to be contained within a conventional form.

Finally, word arrived from Bardot's agent. They were leaving for Rome the following day, Horstig reported, where she and Bardot would be staying at the Hotel Parco Dei Principi. Horstig now wondered if Jewison could film the picture in Europe, as "twelve to fourteen weeks away from home will appear terribly long to Miss Bardot."[35]

"Received your letter. Impossible to shoot in Europe," Jewison wrote back. "Please contact Ilya Lopert or myself as soon as possible."[36]

The next telegram arrived from Rome within days. "Script excellent but Brigitte feels Vicki should be an American or able to speak English with no accent. Hope to meet you one day. Regards, Olga Horstig."[37]

With that, Jewison's opportunity to bring Steve McQueen and Brigitte Bardot together on screen had vanished, and casting "the girl" was back at square one.

* * *

On April 14, Raquel Welch read a half-dozen scenes for the role of Vicki.[38] Jewison was also considering Catherine Deneuve, Claire Bloom, Faye Dunaway, Elizabeth Taylor, and Sharon Tate, who came with complications: Roman Polanski's romantic partner was under contract with Martin Ransohoff (who had tested her for the Tuesday Weld role in *The Cincinnati Kid*), and it was difficult to set up a screen test since she was working on *Valley of the Dolls*. Moreover, Walter Mirisch had already met her and wasn't impressed.[39] The deliberations continued.

Smaller pieces of the cast were falling into place. They picked up Yaphet Kotto ($250 daily) and Gordon Pinsent ($1,000 per week).[40] Television actor Paul Burke agreed to play detective Eddie Malone for $40,000, but his agent drew Jewison into a tiresome negotiation over details including the size of his screen credit. "The billing will be not less than 75 per cent size of Steve McQueen," Jewison responded tartly to Burke's agent. "Since I am sure you must be as bored with this negotiation as I am, and as it is getting a little dark out, I'm afraid this is my last response to your requests. If I do not hear from you in the next twenty-four hours, I will assume we have no deal."[41] No further objections emerged.

Finally, eleven days before starting principal photography, they found "the girl." Faye Dunaway, who hailed from Tallahassee, Florida, was not exactly the refined European ingénue that Jewison had envisioned. He respected Dunaway's theatrical work: she had spent three years in New York's Lincoln Center Repertory Company, after which Elia Kazan recommended her for a role in the Broadway production of *A Man for All Seasons*. What put her over the top, however, was *Bonnie and Clyde*. Director Arthur Penn let Jewison view a couple reels of the film, which was still in post-production.[42] Simcoe Enterprises, Jewison's production company, bought Dunaway's services on a loan-out agreement from Port Bascom Productions, which had her under contract, for $125,000. She was also entitled to $850 per week as a living allowance and a credit comparable to McQueen's.[43]

* * *

We know that principal photography on *The Crown Caper* began on June 6, 1967. Less clear is why the director of *The Russians Are Coming* and *In the Heat of the Night* wanted to make *Crown* at all.

At the time, Jewison insisted that, despite appearances, *Crown* was consistent with his more socially conscious work. Thomas Crown might look slick, decked out in his three-piece suit and $5,000 Patek Philippe watch, but Jewison insisted that he was an agent of the counterculture: robbing bank vaults was a more effective blow against "the man" than picketing in the streets, because it hit the banks and insurance companies where it hurt. Years later, Jewison admitted that what had really attracted him was the heist itself, in which five strangers execute an elaborate robbery orchestrated by Crown. "I just thought it was a fascinating caper," Jewison said, "a film essentially of style over content."[44] Despite intensive rewrites, the script remained thin, alarmingly so in some key emotional beats. Later, Jewison would recite, in bemused disbelief, some of the film's lines: "'What a funny, dirty little mind,' 'What a funny, dirty little job.' I mean, who writes dialogue like that? It's just kind of dumb."

They filmed the heist over a weekend at Boston's National Shawmut Bank. Executives were taken aback by the scale of the enterprise. "There is no question that we were somewhat uneasy at the thought of all the equipment, men, and materials needed for this massive undertaking," an assistant vice president at Shawmut admitted.[45]

The sequence itself was frenetic yet intricately choreographed, demonstrating the assurance and verve of a director ready to experiment. As usual, Jewison was not working from storyboards, but improvising in the moment. At one point, Wexler strapped his camera to a skateboard to follow a flare down a bank hallway, hurtling behind plumes of billowing red smoke. Wexler wanted the scene to have a documentary-like feel; he cited Gillo Pontecorvo's *The Battle of Algiers* (1966) as inspiration. "Cinematically, I've never been as loose," Jewison reflected. "I just had time. Since it was a very short script, we were riffing on a theme and making it up as we went along."[46]

Jewison discovered what would become the film's signature visual technique earlier that summer. At Montreal's Expo 67, the World's Fair that aligned with Canada's Centennial, Jewison had been struck by the Canada Film Board's *Labyrinth* exhibition, an immense conceptual installation inspired by the Minotaur myth. The final section presented an experimental film that made pioneering use of the "multiple image technique," in which images of tribal Africans intermingled with shots of traffic cops and rockets blasting into space to suggest the variety and simultaneity of the human experience. Jewison, in pre-production of *Crown*, saw something rather more prosaic: a groovy set-up for a bank robbery.

"For the next few weeks, I shipped certain key members of my production team to Montreal," Jewison remembers, where they also admired Christopher Chapman's short film *A Place to Stand*, which employed a similar groundbreaking method.[47] Pablo Ferro, who designed the opening credit sequence of *Russians*, was responsible for the visual composition of the multiple-image sequences in post-production. *Crown* used the technique as a device for increasing tension and narrative convergence, showing disparate characters coming together. While the film was not written with the technique in mind, Wexler found creative call-backs to the multiple-image format even within full-screen shots, using elements within the frame (phone booth doors, elevators, door frames, mirrors, and oak panels) to create visual unity with the multiscreen moments that were imposed in editing. "Wherever we could, we were trying to make interesting compositions, with the style emerging from the very moment of making the film," Jewison recalled.[48]

* * *

McQueen arrived in Boston ready to work, driven by impostor syndrome and fear that audiences would find him laughable in the role. He assumed his career was at stake. "If I fuck up now, it's over," he said at the time.[49] McQueen biographer Penina Spiegel reports that the actor worked harder on *Crown* "than he had on any other film. He worked on his speech; he spent endless hours in fitting rooms trying on suits, shirts, ties, learning to move and walk naturally in another man's shell."[50] He practiced polo until his palms bled, mastering a challenging backhanded shot he performed in the film. He had more difficulty with chess, later admitting that the moves his character performed in the film's romantic climax were beyond him. The habits of a cosmopolitan sophisticate didn't come easily to McQueen: when he was stuck, he would adopt the mannerisms (and sometimes even the wardrobe) of his director. Unhappy with his costume in a scene where Crown slips past the police, McQueen borrowed Jewison's hat and jean jacket. He took one of Jewison's cigars for good measure.[51]

The characters in *Crown* were never without cigarettes, thin tendrils of smoke coiling around the margins of the frame. Behind the scenes, the film's creators were also heavy smokers, and not only of cigarettes and cigars. For many, a steady dose of marijuana had become part of the creative process. "It was Hal who introduced me to pot," Jewison remembers. "All of a sudden I saw that, 'Oh, man, this is good!' I feel better and the world doesn't look as bad as it did before."[52]

McQueen's drug regimen was having the opposite effect, exacerbating his paranoia. "Steve would wake panic-stricken in the middle of the night, convinced that someone was trying to harm his family," Spiegel writes. He would telephone Jewison "to say that he saw an intruder at the bottom of his driveway. The police would be called and find nothing more ominous than a couple of teenagers on the beach."[53]

McQueen, as Jewison had learned on the set of *The Cincinnati Kid*, was obsessed with "the Juice"—that is, who had the power in any given situation. "You had to approach him without fear," Jewison recalled. "You had to be strong and totally honest with him. When he saw the director hesitate, he would know the director was having trouble with the scene— and that's when Steve would bore in."[54]

From the outset, Jewison worked to forge a tight bond between himself, McQueen, and Dunaway, keeping the mood on the set light and amicable.

"If he liked the way a scene was going," Dunaway recalled, "it was not unusual for him to come over and grab Steve and me in a great bear hug."[55]

Every production has its inside jokes. On *Crown*, the director had fallen into the habit of taking all of his daily liquids from the same cup. "When he starts the day, we give him coffee in the mug," Nadine Phinney said. "After lunch he has tea. Then at wrap-up, he gets scotch and soda." His collaborators began needling Jewison about his habit, and McQueen, ever concerned with "the Juice," decided that he needed a mug of his own, only bigger. That's when Jewison's competitiveness kicked in. "When we started the picture it was just a cup," Ashby said. "Then Steve got himself a mug, so Norm appeared with a bigger one. Then Steve got a huge mug, so Norm appeared with the biggest he could find. Right now, Steve is ahead. He had a wooden block mounted on the bottom of his."[56]

For the time being, relations between director and star remained jocular. Asked whether his second outing with Jewison was different from the first, McQueen grinned: "Yeah. He's shorter. I always call him Shorty. And he calls me Spanky."[57] Beneath the jokes, however, were neuroses that could quickly warp McQueen's competitive energy into something darker and more menacing.

He could kid about the mug, about Jewison's height, and much else. But he wasn't kidding about what those things represented. McQueen needed everyone to understand: he was the one with the Juice.

* * *

Crown was Jewison's first opportunity to film primarily in an urban *milieu*. He had never seen graffiti before that summer in Boston. He and Wexler made the most of the city, using as many as four cameras, concealed in nearby trucks or behind windows, capturing unscripted moments of Boston and its residents.

"People did things you wouldn't believe," Wexler said, recalling the reaction to Yaphet Kotto waving a gun and loading bags of money into a station wagon in broad daylight. "A lady walked by, she looked, and you could see her perplexed—should I get involved, should I say something? Then she shrugged her shoulders and walked on."[58] Bostonians were giddy about the production. More than two thousand people turned up after a newspaper ad promised extras $16 a day. Many of these extras arrived on location in chauffeured cars, business executives out for a laugh. McQueen noticed that one brought his secretary along and was dictating memos between takes.[59]

McQueen had continued testing Jewison in all sorts of ways, and the director was running out of containment tactics. Increasingly paranoid, McQueen had demanded twenty-four-hour protection of his rental house in Beverly Farms. Boston Police and Pinkerton detectives did the work, and the Mirisch Corporation, to Jewison's annoyance, picked up most of the tab. McQueen squeezed money out of the production in any way he could. At one point, he submitted an invoice for $250 because Jewison had filmed his watch. He would phone Jewison in the middle of the night, grilling him about the scene in which Crown tells Vicki about his next heist. It wasn't scheduled for another couple of weeks, but McQueen always knew which scenes made Jewison anxious. "Why do you do that? Why do you always bore in on my insecurities?" Jewison asked. He later explained that McQueen "knew I was worried about the scene because I kept rewriting it. I felt like I was on the rack."[60]

One day, while shooting on a beach near Provincetown, Haskell Wexler insisted that they wait until "magic hour," those few minutes of sunset when the light was sublime. "We'd waited all day," Jewison recalled, "conditions were perfect, everyone was ready." Then, after the actors were called to their marks, McQueen peeled off in the dune buggy, ripping around the beach. Wexler joined Jewison in an anxious huddle. The light was fading fast. McQueen was way down the beach now, the dune buggy's engine blaring so loud that the actor couldn't have heard the crew's yelling even if he'd wanted to.

Finally, with just a sliver of the sun remaining on the horizon, McQueen brought the dune buggy to a skidding halt and bellowed at Jewison: "What are you waiting for?" Dunaway prepared for an explosion. "If Norman was the kind of director given to screaming, this would have been the moment for it," she remembers. "It was a classic standoff, the kind that happens so often between leading actors and directors. In these moments, a director can lose control of the entire movie if he's not careful. At the same time, he can irrevocably damage his relationship with the actor."[61]

All eyes were on Jewison, the crew in a state of hushed disbelief over McQueen's brazen challenge. Would Jewison ignore the provocation and attempt to salvage a few shots with what remained of the light? Or would he finally snap and call out McQueen's megalomania?

Jewison took a long drag of his cigar, then slowly wandered off. He walked alone for half an hour or more, allowing darkness to completely swallow the beach. When he finally returned, Dunaway noticed that he was carrying a seagull's feather. "Norman devised this absolutely crazy story that the feather had special powers and whoever had the feather would be the director that day," Dunaway remembers. "So he handed the white feather to Steve and said, 'You be the director for a while, then we'll give it to Faye, and then I'll take it back.' Steve looked at him for a minute, then started laughing, and took the feather and stuck it in Norman's cap.

It was exactly the way to handle Steve, who would have fought to the death if Norman had decided to assert his authority as director rather than trying to make peace."[62]

Dunaway may have thought it inspired, but Jewison was churning with rage as the crew packed up. Another day's work spoiled by McQueen's ego, another $12,000 over budget. The front office wouldn't see McQueen's antics on the beach; they would see the overages in time and money, the symptoms of a director losing control.

Rock-bottom arrived a couple of weeks later, when it came time to film "the last supper," the scene Jewison had been dreading for weeks. Alone with McQueen in the back of a limousine, Jewison confessed he was still worried about the dialogue but, for scheduling reasons, they simply had to do the scene that night. McQueen, however, still had his doubts; he did not want to do the scene as written. Jewison focused his atomic level of energy on McQueen and promised, with a look that invoked everything they'd been through, that he would make the scene work. McQueen thought about it. Then he thought about the Juice. He opened the car door and walked off.

An assistant director eventually found Jewison in the back of the limo, tears streaming down his cheeks. "I don't care whether I ever finish this picture," Jewison said. "I'm ready to walk off right now."[63]

* * *

Jewison's spirits received a major boost in August, with the opening of *In the Heat of the Night*. He'd felt skittish about the film's reception since its first sneak preview in San Francisco, where the audience seemed to laugh at everything. Atmospheric details meant to establish verisimilitude, such as Gillespie's busted air conditioner, caused gales of laughter among the audience. "When Steiger asks [Poitier] what he does in little old Philadelphia to earn that kind of money, and he says, 'a police officer,' the audience went *crazy*!" Jewison recalled. "They started to hoot and holler and scream and yell, and I was appalled! I thought, Oh my God! They're laughing at the film!"[64]

It wasn't long, however, before powerful voices reassured Jewison that he had created something special. After seeing an early cut in a United Artists screening room, Jack Valenti offered a perceptive compliment. "Coming on the heels of *The Russians*, [*Heat*] is specific evidence of an uncommon talent for diverse themes," Valenti said. "I was struck by the ingenious scene-setting you created, the dramatic use of extreme close-ups cutting back to let the viewer gulp in the drama!" Valenti wrote. "It was superb!"

The critics agreed, mostly. Given a premise that struck many of them as engineered to convey a sanctimonious liberal message, many of *Heat*'s first reviewers were shaken by the quality and force of the film, as though it was better than it had any right to be. "[T]o their credit and without getting preachy," Richard Schickel wrote in *Life*, the filmmakers "manage to transcend their cute premise and make a sound, serious, and altogether excellent film that is quite possibly the best we have from the US this year." Bosley Crowther praised Jewison for taking a "hard, outspoken script" based on an "undistinguished" novel and turning it into "a film that has the look and sound of actuality and the pounding pulse of truth." Charles Champlin raved in the *Los Angeles Times* that *Heat* was "this year's *The Russians Are Coming*," arguing that both films present "astute and satiric observation of attitudes prevailing in our society."[65]

Jewison's collaborators were also singled out for acclaim. "One can certainly recognize Wexler's hand in the weirdly beautiful compositions and juxtapositions which stud the film here and there almost like abstract paintings," wrote Tom Milne in *The Observer*.

Unsurprisingly, Poitier and Steiger received the most fervent hosannas. The *National Observer*'s Joseph Bell cited some of the film's subtle moments—"Mr. Poitier shaking his head in amusement as a white host hesitates to direct him to the washbasin; the chief picking up the Negro detective's bag in a silent act of respect"—as evidence of sharply observed performances. Steiger, Derek Prouse wrote in *Sight and Sound*, "has become one of the most authoritative and inventive actors on the screen."

Further praise came from unexpected quarters. Meredith Willson wrote to tell Jewison that *Heat* was "the best movie I ever saw."[66] Television producer Roger Ailes, future chairman and CEO of Fox News, effused to Jewison: "I have never written a fan letter, but I must say that I thought *In the Heat of the Night* was the best picture I have seen in a long time."[67] Grace Kelly, the Princess of Monaco, sent a personal note.

> Last week your new film *In the Heat of the Night* was shown here in Monte-Carlo. It was a tremendous success and I want you to know how much the Prince and I enjoyed this exciting picture. It was beautifully done from every point of view! Congratulations on this fine work.
>
> We both send our best wishes to you and your wife, and hope to see you in Monte-Carlo soon again.
>
> Grace de Monaco[68]

Industry colleagues were similarly impressed: in early August, "Superagent" Sue Mengers reached out with a sarcastic offer.

Darling,

I saw *In the Heat of the Night* and I don't care what the critics say—
I liked it!

After all, we know reviews aren't everything and how can you
trust a group of men who didn't like *40 Pounds of Trouble*?

I am willing to represent you now when your career is
floundering because it is much more satisfying to help someone
on the way up. I'll even sign Dixie—everyone knows what a great
job I've done for Marty Ritt's wife . . .

Yours,
Sue[69]

Jewison did not fail to notice that one of the sole dissenting voices came
from Toronto's *Globe and Mail*. In a review headlined "Heat of the Night:
A Pretentious Story," Urjo Kareda derided the "plodding, pretentious
and luridly melodramatic" approach of a director "obsessed with
significance." Kareda devoted several paragraphs to mocking Sidney
Poitier for being well-dressed and speaking in grammatically correct
English, and dismissed Rod Steiger as a performer who "has made a
career out of being obnoxious." Jewison probably took Kareda's review
as the byproduct of a vindictive provincialism endemic to the Toronto
arts scene, although the rough treatment by his hometown press would
continue to rankle in the years ahead.

* * *

One of the most famous scenes in what was still "The Crown Caper"
unspooled from three words in the script: "Chess with sex."

Approaching the end of filming in September 1967, the production moved to the plush interior of Thomas Crown's residence. Dunaway was seated at a chess table, wearing a backless chiffon dress, one of twenty-nine costumes designed by Theadora Van Runkle. Dunaway wore two rows of false eyelashes on top, with another row on the bottom that had to be glued one lash at a time.[70] McQueen, in a three-piece suit, sat opposite, avoiding her gaze. Jewison, bounding around as usual in his sneakers, white slacks, and striped polo shirt, came in to huddle with the actors.

After the scrutiny of the poker game in *The Cincinnati Kid,* Jewison knew that chess experts would howl if the game didn't track. He patterned the moves after an 1898 match between Gustav Zeissl and Walter von Walthoffen in Vienna. But the real game wasn't confined to the board. "Faye, you are playing chess," Jewison said in a hushed tone, "but there is another game going on. Without thinking, your right hand goes up your left arm, lightly caressing, to your throat . . . Steve, let's see your eyes follow her hand . . . She looks up and catches you watching." Jewison cackled. "Good. You're embarrassed. You smile and look down. Great!" Jewison got closer to the stars, whispering direction, mouthing their dialogue. He shut his eyes as McQueen and Dunaway locked lips, silently counting down with his fist, three, two, one, "Cut!" He leapt into the scene and embraced the actors.[71]

Jewison intended "the kiss" to be the longest in the history of mainstream motion pictures, and perhaps it was. Behind the scenes, Haskell Wexler was skateboarding around the lovers in multiple 365-degree turns. In the edited scene, the kiss continues for over a full minute of screen time, gradually dissolving into shimmering fractals of light. Years later, Dunaway would admit, "Every man I've ever met since, if we talk long enough, has mentioned the chess scene to me. And every man I've known since then who has been in love with me has loved that movie."[72]

Dunaway loved working with Jewison. "He's the only man I've ever known who has no hostility in him. He's all love," she said at the time.[73] In *Looking for Gatsby*, her memoir, Dunaway describes herself as being frankly awed by McQueen, who she describes as "such an icon," and a "big old movie star." She recalls a casual dinner with McQueen and their respective spouses, during which her mind wandered from the small talk to the "sexually saturated embrace" they would film the following day. Dunaway allows that McQueen was a "chauvinist" with "very specific ideas about a woman's place." Ultimately, though, she frames even their differences as productive, a source of "chemistry," which she and Steve "had in spades."[74]

Dunaway paints a rosy picture of her experience on the film. She described the role as "groundbreaking" and "the first in what would become something of an archetypal character for me—a woman pushing the envelope. These women who found out who they were, and who were able to function as complete human beings, the way men do in the world."

Perhaps the twenty-six year old was unaware of the slander and gossip that targeted her throughout the shoot. Much of the misogynistic attitude toward the film's glamorous star made its way into a piece of doggerel passed around the set:

Runaway Dunaway
Thick in the belly
Bonnie's Happened, it's Sundown
So back to the telly
Runaway Dunaway
Fat in the assy
You ain't continental
You're sassy not classy.[75]

On-screen, Vicki Anderson proved to be Thomas Crown's stylish, intellectually dextrous equal. Off-screen, Dunaway was ridiculed as coarse and overweight, just one victim of the casual sexism that permeated the entire industry. McQueen was far from alone in having "very specific ideas about a woman's place."

* * *

"What are we going to do about a cast party?" Hal Ashby asked. It was mid-September 1967, and *Crown* was in its final days of shooting.

Jewison was in no mood to celebrate. He had dragged the production across the finish line, but "The Crown Caper" had been frustrating in almost every way. He'd grown to hate the title of the film, although the marketing department loved it. "We get ruined by the advertising and publicity people," Jewison said at the time. "I didn't want to name it *In the Heat of the Night.* Cheap. They talk all the time about 'commercial' words. Good words are commercial. I wanted to call it *Give Me till Morning,* but they said that was too lyrical. Now critics say it is a good picture but a lousy title. I wish I hadn't given in."

As for the cast party, Jewison wanted something low key, heavy on the hors d'oeuvres, light on booze. The trouble with cast parties, he said, was that "people either get very maudlin or they decide to take out all their petty grievances."[76] As an end-of-picture gift, Jewison opened a ten-dollar account (with passbooks and signature cards) at the Shawmut National Bank, the scene of the crime, for the cast, crew, and staff.[77]

Looking back, Jewison would characterize *Crown* as his most cynical work. A new note of frustration creeps into his voice in interviews in the period, as though his second outing with McQueen had sapped some of his own innocence. At a moment when *In the Heat of the Night* was reaping vast profits and critical praise, Jewison sometimes sounded downright jaundiced, both professionally and personally.

"You have to fight. You shouldn't compromise," he said at the time. "There are times when you're tired and you compromise to get on with it. I guess I have. But you shouldn't." Here, a witness describes Jewison pounding the steering wheel of his car, exasperated. He fantasized about doing a couple of pictures in Europe. He was also sick of leaving his family behind for extended periods. "First thing you know," he said, slamming the car door shut, "you'll be messing around with another woman."[78]

CHAPTER 9

The Ambassador at Midnight

ROBERT F. KENNEDY WAS A MAN OF MANY GIFTS. If his performance at New York's Sardi's restaurant on January 28, 1968 was any indication, comedy was not among them.

It was the 33rd annual New York Film Critic Circle Awards, and the toothy kid brother of JFK was on hand to present some of the top honours and crack a few topical jokes, including one about Lyndon B. Johnson saying to Lady Bird, "Guess Who's Coming to Dinner—Eartha Kitt!" (This ten days after a White House luncheon where the singer of "Santa Baby" had excoriated Lady Bird Johnson: "You send the best of this country off to be shot and maimed . . . No wonder the kids rebel and take pot!")[1]

"They're also showing *The Good, the Bad and the Ugly*," Kennedy continued. "President Johnson, Gene McCarthy, and myself—the casting isn't set yet."[2]

Kennedy's jokes left something to be desired, but, for Jewison, the forty-two-year-old senator from New York represented a beacon of hope in a darkening political landscape. It was a special thrill to receive the

Best Picture award for *In the Heat of the Night* from Kennedy. As Jewison would frequently recount in later years, the senator had immediately picked up the thread from their conversation at Sun Valley: "See, I told you, Norman," Kennedy whispered. "Timing is everything. I told you the timing was right."[3]

Jewison understood that timing was everything. But the times were pulling him in two opposing directions at once.

The first was political. Jewison felt that his next film needed to respond to the social unravelling he was witnessing in the United States. Over the previous "long, hot summer of 1967," race riots had exploded across cities including Boston (where Jewison was shooting *Thomas Crown*), Newark (twenty-six killed), Detroit (forty-three killed, hundreds injured) and dozens of others. The Vietnam War was approaching its nadir: that February, 543 American soldiers were killed in a single week. Anti-war protests rocked Washington, D.C., New York, and San Francisco. Jewison's own politics in this period were partially influenced by I. F. Stone's left-wing *Weekly* newsletter, although he was equally influenced by what he'd seen on the ground. Jewison recalls that he, Haskell Wexler and Hal Ashby "just had our heads beat in" by mounted policemen during an antiwar protest at Century City.[4]

Jewison was ready for another socially engaged film, not only because of the scale of the unrest, but also because he worried that *Crown* had been a cop out. He basically admitted as much in an awkward interview:

REPORTER: So what's the point of *Thomas Crown and Company*?

JEWISON: I don't want to waste my time on something that is just a good story.

REPORTER: So what's the point of *Thomas Crown*?

JEWISON: (belligerently, after a pause) Be careful you don't hit below the belt . . . We're all worried about that. Even if it isn't the attack on the establishment that I say it is . . . (Dropping the subject, he flips through theatre-attendance reports on his desk)[5]

Following his brief dalliance with "style over substance" in *Crown*, Jewison was itching to get back into the political fray. But he also felt the allure of the "youth" film, a desire that could only have been sharpened as Mike Nichols was called up to receive the "Best Director" award that evening at Sardi's. Critics would continue to laud *In the Heat of the Night* as the best film of the year, but everyone, including executives at the Mirisch Company and Jewison himself, recognized that *The Graduate* represented something new and invigorating, a generational shift in cinematic sensibility.

And it wasn't just *The Graduate*. The "Summer of Love" had erupted just a few months before.

The new-age musical *Hair* proclaimed "the dawning of the Age of Aquarius." Antonioni's *Blowup* had been an unexpected box office smash, raking in $6 million in 1966. *Bonnie and Clyde* was on its way to becoming a phenomenon. While Hollywood had long targeted the youth demographic, the first forays of the "New Hollywood" represented a tectonic shift. Freed from the constraints of a vitiated production code, their treatment of sexuality was frank and open.* Some New Hollywood creators cast aside the timeworn conventions and drew on a range of influences, from Pop Art, avant-garde cinema, and foreign language films. Jewison, with collaborators like Ashby, Wexler, and designer Pablo Ferro, had been part of this shift, although, at forty-one, Jewison's own youth

---

* The Motion Picture Production Code, which stipulated that "correct standards of life shall be presented on the screen," and forbade movies from "lowering the moral standards" of their audience, was eventually scrapped in 1968 in favour of the MPAA ratings system.

was in the rearview mirror. One reporter at the time described him as a "slightly wizened Puck," whose "cheeks are plump and move upward when he smiles, almost closing his eyes."[6] The director may have been middle-aged, but artistically he saw the need to move decisively in the direction of "the youth."

When Ingwald "Ingo" Preminger (brother of director Otto Preminger) approached him with a project called *Running Scared*, Jewison was all ears. *Running Scared* was the story of Tom Betancourt, a university student who watches his roommate commit suicide, seduces the dead roommate's sister, then dies in a spectacular car crash after feeling his first genuine emotion.[7] A literary descendent of Albert Camus's *L'Étranger* (and forbear of Bret Easton Ellis's well-heeled American psychos of the 1980s), Tom's incapacity for empathy or genuine emotion is partly construed as the product of his emotionally distant parents and privileged upbringing, although his psychosis was also meant as an indictment of the anesthetizing culture of conformity that artists of the period were lining up to attack.

Cold, distant, and awash in the existentialist anxieties of the moment, *Running Scared* was unlike anything Jewison had done, which was partly the point. He was interested in experimenting with a "young man's film." Ashby was on board, although he warned Jewison against filming the picture in a flashy "young man's style," like that of "Truffaut or Coppola." Ashby insisted that the film's aesthetic needed to be "austere" in order to convey the protagonist's existential detachment. Ashby also felt strongly that Ellen, Tom's love interest, should be sexually experienced (not a virgin, as she was in the script).

"You are out to make a 'real' film about 'real' young adults. And real young adults screw," Ashby said, bluntly stating a New Hollywood thesis. With the opening of *The Graduate*, the sexual morality of American youth surfaced as a national obsession in all the magazines. As far as

Ashby was concerned, "There have been too many movies in which the heroine 'holds out' . . . young men today are not particularly 'hung-up' on the previous state of their girls' sex life, and young women are rapidly adopting the much healthier philosophy that fornication is simply a part of life."[8]

Jewison's personal style, the way he spoke and dressed, both reflected and clashed with the ascendant west-coast youth consciousness. In 1968, a reporter arrived at Jewison's geranium-lined bungalow office on the Goldwyn lot to find what he described as a "capitalist hippie" and a "symbol of the New Hollywood." To his standard uniform of striped T-shirt, Levi's, tennis shoes, and baseball cap, Jewison had added a pinkie ring and a beaded necklace with an ankh symbol (the Egyptian hieroglyph signifying life). In a certain mood, he wore a denim jacket over a bare chest. "I don't like to think I'm middle-aged yet," he said at forty-two. "I really feel much more in tune with the thirty-five-year-olds and under than the older crowd. And it's more fun to play to a younger audience. They dig."[9] In common with Hollywood moguls of the past, he had a weakness for cigars. "No doubt about it," the reporter concluded, "Norman Jewison is pretty much what's happening these days."[10]

* * *

Jewison's embrace of the youth culture was motivated by the capitalist as well as the hippie strands of his personality: 65 per cent of the total moviegoing audience at the time, as Jewison was fond of noting, was under 35. Industry scuttlebutt held that he would next direct Arthur Miller's *After the Fall* for Paramount, but in truth he didn't know what to do next. "I have too much to say," he said, "too many pictures I want to make."[11] He knew he wanted something sexy, contemporary, and political.

At first blush, *Gaily, Gaily*—a semi-biographical account of the writer Ben Hecht's arrival in Chicago in 1910—may have seemed a counterintuitive way to connect those dots. Jewison knew Hecht as a major screenwriter of Hollywood's Golden Age, with credits for *Scarface*, *It's a Wonderful Life*, and *A Farewell to Arms*, and uncredited contributions to *A Star is Born*, *Gone with the Wind*, and *Roman Holiday*. Abe Ginnes's script for *Gaily, Gaily* took place before Hecht's adventures in the screen trade, recounting Hecht's formative experiences as a knockabout cub reporter on the Chicago crime beat.

Few filmmakers would have seen anything urgent or contemporary in *Gaily, Gaily*. But for Jewison it hit all the right buttons. He was taken with the parallels between boisterous 1910 America as portrayed by Hecht and the fractious society of 1968: Hecht's descriptions of the anarchist street protests outside the Chicago stock exchange felt akin to the anti-war protests playing out around him. Hecht's portraits of the writers and artists he knew made them sound like the flower children of his time, "Hippies, 1910 style."[12] So struck was Jewison by the countercultural energy of Hecht's memoir that he chose a passage for the film's epigraph: "If you did not believe in God, in the importance of marriage, in the United States Government, in the sanity of politicians, in the necessity of education or the wisdom of your elders, you automatically believed in art."

Most important of all, however, what *Gaily, Gaily* provided was sex. Abe Ginnes's screenplay was licentious enough that the MPAA threatened to slap a "for mature audiences" label on the film, which was fine with Jewison. The stratospheric success of *Tom Jones*, Tony Richardson's historical, sex-filled romp which won the Academy Award for Best Picture in 1963, provided a model for the bawdy epic Jewison imagined.

* * *

The extensive location filming and period detail required of *Gaily, Gaily* would make for an expensive film. To determine just how expensive, Jewison hired a young production manager on contract with the Mirisches, Patrick Palmer—"a tough little guy with a crew cut, reddish blond hair, and a bulldog stance," Jewison recalled—to assist with budgeting and location scouting.[13] Palmer later admitted that he wasn't particularly interested in Hecht or *Gaily, Gaily*, but Jewison was something else. "He sucked me in," Palmer recalled, "he really did. He'd be bigger than life, and he was a great storyteller and very passionate." The pair would work closely together on Jewison's next fourteen films.

Where movie stars of the period would gush about Jewison's affability, Palmer was privy to another side of the director. "Norman was this maverick independent, tough, 'don't fuck with me' Canadian, you know, who was really strong. I was very impressed by his tenacity, and his ability to bluff, and his ability to go for the balls. We pulled off a lot of shit together, the two of us. [Norman] was never afraid to walk away. We walked away on [*Jesus Christ*] *Superstar* and they called us back; we walked away on *Rollerball* and they called us back." The affection was mutual. Jewison was used to working with production managers of the "old school," who (according to Palmer) fixated on details like "How many extras do you want? How many of this and how many of that?"[14] Palmer, however, could operate as a more aggressive and versatile field operative, particularly valuable to Jewison in the winter of 1968 with Ashby locked away in one of his marathon cutting sessions on *Crown*.

Palmer soon became a third point in the creative triad, over which Jewison held a kind of paternal sway. Palmer remembers that he and Ashby would "smoke dope, you know we would fuck off together, and we had this whole secondary life together . . . Hal was a real idealist and I guess I really identified with him in many aspects, like a lot of people did, and Hal was sort of the Pied Piper. He had a lot of people following him down the garden path. Norman was more the pragmatist."

Jewison had his ideals, of course, but he understood that, in the film business, financial success was the most powerful lever to further those ideals. "Norman did more about it and less talking about it. Hal talked more about it and did less," Palmer said. "Norman could separate: alright, I'm a whore but I'll raise a quarter of a million dollars for this liberal cause and I'll support [New York Mayor] Lindsay or I'll do this in New York or whatever, and Hal would say, well that's not pure, you know; he'd get into this issue 'what is pure?' Norman would say, 'Well, you can stand around and talk about it forever while I get the $250,000 and feed these kids or get this medical supply.'"[15]

Jewison believed that his positive influence in the world was tied to the success of his motion pictures. On that score, Patrick Palmer had returned from his *Gaily, Gaily* location scout with dire news. Between locations in Chicago, Milwaukee, and Galena, *Gaily, Gaily* would be staggeringly expensive to produce—as much as *Russians*, *Heat*, and *Crown* combined.

Jewison was fairly confident that 1968 audiences would fall in love with his lascivious reimagining of Ben Hecht's youth. But if he decided to commit, *Gaily, Gaily* would have to be the biggest moneymaker of his career.

* * *

McQueen had continued to bedevil Jewison even after *Crown* had wrapped. They were minor matters, mostly, haggling over the prices of various items used in the film, including the custom-made dune buggy. But McQueen's latest fixation was something bigger: the film's title. After Jewison finally convinced the United Artists advertising department to nix "Caper," the film had been retitled *Thomas Crown and Company*, hardly an improvement. After endless deliberation, they landed on *The Thomas Crown Affair*. Everyone liked it, except the actor behind Thomas Crown.

"I have given great thought to the title of the project," McQueen wrote, portentously, "and really feel that considering the efforts and contributions I have attempted to make, that I must express my feelings to you. I strongly feel that the picture should be called 'Thomas Crown,' and that all of the other proposed titles including 'The Thomas Crown Affair' are not right."[16]

Even at this late stage, Jewison approached McQueen gingerly, fearful of rousing the demon. "I tried to get thru to you on the phone last night, but there were all kinds of disconnections," Jewison wrote, probably fibbing. "UA has really taken the adamant position that since it's been changed for the fourth time, they want to leave it. The only heartening thing in the whole matter, is the title is as good as the picture. I think we've got a fine picture."[17]

For now, *Crown*'s fate was literally in the hands of Hal Ashby, who had sequestered himself in the editing room for another four-month stretch. This time out he would have a collaborator in Ferro, who took the lead on scenes involving the multiple-image technique. Creatively, however, Ashby was not entirely satisfied.

Ashby had taken major creative strides since his days as Bob Swink's assistant cutter, and was ready for another leap. In one letter from "Hal Anxiety" addressed to "Norman Jumpison" (Subject: "Leapin' Lizards"), he opened up about his future aspirations and present discontents. "I should like very much to get myself into finding a property," he wrote, "then having time to develop it into a screenplay." His associate producer duties had provided a real education, but he struggled with the constant interruptions and demands of the business (the "trivia load," he called it), which he was starting to conceive of as a threat to his artistic identity. "I've been pulled out of the creative thing so many times and so often," he confided, "I begin to doubt if there is—or ever was—anything creative or talented inside me to begin with."[18]

Jewison took this to heart. He was passionately invested in Ashby's artistic growth, and shared his creative anxieties. Jewison still yearned for more authentic artistic expression within an industry that seemed bent on euthanizing that desire. Some days, Jewison's "trivia load" was unbearable.

Jewison looked forward to *Gaily, Gaily*, which (he hoped) would provide an outlet for meaningful filmmaking within a commercial package. Over the past few months, however, Jewison had become even more enamored with a project that he believed would follow Ben Hecht's ribald misadventures. At the time, he had no premonition that this project would embroil him in nationwide controversy, bring him death threats, and contribute to his decision to leave Los Angeles and America for the next decade.

For the time being, he felt only that *The Confessions of Nat Turner* would be the most important film of his career.

* * *

Published in September 1967, William Styron's *The Confessions of Nat Turner* was inspired by the bloodiest slave revolt in United States history. On the evening of August 21, 1831, Turner and as many as sixty disciples took up whatever weapons they could find—hatchets, farm tools, then guns belonging to their victims—and slaughtered fifty-seven whites, including children and infants asleep in their cradles, as they rampaged toward the local capital of Jerusalem, Virginia. Turner's insurrection was brutally extinguished by an armed militia who killed perhaps two hundred Black men and women, mutilating and decapitating many.[19] Turner was captured some nine weeks later, tried, and sentenced to death. But before being hung and dismembered, his flesh boiled into grease, leather keepsakes crafted from his skin, Turner relayed the story of the uprising to one Thomas Gray, his court-appointed lawyer. Gray's recording of Turner's "confession" would serve as Styron's source text, although the novelist allowed himself "the utmost freedom of imagination in reconstructing events," as he wrote in an introductory note.[20]

The major critics of the age greeted Styron's novel with rapturous praise. Philip Rahv raved that it was "the best [novel] by an American writer that has appeared in some years."[21] R. W. B. Lewis agreed, calling it the best novel since Ralph Ellison's *Invisible Man*. To poet Robert Lowell, it seemed "an American classic written by a contemporary of Hawthorne and Melville."[22] To these readers, the novel's riskiest aesthetic gambit, Styron's use of the first person to channel (as critic George Steiner put it) "the mentality of an inspired Negro slave who lived briefly and died grimly a hundred and thirty-six years ago," had handsomely paid off.[23]

Readers followed the critics. *Confessions* would spend sixty weeks on the hardcover and paperback bestseller lists, twenty-five at number one. And Hollywood followed the readers. David Wolper, the prolific producer later known for bringing Alex Haley's *Roots* to television, purchased the film rights for *The Confessions of Nat Turner* for $600,000, then an industry record. Jewison was the natural choice to direct: *In the Heat of the Night* had been breaking house records across the nation while Styron's *Confessions* had topped the bestseller lists. Jewison's non-exclusive deal with the Mirisch corporation gave him the right to work with other partners at his discretion; his *Nat Turner* deal, calling for $400,000, was his most lucrative to date.[24]

Jewison, always passionate about his projects, was unusually fervent about *The Confessions of Nat Turner*. He called it "the most important book of the last twenty-five years," and was fascinated by the figure of Turner himself, who he saw as a "heroic, revolutionary figure," a "Black Gideon influenced tremendously by the Old Testament."[25] He felt the film could depict the abomination of antebellum slavery in a way that would resonate with the broader social reckoning over civil rights in 1968.

Jewison felt that *The Confessions of Nat Turner* was at the very centre of a roiling cultural inferno. Martin Luther King Jr.'s ideal of non-violent resistance had curdled into disillusionment and rage. With each race riot, each political roadblock to equality, each swing of a policeman's baton, the archetype of Nat Turner—an exterminating Black angel of divine retribution—felt increasingly prescient. Jewison conceived of *Nat Turner* as akin to *The Russians Are Coming* and *Heat*—socially necessary films that tapped into something deep in the American psyche. He also believed it would be a major box-office success, although he always downplayed his commercial inclination. "I'm more interested in the number of people going to see my film than I am really in the box office. There are easier ways of making money," he remarked at the time.

"You *are* making money though, aren't you?" a reporter pressed.

"Oh, making a great deal of money," Jewison admitted. "It's embarrassing."[26]

* * *

The letter came from an organization Jewison had never heard of: The Association to End the Defamation of Black People. As he would learn later, the group had been formed for the sole purpose of cancelling Jewison's next film. They began:

You are murdering the spirit of Nat Turner, one of the great ethnic heroes of Black Americans. You are distorting and falsifying the history of Black people in this country, and by extension, defaming the entire Black race. You are pandering to white racism and deepening the gulf of alienation between the races.

These are crimes you are committing and will continue to commit if you persist in producing a motion picture based on *The Confessions of Nat Turner* by William Styron.[27]

Jewison was thunderstruck. Did those behind the anti-Turner letter know the director's record on racial issues? Had they seen what he'd accomplished with Harry Belafonte in their 1959 TV special? Had they missed the slap that Sidney Poitier delivered across the flabby cheek of the plantation owner in *Heat*? Did they know about the time and money he'd given to various civil rights initiatives? (The previous month, upon learning from his friend Brock Peters that the Free Southern Theatre was in financial crisis, Jewison had immediately cut a cheque.)[28] Was there a Hollywood filmmaker in 1968 more committed to overcoming the "gulf of alienation between the races"?

Jewison was upset, but assumed he could win the critics over in due course. By March 26, the date of the letter, Jewison was months into preparing the screenplay for *Nat Turner*. After it became clear that James Baldwin (Jewison's first choice for screenwriter) was unavailable, Wolper asked him to consider Arthur Miller and Reginald Rose (*Twelve Angry Men*). But their first serious candidate for screenwriting duties on *Nat Turner* was Dalton Trumbo, the screenwriter of *Exodus*, *Spartacus*, and many others.

Two decades earlier, Trumbo had been summoned before the House Un-American Activities Committee to testify about a suspected communist infiltration of Hollywood. Trumbo, along with the rest of the Hollywood Ten, refused to cooperate, and served eleven months in a federal penitentiary. The MPAA, meanwhile, called for Trumbo to be blacklisted unless he publicly rejected communism under oath. Again, Trumbo refused, and moved his family to Mexico where he wrote screenplays under pseudonyms and front writers, winning two Academy Awards in absentia. For Jewison, the prospect of doing *Turner* with Trumbo was exhilarating.

For Trumbo, Turner was part of a larger story. Influenced by the mid-century existentialism of Jean-Paul Sartre and Frantz Fanon, Trumbo saw Turner as an exhilarating symbol for the anti-colonial struggle playing out in Africa, South East Asia, and Cuba. Still, the writer had reservations, albeit not about the rumoured protests or boycotts by Black performers. What concerned him, he wrote, was the "extreme religiosity" of a character incapable of critical reflection upon how "Christianity not only supported and strengthened the slave system but also weakened the Negro and increased his degradation by persuading him to accept his misery in this world in return for paradise in the next." In the end, Trumbo wrote,

the violence which [Turner] turned against the white man was that same Christian violence by which the white man had made the Negro his slave. Setting the violence of Nat's rebellion in this context, I can't believe that any audience except the lunatic right could fail to understand that Nat's violence was the natural outcome of a situation born in violence, and that to Nat's mind it was completely justified.

Jewison, then working with Michel Legrand on scoring *The Thomas Crown Affair*, was still chewing on Trumbo's first missive when a second one arrived. Further rumination had convinced Trumbo that he couldn't write the screenplay. Any version of Turner that Trumbo could envision would "violate the character Styron has created and which his readers would expect to find in the film." He expressed a desire to work with Jewison and Wolper in the future, and bid them good luck.[29]

Wolper had already begun talking to other writers, including Horton Foote, screenwriter of *To Kill a Mockingbird*, who deemed Styron's novel "a deep and profound work."[30] Jewison, however, had started to think that he could coax a screenplay out of William Styron himself. Who knew what they might be able to accomplish with a few days together in Los Angeles?

"Styron came out to my home in California," Jewison remembered. He "tried to entice" Styron with a sweeping new opening he'd written, beginning with Turner's grandmother in Gambia where she was sold on the slave block, and ending decades later with a young Nat tracing her name on a wooden tombstone. Styron, however, confessed that he was simply "written out on Nat Turner."[31] They spent a profitable few days drafting an outline, and decided that the screenplay itself would be best served by an African American writer. Styron left Jewison feeling invigorated about the project. On March 26, he wrote:

Dear Norman,

Best thanks for the California sunshine and the splendid hospitality. I think I might have added 2½ years to my life expectancy simply by the quarter-gallon of orange juice that they served each morning at the hotel. The outline for the treatment is here . . . I think we've made a splendid start and I hope and trust that we'll keep up the momentum. Fond regards to Dixie and let us talk again soon.

Faithfully,
Bill[32]

By the time Jewison read Styron's encouraging words, *Nat Turner* had gotten a lot more complicated: the letter alleging that he was "murdering the spirit of Nat Turner" was dated the same day. Jewison re-read the accusations. Styron had "distorted and falsified history," they claimed, "to convert Nat Turner from a bloody avenger fighting for freedom to just another Black boy itching to fornicate with white women." Worse, Styron had invented a homosexual encounter between Turner and another slave named Willis, which the letter exaggerated into a "homosexual orgy" that robbed Turner of his "strength, fortitude, and manhood." The signatories, who included Stokely Carmichael, LeRoi Jones (later Amiri Baraka), and H. Rap Brown (later sentenced to life in prison for murdering two sheriff's deputies), ended with a demand that the motion picture stick to historical facts and avoid William Styron's "falsification of history."[33]

Jewison was reflexively opposed to anyone attempting to exert control over his artistic decisions. He was also used to overcoming the resistance of studio executives and others who needed to be convinced of his vision. Those behind this letter might have been especially recalcitrant, but Jewison decided to do what he always did: win them over with his dance. He made arrangements to host a few representatives in his office.

* * *

Over the last few months, Jewison had grown closer with now presidential candidate Bobby Kennedy, and had begun working on his campaign in California and Oregon. Jewison also found that he had ascended another rung on the celebrity ladder. After some reluctance, he accepted an invitation to appear on Johnny Carson in an episode with Bob Hope and Sid Caesar.

With the Oscars approaching and the *Turner* controversy growing more heated by the day, Jewison tried to stay focused on what should have been his top priority: prepping *Gaily, Gaily* for its summer production. The sheer size of the period picture was intimidating. Before committing, Jewison had shared his concerns over the film's "commercial possibilities" with Marvin Mirisch.

"As I see it," Jewison wrote, "the picture would have to gross a minimum of nineteen to twenty million dollars to become a profitable venture. I couldn't even do that with *Russians*." While he had worked to reduce the scope, he still felt the picture needed a major star to work at the box office. After considering Ava Gardner and Lana Turner, Jewison landed on Sophia Loren for the role of Queen Lil, the madam who takes in Ben Harvey (renamed from "Hecht"). When Loren passed, Jewison tried to recruit Anne Bancroft by describing the film as a "lusty, bust, epic, a huge undertaking with, I think, some great significance for the audience of today. It's a song of life."[34]

In the end, the role of Queen Lil went to Melina Mercouri. Best known for her performance in *Never on Sunday*, Mercouri had more recently become heavily involved in campaigning against the Greek military junta, which had revoked her citizenship. Mercouri brought an air of European sophistication, and Jewison was, as ever, drawn to her political commitment; what she did not bring, however, was name recognition or broad box-office appeal to the North American audience.

* * *

If Jewison was anxious about *Gaily*'s box office prospects, there were plenty of distractions to consume his attention. The 40th annual Academy Awards were scheduled for April 8, 1968. The trade papers and entertainment columns were abuzz with speculation about who would win: even at the time, it felt like a remarkable field for Best Picture: *Heat* was up against *Bonnie and Clyde*, *The Graduate*, *Guess Who's Coming to Dinner*, and *Dr. Dolittle*. Only the last picture, the bloated remains from a previous era, had no business being there. As for his own chances for Best Director, Jewison knew that a Mike Nichols win was almost inevitable. Still, some small part of him clung to the hope that April 8 might bring a surprise.

By the morning of April 5, the Oscars, the gossip, the gowns, the pomp and circumstance—all of it felt suddenly trivial. Martin Luther King Jr. was dead. The night before, King, who was in Memphis, Tennessee, to support a striking sanitation workers' union, had stepped out on the balcony of his room at the Lorraine Hotel, where a single shot rang out, piercing his jaw and severing his spinal cord. The knot from King's necktie had been shot clean off. He was thirty-nine years old.

Over the last several years, Jewison had born witness to social disintegration and violence all around him, from the 1965 conflagration in Watts to the anti-war demonstrations to the nation-wide race riots. But the sudden erasure of Martin Luther King Jr., the nation's most visible and eloquent advocate for a peaceful future between Black and white, was hard to fathom. A couple of weeks before, in one of his letters on *Nat Turner*, Dalton Trumbo had ventured that the key to Turner's contemporary appeal was his "doctrine of absolute violence": Turner "is truly a man of the Twentieth Century, which Martin Luther King, unhappily, is not."[35] Now Trumbo's pessimism read like prophecy.

Gregory Peck, the president of the Motion Picture Academy, urged the board of governors to postpone the Awards on the grounds that "it seems somehow the wrong moment for a celebration."[36] Jewison, meanwhile, had dropped everything to attend King's funeral procession in Atlanta. On the morning of April 9, he marched the four miles from Ebenezer

Baptist Church to Morehouse College, King's alma mater, shoulder to shoulder with his friend Bobby Kennedy. He was moved by the simplicity of King's hearse. The next day, chauffeured limousines would convey dozens of movie stars to the red carpet for the industry's annual feast of self-congratulation; today, King was conveyed to his grave on a creaking farm wagon pulled by two prison mules. Jewison saw Vice President Humphrey, who had laughed so riotously at that screening of *Russians* less than two years ago. Trailing them, in the crowd of some 50,000 people, were the Black sanitation workers from Memphis for whom King had died. After the procession reached its destination, mourners joined hands and sang "We Shall Overcome."[37]

The next evening, an emotionally drained Jewison took his seat next to Dixie in the eighteenth row of the Santa Monica Civic Auditorium, listening to Bob Hope explain that "due to the gold drain this year, the Oscars have been made of chopped chicken livers." Gregory Peck attempted to inject the proceedings with some measure of gravitas, affirming that films should "celebrate the dignity of man, regardless of race, creed, or colour."[38] But the show was soon back on familiar rails. If anything, the event (themed "Four Decades of Oscar") offered a particularly lugubrious iteration of the Academy Awards, "twice as turgid and ten times as tasteless," one chronicler wrote at the time, with predictable prattle between the stars and a larger than usual dose of nostalgia.[39] At least the presentation of the Irving G. Thalberg Award felt momentous: the recipient was Alfred Hitchcock, with whom Jewison had taken tea on the Goldwyn lot.

The Best Actor award was presented by a glittering Audrey Hepburn, who introduced, in her crystalline cadences, Warren Beatty, Paul Newman, Spencer Tracy (who died the previous June), Dustin Hoffman, and Rod Steiger. Hepburn bit her lower lip as she slit the envelope, then beamed as she announced Steiger's name. Claire Bloom, stark in black chiffon and white peau de soie, smiled tensely in the audience as her husband took the stage.[40] Steiger cut a formal figure in tails, and addressed the crowd in his baroque manner, rolling his 'r's like English nobility. "I'd like to thank Norman Jewison for his giving an actor freedom to make a mistake," Steiger said. "Most importantly, I'd like to thank Mr. Sidney Poitier for the pleasure of his friendship, which gave me the knowledge and understanding of prejudice in order to enhance my performance. Thank you, and we *shall* overcome."

* * *

It was a good night for *Heat*. Silliphant's adapted screenplay beat out adaptations of *In Cold Blood, Cool Hand Luke*, and Joyce's *Ulysses*. (Best Original Screenplay went to William Rose for *Guess Who's Coming to Dinner*; predictably, Rose didn't show up to accept.) Ashby won for best editing. *Heat* even won for best sound mixing. But Norman Jewison did not appear on stage during the Academy Awards ceremony in which his had been the most recognized film of the year. Mike Nichols took Best Director for *The Graduate*, as expected. And when *Heat* won Best Picture, producer Walter Mirisch accepted the Oscar and addressed the crowd. "Many people have described their emotions at winning an Oscar," Mirisch wrote in his memoir.

> Fewer people have described the emotions of winning the Best Picture Oscar. I stood up, I was somewhat transfixed or enraptured, I don't know how to describe my emotion. I do remember thinking, 'At this very extraordinary moment, all these people, fellow workers, people whom I respect, have selected this piece of work that was my project, and on which I was able to

assemble some remarkable collaborators, have chosen our film as the best piece of work this whole year.'[41]

One of Mirisch's "collaborators," the director, watched the scene play out from his seat. On an evening that supposedly celebrated artistic achievement and imagination (in one cringe-worthy moment, Hope had compared movie pioneers Samuel Goldwyn and Jesse L. Lasky to Martin Luther King Jr., because "they, too, had a dream"), it could not have been more apparent, from Jewison's vantage point, that the Oscars were a celebration of juice.

By the time Jewison was back in his office, the place had been flooded with notes balancing congratulations with condolences. The phone was ringing off the hook. "WE KNOW WHO ALL THOSE AWARDS WERE REALLY MEANT FOR," offered Steve McQueen in a telegram. Lyricists (and now friends) Marilyn and Alan Bergman wrote: "Congratulations on having directed the Best Picture of the Year. Isn't it a shame that the Academy doesn't have such a category?"[42]

An eleven-year-old Oakdale Park Elementary School student wrote to congratulate Jewison, adding, in bubbly blue pen: "I hope some day you will make Dr. Martin Luther King's life story . . . Would you like me to make you some peace and love beads? If you decide to make a movie about children from all over the world I would like a small part in it to show that Americans are not unkind to people who have a different colour of skin."[43]

Jewison was still reflecting on this letter a month later, when he wrote back:

If I ever make a film about children from all over the world, I will make sure that you are a part of it, because it is people like you, Jennifer, who will make this old world a better place to live in.

You did not put an address on your letter, so I am sending this to your school. I hope that you receive it.

Peace and love,

Norman Jewison[44]

* * *

If *Heat*'s Best Picture win further expanded Jewison's industry profile, so too did it intensify the notoriety of *Nat Turner*. Not long after the Oscars, a group now calling itself the Anti-Black Defamation Association took out a full-page ad in the trade papers addressed to "all Black actors and other interested parties." It called Styron's novel a dangerous falsification of history: "Styron's implication . . . is that what agitates the Black man is not a search for freedom but a search for white women. To magnify this inflammatory lie on a mass scale—as only the motion picture can magnify it—is the height of social irresponsibility." Black actors were advised to avoid "such a flagrant libel against one of our greatest heroes." It was signed by Ossie Davis, one of the leading Black actors and civil rights advocates of his age, and thirty-seven groups and individuals, from pastors and professors to representatives from the NAACP and the Black Panthers.

Davis's anti-*Turner* statement became national news: a contemporary report described Jewison and Davis as "being on opposite sides of an issue which may ultimately tear Hollywood—and the racial question—apart."[45] Jewison found himself the public face of a high-profile, pro-civil rights Hollywood film that had been publicly rejected by high-profile African Americans. Yet Jewison had not undertaken the film as a work of public relations. Rather, he believed the film had something important to say to America in 1968, and that belief was only sharpened under the pressure to give up.

Jewison invited three members of the Anti-Black Defamation Association to his Goldwyn office, which was piled high with *Turner*-related materials: months before, he'd written the educational division of Doubleday to request their entire library of books relating to slavery and African American history. Jewison knew that the association's membership overlapped with Black Power militants, but still believed that he could assuage their concerns and turn them into allies.

The meeting did not go as he imagined. "They came in and told me I shouldn't make the film," Jewison remembers, "and if I went ahead and did it, it would be in total opposition to the Black community and I would have a hard time casting and so on. If any film was going to be made on Nat Turner," they said, "it should be made by Black people with a Black director." The tone of the meeting only deteriorated from there.

"They threatened me," Jewison recalls. "I remember this young guy looking at me and saying, 'we're going to blow you away, man, you're going to be blown away, you just don't realize it.' I mean, they . . . there was no doubt that there was tremendous emotional feeling at that time."[46]

The threat of racial violence in 1968 was more than theoretical. The association's belief that Jewison's film would endanger Black lives had given its members extraordinary moral leeway to cancel it.

The director was unswayed. If anything, his public rhetoric was more swaggering than ever. "I'll make the film my way," he said in an *L.A. Times* interview, "and nobody is going to tell me how to do it. I'll listen to all the people involved, but it will be done my way, and my way alone. That goes for the studio as well as protest groups."

"They claim a white man like Styron shouldn't write a novel about a Black slave," he went on. "Well, I am not concerned about the colour of Mr. Styron's skin. I am, however, impressed that he spent six years on his book and that his knowledge of slavery is better than almost anyone." Jewison pointed out that Wilberforce University, the first private all-Black university in America, had recently presented Styron with an honorary degree.[47]

The truth was that Styron had been shaken by the hostile Black reaction to his novel and potential film. In 1963, when Styron had begun writing, "there was still a sense of hope for amicable alliances and white people were still welcome in the struggle," said Alexandra Styron, the writer's daughter. By the time *Turner* arrived in bookstores in 1967, the spirit of non-violence and conciliation had given way to Black Power. "The energy into which the book was arriving was entirely different from what was going on when he started," Alexandra Styron says. "He didn't see it coming," and adds that her father "wore that scar for the rest of his life."[48]

With *Turner* under attack, Styron, never temperamentally inclined to discuss his work in the public arena, decided his novel needed a full-throated defense. He accepted an invitation to debate Ossie Davis, with James Baldwin serving as moderator, in front of nearly 1,000 people. Jewison had cause to believe that his film hung in the balance.

* * *

On May 25, industry players gathered at the annual SHARE Boomtown benefit, a lighthearted charity event featuring comical performances by the stars (including, that year, Gene Kelly, Adam West, Janet Leigh, and others). Dean Martin, attired in full cowboy regalia, served as host. On this particular evening, however, Jewison and Dixie had to leave early. Their houseguest, William Styron, needed a lift to Eugene's, the LA nightclub where he was set to debate Davis.[49] Jewison suspected that Styron could also use some moral support.

Outside the club, a mêlée of protesters chanted and waved signs ("Make Love, Not War!") that seemed strangely unrelated to the debate. The club was packed with industry and intellectual types; the air was thick with cigarette smoke and, Jewison felt, a sense of danger. Styron didn't want to be there. He had stiffened his resolve with drink, although the booze didn't register in his voice. The author took his seat next to Baldwin, who opened the debate by declaring his affinity with both men. Bill—"he's the white cat," Baldwin said with a smile—was right because the province of the writer "is the province of all human life" and "no one can tell a writer what he can and cannot write."[50] But insofar as Davis's complaint was about the film, rather than the book, he was "also right," Baldwin said.

Baldwin turned the floor over to Styron, who confessed a feeling of "extreme embarrassment" to be there at all. He eventually summoned a few stilted words in defense of his "honest" book, and for the historical Turner, "who to me represented what the human spirit could achieve in overcoming the most ruinous and despotic form of human bondage that men have ever imposed on other men."

Ossie Davis, by contrast, blossomed under a spotlight. A "rather majestic man with a sturdy, thoughtful style of delivery," as one reporter described him, Davis addressed the audience in a sonorous voice that sometimes cracked with passion.[51] He, too, paid lip service to Styron's right to "create what he wants to create," and recognized the presumptuousness of speaking out against a film that hadn't even been written. His objection, he said, was not to Styron's art but to its "social consequence," especially regarding Styron's depiction of Nat's lust for a "young white maiden," a form of love toward "which my country can be most immediately psychotic and destructive." These images, "magnified on the screen," Davis argued, could result in renewed anti-Black violence and even lynching.

If the debate turned on a single theme, it was the meaning of Turner's heroism. As Styron insisted in his rebuttal, his intention was to render the character more heroic by granting him an interior life that was not visible in Gray's 1831 *Confessions*. But where Styron had intended to convey moral ambivalence, his critics read the character as a neurasthenic Hamlet in blackface.

"I admired Styron that night. He'd had a few drinks to fortify himself," Jewison recalled with a laugh, "but I admired him because he literally defended his position" in a milieu where "people could say things that they had never said before about race relations." Many in attendance that night were shaken with the force and eloquence of Davis's oration. Jewison understood it on an emotional level, "but I can't understand it artistically. Ossie says that it was Nat Turner's lust for a white woman which motivated him in the book. I didn't get that at all when I read it. If that idea came through in the picture, it would be a disaster."

Jewison's version of Turner would resemble a "Black Che Guevara," he said, rather than "a Black Batman." He came away from the debate convinced that he could make a Nat Turner film that would please everyone.

* * *

On the evening of June 4, Norman and Dixie took Melina Mercouri out for Chinese food in Santa Monica. They planned to drive to the director John Frankenheimer's Malibu home to celebrate what they hoped would be Bobby Kennedy's win over Eugene McCarthy in the California Democratic primary. Bobby and Ethel were to be there by 10:00 p.m.

Over the past few months, Kennedy had become the political vessel for Jewison's irrepressible idealism. Bobby was not only a friend: realistically or not, Jewison had come to think of him as the only presidential candidate capable of pulling the nation back from the brink. For decades, Jewison would keep a framed portrait of Bobby on an easel in his living room.[52]

He couldn't wait to introduce Kennedy to Mercouri, sure they would be fast friends.

Downtown, the noise in the ballroom of the Ambassador Hotel was deafening. It was past midnight, and after winning by a razor-thin margin over McCarthy, Kennedy was prepared to deliver a victory address for his supporters. Now he stood at the podium, trying to get a microphone, any microphone, to work. Finally, a roar from the adoring crowd confirmed that he was live. The loudest applause of the raucous evening came when he talked about ending the war in Vietnam. He concluded with his vision of America as a "great country, an unselfish country, and a compassionate country—and I intend to make that my basis for running over the next few months."

Kennedy would leave the Ambassador via a back exit through the kitchen. Waiting there to greet him were campaign insiders and friends (including the writer George Plimpton), as well as chefs, busboys, and Sirhan Sirhan, a twenty-four-year-old Palestinian with a .22 rolled up in a campaign poster. Timing is everything.

Jewison checked his watch. It was getting late, but he assured Melina Mercouri that Bobby was worth the wait. It wasn't every day, after all, you get to "meet the next president of the United States."[53]

CHAPTER 10

Norman Christianson

THE AIR WAS THICK WITH THE ODOUR OF MANURE. It was late in the summer of 1970, and Norman Jewison was inspecting horses in a musty stable outside Zagreb, Yugoslavia. Jewison was there to choose a horse for Tevye, the Jewish peasant and protagonist of *Fiddler on the Roof*, set to begin filming in Lekenik and Mala Gorica in early August. Jewison had a fondness for animals and had been looking forward to casting his horse. The decision, however, turned out to be a painful one. Jewison was selecting from horses that had been deemed no longer suitable for work: those he didn't choose would be sent to the rendering plant, where their hooves, tendons, and ligaments would be torn from their skeletons and boiled into collagen for glue. He felt responsible, somehow, for sending the horses he didn't choose to their brutal fate.

Sometimes it was hard not to feel a similar sense of responsibility for the actors who wrote to him with such candid, lacerating desperation. "I'm not begging for anything from you," a stranger had written recently, "all I want is a chance to prove myself. A chance to be something. Will you give me that chance? Or will I be tossed away like all your other trash?"[1]

Another wrote, "So my father died an alcoholic and my mother is mentally ill and I'm supporting myself in school and I think I have homosexual tendencies and I happen to be ½ Black and ½ white . . . Oh, how I wish you could talk to me and listen to my plea, my cry for acknowledgment . . . HIT me (at least I know then I exist) but I rather you listen first."[2]

Months later, bemoaning the fact that *Fiddler* had gone slightly over budget, Jewison would admit to sometimes feeling almost overwhelmed with guilt. "I feel responsible for everyone," he said. "It's something I've been trying to get rid of," he went on, speculating that it may be a Canadian trait. "I don't know why we are so full of guilt."[3]

Jewison moved from horse to horse, examining their features, tousling their hair. Eventually, he chose a horse with a "wonderful big nose," because he looked a bit like Chaim Topol, the actor who would portray Tevye. The animal was, if anything, too spry: they would put a pebble in his shoe to give him a limp. "I went back to the hotel and wept," Jewison reflected later, laughing at the absurdity of the situation. "I was so moved by all those poor old horses, that had worked hard all their lives . . . But I chose a horse for Tevye."[4]

* * *

Even by the obscene standards of big-budget Hollywood filmmaking, *The Thomas Crown Affair* enjoyed one of the most extravagant openings in memory, providing (in the words of one Boston daily) "the most glittering show ever staged in the history of show business in the City of Boston."[5]

It was, if nothing else, a masterpiece of what the marketers called "exploitation." Steve McQueen arrived by helicopter before 20,000 horse-racing fans at Suffolk Downs, to present the Thomas Crown purse to the winner of a just-completed race. McQueen (dressed in a seersucker suit, beads around his neck) then joined Boston Mayor Kevin White at City Hall to award the Police Athletic Trophy to fourteen-year-old Richard Mullet, who had rescued another boy from drowning. Meanwhile, a *Thomas Crown*-inspired fashion show took place at Prudential Mall. Then the afternoon yacht cruise, the cocktail reception at the New England Aquarium, the black-tie dinner hosted by the elite ladies' auxiliary of the exclusive Brockwood School. For an "anti-establishment" film, *Thomas Crown* certainly struck a chord with the establishment.

Leading up to the screening, a parade featuring five marching bands, cars from the film (Crown's Rolls Royce and dune buggy), limousines packed with industry executives, bus-loads of dignitaries, and Lord & Taylor models, made its way from the State House to the Music Hall, where a forty-piece pit band entertained the gathering guests. Fireworks lit up the night sky. Boston's Channel 4 devoted ninety minutes of live coverage to the extravaganza. The following morning's *Boston Globe* described "a spontaneous and sometimes frightening scene" of "mass hysteria" as police struggled to keep a single lane of traffic open for the *Thomas Crown* parade: "the crush was so great, ticketholders had to be assisted by police into the theatre." A band of bemused hippies sauntered over from Boston Common to check out the action.[6]

The film itself produced a more muted response. Critics fixated on *Crown*'s style, and noted the lack of political engagement that they had expected from the director. *Crown* "strips away the thin patina of social significance in favour of pure fashion," wrote *The Hollywood Reporter*. "It is a flashy, undemanding technical achievement . . . essentially the story of a director directing."[7]

Crown was "the most stylish American feature in years, perhaps ever, but it is also a depressing reflection of the vapidity of the times," wrote the *Milwaukee Journal*.[8] "Clearly, [Jewison, Ashby, and Wexler] have shed their commercial inhibitions and the result is dazzling."

"I am not so old-fashioned as to demand that every movie explain itself, that every plot mesh like the great grind-wheels of Victorian literature," wrote Roger Ebert, but *Crown* is "possibly the most under-plotted, underwritten, over-photographed film of the year. Which is not to say it isn't great to look at."[9]

European critics, and particularly the French, were far readier to embrace *Crown*'s high style without qualification: "Brilliant direction" (*Paris Match*), "the direction is a marvel of intelligence, of movement, of precision" (*Cinémonde*), "Voila, the true cinema" (*L'Aurore*). *Télérama* declared the chess sequence "a classic masterpiece of style. Hitchcock has not done better." *Parisien Libéré* called the film "sheer perfection," and declared "that from now on each of Norman Jewison's new films will constitute a cinematographic event of importance."[10]

While Jewison's disenchantment with the United States increasingly caused him to look toward Europe as an escape, his cinematic sensibilities remained firmly American, even populist. ("Andy Warhol's films just bore the hell out of me," he said at the time. "There's very little effort made by many of the filmmakers in the underground cinema to reach anybody. That's their problem.")[11] He basked in the French critics' praise but suspected that the American critics were right: *Crown* was bereft of "social significance."

Jewison was determined to re-engage the political world on his next film, as he brought all of his prodigious energies to bear on *Gaily, Gaily*. Observers in this period were amazed by the all-encompassing power of Jewison's emotional ecosystem: the way in which the director's own attitudes were like a second weather. "Jewison's rapport with his professional intimates is profound, almost tribal," remarked the reporter

Arthur Zeldin. He appeared to communicate "his feelings to groups without actually saying any one thing to any one person."

The nineteen-year-old Margot Kidder, making her debut in *Gaily*, had noticed the same thing. "When he's directing, he doesn't really say that much to me aside from, you know, 'keep it 1910 and not 1968.' But somehow he manages to communicate—God, does he communicate."[12]

Roger Ebert, who spent time with Jewison on the Chicago location, noted that he "seems to have more fun than most directors. He wears sneakers, moves around rapidly, joins in exchanges of one-upmanship."[13]

That was the director's popular image, but Zeldin noticed something else behind the "laugh-a-minute geewhiz bundle of amiability and jes' plain folks." He believed Jewison's famous energy had acquired a serrated edge. "If he is displeased by a question, say, about money, the extent of his ownership of some of his films, he can freeze you with thirty seconds of breathtaking silence before he coolly resumes the conversation with an absolutely unrelated topic." Riding between locations with Jewison "in his chauffeured station wagon as he receives memos from his secretary, signs cheques, scans reviews, tabulates grosses, issues instructions, you are in the presence of a big-time Hollywood producer," a businessman who could "be quietly, imperiously aloof, not to say rude, when he chooses."

"In good moments or bad," Zeldin said, "for those within ten yards of him, Jewison is the source of energy by which you define where you are and what is happening, and you can't help admiring a man who possesses that kind of vitality."[14]

* * *

Jewison's decision to direct *Fiddler on the Roof* officially ended his association with *Nat Turner*. David L. Wolper lumbered on with Sidney Lumet as director for another year or so, before *Turner* was finally cancelled. According to James Earl Jones, who was set to play the title role, the protest groups "supplied just the excuse the power structure needs not to do these kinds of projects." Jones believed that stories like *Nat Turner* offered "an alternative to racism and the order of the day. If these things don't get made, it doesn't matter who's right and wrong. If they're killed, everyone's wrong."[15]

Fiddler on the Roof came with a different kind of pressure. By the time Jewison signed on, *Fiddler* was on its way to becoming the longest running musical in Broadway history. The first run collected ten Tony Awards and ran for more than 3,000 performances. Songs from *Fiddler* penetrated broader American culture in ways that even the savviest of PR professionals could never have predicted, and subsequent productions had been mounted all over the world.[16] Just what did Jewison think he could add to *Fiddler on the Roof?*

There were two answers to that question: magnitude and authenticity. Audiences for theatrical performances were, by film's standards, miniscule. Jewison, ever the universalist, was interested in bringing Sholem Aleichem's stories to large audiences the world over. But he also felt that this material could achieve greater emotional heft through a more naturalistic approach. A *Fiddler* rooted in the specific textures of place and ritual could be even more powerful than the Broadway version.

Jewison had not been a religious person in any conventional sense. If he'd had a personal credo until this period, it may have been the epigraph that appears over the first, pastoral shots of *Gaily, Gaily*: "If you did not believe in God, in the importance of marriage, in the United States Government, in the sanity of politicians, in the wisdom of your elders, then you had to believe in art." Jewison's own belief in art could seem jarringly out of place, if not downright quixotic, in the film business.

Listen to him wax poetic about the power of the cinematic medium, or about film's *raison d'être*, to politely baffled reporters in the Midwestern backwaters where he shot on location, and Jewison sometimes sounds like a religious proselytizer for cinema itself. Yet as he approached his mid-forties, Jewison felt the pull of religious tradition and consolation. And he felt the particular pull of Judaism. It began under the relatively routine auspices of research he was undertaking for his next film, *Fiddler on the Roof.*

In late September 1969, with *Gaily* wrapped, Jewison and Pat Palmer flew to Jerusalem and spent a few days immersing themselves in Jewish culture. Their visit was coordinated by Moshe Davis, a rabbi and professor of Jewish history at Hebrew University. Jewison wanted to spend time embedded with descendants of the Eastern European Jews depicted in the Sholem Aleichem stories that were the basis of *Fiddler on the Roof.* He greeted the Sabbath with residents of Shaare Hesed and visited a synagogue for Simchat Torah. He shared the Sabbath meal with an Orthodox Jewish family, following the customs and traditions as they had been observed in the shtetl. He sang the Smiroth, the family songs of Sabbath. Saturday morning, he took a guided tour of the Meah Shearim, the Hassidic Quarter, and attended prayer at the Western Wall with Professor Davis. He wanted to spend a day riding along with an Orthodox milkman, a modern Tevye, but time was short.[17]

The experience had been unexpectedly moving. Jewison was touched by the strength of the familial bonds of the Orthodox Jews, their reverence for tradition, and what struck him as the clarity of their lives. He loved the theatricality of their traditions, their devotion to the details of its performance. Mistaken for a Jew his entire life, Jewison discovered a deeply felt connection with his Jewish hosts and their historical burden.

"I spent quite a bit of time in Jerusalem," Jewison said later. "It was quite possible for me to identify with Tevye, and with the Jewish religion.

The more I studied it and the more I exposed myself to Jewish homes, more Orthodox homes . . . I identify with certain aspects of the Jewish religion. I find it a very personal religion. Any deep feelings I have at all about God, and about my own religion, are very personal."

Rumours later circulated around the production that Jewison was thinking about converting, but he shrugged it off as a joke: sure, he'd convert to Judaism and change his name to Norman Christianson.[18]

From Israel, the team moved on to scout *Fiddler*'s locations throughout Eastern Europe, including Romania, Austria, Hungary, and Yugoslavia. (Jewison considered filming in Russia, but Soviet authorities deemed the play anti-Russian because of its sympathetic portrayal of Jews suffering under the Tsar's pogroms.) Filming in Eastern Europe, while rare, was nonetheless "technically feasible and economically advantageous," according to a 1967 internal report for United Artists. Arrangements were straightforward, given that such countries had a single, state-owned company to facilitate foreign film production. State control manifests in "a visible tendency to overstaff and in a vitiation of enterprise on the part of the workers, technicians, and non-creative participants in general. Since these latter are salaried annually on a low-level, no incentive exists for work to be accomplished at more than a minimal rate of speed," the report went on. Requests for overtime went to a workers' committee and were often denied. The report added that dressing rooms ranged from "barely passable to fair," that "bringing wives and family should be discouraged," and that "life is generally drab."[19]

Jewison loved what he saw. To his eye, Yugoslavia in 1969 still looked much as it would have at the turn of the century. Agriculture was accomplished with horse-drawn ploughs; the countryside offered "the last vestiges of old wooden villages and Eastern European architecture." He was also glad to see that the landscape was blanketed with snow. Jewison planned the structure of the film to revolve around four seasons, and an abundance of snow was crucial for how he envisioned the film's winter movement.[20]

Jewison took an immediate liking to Yugoslavia and its people. "There's something about it," he said at the time. "Maybe it's because it reminds me of Canada a little bit. Maybe it's the people, the simplicity. I like their form of Communism, even if the individual isn't as important as I think it should be . . . Life is very simple here. It's so refreshing."[21]

* * *

Jewison sought a similar authenticity in the actor who would portray Tevye. Conventional wisdom around United Artists held that the part was indelibly linked to Zero Mostel, who created the role on Broadway. But Jewison, whose first concern was believability, worried that Mostel's broad, comic approach would be too "big" for film. He imagined a soulful, authentic *Fiddler*, not a comic "7th Avenue entertainment." The dance numbers were to convey the intensified emotional reality of the characters, and not appear overly rehearsed or professional. Earlier that year, Jewison had been moved by Chaim Topol's forceful portrayal of Tevye in the London production. "I felt that Topol brought to the role a strength, a reality. And being Israeli, he also brought to it a kind of toughness, a dignity." Topol was also "kind of sexy," Jewison thought.[22]

Topol proved to be a hard sell to executives. United Artists had a lot riding on *Fiddler*: the struggling studio had paid over $2 million for the rights, and Topol added nothing to the box office draw. Executives, producers, agents—everyone was pressuring Jewison to go with a recognizable star. "Luckily for me he was stubborn, as he usually is," Topol said, "and he won the battle for me."[23]

Jewison's first choice for Golde, Tevye's wife, was Anne Bancroft. "My impulse is to cast Golde with a genuinely warm sensitive personality to prevent the character from becoming too hard," Jewison wrote Bancroft.[24] She turned him down for the second time in a row. Jewison then invited the Israeli actress Hanna Maron to sing for him in London. She would never arrive.

Jewison would recall the anguish in Topol's voice when he phoned with news of the terrorist attack on El Al passengers at the Munich airport. "An act of cowardice perpetrated by people who are incapable of fighting on or within the frontiers of Israel," was how the Israeli Minister of Transport described the attack. Terrorists fired submachine guns and threw grenades at a bus conveying passengers to a London-bound Boeing 707. Rival Palestinian guerilla groups took credit for the attack, which killed one passenger and injured twenty-three.[25] Hanna Maron lost a leg and would be convalescing for months. The American actress Norma Crane would eventually take the part.

Anti-Semitic violence was a fact of life for the creators of *Fiddler*, as it had been for the Old World Jews depicted in the musical.

* * *

One of those Jewison passed over for the role of Tevye was Theodore Bikel, the Russian submarine commander in *The Russians Are Coming*. Given their friendship, Bikel, who played Tevye in the Las Vegas production of *Fiddler*, was stung by the decision. "I gave the fullest and most deeply felt performance of my life those 350 times (370 by now) that I played Tevye," Bikel wrote Jewison. "According to people like [UA president] Dave Picker and [composer] Saul Chaplin who had seen most or all Tevyes I seem to have brought things to the part—not just musically but emotionally and artistically—which they had never seen before . . . I am certain these and similar opinions somehow reached your ears. That might have been enough, one could have hoped, to make you curious. Apparently not." Bikel concluded:

> One might have assumed that our friendship alone would have been inducement enough for you to take the forty-five-minute trip to Las Vegas to see my Tevye. Perhaps not. Friendship or no, you certainly didn't owe me anything. But as director and producer, you did owe yourself a look.[26]

Jewison probably should have ignored Bikel's letter. He had done what was best for the film, his first responsibility. Yet Jewison could not suppress his gnawing sense of guilt. He was not the sort of director, or person, who tossed people aside. He tried to explain himself.

Dear Theodore,

This letter is one I should have written long before receiving yours. Although I do not feel I have to justify my position, I will attempt to explain it.

As you know, casting is probably the most traumatic and soul-searching task for a director. The choosing of every part affects the total film. Yet, at some point, he must be arbitrary. That is usually the time when he makes a very personal and sometimes instinctive decision. Not always right. Many times, unpopular, and sometimes . . . not even understandable.

In casting important roles, many actors who are more than capable are often passed by. There is no scarcity of talent in this world. There are probably many unique and undiscovered talents that could be exposed, if one were only to look about and take the time.

I searched my heart and mind for many months before casting this role. Maybe it took so long because there have been so many effective "Tevyes" . . . But since I feel there is little relationship between the stage and film, I did not want a theatrical performance to affect my cinematic image of "the man . . ."

Our personal friendship means a great deal to me, and I can only hope your present feelings and personal disappointment in my actions will not totally destroy our friendship.

There are many directors who are capable of directing *Fiddler on the Roof*—that is a fact. There are a few actors, other than Topol, who could play Tevye—that is also a fact.

What more can I say. The only other excuse I have for not flying to Las Vegas was that I was totally involved with the Ben Hecht film, from May through September.

Much love and peace attend you,

Norman[27]

* * *

Jewison spent more than two months travelling and researching in Israel and Europe in the fall of 1969. He returned to an America from which he was eager to escape. Always restless, he had fantasized about leaving Los Angeles almost from the day he arrived. By the time Dixie visited him on the *Gaily* location in the summer of 1968 (it was their fifteenth wedding anniversary), they may have already been planning to decamp to the UK, as Stanley Kubrick had done a few years prior. Feeling professionally thwarted after his *Nat Turner* experience, Jewison had also earned something of a reputation among industry colleagues for his brash (some said obnoxious) public criticism of American politics. If his mind had not already been made up to permanently leave Los Angeles, the reception of *Gaily, Gaily* might have clinched it.

Jewison knew going in that *Gaily, Gaily* would have to be his most commercially successful film to earn back its budget (which exceeded the operating budget of the National Film Board of Canada).[28] Critics mostly liked what they saw. Rex Reed called the film a "triumph," shot through "with so much opulent dash and style that I can't think of anything in recent memory that has given me more pleasure."[29] Vincent Canby praised the seemingly old-fashioned film in postmodern terms, arguing that *Gaily, Gaily* "pays homage to the classic conventions of American farce" while signaling an "awareness of its existence as a movie." Canby pointed to the "last, lovely moment," a banquet scene in the bordello, where "the camera slowly withdraws to reveal the movie set, the lights hanging overhead, the power cables, the camp chairs, all isolated in a huge, dark soundstage." If nothing else, the film believed in its own art.[30]

While a handful of critics picked up on the contemporary relevance of *Gaily, Gaily*, audiences failed to make the connection. Far from the "youth film" he imagined, the final product (with Chaplinesque chases set to rinky-plinky nickelodeon music, arcane references to the Wobblies and Anarchists and Reformists) struck audiences as nostalgic. In some markets, *Gaily, Gaily* played concurrently with *Easy Rider*; viewers were not confused about which of these was the genuine "youth picture." The film soon vanished from theatres and from public awareness.

There was always a temptation to blame the marketing. Jewison often bridled at the crass ways in which his movies were sold. As David Picker remembers, however, Jewison had become smitten with Konheim, Gould & Ackerman, *Gaily, Gaily*'s advertising firm. "I nearly went crazy because he wanted to use this Madison Avenue advertising firm to do the campaign," Picker recalled, "which we felt was dead wrong but we gave into Norman. He had enormous muscle with us because he had very, very successful movies, despite our better judgment. I was very upset with [the campaign] because I felt it was bullshit—just very specialized, very expensive, and pretentious, and we knew it."[31]

Gaily, Gaily's box-office performance was not enhanced by its title, which came via Hecht from the poet Bliss Carman ("but life went gaily, gaily, / In the house of Idiedaily!"). "At that time, the word 'gay' was just starting to be used to designate a homosexual," said Marvin Mirisch. "I remember our discussing . . . Are we telling people that this is about gays?" They stuck with *Gaily, Gaily*, remembers Mirisch, because "nobody came up with a much better title," and because of a prevailing attitude that film titles didn't matter.[32] The film did better business in Europe, where it was called *Chicago, Chicago*.

Jewison had estimated that the film would need to do $20 million to break even. All told, it would struggle to make $1 million. In some ways, *Gaily* had been his most accomplished (and certainly the most technically ambitious) production. But the audience, for whatever combination of reasons, did not come. He'd tasted commercial failure before with *The Art of Love*, but that was a studio picture, with the studio to blame. *Gaily, Gaily* was a Norman Jewison Production, and Norman Jewison would take the blame. Commercially, it was a catastrophe.

* * *

"Hit the fans! Cue! *Aaaaaction!*"

Jewison, dressed in a grey trench coat and white pants tucked into mid-calf length leather boots, was attempting to direct an outdoor scene involving a flock of geese in the village of Lekenik, Yugoslavia, which would pass for Anatevka in *Fiddler on the Roof*. But the shot was spoiled almost before it began.

"Son of a BITCH!" Jewison bellowed. "Cut Cut Cut Cut! What the hell's the matter with those people! What the hell is the matter with them! We had a beautiful shot of the geese going and anything else . . . shit!"[33]

Jewison was now heavily bearded, long grey hair cascading out from beneath a well-worn baseball cap. It had been a long shoot, the longest of his career, and the weather was not cooperating. He'd chosen the Yugoslavian location because he needed snow; a year ago, when he'd scouted the location, "I'd been standing in snow up to my waist." Today, he said, "the bloody crocuses are coming up."[34]

A clear note of frustration had entered his voice: at one point, in *Norman Jewison, Filmmaker*, a Canadian National Film Board documentary on Jewison and the making of *Fiddler*, he can be heard yelling at a chicken for making noise on set.

Norman Jewison, Filmmaker captures what reporters had described for years as Jewison's "energy." He seems intimately, almost physically connected with the actors, like an orchestra conductor crossed with a ventriloquist. He mouths the dialogue along with the actors, occasionally breaking in with a direction. At any given moment he's pumping his fist, yelling, snorting with laughter, roaring curses at something that's not working. In emotional scenes, his eyelids are rimmed with tears. Film sets, as the director Bruce McDonald observed years later, can be hectic, crazy places. Directors "have a million things going on, and everybody's like 'when's lunch?' or 'I'm on overtime.' Somebody is always pissed off.

And to have [Jewison's] level of focus, that level of empathy—to lock into that twenty-five times a day—wow, that's kind of amazing."[35]

* * *

After the *Thomas Crown Affair*, some critics accused Jewison of being a soulless technician, a virtuoso craftsman whose films were emotionally distant. *Fiddler on the Roof* was in some ways a direct rebuttal of that criticism. "I'm not interested technically in the making of films," Jewison claimed at the time. "I'm not an intellectual filmmaker. I'm not a cerebral filmmaker. I make emotional films. And I want my audience to become emotionally involved in what I do."[36]

The pressure was mounting on Jewison to deliver a commercial success after the failure of *Gaily, Gaily*. "If *Fiddler* doesn't make it, well . . . maybe there's still that television spot back in Toronto," he said at the time. But he also felt a deep affinity with Tevye and his people. Indeed, Jewison became a physical part of Topol's performance: make-up artists plucked precisely fifteen grey hairs from Jewison's beard, gluing seven on the left brow and eight on the right brow of the thirty-five-year-old actor. Jewison had earned Tevye's grey hairs.[37]

Jewison was conscious of the fact that many of the characters portrayed in the film were future Holocaust victims. "Not all of them go to America or Canada or Israel," Jewison said of the residents of Anatevka. "Many of them ended up in the ovens at Buchenwald and Dachau and Auschwitz."[38] The pathos *Fiddler* evokes in the village's Sabbath prayer—"May the Lord protect and defend you / May the lord preserve you from pain"—is deepened by our knowledge of what history has in store.

Fiddler's enormous success on the stage was partly attributable to its universal story about the conflicts between parents and children: Tevye, the quintessential Old World father, is torn between the tradition of arranged marriage and his three strong-willed daughters, who want to marry for love. It was "about the breaking down of traditions, which applies to all cultures, in every country," Jewison said. While *Fiddler*'s music was distinctively Jewish—composer Jerry Bock conceived the score as an affectionate amalgam of Russian and Hungarian composers who preferred the minor to the major key—John Williams, tasked with adapting Bock's score for film, believed the play's worldwide success resided in universal musical principles that bridge cultures. Williams wrote a new cadenza for Isaac Stern, the world's most accomplished violinist, who would bring the sounds of the fiddler to life.

Williams was amazed to find that Jewison could "actually perform the numbers himself. He would go through the song and perform it himself with this little twinkle in his eye, and a sense of fun, or drama, or whatever it happened to be, that people ended up imitating."[39] Williams would win his first Academy Award for his work on the film.

***

Fiddler told a universal story, but one aspect felt especially personal to Jewison. In the film's final scene, Tevye packs all his family's belongings onto an old cart and bids farewell to Anatevka. A version of that scene had recently played out in the director's own life. Jewison would never have compared his personal circumstances to the pogroms and anti-Semitic violence that forced Tevye to flee to America. Still, he understood what it meant to uproot his children from their home. Kevin, Michael, and Jennifer—now fourteen, twelve, and ten—had been comfortable in Brentwood, and did not understand their father's sudden need to leave that home behind.

Jewison had never felt completely at home in Los Angeles, and his family had lived through a violent period of its history. The Jewisons resided in the city during the Watts riots, the intensifying anti-war protests, and the assassination of Bobby Kennedy. The previous summer, the actress Sharon Tate and five others (along with her unborn baby) had been massacred by the Manson Family at 10050 Cielo Drive, a fifteen-minute drive from the Jewison home.

Norman later described the decision to move as "a terrible, wrenching moment."

"I had to make certain choices," he reflected, "and it got to the point where the choice was to change my life, change my home, change where my children grew up and went to school, change my friends, sell my house, give up membership in every group, every party."[40]

Those who knew him were not shocked by the move. Friend and songwriter Marilyn Bergman remembers walking out of the dining room on the Goldwyn lot when he broke the news. "It was at the height of the Vietnam War, and I think they wanted their kids to have the experience of living in another part of the world and have some perspective," Bergman said.[41]

David Picker, president and COO of United Artists at the time, said that Jewison "is not a Hollywood director," nor was he ever "seduced" by Hollywood. "There are people who fall into that trap, and start to believe all the publicity, the adoration, and all the nonsense that goes on . . . A lot of us fall prey to it, at some time," Picker added. "Norman has never been that way. Norman basically cared about his films. He loves things that grow; he loves animals, his kids, his family. He's been able to keep a perspective that you need and I think it reflects that he never played the game."[42]

Certainly, there were some who believed that, by refusing to play the game, Jewison was throwing his career away. Jewison felt that he was doing what was needed to save it. Los Angeles, he would later say, was sapping his energy, killing his sense of humour.

Hardest to part with was the garden. For years, Jewison had tended to the flowers and vegetables each morning before driving to his Goldwyn office. Now, many of those flowers were uprooted and given to friends. He gave away his Bonsai collection, and offered his orchids to Wayne Varga, a journalist at the *L.A. Times*. Jewison wrote to a friend about the "heart-breaking" feeling of seeing the "bare and lifeless" patch of earth that he had cultivated for years—plants that had grown up along with his children.

"What do we leave? Nothing much," the cast would sing in *Fiddler*, as Tevye piled up the cart. "Only Anatevka."

Now, the Jewisons were trying to establish new roots in London. "We are living in a nutty house in Chelsea," Jewison dashed off to friends. "Red carpets, red sheets, pink bannisters—it's like living in the middle of a boutique."[43] If the quirky English décor would take some getting used to, so would much else. A new chapter of family life had begun.

* * *

"You might say every one of us is a fiddler on the roof, trying to scratch out a pleasant, simple tune without breaking his neck," Tevye says in the opening of *Fiddler*. "It isn't easy." For Jewison, the fiddler represented "the spirit of the Jewish people. Whatever that is, whatever it means. It's magic."

If there was a visual manifestation of that magic, it was in Marc Chagall's paintings of shtetl life, especially *The Fiddler* (1912). By February 1970, Jewison was into negotiations with Chagall to film the artist's paintings for *Fiddler*'s opening credits sequence. The discussion went on for several months; at one point, staff translated an extensive French synopsis of *Fiddler* for Chagall's consideration.

However, as publicist Saul Cooper reported to Jewison, Chagall remained "so annoyed at not being involved in the original stage production and upset by what he considers the plagiarism of the set designs and advertising, that he wants absolutely no part of *Fiddler on the Roof*. In any case, it's a little hard to reason with a very proud eighty-four-year-old multi-millionaire."[44] Cooper suggested that the Mirisch Company purchase the rights to a documentary film that contained images of the paintings, but Jewison was more equanimous.

"I am disappointed to say the least," Jewison wrote to Walter Mirisch, but "like the entire film, the titles perhaps need only the spirit of Chagall, as our script possesses the spirit of Sholem Aleichem."[45]

* * *

Gruelling as *Fiddler*'s production had been for Jewison, it was incomparably worse for Norma Crane, the female lead. On December 12, she had been admitted to London's Royal Marsden Hospital; two days later, her physician confirmed that a malignant growth was carcinoma of the right breast.[46] Physicians recommended radiation and a single mastectomy.

"She was terribly distraught," remembers Walter Mirisch. Crane didn't want to lose her breast, but she also didn't want to lose what she considered the role of her career. "I told her," Mirisch said, "as probably everyone did, that the film was secondary, and that I didn't know what we were going to have to do or how long she was going to be away, but her primary consideration had to be her well-being."[47]

Crane stayed with the picture, working until 3:30 p.m. on days when she had to be at the hospital for radiation treatments by 4:30 p.m. She asked Jewison to keep her condition under wraps. Topol was the only cast member who knew.[48]

Exhaustion was general among the cast and crew. Jewison wanted nothing more than to break for a couple of weeks; the result would have been stronger performances and a better picture. But the financial burden was increasing with each passing hour. As Walter Mirisch euphemistically put it, they were under "considerable pressure to organize the production as cost effectively as possible."[49] The Mirisch Company was coming off a string of painful flops, not least *Gaily, Gaily*. And it wasn't just Mirisch: the entire industry was in freefall. "Columbia and Twentieth Century-Fox had come to the brink of bankruptcy, and United Artists had the worst year in its history in 1969," recalls Walter Mirisch. The industry "simply couldn't connect with its audiences."[50]

David Picker, recently appointed President and COO of United Artists, had a mandate "to really cut costs tremendously," according to Marvin Mirisch. "They came to us and said, we have got to cut down," Marvin remembers. "They used to pay our overhead. We had twenty to twenty-five employees who were making an average of four to five pictures a year. He said we want to cut down on the number of pictures, and let's get rid of a lot of the help."[51] *Fiddler on the Roof* would be the last collaboration between the Mirisch Company and United Artists.

By this point, *Fiddler* was at least two weeks behind and $300,000 over budget, which gave executives leverage. "There's been a certain amount of pressure, but so far it has only developed into one screaming phone call," Jewison said at the time. "They insisted I shoot the Hotel farewell scene"—Hotel was Tevye's second-oldest daughter, who leaves the family to join her revolutionary fiancé in Siberia—"they insisted I shoot that regardless of the weather in Yugoslavia, but I refused and came back to London. So, we still don't have the scene and now we're at an impasse."

In some shots, he'd used limited amounts of marble dust to create the appearance of a light sprinkling of snow; in Jewison's vision, however, the final movement was to play out in the depths of winter. Despite the delays and mounting pressure, Jewison decided to stand pat. "If the film is good and they're in this far . . . I've just got to hang in there, that's all. It's going to be tough, because I've never been this far over budget. It's difficult to talk to people who can look at me and say, 'you're behind.'"[52]

Eventually, Jewison pushed his executives as far as they could be pushed. They ordered him to finish shooting the picture. "I was heartbroken," Jewison admitted, recalling that they'd told him to "Shoot the goddamn scene at night" to hide the snowless landscape. "You can hardly blame them," he went on, "since the industry is flat on its ass . . . they say, what the hell's he *doing* over there? He's over budget, he's waiting for snow! Then the rumours start. They get incensed, they get annoyed. They say, 'Oh, this Jewison's being *cavalier.*' That's the word they use."[53]

David Picker, Jewison remembered, was insulted by the director's candid frustration with executives, which was caught on film and included in the NFB documentary. Who exactly was this "they" that Jewison was ranting about? Picker wanted to know. (Picker later said he couldn't remember the incident.) "I said 'they, David, is everyone but me,'" Jewison recalled. "No matter if you put up all the money for it; it doesn't even matter if you were the person who hired me. *We* created this film, not you."

"He was very offended," Jewison said, looking back. "We are very, very close friends. And we still are today, but I'll never forget how . . . it shows how insensitive we all are. We are very egotistical, very possessive, very single-minded—filmmakers, or directors, or whatever you want to call us. Producers, 'cause some days I feel I'm a producer and some days I feel I'm a director and some days I feel I'm an actor, some days I feel

I'm a writer—but I do know that you are alone. You are alone, no doubt about it."[54]

* * *

Fiddler opened with a blaring ode to "Tradition," overlaid with flashes of the village synagogue that embody the ancient pedigree of those traditions: the aron kodesh ("holy closet," containing the Torah scrolls), the ner tamid (sanctuary lamp), a menorah, mock stone tablets on which are written the Aseres Hadibros ("the ten expressions"), and portions of Psalms from King David written on the walls of the Shul. The song's celebration of traditional values, of the papa's right "to have the final word at home," is gradually softened over the course of the film, as Tevye gradually accommodates his daughters' individual passions. The story mirrored struggles in countless individual households, while also encapsulating, in miniature, the story of the twentieth-century Jewish diaspora's successful adaptation to liberal modernity.

While Tevye's ability to adapt is the essence of his strength, his story also exudes nostalgia for tradition, a nostalgia animated by Jewison's personal desire for a thicker web of connection to history and society. Certainly, the markers of tradition were suddenly more apparent to the director's children. Since moving to Putney Heath in southwest London, Jennifer had enrolled in Miss Lambert's School for Young Ladies; Michael and Kevin attended Herringswell Manor, a boarding school, and "learned to live with shirts and ties."[55] The backyard swimming pool in Brentwood must have felt like something from another life.

Fiddler on the Roof completed principal photography on February 12, 1971, after 130 days of shooting. Relations with the front office may have frayed, but Jewison remained on good terms with the cast. "He's really the

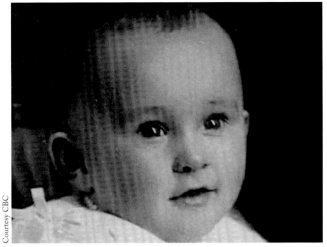

Sidney Poitier recalls Norman's "mischievous" smile: "there's just a little bit more going on underneath than you can read in that smile."

The "Pixie of Jarvis Street," one of CBC-television's pioneers, mid-1950s.

"You had to approach him without fear," Jewison said of Steve McQueen, here with Tuesday Weld on *The Cincinnati Kid*, 1965.

[Left] "Normy" had a way "with the most pampered of prima donnas" while at Universal, said producer Ross Hunter.

[Right] *In the Heat of the Night* was "so fucking revolutionary we don't realize it now," said Sidney Poitier. Haskell Wexler looks on.

[Left] Getting a second opinion on a shot, 1968.

[Right] Some down-time with Faye Dunaway on the set of *The Thomas Crown Affair*, 1967. Dunaway said of Jewison, "He's the only man I've ever known who has no hostility in him. He's all love."

"I don't think I ever loved another man as much as I did Hal." With Ashby, late-1960s.

Jewison felt that Topol "brought a kind of toughness, a dignity," to the role of Tevye in *Fiddler on the Roof*. Plus, he was "kind of sexy."

Directing Ted Neeley in *Jesus Christ Superstar*. "What was going on with us was emotionally overwhelming," Neeley said.

With James Caan on the accident-prone set of *Rollerball*, 1974. "The insurance companies made an absolute fortune out of us," Jewison remembers.

Filming *Moonstruck*. "I don't think I've ever worked with anybody who enjoys it so much," Cher said.

Norman and Dixie were married for more than 50 years. "She's strong," daughter Jennifer said, "I think that's what dad loves about her."

Courtesy Alamy

"You are an actor of immense talent and power," Jewison wrote to Denzel Washington, here on the set of *The Hurricane*. "I will always be there for you."

Winning the Thalberg award in 1999. "Just tell stories that move us to laughter and tears," he told the audience, "and perhaps reveal a little truth about ourselves."

Courtesy ABC

first director I've worked with who deserves the title," said Topol. He was impressed with how Jewison could subtly nudge actors into "discovering" what he was demanding of them. "With little remarks, smiles, very little talk—he'll let [the actor] come to what Norman actually wants to happen."

Norma Crane courageously finished the shoot, concealing the effects of her radiation treatments. *Fiddler on the Roof* was her last film. The cancer claimed her in 1973, at the age of forty-four. "I've heard it said many times, as a criticism of *Fiddler on the Roof*, that she was the weakest member of the cast," Walter Mirisch wrote. "I know she was the strongest member."[56]

After filming had wrapped, Jewison did what he could to protect another member of his cast. Concerned that Tevye's horse might yet end up at the glue factory, Jewison arranged for a small monthly sum to be sent to a farmer near Lekenik who had agreed to take in the animal. The horse lived for another three or four years, grazing on the rustic farm.

"He lived to be quite an old horse," Jewison remembers, and was "happy in his retirement."

CHAPTER 11

Super Double Dynamite
Love and a Couple
Tons of Peace

JEWISON SOON SETTLED INTO THE RHYTHMS of English life. It must have felt comforting, for an Anglo-Canadian of Jewison's generation who had grown up singing "God Save the King" each morning before school, to be surrounded by the familiar symbols and ritual. "Norman really belonged in Putney Heath," said his friend Gary Smith, who met Jewison on the CBS Hit Parade in 1958. "He was a mayor of Putney Heath. He loved going out with his dog in that tall grass and running around. He loved that period of his life." Smith remembers the mouthwatering omelets that were Norman's breakfast specialty.[1] The family also spent time outside the city ("living as the local Squire," Jewison said) near Henley-on-Thames, northeast of Reading. "It's beautiful in the country and the children are running around and I am gardening like mad. Love it!!" he wrote to his friend Chiz Schultz. "This is truly a civil country so far."[2]

Jewison's praise of England as "civil" hints at what perturbed him about his American life. Friends said that Norman and Dixie worried about their kids growing up in Los Angeles. As their friend Henry Mancini explained, "the Californian environment tends to . . . I don't know. It has an effect. It has a laidback effect. It's not like growing up on the streets of New York or anything like that. It's a little detached from the real world." Mancini, along with all of Norman's friends, felt the Jewison kids had turned out to be remarkably well-adjusted—which he attributed to "having the discipline laid on them" during their time in England.[3]

For her part, Jennifer Jewison doesn't remember those years as draconian. Her father wasn't uptight about boys or drugs or other typical sources of parental angst. "I mean, he knows that we all smoke pot—he smokes pot. He can't really say much about it because we know he does it, you know, I mean I've found pot in his room."

Soon after *Fiddler* wrapped, Jewison left for a couple of weeks to Klosters, Switzerland, where he could ski "out all my hostilities and fatigue and depression and feel almost whole again." He often bottomed-out after finishing a film, and *Fiddler* had been particularly arduous. "After all the delays," he wrote to Ashby, alluding to his standoff with the studio, "and the return to Yugoslavia, I still missed the fucking snow. It had melted five days before we returned and got nothing but bright sunshine so I had to scramble around and wait for clouds and so on trying to get as bleak a feeling as possible. I must say I'm glad it is over. After seven continuous months I was beginning to feel my age. It really has been a brute of a film to shoot."

Jewison's move to the UK had necessitated a new logistical approach to film production. *Fiddler* would provide the template for future projects. He would avoid British studios, which he found "too slow, hampered as they are by tradition, management-union hostility, reluctance to work past the hour and tea breaks."[4] Instead, he would bring experienced British crews to European locations. "There is such a different atmosphere about filmmaking in Europe," he wrote to Ashby. It "somehow always feels much more personal and removed from the influences of producers, distributors, exhibitors, banks and the rest of the bullshit."[5]

But while Norman had gained a bit of distance from the industry "bullshit," Hal was still very much in the thick of it.

* * *

In 1966, Jewison had taken out an option on Kristin Hunter's novel *The Landlord*, about the scion of an aristocratic WASP family who buys a run-down property in the ghetto to provide himself with a vocation. Critics were split on the book, but Jewison saw an opportunity for "the screen's first Black comedy." He imagined a "bold, funny, avant-garde kind of film" with an almost entirely Black cast.[6] Boaty Boatwright thought the project sounded "perfect" for Norman, "plus how refreshing to see a film about coloured people as PEOPLE, rather than just another film about civil rights."[7] With other projects consuming his attention, and the years passing by, Jewison wondered if the project could be right for Ashby. He decided to take a chance, and gave Ashby his first opportunity to direct.

"In all the time I had known Norman," Ashby remembered, "we had never once touched upon the subject" of Hal directing his own film, "and here this beautiful, sensitive dude was standing there asking me about my dreams."[8]

Norman stayed on as producer of *The Apartment*, supervising Ashby's work mostly from afar. The finished product would impress critics but failed to find an audience. Ashby remained under contract with Simkoe/Cartier II, Jewison's production company, casting around for new projects and alienating more people than usual without Jewison's restraining influence. For years, the two men had enjoyed an enriching creative partnership alongside their deepening friendship. Now, with Jewison based out of the UK, they barely spoke. "I often think of you and wish we could talk," Jewison wrote. "I have tried to reach you a few times but there never seems to be an answer."[9]

* * *

When Jewison did receive the occasional letter from his good friend, the news was not encouraging. One letter, addressed to "My Beautiful Norman," was dated January 8, 1970.

> Norman, if I could just find the words to let you know what's going on inside me. It just all hurts so fucking much that I can't even stop the tears from coming, while I sit here trying to write this damned note. I guess I have spent too many hours this past few weeks, sitting alone in this office, trying to cope with the pain in my life, and I feel like I'm losing, while it's gaining. It's a weird thing to sit alone in the wee hours, and hear those moans come out of my aching soul. It hurts! It hurts! Oh, Christ, it hurts![10]

The immediate cause of Ashby's anguish was an awkward conversation he was about to have with Neil Young. According to Ashby biographer Nick Dawson, Young and Ashby had collaborated for six weeks on original songs for *The Landlord*, and "Cinnamon Girl" was to be the film's theme.[11] Only later did Ashby learn that United Artists would take 50 per cent ownership of the soundtrack publishing rights, leaving him in a position where he would have to ask Young to donate his songs to the film for free. Ashby regarded the financial limitations imposed by executives (the "money people") as painful amputations of his vision. "I will never again be fucked by those who find money more important than my life," he seethed to Jewison. "It hurts too much, and I don't even want to find the strength to withstand that kind of pain."[12]

While Ashby had absorbed any number of professional lessons during his five-picture apprenticeship with Jewison, few left a more lasting imprint than Jewison's conviction that the "money people" cannot be trusted. "Hal can be quite persuasive and quite charming [with executives] until the film's sold, and then he realizes—and this is something I think I was responsible for teaching Hal—that we are alone, *they* are the enemy, always will be," Jewison recalled.

It was a message Ashby took to heart, one that would exact a heavy toll on his career and his mental health. "Hal by nature is anti-establishment," Jewison said, "therefore it developed I think unfortunately into a paranoia."[13]

That paranoia blossomed in Ashby's letters to Jewison throughout post-production of *The Landlord* and beyond. "There isn't a day when I don't think how much positive energy they drain away from us with their negativism," Ashby wrote. "It seems my frustration and anger at the Miri and UA grows with each and every day . . . I have absolutely no contact with any of them, which is just as well, as all I would want to do is yell 'Fuck You!' at them until my voice gave out. Beyond a doubt they are all the prize assholes of all time, who have not one ounce of talent aside from that of really knowing how to be super liars, cheats, and generally bad people. As stated, fuck them."[14]

Jewison knew that he, too, could be paranoid when it came to executives. "I think many, many directors are guilty of it," he later said. He believed that directors were fundamentally alone in their commitment and responsibility for their films: each film represented two years of his life (or more), and the financial interests of executives were often inimical to the creative aspirations of the director. Jewison approached these battles strategically. The key, he felt, was to make those in power confident that "you will deliver them something that will make them even more powerful."

Ashby lacked Jewison's instinct for strategic triangulation. His relationships with the "money people" were mostly oppositional. Moreover, while Jewison's family provided a solid emotional anchor in times of professional tumult, Ashby's personal life was proving to be its own wellspring of chaos.

* * *

While shooting *The Landlord*, Ashby married his fifth wife, a struggling actress named Joan Marshall. (In the film's opening shot, the bride can be seen kissing Jewison, who'd given her away at the actual ceremony: symbolic recognition of the man who made the film possible.) Jewison had not been enthusiastic about Ashby's choice. Marshall came with heavy familial baggage, including a son incarcerated on drug charges, and she was emotionally unstable. Shortly after the wedding, she threatened to leap out of a hotel window.[15] It wasn't long before the relationship imploded.

"Things are still not well with the me and Joan thing," Ashby wrote to Jewison, "and to top it off, her craziness has extended into the money area. To make it plain without explanation, she has indeed fucked it up—and me—on the money thing."[16]

Ashby was now sleeping in his office, which he was in the process of losing: Mirisch, in the process of downsizing, asked Ashby to move his office to a third-floor cubicle, one of those "dumb little boxes, which I absolutely refuse to sit in for one hour. I would, and will, conduct our business on a street corner before I would sit in something like they offered, and just get depressed."

Ashby was in the midst of a contract negotiation with United Artists, which was going about as well as everything else at the time. "To date, my conclusions have been thus: fuck them!"[17]

There is much genuine affection amid the torment in Ashby's correspondence with Norman. Before subjecting him to his expanding catalogue of woes—"getting into any of the bummers," as he put it— Ashby would begin with unironic avowals of love.

"I do want you to know how much I think of you each and every day," Ashby would write, "and how much I hope all is going as well as possible now you are shooting."

Hal closed his letters with hand-written x's and o's, and instructions to "give Dix, the kids, Pat, and anyone else around a big love hug and kisses from me."

He would sign off (sometimes from "Princess Hal") with "Eighteen Loads of Super Double Dynamite Love," or "Some Super Double Dynamite Love and a Couple of Tons of Peace."

Then, in March 1971, Hal wrote the letter that would effectively end his partnership with his friend and mentor. The lengthy missive, addressed to lawyer Irving Klein, Jewison's US manager, with carbon copies to Ashby's lawyer and to Jewison, began:

My dear Mr. Klein,

Some time ago, when Norman first moved to England, it seems he made an unfortunate mistake and assigned you the task of handling his business affairs here in the States. Since then, your performance in conducting the business side of Simkoe/Cartier II (as it relates to me) has been nothing short of disgraceful, disrespectful, shocking, and dishonest, to say the least. As a result, I'm still not certain if your actions during these last few months were motivated by some weird kind of malice, or if they are just an outward display of plain stupidity and ignorance. Whichever, your business acumen leaves me with nothing more than a desire to throw up.

Ashby accused Klein of sitting on weeks' worth of wages that had already been paid by Paramount for *Harold and Maude*, offering "some bullshit story of how I would be paid off prior to the end of shooting" because Cartier II would be responsible if Ashby quit the project before completing it. "That you would put me through all of that, while I was involved with the frustration of trying to prepare a film, is unforgivable," Ashby railed.

Even more infuriating to Ashby was that Klein had directed $6,500 of Ashby's withheld wages toward his William Morris agents, "without even having the courtesy to ask me if it was alright. Now, I say, bullshit, and fuck you, Mr. Klein." Ashby continued:

At one time, Norman used to tell me how I was to participate in some percentage of the profits of RUSSIANS, HEAT, THOMAS CROWN, etc., but when these dreams failed to become a reality, I could only assume Norman had second thoughts, or his business manager had persuaded him that so generous an act might be foolish, or some such thing, so I never brought it up again, and from there on, all I know is that Norman made it possible for me to realize a lifelong dream, I became a film director. On top of this, he gave me a brand new Jag, and loaned me $10,000. Aside from the fact that he is a most beautiful, warm-hearted man, and my dearest friend, I could only imagine he did all of these things because of some kind of gratitude for whatever creative force or help I might have brought to his films. As a matter of fact, it would sadden me deeply if this were not the case . . .

Needless to say, both gestures were much appreciated, but now you, Mr. Klein, have managed in your crummy way to put an awful and terrible taste in my mouth, and all I want is to be released from ever having one God damned thing to do with the business side of Simkoe/Cartier II.

With the exception of Roger Sherman (an honest man, I believe), Norman would be wise to dump the whole lot of you, but that is his business, and I digress, so back to the point. The only way I can think of to be rid of all contact with you is to let you know I will only be in contact with Norman from now on, while you my dear Mr. Klein, can fuck off!

Hal Ashby[18]

For decades, industry players would wonder what happened between Ashby and Jewison. "Of all the stories I don't know," said Patrick Palmer, "that's the one that mystifies me the most, because I maintained the relationship with Hal for about ten years after the split up. Norman and I talked about it a lot and I'm not sure Norman has ever really admitted what happened."[19]

In later years, Jewison claimed to have "repressed" the details. Letters indicate he had been in conversation with Irving Klein about Ashby's compensation on *Harold and Maude*; he would have known if Klein was withholding payments through the project's completion. In his response to Ashby and his lawyer, Klein insists that Ashby had been paid on schedule, claiming that the "pitifully transparent" motivation of Ashby's letter was to "slash at your deals with Norman Jewison while feigning undying gratitude and friendship with your benefactor." He couldn't decide if Ashby's missive "was basis for a lawsuit or for psychoanalysis."[20]

The Jewison-Ashby relationship was coming to a frayed end. Ashby couldn't stand working with Jewison's business representatives in North America; Norman, like so many others, eventually found Ashby impossible to work with.

Norman's competitive spirit may have contributed to the split. Their falling out occurred at the beginning of an incredible run of work from Ashby, who reached the heights of his directorial power in the 1970s with *The Last Detail* (1973), *Shampoo* (1975), *Bound for Glory* (1976), and *Being There* (1979). Jewison would never admit it, but it is possible that Ashby's success complicated any possible reconciliation.

There were traces of Jewison in Ashby's great films of the 1970s, such as the hilarious homage to *Thomas Crown*'s famous kiss in *Being There* (1979). Ashby continued to work with Jewison's collaborators, including Haskell Wexler on *Bound for Glory* (1976) and *Coming Home* (1978). But it was never the same between Hal and Norman. Both men realized what they'd had, and what they'd lost.

"Being loved by you has been a very groovy trip for me," Ashby once wrote. "I can't even imagine what my life would have been without it."

Asked about their relationship in a 2016 on-camera interview, Jewison, who had not had regular contact with Ashby for forty-five years, half of his life, began to cry. "I don't think I ever loved another man as much as I did Hal," he said.[21]

* * *

If Jewison had limited bandwidth for Ashby's emotional breakdown in the summer of 1971, he may have been preoccupied with another professional relationship that was imploding at a distance.

Jewison's move to the UK had complicated many of his business dealings, not least his association with Foster, Ingersoll & Weber (FIW), his PR firm. It was harder to drum up publicity for a client who had deliberately moved away from the action, especially in an age when that business was conducted mostly by post. Still, Jewison was not alone in feeling that FIW was failing in its responsibilities to promote *Fiddler* and its director. In December 1970, Quinn Donoghue, *Fiddler*'s unit publicist, who was responsible for liaising between the production and external publicists, complained to Rick Ingersoll that *Fiddler* "has become a secret rather than a sensation."[22] FIW was tasked with generating earned media, primarily through planting news stories. From what Jewison could tell, the campaign to promote *Fiddler* was almost nonexistent, and the firm was not earning the $100 per week he paid them for personal publicity, either. By the summer, with no discernable improvement, he was fed up.

"This is a difficult letter for me to write especially since we have had a long association both personally and business wise," Jewison wrote to Ingersoll. He could no longer ignore the "almost total absence of personal publicity in America."

Ingersoll mustered only a feeble reply to Jewison's accusations; he claimed that "the picture has had respectable coverage," that the firm had planted all the information they could. Anyway, how could they promote a director who was never available for interviews?[23]

Jewison told Irving Klein to "terminate my payments at the end of the month."[24]

His disillusionment with FIW was part of a larger falling out with the Mirisch Company. In 1964, when he had still been under contract to Universal, the directorial freedom offered by the Mirisch Company seemed like a godsend. By 1971, the Mirisch's fortunes had declined roughly in proportion with Jewison's personal success. Jewison had come to view Walter Mirisch as a creative rival, even if they were ostensibly working toward the same end. Jewison noticed how the trade papers used phrases like "the Mirisch *Fiddler*" or "if plans by Mirisch work out," implying that Mirisch was in creative control of the film. Jewison felt that he was losing a war that his PR firm didn't even know it was fighting. Jewison spelled it out in a follow-up to Ingersoll:

> It is common knowledge that the Mirisch Company are undergoing a severe decline in prestige and production. They have begun an intensive campaign to ensure that *Fiddler* is a Mirisch production . . . Since he also took a co-production credit on *In the Heat of the Night*, he received, and accepted, the Academy Award and never mentioned my name. The same situation can happen on *Fiddler on the Roof*. The annoying fact is that he is not the producer of the film and yet they seem determined to turn this film into a possessive credit.
>
> Without being excessively pretentious or egotistical, I intend to do everything possible to assure that this does not happen. I have little patience or tolerance with non-creative people who continually put their personal brand on the work of others. This includes Sam Spiegel; Joe Levine; Ross Hunter; Carl Foreman; Dino De Laurentiis; Marty Ransohoff; Mike Frankovich; Bobby Evans; and the Mirisch Company. To avoid this from happening requires not naiveté but constant vigilance and consistent pressure and saturation in the Public Relations field.[25]

His characterization of his relationship with the Mirisch Company contained at least one major inaccuracy. He remembers that Walter Mirisch "never mentioned my name" while accepting the Best Picture

Oscar in 1968. In fact, Mirisch had declared his "deep gratitude" for "my friend and partner Norman Jewison, whose brilliant direction brought it so vividly to life."[26]

Jewison's failure of memory on this point suggests, perhaps, the depth of animosity and paranoia that now characterized his relationships with Mirisch and other "non-creative" producers masquerading as artists. He decided to re-engage FIW to lead a strong PR counterattack in the lead-up to the Academy Awards, which would be decisive in cementing *Fiddler* as "a Norman Jewison film." He even increased their fee to $600 per month, which his own operations would have to absorb: Jewison hadn't received salary or expenses since the film wrapped in February.

In October 1971, Walter Mirisch wrote Jewison a heartfelt message reflecting on the "long, long journey" that had been *Fiddler on the Roof.* Attempting, perhaps, to salvage his relationship with the disenchanted director, Mirisch wrote that *Fiddler* was "most unique in my career for the amount of love, devotion, and dedication which was brought to it."

I have expressed to you before my deep appreciation for your efforts and my high regard for your talent and the huge contribution you made to this film. You know, I am sure, my deep feeling of friendship toward you personally.

I feel certain that of all the fine films on which we have worked together over the years, this will be the crowning point. I hope there will still be another film, sometime in either of our lives, that will be as richly fulfilling in all areas, as this one has been.

Most sincerely,

Walter M. Mirisch[27]

Jewison never worked with Mirisch again. "The relationship sort of deteriorated," recalled Marvin Mirisch. "We have given him a couple of things over the years, that I guess haven't interested him, and so that's what happened. I think we are still quite friendly. Every time I see him we throw our arms around one another and I mean it and I think he does."[28]

* * *

Leading up to the worldwide release of *Fiddler on the Roof* in December 1971, Jewison was more concerned than usual about the quality of the theatrical presentation. He campaigned to release the film in four-track magnetic sound, which would require retrofitting some theatres.[29] He was particularly concerned about the smaller markets, where exhibitors with sub-optimal equipment would likely present the film in poor conditions. He reviewed the technical specifications of theatres in dozens of cities around the world, from the Paramount-Elysées in Paris to the New Ostnamba Roxy in Osaka to the Presidente theatre in Guayaquil, Ecuador.[30] He was "dismayed" to find that the Chen theatre in Tel Aviv could not handle magnetic sound.[31]

He also wanted a strong VIP presence at premieres of *Fiddler* around the world, a desire that met with mixed success. When Queen Elizabeth II sent her regrets for the London premiere, Jewison told a publicist that there was "absolutely no excuse" that the film did "not have a Royal premiere."[32] (Princess Margaret attended the premiere in Edinburgh.)

On November 10, Jewison attended *Fiddler*'s Canadian premiere at Toronto's University Theatre, a five-minute walk from where he'd directed his first musical sketches as an undergraduate at Victoria College. Tickets to the black-tie event specified "Fiddler on the Roof on the Screen," to avoid confusion among audience members expecting a stage play. The CBC scheduled the NFB documentary *Norman Jewison, Filmmaker* to premiere on television at 10 p.m. the same evening; friends unable to attend the *Fiddler* premiere wrote Jewison to say that they would be watching and toasting his health from their living rooms. That Friday, Toronto Mayor William Dennison would present Jewison with the Key to the City.

It should have been a triumphant return for Jewison, although his spirits dampened by the fact that he couldn't share the experience with his parents. Jewison's father, who had suffered a stroke years earlier, was again unwell and unable to attend the opening.[33]

In her review of *Fiddler on the Roof*, Pauline Kael predicted "that people of taste have been so indoctrinated now with a narrow conception of cinematic values that a movie in a broad popular style will be subject to a snobbish reaction." Kael's prophecy proved true for film critics in Jewison's hometown: the *Toronto Star* bemoaned the vulgarity of Jewison's big-budget production, while the *Globe* dismissed *Fiddler* as just another stale Hollywood musical. Vincent Canby sounded a similar note in the *New York Times*, arguing that *Fiddler* was gratuitous and unnecessary.

For her part, Kael wrote that *Fiddler* "is an absolutely smashing movie," and "the most *powerful* movie musical ever made." Kael criticized some of Jewison's directorial choices as "square," and wished that his camera simply recorded the dancers in motion rather than becoming one of the dancers. But Kael spoke for many viewers when she praised the cumulative force of Jewison's three-hour epic. "The music is certainly not operatic, but the movie of *Fiddler on the Roof* has operatic power," she wrote. "It's not a soft experience; you come out shaken."[34]

Jewison was stung by the dismissive reviews in his hometown papers, but knew by now that even bad press could help drum up business. "The more controversy we can get going, the better," he wrote to Gabe Sumner, a United Artists vice president.[35]

Accordingly, he unleashed two withering letters to the editors of the *Globe* and the *Daily Star*. "I realize Mr. Gilmour has been reviewing films for many years; however, it's amazing that he is still provincial enough to dismiss the emotional impact of a film," he wrote the *Daily Star*.[36] As for *Globe* critic Martin Knelman, Jewison felt sorry "that he cannot allow himself to be moved by the music of Isaac Stern or to feel compassion or even shed a tear," the director wrote. "However, you may assure him that long after he has ceased to write film reviews, Sholem Aleichem will still be read by millions and the sound of the Fiddler will continue to be heard."[37]

Meanwhile, UA had been setting up screenings for religious leaders (including Billy Graham) around the country. All publicity was good publicity, and those with a stake in *Fiddler* were not above old-fashioned shenanigans in service of the film. Sumner and Fred Goldberg, another UA vice president, borrowed friends' stationery and were singing *Fiddler*'s praises in letters to various newspaper editors under false names. Sumner advised Jewison to keep this particular publicity tactic under wraps: "Please, let's keep this sneaky little thing *entre nous* because if it gets back to [*New York Times* editor] Sy Peck we'll all be in the crapper."[38]

CHAPTER 12

Strange Thing Mystifying

W HILE SOME CRITICS WOULD LATER STRUGGLE to find a thematic through-line connecting Jewison's works, the director often identified betrayal as his signature theme. *Jesus Christ Superstar* allowed Jewison to tackle the archetypal story of betrayal in Western culture, while simultaneously creating something completely original: the first filmed rock opera. The project brought him back to Israel, which continued to exert a strong hold upon his imagination. Plus, coming off *Fiddler*, "I thought I should do something for the goyim," he joked to a friend.[1]

Andrew Lloyd Webber and Tim Rice had begun writing the songs that would become *Jesus Christ Superstar* in 1969, when they were twenty-three and twenty-five years old. Rice was inspired by a few lines from Bob Dylan's 1964 protest song, "With God On Our Side":

Through many a dark hour
I've been thinkin' about this
That Jesus Christ was

Betrayed by a kiss

But I can't think for you

You'll have to decide

Whether Judas Iscariot

Had God on his side[2]

Before it was an album, musical, or film, "Jesus Christ Superstar" was a hit single. Attuned to the countercultural wavelengths of the moment, the song came from Judas's perspective, raising questions about Jesus's motivation and about Judas's culpability for a murder that was God's will. Tim Rice remembers sitting in his parents' home one Sunday morning where he penned the final lyrics:

Did you mean to die like that, was that a mistake or

Did you know your messy death would be a record-breaker?

Don't you get me wrong

I only want to know

Jesus Christ, Jesus Christ

Who are you? What have you sacrificed?

Jesus Christ, Superstar

Do you think you're what they say you are?

Webber and Rice knew their material justified something bigger. The resulting *Superstar* album would approach timeless theological questions through the frame of modern celebrity culture. Perhaps Christ was the son of God; perhaps he was also a proto-rockstar, the tabloid fodder of classical antiquity. Jewison would represent the character of Mary Magdalene as a kind of groupie: washing his feet, anointing him with oils, "in love with the idea" of Christ, Jewison said, in much the same way that young fans might dote on a "superstar." Yet Jewison also felt that Mary's song "I Don't Know How to Love Him" expressed "an emotion that is perhaps one of the most beautiful in the whole film, because many people do not know how to love Him—indeed many people do not know how to love anybody."[3]

The *Jesus Christ Superstar* double-LP "Brown Album," released in the UK in October 1970, was an immediate disappointment. "It was met with a massive dose of British indifference, even condescension," remembers Andrew Lloyd Webber. "There were a few nice comments but as there were no big names involved, I doubt if any of the major rock critics heard the whole thing out."[4]

Jewison, by contrast, had found himself both "curiously moved" and "flooded with exciting visual images" upon first hearing the album while on location in Yugoslavia.[5] By chance, the actor Barry Dennen, who had a bit part in *Fiddler* and voiced Pontius Pilate on the *Superstar* album, had given Jewison a copy. Patrick Palmer remembers Jewison's excitement about this "obscure album from England . . . He said, 'You've got to listen to this . . . I'm going to make a film out of it.'" Before long, Jewison set up a meeting with Lloyd Webber and Ned Tanen, an executive at Universal.

For Rice and Lloyd Webber, Jewison's interest in *Superstar* was a major boon. *Fiddler* had given Jewison "street cred not only with steering a musical from stage to screen but also with a Jewish story," Lloyd Webber recalls. Jewison seemed "the perfect fit and the meeting was positive as meetings always are in Hollywood. Ninety-nine per cent of the time you leave buzzing with the fantastic power powwows you've had and then never hear from anyone again, but this meeting proved the exception."[6]

* * *

From the outset, everyone agreed that the film would be "sung-through," consisting only of the album's songs with no added dialogue. Rice had first crack at the screenplay, and turned in a monumental *Ben-Hur*-style epic. He remembers approaching it as though it were simply "a question of pointing out which massive visual effect accompanied which song. Should the procession of camels enter from the left or right of the frame? What was the best marching formation for the Roman legions?"[7]

Jewison didn't see *Superstar* as an old-fashioned sword-and-sandal epic. He wanted to devise a film idiom as hip and contemporary as the rock opera. In the weeks ahead, he and the English novelist Melvyn Bragg developed a "pastiche" approach that blended the biblical and modern eras. A new framing device would deposit a theatre troupe in the Holy Land, where they spontaneously mount the passion play amidst the ruins. Jewison and Bragg drafted scenes while scouting locations in Israel, walking through desert locations listening to *Superstar* from a tape recorder, immersing themselves in the landscape and music.

Budgeted at slightly under $3.5 million, *Superstar* would be Jewison's leanest production in years. The actors eventually cast in the three principal leads of Jesus, Judas, and Mary would make just $16,500 each. Jewison took a significantly reduced director's fee (at $150,000) in exchange for 10 per cent of the worldwide net profit. (According to Patrick Palmer, the film had done $40 million in business by the mid-1980s.)[8] The low budget was also made possible by the Israeli government, who offered a 23.5 per cent rebate on foreign currency brought into the country. Jewison also received support from senior officials, including General Chaim Bar-Lev and Ze'ev Birger, the director of Light Industries, who was then working to establish a new Israeli Film Center. In return, Jewison recommended the experience of shooting in Israel in the Hollywood trades. "There is a spirit in the country and among its people that grabs you," Jewison wrote in an article for *Variety*, "and if you spend any time there you will never be the same."[9]

While filming *Superstar* in Israel, Jewison and Palmer would also produce *Billy Two Hats*, a "kosher western" directed by Ted Kotcheff; the two productions would shoot simultaneously, sharing equipment and logistics. After a failed bid to secure Marlon Brando, Jewison cast Gregory Peck and Desi Arnaz Jr. in the leads.[10]

The Mirisches may have been out of the picture, but it didn't take long for conflicts to ignite with Jewison's new executives. Universal wanted a 200 per cent recoupment penalty written into his contract: if he went 10 per cent or less over budget, the studio would recoup in full, but if he went more than 10 per cent over, Universal would recoup as though he'd gone twice as much over his budget than he actually had. The penalty was "just another attempt by Universal to increase the pressure," Jewison wrote to the entertainment lawyer Harold Berkowitz. "It's points like these that continue to widen the gap between the studios and the independent artist." In the end, Jewison felt he had little choice but to "accept their unfair conditions."[11]

* * *

Principal photography of *Jesus Christ Superstar* began on August 18, 1972 in the caves of Beit Guvrin, near the valley in which David is said to have killed Goliath. Today, the vast network of underground caves is part of Beit Guvrin National Park, although Jewison remembers that it "took days to clean out all the pigeon shit and bat dung" before they could begin filming the songs "What's the Buzz?", "Strange Thing Mystifying," and "Everything's Alright."[12]

Jewison had chosen for Christ's refuge the vast, cathedral-like bell cave not only for its primal beauty but also for its implicit symbolism: Jesus and his Apostles were an "underground" movement, literally and figuratively.[13] He'd cast the picture from top to bottom with unknowns— he told a casting agent he wanted "mainly young rock singers who can also act and dance"—just two of whom had prior film credits.[14] A running joke was that their careers had taken them from *Hair* to Eternity.

Among the *Hair* alums was Ted Neeley, who had played the male lead in the 1969 Broadway production. A rock-and-roll drummer from Ranger, Texas, Neeley wasn't an obvious choice for the son of God; indeed, casting notes Jewison scribbled on a piece of Beverly Hills Hotel stationery reveal a list of actual superstars he was considering for the part, including Mick Jagger, John Lennon, Paul McCartney, Barry Gibb, Ian Gillan, and Robert Plant.[15] Sometime in 1971, Neeley's agent invited Jewison to watch the singer perform in The Who's *Tommy* in Los Angeles. Jewison, then in Palm Springs, made the two-hour drive to LA for an evening performance, only to discover that Neeley had the night off. Jewison returned to his hotel, irritated that he'd wasted his time.

"The next morning," Jewison recalls, "I opened the door of my motel room to find a short young man in Levis wearing a false moustache and beard." Neeley, wearing the cosmetics to show Jewison what he could look like with facial hair, had tracked the director down to apologize and explain that he'd been out sick. "I agreed to meet him for a coffee in the cafeteria and we chatted for twenty minutes," Jewison recalled. "That afternoon on the plane to London I told Pat Palmer that I had a hunch that I had found our Jesus, and I hadn't even seen him perform." They would test more than two dozen actors for the role, but no one could match Neeley's combination of swagger and vulnerability.[16]

Jewison knew that he was courting controversy by casting Carl Anderson as Judas. As a member of the Vatican Press would ask: "Mr.

Jewison, why did you choose a Black Judas?" His response was categorical: "I think discrimination is evil," he said. Anderson "tested along with many others in London, and as always happens, the film really told us what to do. The test was so successful that there really wasn't any doubt in my mind at all that he was the most talented actor to play the role."[17] (Elsewhere, Jewison conceded that "nobody would believe" that explanation, but he didn't care).[18] Yvonne Elliman, the exquisite twenty-year-old Japanese-Irish singer from Honolulu who voiced Mary Magdalene on the album, would embody the part in the film version.

From Beit Guvrin, the production moved to the "Occupied Area," territory taken by Israel in the Six Day War just a few years earlier. Robert Iscove, the film's choreographer, remembers an incident where "Arabs with machine guns came over the hill, pointing at us. They were from a neighbouring village and there had been some tiff that had nothing to do with the actual war, but, the whole experience—I mean from beginning to end it was fraught."[19]

Everything about *Superstar* was infused with a sense of place. One of their main locations was Herodian, a palace fortress built by Herod the Great between 23 and 15 BCE. On a clear day, Jewison could perch on the highest of the walls and see Bethlehem and Jerusalem to the north, and the Dead Sea to the east. He shot Jesus's climactic number, "Gethsemane," in which a spiritually tortured Christ implores God to reveal "just a little of your omnipresent brain," amidst the imposing crags and cliffs of the Siluad Wadi. The area was completely inaccessible by the company's buses and Land Rovers, so their generators, lights, and other production equipment was hauled in by donkey.

Sequences involving the Roman priests were shot at Avdat, a 2,300-year-old Nabataean city near the centre of the Negev desert. Crews added a steel scaffold to create visual interest and foreground a sense of chronological tension, heightened in other scenes with tanks and jets on loan from the Israeli army.[20] Jesus's theatrical moment of tearing down the temple ("our little swing at the materialistic world," Jewison recalls) contained images of modern weapons and a bag of marijuana—"Which there was a lot of around as I remember," Jewison recalls with a laugh.[21]

In the end, Jewison used more than twenty locations from four base camps, in Jerusalem, Beersheba, the Dead Sea, and Nazareth. Not a single frame of *Superstar* was shot on a soundstage.[22]

While a small handful of sequences, such as Herod's number and the title song, were "absolutely set," remembers the choreographer Iscove, most dance numbers were worked out on the spot. Iscove recalls, "We would get out to the set, see the environment," and Jewison would say "this is what we're doing today guys and the camera will be roughly over here," and the rest was devised in relation to the landscape. "I mean, there was just so much history all the time, every place. You just absorbed it by osmosis," Iscove said.[23]

* * *

Jewison brought his entire career's worth of experience to bear as a director on *Superstar*. The lessons he'd learned working in live television on CBC, his musical specials with Belafonte and Judy Garland, and everything he'd learned since proved useful in staging Christ's final hours. Jewison shot in 70 mm with Todd-AO lenses, which provided an image of remarkable clarity; an immense crane imported from Italy (complete with three Italian operators) allowed for dramatic set-ups. MTV was still a decade away, but Jewison's camera, swirling around a wailing Jesus Christ perched on an Israeli cliffside in "Gethsemane," provided an influential model for the music video genre.

Director Atom Egoyan remembers seeing *Superstar* "over and over again" at the Haida Cinema in Victoria, British Columbia, in 1973. *Superstar* "was pretty fundamental in making me understand what a camera does," Egoyan says. "The way the camera is moving, the way it moves in time to the music, the way the film is cut, the production design, the framing device . . . it was just brilliantly conceived as this pageant within a film."[24]

Much of the film's sense of spiritual abandon reflects the heady atmosphere that presided among cast and crew that summer. Jewison had assembled a tribe of flower children in the Holy Land and completely isolated them from the secular world. They spent their days blasting the rock opera at deafening volume in the Israeli desert; when they weren't working, they played beach volleyball: team Judas against team Jesus. The film had taken over their lives.

"We were all hippies, we were all kids," remembers Rob Iscove. *Superstar* "was bringing what we were doing in our personal act together with our craft . . . we were all reading the *Aquarian Gospel of Jesus the Christ*," a central text for New Age astrology. The average age on set was about twenty-five.

Jewison, who turned forty-six that summer, was no longer interested in pretending to be one of the kids. "Norman was a little bit of a fuddy-duddy," remembers Iscove. "He didn't spend a lot of time with the cast and I don't remember a lot of dinners or a lot of cast parties at that time. He did remove himself."[25]

With the crucifixion scene looming, the highly emotional, spiritually intoxicating vibe was almost too much for Ted Neeley. He and other cast members believed that they were walking on the very soil upon which Christ had walked; that the thorns that pricked them were the same thorns that had made up Jesus's crown. "The emotional power we experienced . . ." Neeley said, struggling to find the right words. "What was going on with us was emotionally overwhelming."[26] Neeley's performance on the cross brought the cast and crew to tears. Everyone felt the full spiritual weight of what they were doing. Neeley remembers falling apart emotionally after embodying the crucifixion.[27]

While Rice and Lloyd Webber's album had been denounced as blasphemous in many quarters, including the BBC, where it had been banned from the airwaves, Jewison's film feels less confrontational, and contains more room for reverence. At times, Christ looks up and addresses the camera lens as God, in precisely the same way that Tevye had in *Fiddler on the Roof*. The instant that Christ resolves to die, the viewer is assailed with a lightning-fast montage of canonical paintings (by Goya, Tintoretto, Velázquez, Grünewald, Bosch, and others) evoking Christ's agony on the Cross. The director may have had another montage in the back of his mind. Medgar Evers, Martin Luther King Jr., Bobby Kennedy: Jewison didn't have to look two-thousand years into the past to find a leader who had been killed for preaching peace.

* * *

Jesus Christ Superstar ends with an air of religious mystery: after Christ's crucifixion, the performers, having completed their pageant, re-board the bus that will carry them back to 1972. The actor who played Jesus is not among them. When we first encountered this troupe, they leapt off the bus with wild ebullience; now, they seem burdened with a profound sense of loss. The film ends with the silhouette of an empty cross, a shepherd and his flock barely visible in the sunset. The credits roll in total silence.

"I am so convinced that in the hands of anyone else this film would not have had the magnificent spiritual content it does," Neeley said of Jewison. "It is what it is, and it's so simply stated that everyone can understand it."[28]

Superstar wrapped on November 24, 1972, exactly on schedule. This time, the bumps along the road of production had been relatively minor. At one point, Universal had demanded a minimum running time of ninety-seven minutes to make it an easier sell for TV networks. Jewison was flabbergasted. "Everyone should be aware by now that I am trying to make a motion picture out of a record album," he stormed. "What the hell does Rudy Petersdorf and Universal think we are making—film by the yard?"[29]

Jewison had also gotten wind of foreboding rumours emanating from across the Atlantic, where *Superstar*'s Broadway opening had incited charges of anti-Semitism. But Jewison honestly believed that his film was incapable of offending anyone, and, besides, who could accuse the director of *Fiddler on the Roof* of creating an anti-Semitic film?

CHAPTER 13

"Crucify Him! Crucify Him!"

ON JULY 1, 1973, AT A CEREMONY at the Beverly Hilton Hotel in Los Angeles, Norman Jewison received the California-Israeli Chamber of Commerce Achievement Award. It was far from the most prestigious accolade of Jewison's career, but he cherished the honour. His recent experiences of bringing *Fiddler* to the screen and living in Israel while shooting *Superstar* had allowed his longstanding fascination with Judaism to blossom into something deeper. He told his old friend Carl Reiner that in making *Fiddler* he had "even found, in a way, in myself my own Jewishness."[1] At one point, he hired a researcher to investigate whether Jewison's family didn't have a long-lost link to Judaism after all. (He found a Jewless lineage extending back to Yorkshire in 1116).[2] Decades later, when he finally wrote his memoir, he would begin by declaring: "For as long as I can remember, I've always wanted to be a Jew."[3]

It wasn't only spiritual. For the last couple of years, there had also been a business side to Jewison's friendship with Israel. In negotiating the favourable tax inducements for *Superstar* and *Billy Two Hats*, Jewison had developed a relationship with General Haim Bar-Lev, the Minister of Commerce and Industry under Prime Minister Golda Meir. Bar-Lev, a celebrated military tactician, would soon be pressed back into military service after Egyptian President Anwar Sadat launched a surprise attack in October 1973, inciting the Yom Kippur war. During his brief spell in politics, Bar-Lev and Jewison enjoyed a prosperous relationship. "I wanted to let you know how grateful I am personally, and in the name of the Israeli Government, for the contributions you are making to our growing motion picture industry," Bar-Lev wrote. "You have constantly promoted our industry in remarks to the press and to members of the motion picture community throughout the world."[4]

By the time Jewison was to receive his award from the California-Israeli Chamber of Commerce, however, there was an ominous chill in the relationship, at least from the Israeli side. In his remarks that evening, Jewison spoke glowingly of Israel and its people. But he had been stung by the fact that Ze'ev Birger, head of the Israeli Film Center in Jerusalem, had abruptly declined to attend the ceremony. Worse, Jewison had reason to believe that *Jesus Christ Superstar* was fast becoming a political liability, indeed perhaps even an embarrassment, for his friends in the Knesset. Some were even questioning whether the Israeli government had become party to a work of rank anti-Semitism.

* * *

Only a few months earlier, Jewison had been aglow with the usual consolations of spring. "We have wild ducks in the pond and all the trees are in blossom and the spring flowers are at their best," he wrote to Nadine Phinney back in LA. "The boys are doing well at school in Switzerland and Jenny had taken to speaking very proper English."[5] He and Dixie would soon commence on a trip to Japan, Hong Kong, Bangkok, and Tehran to support *Jesus Christ Superstar*. The only cloud on the horizon was the lingering suggestion of anti-Semitism—which, Jewison believed, would be swiftly eradicated when the film saw the light of day.

The accusations of anti-Semitism that dogged the Broadway production of *Jesus Christ Superstar* were rooted in an investigation commissioned by Rabbi Marc H. Tanenbaum, Director of Interreligious Affairs for the American Jewish Committee (AJC). The eventual report, written by a Presbyterian advisor to the AJC named Gerald Strober, was methodical and damning. He compared *Superstar* to ancient Passion Plays (such as the Oberammergau) which implicated the Jewish people in the act of deicide, and found that the musical "unambiguously lays the primary responsibility for Jesus's suffering and crucifixion to the Jewish priesthood."[6] Strober's report was widely circulated; various parties sent it to Jewison before he began production. The director promised friends in Israel that his version of *Superstar* would be neither anti-Semitic nor anti-religious—a promise which was reiterated on the floor of the Knesset by General Bar-Lev to calm anxious Israeli politicians. Officials there requested a copy of the script for their approval prior to the start of production, and Jewison provided it.

Jewison poured over the Strober analysis, and consulted widely. He talked it over with Ned Tanen, the Universal executive. He held a cordial phone conversation with Morton Yarmon, Director of Public Relations with the AJC. He reviewed the specific recommendations concerning the filming of *Superstar* prepared by the Anti-Defamation League of B'nai Brith, and claimed he would take them under advisement. Jewison talked to Tim Rice and Andrew Lloyd Webber about possibly changing a few lyrics. "I myself cannot see anything in *Jesus Christ, Superstar* that could remotely offend anybody," Lloyd Webber wrote to Jewison, "and I cannot help feeling that the reaction is over emotional and possibly based on the Broadway production which tended to over-play certain aspects."[7]

Jewison agreed. While he maintained the appearance of cordiality with *Superstar*'s Jewish critics, the director (still stinging from the defeat of *Nat Turner*) detested censorship and pressure applied by special interest groups. Mostly, however, he believed that the concern was simply unfounded. Jewison was not an anti-Semite. He believed that he was incapable of making an anti-Semitic film. He urged critics to familiarize themselves with his work: virtually all of it, he told Allen Rivkin of the Jewish Film Advisory Committee, advanced the idea that "discrimination, in any form, [was] an evil." His version of *Superstar* would "not be found offensive, blasphemous or distasteful to <u>any</u> religious group. What more can I say?" *Fiddler on the Roof* had recently earned Jewison the 1971 Inter Religious Award granted by the Broadcasting and Film Commission of the National Council of Churches, the Committee on Films of the Synagogue Council of America, and the Division for Film and Broadcasting of the United States Catholic Conference. Once his critics saw his vision, Jewison believed, they would shower *Superstar* with similar praise.[8]

* * *

Few musicals are as beloved as *Fiddler on the Roof*, so it was no surprise that aficionados subjected Jewison's adaptation to microscopic scrutiny. One woman, who had grown up in a Russian village not unlike Anatevka, wrote to upbraid him for showing Golde using an "American" style rolling pin (comparatively short and thick) rather than a proper European rolling pin (long and narrow); another viewer was moved to inform Jewison that "there were no clothespins in Russia, and certainly not in a small village."[9] Still, while some viewers' devotion to *Fiddler* had excited particularly fine-grained inspection, *Superstar* was about to be subjected, in certain quarters, to the sort of intensive textual exegesis normally reserved for sacred texts.

The substance of the public case against *Superstar*, the movie, was provided by Strober, who had led the charge against the musical the year before. His method was to compare specific aspects of Jewison's film to their portrayal in the New Testament, quoting chapter and verse. Where the New Testament priests took Jesus seriously, *Superstar*'s Caiaphas was akin to a B-movie villain, Strober said, "full of arrogant contempt for Jesus and the people who acclaim him." Strober claimed that Judas "is represented as a victim of Jewish perfidy," and that Jewison included modern Israeli tanks and planes to "caricature the supposed 'ruthless power' of modern Israel."

Worst of all was Jewison's portrayal of the chanting crowd in Jesus's final moments ("Crucify him! Crucify him!") which "asserts a collective Jewish guilt for the crucifixion." Strober concluded that Jewison had "pressed into service every device of cinematic art to spread the old falsehood of the Jews' collective responsibility for Jesus's death" and exploited "a tradition that has scarred Jews and Christians from the time of the Church Fathers, through the Middle Ages, to the era of Auschwitz."[10]

Jewison could not have been particularly surprised by Strober's Jeremiad, much of which was recycled from his denunciation of the musical. Still, the charge that he had personally represented the Jews as Christ-killers, participating in a "tradition" of anti-Semitic propaganda that had culminated in Auschwitz, was galling. The AJC broadcast Strober's findings across the world. Shortly before the American release of the film, the *B'nai B'rith Messenger* published a front-page condemnation under the headline "'Superstar' Super-Demeaning." Strober called the film "nothing less than a catastrophe," while Rabbi Tanenbaum opined that the film's "G" rating "means that masses of Christian children of

Sunday school age will be exposed, in most compelling fashion, to an anti-Jewish presentation of the gospel story."[11]

Jewison, who continued to believe that the film was its own best defense, arranged an advance screening of *Superstar* for members of the Jewish community in New York. Soon after, Ze'ev Birger, of the Israeli Film Center, wrote to Jewison in a nervous frenzy. Some "prominent" Americans, "deeply shocked" by what they'd seen, had approached members of the Israeli government to "express their fears of possible damage to Israel."[12]

Their specific concern, according to Birger, was one "thirty-second sequence"—probably the moment when Israeli tanks emerge from behind a hill to threaten Judas—which might prompt audiences to connect the film with "present-day Israel." Jewison later insisted that the tanks were meant to symbolize Judas's personal guilt over his betrayal of Christ's pacifism.[13] For Birger, a Holocaust survivor who had been reduced to a "typhus-ridden living skeleton" before the liberation of Dachau/ Kaufering, this was no mere debate about aesthetic autonomy.[14] Birger was convinced that Jewison's artistic choices could spill over into actual violence and death. He reminded Jewison of the mass shooting that had taken place at the Lod Airport near Tel Aviv the previous May, in which twenty-six people had been killed and another eighty injured.

Dear Norman, one <u>never never</u> knows what makes a young Japanese boy pull the trigger on innocent women and children at an airport terminal . . . This is now snowballing, getting out of control and nobody—nobody will be able to stop it.

People who called me from the States, mostly friends—told me that the film is so good—so excellent that it stands on its own with or without that sequence.

The burden of carrying such responsibility is too heavy for anyone and I took the liberty of writing you these few lines only out of my deep respect for you—your personality and friendship to Israel.

Before it will be released in N.Y. it's time to do it. After the demonstrations—that will be in N.Y. —it will be too late! My premonition is that you are able to prevent a catastrophe.[15]

Jewison deeply resented the implication that *Superstar* could lead to violence against Jews, but understood that his reputation and future film projects were in grievous danger if Birger's hysteria spread among the Israeli government. Universal Pictures released a statement denying the accusation, and the public relations people did what they could.

Jewison sat down at his typewriter and let loose a flurry of letters to Israeli officials and well-connected journalists in an effort to salvage the situation, emphasizing his personal disgust at the insinuations of anti-Semitism and portraying himself as the victim of a "secular" attack on the film. He also sent a reassuring message to General Bar-Lev, the Industry Minister, reiterating his desire to proceed with a new film in Israel about the military tactician Orde Wingate, and recognizing the political pressure he had inadvertently caused. "I apologize if this secular attack on the film has caused you any personal discomfort or embarrassment," Jewison wrote. "At the moment, my concern is only for my friends in Israel and any discomfort I may have brought to them."[16]

Such was the public uproar over *Superstar* that Jewison felt compelled to write directly to Prime Minister Golda Meir, the seventy-two-year-old "Iron Lady" of Israeli politics. He had been almost overwhelmed with emotion when, after the Jerusalem premier of *Fiddler*, Meir squeezed his hands in approval.[17] "Your words that night meant more to me than all the Oscars or critical praise the film ever received," Jewison wrote to Meir.

> As you are aware [*Fiddler*] reached millions of people in almost every country in the world and has engendered a deeper understanding and appreciation for Jewish history and culture. It pointed out in strong visual terms the persecution of the Jews during the Russian pogroms and brought the writing of Sholem Aleichem to a world audience.

He wanted Meir to know that his support for Israel was as strong as ever, and that the accusations against *Superstar* were bunk. He'd screened the film in locations around the world, including in Israel, and "Not one member of any audience has complained that *Superstar* is anti-Semitic or in any way detrimental to Israel or Jewish-Christian relations."

Finally, Jewison turned his attention to Ze'ev Birger, who had attempted to use the prospect of violence against Jews as a veto. "Your letter upset me very much," Jewison wrote.

> For me, as a creative filmmaker, I must stand behind what I have done in this film and, as in the past, I have no intention of cutting or changing my films because of hysterical and untrue charges from a fanatical group.
>
> Ze'ev, you must understand I could not live with myself if I gave in to these secular and absurd pressure groups. Please believe me, there is no unanimity in the controversy. We are playing in fifty American cities and there has not been one demonstration from the Jewish community. Therefore, I feel strongly that the responsibility for any demonstrations that may occur in New York

should be borne by the people who incited this absurd attack in the beginning.

These people . . . who can interpret this film as anti-Israel to fit in with their own political beliefs are obviously fanatics for whom I cannot remake my films. For you to suggest that *Superstar* carries a message of hate is both unacceptable to me and rather surprising, coming from you. For I believe the exact opposite to be true.

Ze'ev, your letter has taken on a note of hysteria and dramatic exaggeration that I cannot accept. I have deep respect for you and our friendship but I must tell you honestly that I resent the reference to the type of responsibility you now wish to put upon my shoulders.

In the end, Jewison's argument for creative autonomy and the purity of his intentions fell upon deaf ears. On July 13, the Israeli Foreign Ministry announced that its consular officials in New York and Los Angeles had been forbidden from attending openings of the film. An official statement from the Israeli government followed: "The fact that the film was shot on location in Israel in no way constitutes any agreement whatsoever to it on the part of the Government of Israel . . . The creators and producers of the film are alone and exclusively responsible for its contents."

The *New York Times* reported that the National Jewish Community Relations Advisory Council, an umbrella organization that included the 500,000-member B'nai B'rith, the American Jewish Congress, the National Council of Jewish Women, the Jewish War Veterans, and other organizations, denounced *Superstar* as "insidious" and accused Jewison personally of distorting Biblical history.[18] Three days later, Jewison received a response from the Israeli Prime Minister.[19]

Dear Mr. Jewison,

I have received your cable.

I am fully aware of your friendship for Israel which I value highly. I do not for a moment question your good intentions. However, I sincerely hope you will understand that I cannot pass judgment on the film which I have not seen. At the same time, I am sure that you certainly understand the sensitivity of the subject.

The reports that I have received from Jews in the United States, as well as some Israelis, are most distressing.

Sincerely yours,

Golda Meir

* * *

Jesus Christ Superstar elicited a polarized response from secular critics. For once, the hometown scribes admired a Norman Jewison film: "A powerful and fascinating experience," Clyde Gilmour wrote in the *Toronto Star*, "the best thing Jewison has ever done."

Roger Ebert declared that "Jewison, a director of large talent, has taken a piece of commercial shlock and turned it into a Biblical movie with dignity."[20]

Yet most reviews were negative, with many critics lashing out at what they considered a manifestation of decadent youth culture. Howard Thompson of the *New York Times* grumbled about the "deafening" music, the "mod-pop glitter," and the "bizarre garb, ranging from Ali Baba to platinum-blond transvestite."[21] Pauline Kael complained that the film treated Jesus as a "misunderstood kid" (which was in fact Jewison's intention).[22] Many of these critics registered its alleged anti-Semitism: even if they fell short of condemning the picture, critics treated *Superstar* as though it were distasteful.

Audiences were generally less concerned with *Superstar*'s supposed blasphemy or decadence. Countless fans wrote to express their gratitude; many had been profoundly moved. Industry colleagues were blown away by Jewison's technical achievement. "Your approach to *Superstar* is so breathtaking that I can only say that it takes filmmaking beyond an art so that it becomes an experience," wrote the Chairman of the Guild of British Film Editors.[23]

"I cannot remember ever seeing a film that emotionally exhilarated me, where I felt so spiritually uplifted," wrote Don Siegel, the veteran director of *Dirty Harry*. "I absolutely flipped out over the picture—and I am an atheist."[24]

Roger Moore advised Jewison to "Buy a big suitcase for next Oscar time."[25]

For every viewer who admired the film, however, there was another who loathed it. A self-identified Jew informed Jewison that his "main accomplishment was to stir up feelings of hatred that have taken thousands of years to subside."[26]

A self-identified Christian wrote to "Mr. Director" that she was "still trying to salvage my own self-dignity" after suffering through Jewison's "sick" and "objectionable" film, which "seems to depict Christ as a craze, a fad. Would you call a 2000-year-old belief caused by a lifetime of thirty-three years a FAD?"[27] Jewison replied: "Your faith must be very shallow indeed if it was shaken so completely by my film."[28]

While Pope Paul VI had supposedly given the film his blessing, one vigilant Italian priest had exorcized the opera house in Rome where the film had premiered.[29]

Patrick Palmer didn't mince words when reflecting on what the conflict had cost Jewison. "We live in a community where you don't fuck around with certain feathers, you really don't," he said. *Superstar* was "inadvertently a good example of fucking around with the Jewish Anti-Defamation League." Palmer believes that Jewison "listened to the wrong advice from the quote unquote 'People in the Jewish Community' at Universal who sold us down the fucking drain."

According to Palmer, Jewison—self-conscious of his status as a "goy"—had been overly receptive to advice from Jewish voices at the studio urging him to set up an advance screening for Jewish leaders in New York. "I remember sitting in the screening room," Palmer recalled, "Jewison was flying in from London; I got the chore of doing it, and you know . . . they hated it. I mean, I sat there, and it was the worst screening of my life. They saw everything in black and white." Any hope of bringing the ADL in line had been permanently dashed, and Jewison had gifted his opponents with precious lead-time to take control of the narrative in the press. As a result, the opening Jewison had envisioned, an extravagant outdoor happening in Central Park, was cancelled for fear of protests.

"We never opened the movie in New York," Palmer recalls. "We played behind in New York, which is suicide."

In his reply to the Anti-Defamation League, Jewison argued that *Superstar* unambiguously portrayed Jesus as having "made up his mind to die on the cross," and that the audience "knows that he is in complete control of his destiny."

It was to no avail, of course: members of the ADL had made up their own minds about *Superstar* long before seeing the film.

"We should have never ran the fucking picture for them in New York City," Palmer said.[30]

* * *

Like *Fiddler* before it, *Superstar* was a runaway commercial success. Thanks to his participation in the profits, it was also the most personally lucrative film of Jewison's career to date. The controversy over the film's anti-Semitism, however, combined with the fact that the Yom Kippur war had broken out in Israel, scuttled Jewison's plans for his film on Wingate.

He had been drawn to Kurt Vonnegut's *God Bless You, Mr. Rosewater*, which Margot Kidder sent him after *Gaily, Gaily* had wrapped.[31] He had also developed a friendship with Mordecai Richler, a fellow Canadian ex-pat in London, and was now seriously considering a film adaptation of Richler's *The Incomparable Atuk*, the story of an "Eskimo" poet who immigrates to (and is soon corrupted by) city life. He met with Dustin Hoffman about playing Atuk, but wondered if Alan Arkin wouldn't be better in the role.

Jewison burned through two screenwriters on *Atuk*, including Marshall Brickman, Woody Allen's cowriter on *Sleeper* and *Annie Hall*. Brickman's treatment, called "Lunch," followed a New York academic named Maurice who "discovers" Atuk in the Arctic, and boasts that he can turn the Eskimo into "a model of completely assimilated urbane sophistication" in six months. Much broad ethnic comedy ensues (Atuk in the art museum, the jazz bar, learning to drive), plus the requisite love plot. In the end, after getting stranded in the far North, where they travelled for a photo opportunity, Atuk eats Maurice (the eponymous "Lunch"). After three years of intermittent work on the project, Jewison wrote to Brickman: "The idea behind your treatment made sense, but somehow the whole project has lost some of its attraction for me. It seems so thin . . . I feel we are straining to flesh out a one-joke situation."[32]

Jewison continued searching for his next project, and Richler remained (as he bemoaned in a letter to Jewison) "the most optioned, least produced, famous lower Montreal Orthodox Jewish writer."[33]

CHAPTER 14

Blood on the Track

C HRISTMAS 1973 WAS HECTIC. The Jewisons had once again spent the holiday in Klosters, Switzerland, where Jewison had "skied off all my fat and a lot of hostility." That year, the family had been joined by a seemingly endless procession of teenagers visiting from Kevin and Michael's Swiss boarding school. Twenty-four people had crowded around the table for Christmas dinner, including the designer Tessa Kennedy and her husband, the film producer Elliot Kastner, along with their five children (one of whom was the budding actor Cary Elwes, who would star in *The Princess Bride*). Norman enjoyed the hubbub, although Dixie found it a bit much.[1]

After ringing in the new year, Jewison loaded up the Land Rover with luggage and Christmas presents, and undertook the return trip with his daughter Jenny. They'd always had a special bond. "Dad and I can look across the table at each other and know what each other's thinking," Jennifer said later. "I've always had that thing with Dad, I don't know what it is."[2] On the two-and-a-half-day drive through France, Jewison could not help but notice some "distressing" looks from fellow patrons of their hotels. Jenny was wearing her mother's fur coat, and the French ogled them "like a truck driver with his child bride."[3]

Back in London, the atmosphere dreary, Jewison found himself increasingly anxious about what would come next. For the first time in a decade, he found himself without an active film project. He and Patrick Palmer had been reading scripts "like mad," but so far inspiration had failed to strike.

After the spiritual turn of his last two pictures, Jewison was longing to re-engage the material world, especially with something about the rising power of corporations. His entire career had unfolded against the backdrop of corporate takeovers of the major film studios: in 1962, the year he started at Universal, that studio was acquired by MCA; Gulf+Western swallowed Paramount in 1966; Transamerica took over United Artists in 1967; Kinney National bought Warner Bros in 1969; the Vegas tycoon Kirk Kerkorian bought MGM the same year.

In almost every case, the purchasing party in these buyouts was motivated by the studios' depressed stock value and had virtually no experience in film production.[4] Creative decisions were now in the hands of lawyers and business executives, "money people," as Jewison and Hal Ashby called them, who lacked creativity and aesthetic ambition. Such takeovers were hardly limited to the film world. Around this time, Jewison read Richard Barnet and Robert Muller's bestselling *Global Reach: The Power of the Multinational Corporations*, which argued that the most basic functions of the nation state, "the power to raise revenues, maintain employment, provide adequate social services, [and] encourage the equitable allocation of income and wealth," were being undermined by corporations.[5]

Jewison was still combing through properties when his New York agent sent him a short story that had appeared in *Esquire* a few months before. "Roller Ball Murder," by William Harrison, was set in just the sort of post-national future predicted by *Global Reach*. The story focused on Jonathan E., a legend in the invented sport of rollerball who still yearned for knowledge and tradition. Jonathan, who comes from a time before "the corporate police forces supplanted the world's armies," remembers reading Rousseau and T. E. Lawrence, but literature and philosophy (along with war and famine) had been rendered obsolete by the new corporate order.

"Roller Ball Murder" didn't offer much by way of narrative. The story consists of brutal game sequences (quidditch with roller skates and motorbikes instead of brooms) interspersed with the existential musings of the disconsolate narrator. Still, Harrison's description of a world run by six mammoth corporations—ENERGY, TRANSPORT, FOOD, HOUSING, SERVICES, AND LUXURY—a world in which the anesthetized masses sing corporate hymns instead of national anthems and require more extreme forms of gladiatorial entertainment for cathartic release—dovetailed with Jewison's anxieties. While he wasn't a fully developed character, Jonathan E. allowed Jewison to return to the concept of superstardom from a different vantage.

Most important for getting the project green-lit, of course, was the bloody spectacle of rollerball itself. Jewison may have been interested in the critique of transnational corporations, but he knew that the ultraviolent game sequences were what would cause film executives to sit up and take notice.

Jewison set up a meeting with the United Artists board, then chaired by Arthur B. Krim. He remembers extemporizing a pitch based on Harrison's scenario, counting on his own boundless enthusiasm to sell the concept. "Somebody asked me, 'how do you play the game?' Well, I didn't know how to play the game. I just read this short story in the magazine, so I started to spin and make it up as I went along."[6] He pointed to the recent box office success of *A Clockwork Orange* (another violent film set in the future) to bolster his case. When the board decided to commit enough money to develop a screenplay, Jewison pushed back: "I just don't want to develop another screenplay and have you say, 'Well, I don't know whether I like that or not.' I want you to commit. I need some security here."

On March 14, 1974, United Artists announced that Jewison would produce and direct *Rollerball*. He had $4,674,935 to work with.[7] All he had to do now was turn a 5,000-word "experimental mood piece" (as William Harrison later characterized his story) into a two-hour blockbuster while creating a whole new sport and making sure nobody got killed.

* * *

Compared to the rights to some of his recent properties—$600,000 for *Nat Turner*, $2,000,000 for *Fiddler*—"Roller Ball Murder" was almost comically cheap. United Artists paid Harrison $10,000 for the rights to the *Esquire* story. When Harrison asked for a chance to write the screenplay, Jewison offered him $10,000 more.[8] A creative writing professor at the University of Arkansas at Fayetteville, Harrison joined Jewison in England while on sabbatical. "I started going to [Jewison's] office at Pinewood every day or so," he remembered. They began fleshing out the story's meagre narrative. Both agreed that it needed a central conflict. "I suggested that Jonathan E., the main character, should be given an ultimatum by the executives who ran the game. They would try and force him out of the sport. So this became the new conflict . . . It was probably a gigantic mistake," Harrison reflected, "but everyone seemed happy."[9]

In truth, United Artists was less than enthusiastic about the state of the screenplay. Dan Rissner, head of European production for United Artists, shared several concerns: "Script is over-written and dialogue needs work. I'm sure Jewison is aware of this as script is only a FIRST DRAFT. WE

<u>NEED MORE INFORMATION ABOUT THE TOTAL SOCIETY,</u> <u>RATHER THAN THE SOCIETY AS IT EFFECTS THE ROLLER</u> <u>BALL SITUATION</u>. We need to find out how the 'corporation' effects the total structure of the world-at-large."[10] It was a valid objection: the script provided virtually no indication of how the corporations controlled the lives of their citizens. Jewison, partly out of fear of a ballooning budget, wanted to keep the focus squarely on the game. He would rely upon cinematographer Douglas Slocombe, and a few shots of the new BMW headquarters in Munich, to give the film a futuristic feel.

* * *

Jewison's first choice for the role of Jonathan E. had been Clint Eastwood— an actor who had, in the *A Fistful of Dollars* trilogy and *Dirty Harry* films, become closely associated with the hyper-violent entertainments that Jewison set out to satirize in *Rollerball*. Jewison's meeting with Clint lasted all of ten minutes: Eastwood dispensed with the pleasantries and said he'd participate only if he owned the property. Jewison thanked him for his time and left.

"Clint was at Malapaso," his production company, Palmer explains, "and they consumed [properties] like we did. If something came in you considered it and pushed everybody else off of it."[11]

"I would have liked to have worked with him," Eastwood later said of Jewison, "but it just didn't happen."[12]

Jewison's next choice for Jonathan E. was James Caan, who took the role for $375,000 plus five per cent of the gross after breakeven.[13] Best known for his Academy Award-nominated turn as Sonny Corleone in *The Godfather*, Caan specialized in tortured athletes in films like *The Rain People*, where he played a brain-damaged football player, and *Brian's Song*, where he played a Chicago Bears running back with terminal cancer. Jewison had been "knocked out" by Caan's performance in the latter film, particularly by Caan's seemingly monomaniacal obsession with winning.

Caan was ultra-competitive by nature, and some of the testiest moments between *Rollerball*'s director and star came when Jewison tried to rein him in. "I was always afraid he was going to get hurt," Jewison said. "I kept telling him that one accident would finish us . . . It was difficult, because Jimmy was very athletic and he loved playing the game."[14] Caan insisted that he had to do the game sequences because his stuntman didn't look like him. "You could tell every time it was him," Caan said. "He had these long, geeky arms—so I wound up doing most of the stuff myself. I enjoyed that more than any of the other stuff."[15]

Caan's public image was that of an irresistible brute whose sexism made him even more attractive to women. On the Pinewood set, Caan would initiate crude banter with his female co-stars for the amusement of the crew. Between takes with Pamela Hensley, a love interest dressed in a diaphanous dress, Caan told the actress: "Stand in the light. The boys in the crew will love it." When she ignored him, he bellowed, from three feet away, "Pamela! I love your crotch."

Far from being considered problematic, Caan's treatment of women was sold as part of his appeal. As a 1975 *Cosmopolitan* profile of the actor noted:

No woman seems safe with Jimmy Caan. He's always testing, testing. When he isn't actually swinging his caveman's club, he is in there probing with his tongue. "How was your weekend, sweetheart?" he'll ask a waitress, giving her an exaggerated leer. "Not so terrific? That's too bad. Listen you should have spent it with me." The poor little waitress blushes magenta and almost drops a plate. She can't think of a thing to say. Jimmy keeps staring at her until she retreats to the kitchen. He turns to me and shrugs. "What can I tell you? I bequeath her to you."[16]

Jewison played the "boys in the locker-room" routine with Caan, swapping stories and crude jokes. He once ended a letter to Caan advising him to "take care of your thumb [and] your cock."[17] Much of Jewison's success as a director, of course, hinged on his ability to modulate his performance according to the needs of his performers. In a short letter enticing Orson Welles to play the role of a top corporate executive in *Rollerball*, Jewison ditched the ribaldry and assumed an air of gravitas and formality befitting the director of *Citizen Kane*.

Dear Orson,

My fellow director, Peter Bogdanovich, has very kindly arranged to try and get this script to you.

Since I believe the corporations today control the resources of our society, the direction, the production, the jobs, and the nature of work, this script has, I believe, an important statement to make . . .

There is no other actor I can think of who could play the role of Bartholomew with greater impact than yourself. I believe you would bring to this part a depth of understanding that would result in a great film performance.[18]

In the end, the role of Bartholomew went to John Houseman, Welles's collaborator at the Mercury Theatre. Houseman, who took the Best Supporting Actor Oscar in 1974 for his role in *The Paper Chase*, received $50,000 for six weeks on the picture.[19] Jewison considered Houseman a consummate embodiment of "the ultimate evil of the corporate society," though, as William Harrison recollected, Houseman "couldn't remember any of his lines—ever." Jewison had the actor dub his own lines over the edited version."[20]

Sir Ralph Richardson added some flair to the cast as the bumbling "Librarian" who tends to Zero, the failing supercomputer and "world's file cabinet." The whimsical actor was the perfect human counterpart to the absent-minded supercomputer: where Kubrick's HAL 9000 was a vision of murderous efficiency, Jewison's Zero, the sole repository of all human knowledge and culture, at one point manages to misplace the entire thirteenth century. "Not much in the century," Richardson's character consoles himself, "just Dante and a few corrupt Popes."

With the principal leads in place, all Jewison needed was perhaps two dozen of the best stuntmen in the business. That April, he received a letter of inquiry from one Boris Spyztych.

Dear Sirs:

You are I understanding shooting movie w/ motorsickles & roller skaters. I apply now for Stuntman Extraordinaire, for I was Rumanian champion, 1958-59 & got no broken bones now. I do barehead crash into Brickwall, you provide the motorsickle. Also Evil Kneeval-type flips, I got my own pads & my brother (you get him for extra $15 cash) is doctor . . . Also willing catch nose, cheek, earlobs or nether parts in sickle chain for extra Overtime pay! Brother asks, pleeze, he can work also in Female Skater's dressing & makeup Travel Trailer?

Flying thru air for you, I am,

Boris Spyztych
"The Flying Fool"

Needless to say, "Mr. Spyztych" was not given the opportunity to mangle his earlobes or nether parts in *Rollerball,* and probably existed only in William Harrison's imagination. Thankfully, there was no shortage of real-life "flying fools" to satisfy Jewison's needs.

* * *

The noise inside the Munich stadium was almost unbearable.

Jewison and his production team were on location in an Olympic stadium in West Germany, where they would shoot the film's game sequences over several weeks; they would return to Pinewood to shoot the "walk and talk" scenes after that. A thundering herd of fourteen men were now roller skating around the inclined hardwood track of the converted basketball stadium. Six motorbikes, echoing in the closed stadium, added to the ungodly din. Jewison bellowed his instructions through a bullhorn. "You couldn't get away from the sound," Patrick Palmer remembers. "As soon as you walked in, in the morning, the skaters would be there, the bikes would be there . . . it was just like combat in a way."[21]

Working first with paper mock-ups, then with stuntmen on the track itself, Jewison and his designers had devised a playable sport around the mayhem described in Harrison's story. Two teams, seven skaters, plus three bikers per side, moved counter-clockwise around the 557-foot track, trying to throw the ball into a magnetic goal. To start the action, a cannon fired a steel ball around the track at randomized pressures; Jewison said he got the idea from playing roulette in Vegas. Full body contact was permitted, including the in-game beating and murder of opponents. In Harrison's story, one player's "brains" are stomped out on the track.[22]

It was one thing to imagine this perilous game, and quite another to see it played in the flesh. Jewison was constantly on edge that someone would be severely injured or even killed. The mainstream use of digital special effects was still decades away: each of the film's dozens of stunts—actors leaping from motorcycles, smashing through fences, and pummeling one another on roller skates at high speeds—would have to be physically executed. Jewison had hired an elite team of American, British, and German stuntmen, but injuries were inevitable.

On one day of filming in late July, one skater suffered a concussion and another was hospitalized with a pulled ligament. More concussions followed in the days ahead. Another stuntman broke his ankle after smashing his motorcycle into a wall. Patrick Palmer remembers "a couple of broken legs." Toward the end of their shoot in Munich, filming was delayed due to a gas leak from fire effects.[23]

"The insurance companies made an absolute fortune out of us," Jewison said in 1975. "There were doctors on the set the whole time . . . but if a man falls off a motorbike when it's going at forty miles an hour he's obviously going to get hurt."[24]

The commercialization of violence, the increasing desire for blood and mayhem in professional sports and popular culture in the 1970s, was one impetus behind the film. "There was a lot of Evel Knievel stuff on television. Stunts in which stuntmen got burned and hurt and all this for the ratings," William Harrison remembers.[25] Bench-clearing brawls were becoming routine in hockey; riots were breaking out at soccer matches. While Jewison saw something fundamentally decadent about violence as entertainment, as though televised sport was ushering in the return of the Circus Maximus from Ancient Rome, he was also presiding over a Hollywood spectacle in which his own performers were snapping bones and suffering concussions.

"He hated shooting the violence, you know," Palmer remembers. "He really did and he had to shoot it."

Jewison eventually dreaded coming to work each morning and wanted Max Kleven, the second unit director and stunt coordinator, to finish filming the game sequences. But Palmer insisted that Jewison direct the violent scenes "because I knew he would make them interesting . . . there would be humanity within the framework of the violence, so that the violence wouldn't just be shots."[26] Jewison soldiered on, but Palmer knew he was suffering.

* * *

Looking back, Caan almost couldn't believe what they went through on *Rollerball*. "Oh, God—it was just . . . I mean we had quite a few accidents . . . We were doing something like close to forty mph behind those bikes," he says. "We actually tried to play the game which lasted about three minutes and these fucking monstrous fights we got into, you know."[27]

Jewison approached the dramatic scenes surrounding the carnage with a deliberately cerebral aesthetic. He characterized the style as "more European than American. I think I moved the camera a little slower. I took my time. Editorially, I wasn't trying to please an audience." The Bach, Shostakovich, and Albinoni on the soundtrack further signaled his high-art ambitions (as well as the influence of Stanley Kubrick). Jewison wanted "a little more depth and grace" than the standard genre fare, more *2001* than *Planet of the Apes*.

Jewison expected things to get easier after they finished the game sequences, but it didn't turn out that way. The holes in the screenplay, which seemed manageable enough when Jewison and Harrison had been swapping ideas at Pinewood the previous spring, suddenly were vast chasms. The corporate leaders were forcing Jonathan to retire from the game to demonstrate the futility of individual action. But what did that have to do with Jonathan's ill-defined quest for knowledge? Jewison worried that he was into a film that didn't make any narrative sense, filled with inert dramatic scenes that didn't amount to anything. One day, confronted with a particularly nebulous scene, Jewison hit a wall. "I can't shoot this scene," he told Palmer. "It doesn't work."

"You know, you're right," answered Palmer.[28] Jewison halted production until he got the remaining scenes into filmable shape.

Caan knew Jewison struggled with the screenplay, and wondered if the film was too blunt with its allegorical message. "You know, you don't want to hit [the audience] over the fucking head too many times, and say this is a corporate world, there's no room for individualism," Caan said. "You go one step too far and they get insulted and they feel their intelligence is underestimated and they become upset with you. And I think that was a major problem for Norman, and I'm still not quite sure whether we did right or wrong."[29]

Rollerball may have been an instance of Jewison getting carried away with his own enthusiasm: he seems to have convinced everyone, including himself, that the film was ready for production. It wasn't.

Rollerball "was not a good experience," says Palmer. In fact, of the eighteen films on which he and Jewison collaborated, if he could "pull one back," it would be *Rollerball*.[30]

* * *

That April, Jewison received a courteous letter from Richard Hefner, chair of the MPAA's Classification and Rating Administration (CARA), explaining that *Rollerball* would be rated "X." That rating, barring those under seventeen and normally reserved for pornographic or extraordinarily violent films, spelled financial disaster for *Rollerball*. It wasn't that *Rollerball* was puerile or exploitative. In fact, Hefner called it a "masterpiece." Yet he believed that Jewison's film was dark and gruesome enough to have a detrimental effect on "not-yet-mature minds."[31]

From the moment Jewison had done his dance for UA, he'd had no illusions about the importance of the film's violence to its commercial appeal. To fight off CARA's X rating, however, Jewison adopted a sanctimonious tone. "I abhor the increasing violence in our society and find the fascination of television and the press with people like Evel Knievel absolutely obscene," he wrote to Hefner. "Violence in professional sport is being merchandised today for the public by three major networks at an alarming pace. Let's hope *Rollerball* in some ways can show them where it may end."[32]

CARA eventually settled on R rather than X. Jewison then tried, and failed, to get it down to a PG. Yet even as he was arguing that *Rollerball*'s violence was intended to repulse viewers, the film's marketing team was devising an advertising strategy built around its mayhem.[33] United Artists bought advertising space during major sporting events for TV spots showcasing the film's carnage. James Caan appeared on ABC's Wide World of Sports and delivered colourful commentary on various clips from the game, introducing Americans to the new "sport." In addition to the usual soundtrack album and book tie-ins, ancillary merchandizing included *Rollerball*-themed skates, an Adidas sponsorship, partnerships with Honda and BMW, T-shirts, badges, handbills, and a charity game.[34] It also inadvertently spawned *Rollerbabies*, a pornographic film about a corporate future in which sex is limited to a select few, who must fuck on roller skates.

So successful was the film's marketing that a US consortium offered one million dollars to purchase the worldwide licence to the game of rollerball, intent upon turning Jewison's nightmarish parody of the future of professional sports into a reality. Jewison was not surprised—indeed, he took it as evidence of his own prescience—and refused the offer. He also had to quash rumours that he was working on a sequel ("I think one film on the subject is quite enough," he wrote to an inquiring actor).[35]

Rollerball was another major success at the box office, taking in $30 million. Reviews, however, were largely negative, with some critics picking up a scent of hypocrisy. "It works best as the thing it is in effect condemning, exciting blood sport," wrote Joseph Gelmis in *Newsday*.[36]

Another critic called *Rollerball* an "eating-its-cake-and-having-it film using a stereotyped character to attack conformity and strong-arm tactics to deplore violence."

Worse, the raucous film audiences "were identifying with neither teams nor players but rather with the film's mindless masses, cheering and clapping every kill."[37]

Jewison was disconcerted that so much of the viewing audience did not see the film he'd intended to make. Like *Jesus Christ Superstar* before it, *Rollerball* seemed to Jewison to reveal how little control the director had over his work's reception. "It's interesting how Europeans seem to realize the significance of the film whereas most of the American press treated the film as some sort of rip-off, pretentious statement," he vented to collaborator Ed Apfel. "By the time they had finished with me I felt like Stanley Kramer," whose name had become synonymous with liberal message pictures.

"Well," Jewison said, "fuck 'em . . . I'm not going to apologize for wanting to change the world. I will just keep making my films and hope that somewhere . . . somehow . . . they find an audience."[38]

As the dismissive reviews kept piling up, Jewison felt a particular responsibility to William Harrison. "It is difficult for both of us to have received such bad critical appraisal on *Rollerball*, from almost every side," he wrote.

> Looking back on it, I guess I spent too much time and effort on the game sequences and not enough on the dramatic content. However, I am still firmly convinced that the message and idea behind *Rollerball* is valid, thought provoking, and—even revolutionary in essence . . . Looking back on it, maybe [the UA advertising campaign] pushed too hard and, as a result, we became the victim of a psychological backlash. In the last analysis, I will always be personally proud of the effort and of my close association with you.[39]

CHAPTER 15

The Little Guy

J EWISON HAD SPENT MUCH OF HIS ADULT LIFE yearning
to be elsewhere. By 1974, just a few years after leaving LA
for the UK, he was fantasizing about living on "one of those
marvelous, well-established, gentleman farms somewhere within an
hour of Toronto," he wrote family friends in Ontario. "You know—just
a simple little thing with a pool, tennis court, old established trees, etc.
You never can tell—maybe you will find something."[1] By the following
October, they had found something: thirty acres for sale near Caledon,
north-west of Toronto. "Why is he selling it?" Jewison wanted to know.
"Are there any other well-established farms in the area? As you know, we
both prefer older houses and well-established places."[2] Jewison didn't buy
that property, but the search was on.

According to most observers, life in the UK had suited Jewison. And
yet, perhaps owing to a temperamental restlessness and supercharged
ambition, he had trouble settling down. By the mid-1970s, after a
nomadic couple of decades, approaching fifty years of age, Jewison was
thinking more deliberately about where he belonged. If Stanley Kubrick

had provided a model for absconding to the UK, his friend Mordecai Richler provided the model for going home. For his part, Richler had worried about his creative work being "thinned by too long an absence from roots."[3] Jewison conceded that "it sounds rather sentimental, but that was part of the reason." He wanted to re-connect with his own roots and "see if I was more comfortable living there."

With the image of his grandfather, the farmer Joseph Jewison, in the back of his mind, Jewison associated the idea of belonging with a farm of his own. Moreover, on recent trips back he'd noted an "excitement about [Toronto] and the country that wasn't there twenty years before, and I wanted to be a part of it."[4]

There were more pragmatic reasons to leave the UK. In 1974, the new Labour government increased his income tax bracket to 83 per cent.[5] According to Larry Auerbach, Jewison's William Morris agent, it would have been financially "disastrous" for him to stay. "So, it wasn't like he decided to make peace with the United States?" an interviewer inquired. "Oh, no, no, no, no, no, no," Auerbach said.[6]

By now, the Jewison children were mostly grown up. Kevin was at home in London preparing for university; Jennifer had recently joined Michael at Aiglon College in Villars, Switzerland, one of the most exclusive boarding schools in the world.[7] Norman and Dixie would soon have an empty nest.

They eventually settled on a ninety-eight-acre plot in Caledon East, forty-five minutes north of the city. Dixie felt apprehensive about moving to rural Ontario after almost two decades in New York, Los Angeles, and London; she worried that her husband was chasing a fantasy. But he had seized upon the idea, and Dixie agreed on the condition that the farm was "no further than twenty-five minutes from the airport."[8] Even Norman's desire to put down roots was marked with a certain ambivalence. Around the same time, he bought an apartment in Toronto and a beach-front home in Malibu. The plan was to shoot his films based out of Malibu in the winters, and spend the warmer months of each year in Caledon.

Before returning from the UK, however, Norman had some bridges to repair. As Larry Auerbach recalled, Jewison "was not very popular" among industry types when he left for Europe.

"I don't know how much was his ability to be brash and outspoken, I don't know how much was running off to England and making speeches about this country," said Auerbach. Jewison was known for "mouthing off" about America while "making his money here," which didn't sit well in some quarters. "There was definitely an undercurrent" of resentment, he remembered.[9]

Jewison's tendency to ruffle feathers was no secret from friends in those years. Marilyn Bergman remembers that Jewison always spoke of himself as a "dissident," and kept "reminding people at critical points that he is not a part of the system."[10] Henry Mancini vividly recalled dinner parties where Jewison would get carried away in an argument. "He doesn't hold back as far as stating his view," Mancini said, "even though it is a friendly gathering, and sometimes it gets—you know, the knife comes out."[11] By the time Jewison was thinking about returning to North America in the mid-1970s, he wanted to sand some of the rough edges off his reputation. "I know it's something that bothered him," Auerbach said, "and I think he made a lot of amends."[12]

* * *

Around this time, Auerbach approached him with an intriguing idea. *F.I.S.T.* (the acronym stood for Federation of Interstate Truckers) was a sweeping fable of the rise and eventual corruption of Johnny Kovak, a Jimmy Hoffa-like union leader. It came in the form of a massive treatment by first-time screenwriter Joe Eszterhas, and it was unlike anything Jewison had seen. It wasn't non-fiction, it wasn't fiction, and it certainly wasn't an outline, but the subject matter was appealing. For years, Jewison had been interested in making a film about the American labour movement. Here was an opportunity for his *On the Waterfront*. Eszterhas's well-researched (if unconventional) treatment struck Jewison as the basis for an epic film on a rarely told story.

The project had taken an unusual path. Eszterhas had been working at *Rolling Stone* in San Francisco, where he began fleshing out one of his magazine pieces into a book. *Charlie Simpson's Apocalypse* was nominated for a 1974 National Book Award (others in the same category included Studs Terkel's *Working*, Robert Caro's *The Power Broker*, and Bernstein and Woodward's *All the President's Men*), and caught the attention of United Artists production vice president Marcia Nasatir, who found the writing cinematic and asked Eszterhas if he'd try his hand at an original film idea.

Eszterhas was a self-fashioned literary dude, more interested in writing the great American novel than in becoming a Hollywood sellout, but he shared an idea with Nasatir that came out of his childhood *milieu*. "I had grown up in Cleveland, around working-class people," said Eszterhas, whose family fled from Hungary to America when he was six. "A lot of the guys who lived in my neighbourhood had been through the labour wars and labour action in the '30s and '40s. And I'd heard these stories as I was growing up. So I thought I'd do a piece about that: about these old labour guys and the wars they'd had against the companies." Nasatir found the idea promising, and Eszterhas spent six months driving around the mid-West, interviewing former labour activists in Detroit, Pittsburgh, and elsewhere.

Eszterhas knew nothing about screenplays or film treatments. "I was so ignorant about screenwriting," he said, "I didn't even know that one page of script was one minute of screen time." Yet the research summary he produced was promising enough that Nasatir decided to bring a director on board, and Jewison's was the first name on the list. As Eszterhas recalls, a rival studio had been courting Jewison to do a film adaptation of E. L. Doctorow's *Ragtime*, but nothing had been confirmed. After reading his "bastard mutant treatment," Jewison agreed to a meeting in LA.

Eszterhas took an immediate liking to Jewison. "He had a great twinkle in his eye," Eszterhas said, yet "there was an orneriness about him, a feistiness. He viewed himself as a combatant against the studios."[13]

"I think he was amused by me," Eszterhas went on, "because I had come from *Rolling Stone*, my hair was real long and I had torn jeans, and I had this holier-than-thou feeling about corruption in the movie business. I think he sensed that attitude."

For the next few days, Jewison and Eszterhas continued their conversation about US labour history and how the movement had become entwined with the mob. Drawing on his childhood recollections and research, Eszterhas's approach differentiated the roles of particular ethnic groups (Hungarians, Lithuanians, and Italians) in the labour strife. "The company always had an army of guards and goons that went after people in any kind of strike situation," Eszterhas explains. "So these people, most of whom were ethnic people, turned to their own neighbourhood tough guys, who were mob-connected. And the mob gradually infiltrated the unions and became very powerful."[14] Before parting, Jewison asked Eszterhas if he wanted to take a crack at the screenplay, and he agreed.

* * *

If the script for *Rollerball* had been too thin, Joe Eszterhas's first-draft screenplay for *F.I.S.T.* had the opposite problem. He delivered a 360-page experimental mélange of fiction and non-fiction, long enough to sustain a 6.5-hour film. "This weighs like *War and Peace*," Jewison said. "It doesn't *read* like it, but it weighs like it." Much of the material, including a fourteen-page-long monologue, would have to go.

"I was so ignorant, and so ornery," recalled Eszterhas, "I said, 'yeah, but if the words are good, so what. That's what matters.'"

"You don't get it," Jewison replied. "They're going to throw fucking tomatoes at the screen."

"And I argued with him, like a complete asshole," says Eszterhas.

Jewison proposed that the two of them sit down and work through Eszterhas's monstrosity page-by-page, scene-by-scene. It would become almost a year-long collaboration, with Eszterhas spending stretches of time with Jewison in Toronto and living in the director's newly purchased beachfront home in Malibu. "I quickly realized, and I certainly understand now, that this was one of the most generous people I'd ever met," says Eszterhas. "But I still argued with him over nonsensical fucking reasons that I don't really understand at this point, which he tolerated and overlooked."

Jewison won all the arguments, even if it took some ingenuity to do so. Eszterhas had been given his own room in the director's Malibu home, where he had been made to "feel like a member of the family." Joe and Norman began each day walking down to the beach, where they would turn over problems in the script, particularly the ending, over which they strongly disagreed. At one point in the writing process, their differences had grown so severe that, despite living under the same roof, they hadn't spoken for a couple of days. One evening, after Norman and Dixie had gone out for dinner, Joe emerged from his room and "noticed that on the table was an envelope for Norman marked PERSONAL AND CONFIDENTIAL."

"It was just lying there," Eszterhas recalls. "And I was looking at it, feeling more and more curious. I saw the 'personal and confidential,' but ultimately that didn't stop me. So I opened the fucking envelope and read what was there. And what was there was a statement from his accountant on the vast amount of money that he had made the year before."

"So the next morning we go to work down on the beach, and are sort of at war with each other. And he suddenly looks at me and says, 'You read it, didn't you.' And I said, 'I'm sorry?' And he said, 'you read the fucking thing. Didn't you?' And I said, 'read what?' And he said, '*you know what.*' And I sort of looked at him and sort of semi-admitted it. I didn't know what to say. And he said, 'Now you listen to me. If you listen to the shit that I'm suggesting to you, and if you learn, it's just possible that one day you'll get an envelope like that from *your* accountant too.'"

Jewison had planted the 'confidential' letter, and the point had been made. There was no further protest from the rookie screenwriter.

* * *

Arthur B. Krim, head of United Artists, initially wanted nothing to do with *F.I.S.T.* It was a period piece, it was expensive, and (as far as Krim was concerned) nobody cared about the history of the American labour movement. Jewison was able to change his mind, but Krim insisted upon one condition: Johnny Kovak, the union organizer and protagonist, would be played by Sylvester Stallone. Krim may have associated Stallone with the property even if it wasn't called *F.I.S.T.*, but the title probably helped. Marcia Nasatir, the production vice president responsible for initiating *F.I.S.T.*, had also developed *Rocky* for UA, and Krim was itching to line up Stallone's next vehicle.

Jewison remembers being completely "carried away" by *Rocky*, which he saw prior to its release. "I thought he gave a brilliant, sensitive performance," he said of Stallone, "and I thought he had the kind of passion that Johnny Kovak needed."[15] He sent the actor the latest draft of *F.I.S.T.* Within about twenty-four hours, Stallone had committed to the project. The eventual loan-out agreement with Moonblood Productions (Stallone's company) guaranteed the actor $21,875 per week of work, plus 7.5 per cent of net profits.[16]

"Originally, when I met Sly, I loved him," remembers Patrick Palmer. "I mean, I really got quite caught up in the whole *Rocky* thing, against the system and all."

As the magnitude of *Rocky*'s cultural impact became clear, it seemed that everyone in Hollywood was getting caught up in the Stallone phenomenon, no one more so than Stallone himself. The actor was in a volatile place by the time he began working on *F.I.S.T.* For years, he had toiled in the margins of the industry, with few prospects for success. He did a soft-core porn film for $200 ("It was either that or rob somebody," he said). In 1972, he auditioned to be an extra in *The Godfather* and was rejected. Five years later, he had conceived, written, and starred in *Rocky*, which became the highest earning film of the year. It beat *Taxi Driver*, *Network*, *All the President's Men*, and Hal Ashby's *Bound for Glory* for the Academy Award for Best Picture.

Stallone attributed much of his sudden ascent to Jane Oliver, his beloved personal manager. "She basically found me when I was a struggling actor and nobody believed in me," he said.[17] Oliver died of cancer at the age of forty-six, before *Rocky* was released. Stallone was devastated. Those who knew him believed he had lost an important stabilizing influence in his life.

"Within two weeks" of *Rocky*'s release, Jewison remembers, "Sly's whole world had changed. He came to me and said, 'Some crazy guy is offering me a million dollars to do a picture.' I offered to let him off the hook, but he still wanted to do *F.I.S.T.*"[18] They had made the deal on a handshake, and Jewison respected Stallone for honouring an agreement that now reflected less than half of his market value.

About a month before *F.I.S.T.* went into production, however, Stallone informed Jewison and Palmer that he was interested in touching up a few of his scenes. Jewison was uncomfortable with the idea, but now felt beholden to Stallone. According to Palmer, Stallone "really got caught up in his own personification" as Rocky and was now "rewriting" the character of Kovak to fit that image. His heroic vision of Kovac was hard to reconcile with the part as written by Joe Eszterhas and Jewison, who had already undertaken a long and arduous process of revision to arrive at the shooting script. Stallone pressed on with his own draft, and now wanted a cowriting credit.

Jewison initially tried to keep news of Stallone's rewrites from reaching Eszterhas. When the writer eventually found out, he was apoplectic. *F.I.S.T.* was *his* story; he'd grown up with those guys in Cleveland. He'd done the research. He'd written the 500-page screenplay and spent a year of his life revising it with Norman. Now Stallone had minced into the ring with his vain, self-aggrandizing rewrites, demanding cowriter status.

Jewison suddenly found himself in perilous circumstances, mediating between an unstable star and a volcanic writer. He felt a deep responsibility to Eszterhas, whom he liked personally (he would later describe himself as Joe's "mentor") and who had hatched the entire project. But Krim had been unequivocal: *F.I.S.T.* doesn't exist without Stallone.

As always, Jewison did what he believed was necessary for the film. Stallone got his writing credit, along with $150,000 and 2.5 per cent of the net profits for his writing services.[19] The fee alone was more than double what Eszterhas would make from the project. A provision in the agreement guaranteed Stallone writing payment if the film was "substantially" based on his revised screenplay "or" if he completed his acting services. Clearly, the actor—and now the cowriter—had the Juice.

* * *

Jewison's production team based their operation in an office complex at 11ᵗʰ and Jackson Streets in Dubuque, where they worked through daily logistics of shooting a film set in the 1930s. Every barber in the city, it seemed, was busy cutting the hair of almost 1,000 extras into Depression-era style. Prior to filming in residential neighbourhoods, a crew member went door-to-door offering home-owners twenty-five dollars to move their cars off the street. An unexpected problem arose when Dubuque, swamped with people working on the film, began running low on toilet paper. Jewison dispatched a location manager to solve the tissue issue.[20]

Stallone spent much of his time sequestered in a guarded room at the Hotel Julien, once supposedly owned by Al Capone, in the city's Old Main district. He painted and piddled away on the scripts for a *Rocky* sequel and his next film, *Paradise Alley*, which he would also direct. Legions of fans had staked out the hotel, mauling the actor every time he tried to walk from the elevator to a waiting car. To reporters, the frenzy seemed like something out of *A Hard Day's Night*.

Stallone's freedom of movement became so limited that local reporters began to joke that he was being held prisoner in his hotel room. Most days, however, the actor walked over to greet a line of waiting fans, shaking hands and kissing some of the women. He refused autographs, telling fans they'd only lose it anyway, but "a handshake lasts forever." Occasionally, he went out for a drink with his driver and bodyguard.

Inevitably, some young buck, fortified with liquid courage, would loudly proclaim his intention to kick Rocky's ass.

"A lot of people want to take a poke at me," Stallone observed, "even those who don't come out and actually do it. I can feel it. They suck in their stomachs and become very protective of their girl."[21] Still, Stallone partook of the Dubuque night life at such hot spots as the Holiday Inn lounge. He flirted with women selling jewelry in the lobby and joked around with the band. At the end of the evening, he tipped his waitress twenty-five cents.[22]

Jewison knew that Stallone wasn't coping well with his sudden celebrity. "Every time I go out, I think about putting a paper towel with eye-holes cut in it over my face," Stallone said around this time. "But it wouldn't do any good anyhow. They'd still recognize me. The only way I could walk around unnoticed would be by putting an ash can over my head."

When a journalist speculated that the actor had undergone a psychological "metamorphosis" since *Rocky*, Stallone objected. "Money hasn't changed me, that's for sure," he said. "My wife, Sasha, is the same way. Her entire wardrobe costs $3.98." (They separated shortly thereafter.)

"What I'd really like to do with my money is buy land, a rocket ship— maybe even a pyramid," Stallone said. "I don't want to waste it buying things like a pair of Gucci loafers."[23]

* * *

Jewison's own relationship with the star was growing increasingly tense. The director had tried to emphasize that the character of Johnny Kovak was "a long way from the character of Rocky."

"I mean he's intelligent, he's confident," Jewison said, "he's a man of depth and passion, and he suffers."[24]

Initially, Stallone seemed to agree. He took the role, he said, as an "acting lesson."

"I knew that I was going to do a sequel to *Rocky*, but I had to do something first to flesh out other sides of my personality. I knew if I'd done a couple more street movies, that was it for me," said Stallone. "I was locked into that mode of acting forever."[25]

As the shooting continued, however, the lines separating Rocky, Stallone, and Kovak began to blur. "The Kovak character and I were beginning to overlap," Stallone said. He felt himself absorbing the "abrasive" habits of his character. "I was going home a depressed labour leader. My voice was down. I was getting rough, overweight, angry, and no one liked me around the house. Even the dog sensed the difference."[26] Verified an unnamed actor who worked with Stallone on *Rocky*: "He's become such a bastard that even his dog, Butkus, turned on him and bit him."[27]

Stallone had become convinced that the audience would reject his character in *F.I.S.T.* as too unlikable. From Jewison's perspective, the gradual corruption of Kovak was the narrative crux of the film. Over the course of thirty years, Kovak's rise to power within the labour movement is shadowed by mafia connections who inevitably call in their debts. On the final page of Eszterhas's script, Kovak was gunned down at home after a Senate investigation (led by Rod Steiger in the film) threatens to expose the extent of his mob ties. Stallone didn't like the fact that his character transformed from an idealist into a "vengeful, sadistic hate-monger."[28] At stake was something larger than Johnny Kovak, or the fate of the movie: it was about the image of Sly Stallone, now the most valuable commodity in motion pictures, a resource that could not be tarnished by Jewison's artistic pretensions.

The ending was a particular point of contention. Stallone's version would close on a moment of triumph, with Kovak pumping his fists like a boxing champion outside the senate hearing, rather than with the character being shot to death. "I begged Norman to change the ending," Stallone said. On the day they were to shoot the death scene, Stallone found that a health problem would prevent him from acting. Eventually, Jewison persuaded him to do a single take, promising that he would also shoot Stallone's version. The actor made sure Jewison understood that he would not promote the film if his ending wasn't used.[29]

Jewison, meanwhile, was busy triangulating his writer and star. He told Stallone that Eszterhas didn't want to meet him. He told Eszterhas to stay away from the set because his presence would enrage Stallone. Each of *F.I.S.T.*'s writers now publicly blamed the other for failing to work collaboratively. Their feud was catnip for entertainment writers, who played up the threat of a physical altercation between the two alphas. "Eszterhas thinks he can go fifteen rounds with me," Stallone told an *Esquire* journalist. "I'll show you what I can do to Joe Eszterhas," Stallone said, before walloping a punching bag.

While Jewison's entire career had been defined by idealism tempered by pragmatism, the concessions Jewison made for *F.I.S.T.* were, in Patrick Palmer's opinion, too high. "We both sat and let Stallone fuck it up. Probably still his best piece of acting ever," Palmer said. But Jewison and company had "spread their legs" to accommodate Stallone and get the picture made. "A lot went down. We sold ourselves on the pretext that if we didn't do that, we wouldn't get the film made. We both felt, I think, deep down, that we had betrayed Joe in a way."

Larry Auerbach had a similar understanding of the situation: Jewison "had such a desire to make this film that he succumbed to a lot of pressure from United Artists. Also, the experience with Stallone was horrendous. Norman's pretty good with stars, he pretty much doesn't let them run around, but Stallone was impossible. That was one of the worst experiences."

It was a point on which everyone could agree. "The whole experience was very unpleasant," Stallone said after the fact. "*F.I.S.T.* was not what you'd call a blissful experience. If I were on the set for another day or two there would have been some tremendous volcanic explosions. I couldn't have taken another day."[30]

* * *

Jewison was always burned out by the time he finished a film. Maybe it was because he was getting older, but *F.I.S.T.* seemed to bring him to a new depth of enervation.

"It's really exhausting," he admitted, "because you're beset with a lot of emotional problems as well as physical problems. If you get worn down, well . . ."

Observers still spoke of Jewison's impish energy, but the director was now fifty-one, his hair a mop of steely grey. His face, tanned and clean-shaven, had grown slightly jowlier with the passage of years. Stallone's character aged by several decades over the course of *F.I.S.T.*, ending up at about Jewison's age. (Kovak's teenaged sons were named Kevin and Michael after Jewison's own boys; one of them was played by Anthony Kiedis, future front man of the Red Hot Chili Peppers.) "Fifty years is a tough age," Jewison said. "You don't even want to think about it. You know you're getting old."[31]

If *F.I.S.T.* had an upside, it was that Jewison again had the opportunity to work with Rod Steiger. The actor delivered a nuanced performance as Senator Madison, loosely based on Senator John H. McClellan, who investigated links between labour and organized crime. Steiger's scenes with Stallone crackled with Oedipal energy akin to the contest between Edward G. Robinson and Steve McQueen in the *Cincinnati Kid*. Steiger complicates any straightforward moral reading by imbuing his character with a preening vanity.

F.I.S.T. turned out to be an important film for Steiger. "Things were not going too well at the time," he said, "and I was having trouble with a depression." He was nervous throughout the shoot, even worrying that he'd lost his ability to act. Norman noticed that Steiger had stopped giving his usual thumbs-up sign, which he'd always done to signal that he liked a take. After the shoot, Steiger admitted that he'd been too nervous to flash the sign, because he wanted to ensure Jewison liked the take first.

"I'll be a son-of-a-bitch," Jewison responded. "I was waiting for you to stick your thumb up to tell me if *you* liked it."

Steiger, who had acted opposite Marlon Brando in *On the Waterfront* in 1954, was flabbergasted by Hollywood's changing norms and its progressively entitled actors. "I can't believe these days, what so-called would-be actors are doing—coming two hours late to the set, stopping the picture saying, 'I want a hamburger.' I mean, John Barrymore wouldn't have gotten away with that. Cocaine, all this stuff. In my generation, booze was the big thing, but the actor never dreamed of stopping the picture or being late." He might "fall on his face," said Steiger, and be unable to move, "but he'd get to the studio somehow."

* * *

Critics were ambivalent about *F.I.S.T.*, lauding its outsized ambition but bemoaning its execution. Vincent Canby called it a "massive, essentially shapeless film" about "a terrifically interesting, complicated subject."[32] If most reviewers found something praiseworthy in the film, they also found that Stallone's performance lacked credibility, particularly in the section set in the 1950s. The *Globe and Mail*'s Ray Conlogue praised the film's attention to detail—the Hungarian angel atop a Christmas tree, or the reckless swilling of Mass wine—but believed "Jewison lost control of his epic canvas."

The problem was that the director and star were making two different pictures: Jewison intended *F.I.S.T.* as an illustration of Lord Acton's famous proverb about power corrupting. Stallone thought it was about gaining recognition for the little guy.[33] Eszterhas always thought the film was "pro-union and anti-corruption."[34] Viewers didn't seem to think much at all. *F.I.S.T.* generated a modest return on investment, edging out *The Boys from Brazil* to become the twenty-eighth highest-grossing film of 1978.

For a time, it looked as though Jewison would be able to muffle the feud between Eszterhas and Stallone. The three men had appeared amicable enough at the film's Los Angeles opening at Century City, where *F.I.S.T.* had been chosen among three-hundred films from thirty-five nations for the Filmex Festival's opening night showcase. Stallone, who attended the event flanked by three bodyguards in identical green blazers, even apologized for some of his opprobrious remarks to *Esquire* magazine.[35] Before long, hostilities had resumed, and Jewison no longer felt any need to hold back.

Casting Stallone had been "a big mistake so I accept it. I thought he was right for the part," Jewison said in an interview. "But why would I work with him again? I can't take that kind of ego. It's got to be incredible. His next picture he produced, directed, wrote, starred in, and sang the title song . . . I don't know whether he thinks he's a good actor or singer or writer or producer or distributor or what the hell he thinks he is, but if *Paradise Alley* is the result, it's kind of embarrassing."[36]

* * *

As time went by, Sylvester Stallone would dramatically re-evaluate his experience on *F.I.S.T.* By the mid-1980s, he described the film as "one of the most enjoyable experiences of my life. I didn't think it was at the time but in retrospect it is. I don't enjoy the presence of directors all the time. It's nice just to sit back in competent hands and work on a film of such magnitude and size." Stallone phoned Jewison to apologize for some of what he'd said in the press.

"It was a wild scene. I made some political blunders," Stallone later admitted. "I think I've atoned for it. I've been up and down. *F.I.S.T.* was one of those little up moments. Jewison and I should do [one] more."[37]

For his part, Joe Eszterhas was rattled by some of the negative reviews. A piece in *Time* magazine—headlined "J.U.N.K."—had especially gotten under his skin. "It became obvious, two weeks after the movie came out, that it wasn't going to do well, commercially or critically," Eszterhas said. He dreaded heading into a post-release debrief with Marcia Nasatir, the UA executive who had initiated the project. Eszterhas was concerned about his future in the film business. "What's going to happen now?" he asked.

"Well, honey," Nasatir replied consolingly, "what's going to happen is that Norman Jewison will go on to direct many great hits. Sylvester Stallone will be one of the biggest movie stars in the world. And you— because everyone read *your* pages—you will go on to write many more screenplays."

"So who will take responsibility?" asked Eszterhas.

"In Hollywood?" Nasatir smiled. "Nobody."[38]

CHAPTER 16

Almost Famous

IN OCTOBER 1977 NORMAN AND DIXIE undertook a two-week expedition through China to lay the groundwork for a film based on the life of Norman Bethune, a Canadian doctor who worked with a mobile medical unit on the front lines of the Sino-Japanese war and established teaching hospitals before dying of septicemia at the age of forty-nine. Basically unknown in his native Canada, Bethune was like a saint in China, where he was commemorated with statues, posters and stamps. Mao Tse-tung praised "Comrade Bethune" for embodying the international spirit of the proletarian struggle.[1] To Jewison, whose last three films had centred on embattled revolutionaries, Bethune was another fascinating model of ideological commitment. The prospect of shooting the first Hollywood production in Communist China was also alluring.

Norman and Dixie had travelled extensively in recent years, but China struck them both as exotic. Peking was colourless except for the ubiquitous red flags and gold tile roof over the Forbidden City, and there was not a flower, not even a blade of grass, to be seen, yet it was undeniably beautiful.

Thanks to zoning rules prohibiting tall buildings, Jewison could stand in the middle of the vast Tiananmen Square and see for miles in every direction. Dixie was self-conscious about her frizzy hair in the October heat: the Chinese stared at them, and sometimes even followed them around. It was like they were famous. They worried about being hit by one of the thousands of identical black bicycles rattling down the streets; Dixie wondered how the owners could tell them apart. One afternoon, Dixie was offered a guided tour of a school, which had its own factory that made chess pieces. A kindergarten class sang and danced for the visitors. Dixie cried, she found it so adorable.

A few days later, the party set out in the pre-dawn mist, past men doing their rhythmic exercises in the streets, to catch a train to Hebei, where Bethune had served with the Guerilla 8th Route army. Jewison saw the terraced rice and cotton fields, teeming with workers, as a succession of shots—like something from a Cecil B. DeMille movie, he thought. They met with veterans who had known Bethune: frail and toothless old people who felt they owed their lives to the doctor. At the Bethune Memorial Hospital, they witnessed an acupuncture demonstration. Dixie excused herself while the men observed a hernia operation. The hospital director then asked if Jewison wanted to see a woman having her thyroid removed, and he did. They exited through a gift shop full of Bethune-related junk.

Despite the extravagant hospitality, permission to shoot *Bethune* was not immediately forthcoming. Jewison couldn't help but feel optimistic. Nor could he help doing the math. He'd seen some very large cinemas in Peking. How many theatres were there in China, he wondered? Say 100,000 35mm outlets, selling tickets at five cents each, with a total population of 950 million. The sheer size of that audience was tantalizing.

One day before they left, Jewison and Dixie perused one of the department stores that sold luxury goods to foreigners. Feeling pangs of guilt over his relative affluence, Jewison bought some walnuts and started handing them out to children outside. His good intentions didn't translate. The children felt ashamed, perhaps even offended, by the gesture.

It was a minor embarrassment, probably soon forgotten amidst the whirlwind trip, but the walnuts pointed to a larger pattern. So often, Jewison's actions sprung from an irrepressible generosity of spirit. Not infrequently, however, that generosity would elicit something like the opposite of its desired effect.

* * *

Jewison was shielding himself from a biting winter wind on a Baltimore airstrip, using a radio mic to direct Al Pacino and Jack Warden, who were sitting in a helicopter. Warden's character, a gregarious (if also deranged) judge, was supposed to be taking Pacino's character, a squeamish lawyer, out for a private helicopter ride. The real helicopter would not leave the tarmac; Jewison was using a rather rudimentary camera trick (filming the chopper from below) to give the appearance of flight. Jewison listened to another take over his headset; he could tell from the sound of Pacino's voice that it wasn't going well.

"Damn!" Pacino finally snapped. "I'm not feeling it. It's not happening for me." A car soon appeared to drive Pacino, sulky and dissatisfied with himself, back to his trailer.[2]

While Jewison was known as a socially conscious filmmaker, . . . *And Justice for All* was the director's first representation of contemporary social reality since *The Thomas Crown Affair* eleven years before. Part black comedy, part gritty exposé of a shattered American criminal justice system, the film followed a strung-out public defender named Arthur Kirkland (Pacino) forced to defend a powerful judge who he knew was guilty of rape.

In some ways, *Justice* was another take on a familiar Jewison narrative: like *Superstar*'s Jesus or *F.I.S.T.*'s Kovak, Kirkland's calling was to defend the powerless masses from a callous, decadent elite. Where *Rollerball*'s Jonathan E. defied shadowy corporate executives, Kirkland would face off against a mysterious "committee" tasked with bringing rogue lawyers to heel, and, in a blockbuster final scene, turn upon his own depraved client.

Jewison's politics, his distrust of corporations, and sympathy for the downtrodden informed each of these films. But they also provided allegories for Jewison's own battles with studio executives to get those films made. *Superstar*'s critics had seen Caiaphas and the other priests as representing Jews, but they also stood in for studio heads. The reptilian corporate leaders in *Rollerball*, too, were film executives bent on anesthetizing the masses with increasingly violent spectacle. Stallone's scintillating speeches in *F.I.S.T.*, in which he excoriates the company bosses for leeching off the creative energies of their labourers, distilled Jewison's attitude toward producers who took creative credit. For most of the 1970s, Jewison had convinced studio bosses to fund films in which their own "executive" proxies were flouted and condemned by heroes who embodied Jewison's ideals. The parallels may have been unintentional, but the films inevitably refracted Jewison's own anxieties.

. . . *And Justice for All* fit the same mold, although it also brought Jewison closer to conventional 1970s New Hollywood filmmaking. Until *Justice*, Jewison operated largely outside the dirty realist aesthetic that had defined the first half of the decade. *Superstar* and *Rollerball* had taken place in timeless, anachronistic counter-realities, while *F.I.S.T.* was deliberately photographed in what he called the "crisp and clear and hard" look of a 1930s film.[3] *Justice*, by contrast, was recognizably of the moment. "It'll be very crisp, cutty, but terse," he said at the time. "Semi-journalistic, maybe, because it's about the law."[4]

Once again, Jewison had no say in casting his lead. Columbia's funding was contingent upon the star's involvement. Pacino, who considered himself primarily a stage actor, wanted to read the script in New York with a company of actors before committing. "It was a very strange thing to do for a screenplay," Jewison said, but the reading was enough to convince Pacino to take the role.[5]

Pacino's "difficulty," Jewison soon discovered, came from the same intensity that made him such an electrifying presence on screen. Pacino would have rehearsed for more than the allotted two weeks, "but agents regard rehearsals as tying up the working potential of their clients," complained Jewison.[6] He observed trials and embedded himself with public defenders. Once filming began, he kept to himself, and practically lived in the slovenly brown suit that his hangdog character wore in the film.[7] Jewison had never worked with an actor so dedicated to remaining in character.

"At one point," said Pacino, "a friend said to me he was having trouble with a contract, and I just instinctively said, 'Let *me* see that.' You get the feeling that you are able to *do* these things. It's crazy. I literally took it from him and said, 'Well, maybe I can help you with this.' Can you imagine that?"[8]

Pacino took the role for the same reason Stallone had done *F.I.S.T.*: it was an opportunity to play against type. "Every actor has a tendency to be typed, and Al's done one thing after the next that drives home the same tone," said Lee Strasberg, Pacino's teacher and one of the founders of Method acting, who took a small role as Pacino's grandfather in *Justice*. "This film is good for his sense of humour."[9]

Pacino praised Jewison in terms that mirrored the director's praise for the actor. "He was different from anybody I had worked with before. The thing I like most about Norman is his sense of involvement," Pacino said.

"He's constantly about the movie. He broods about it. Even after it's over, he's with the picture."[10]

* * *

Sometimes, Jewison brooded about his own lack of fame. In 1978, he was fifty-one years old, an esteemed veteran of the film industry, entrusted with Hollywood's biggest stars. It might have been the prime of his career. Yet he walked the streets around the Baltimore location of *Justice* in complete anonymity.

The subject came up over lunch one day with a reporter. Jewison had been discussing the courtroom scenes he'd shot that morning, pecking at a plate of prime rib between questions, when a young woman interrupted their conversation to ask, sheepishly, if he "was someone."

"Oh, I'm nobody," Jewison said with a slight chuckle.

"What's your name?" the woman asked.

"Norman Jewison. Nice to meet you," he replied, shaking her hand.

The woman excused herself, saying she knew the name, although Jewison wasn't fooled. To that point, he had been discussing *Justice* in his usual, animated manner. But now, the reporter noticed, "when talking about himself, his benign voice takes on a melancholic tone as it trails off: sentences dangle in silence."

"Nobody knows who I am," he announced, forcing a grin. He speculated that his name itself may have been part of the problem. Those distinctive German names, Erich von Stroheim and Otto Preminger—he pronounced them with a parodic German accent—were somehow weighty and memorable. But "Norman Jewison"—he squealed his own name, like a child refusing spinach—"Who was that? It's a Jewish name," he whinged.

Jewison thought he'd been growing *less* famous over the years, that he had been better known to the public back in his television days.[11]

His friends would sometimes speculate over why he wasn't more famous. Some insisted that he never sought fame. Others, like the writer William Goldman, believed that Jewison simply hadn't played the media game. "It has cost Norman," Goldman said. "I think it ultimately damaged him. Not in terms of the money he has made because he is obscenely successful, and not in terms of the prizes he has won, because he is recognized around the world as a great director, with major pictures. But I think in terms of Hollywood, ultimately he doesn't do that [cooperate with the media] as well as he should, and he could, because he is very charming—he can bullshit with the best."

Jewison was hardly alone, of course. Goldman put him in a camp of invisible titans alongside Walter Hill and Sidney Lumet: "They are these giant figures in the industry," Goldman said, and "they could walk down any street, in any city in the world, and no one would know who they were."[12]

Maybe Jewison had expected too much. He had aspired to be in the same rank as Fellini and Billy Wilder, but it was now harder than ever to get his films made. The recent negotiations with Columbia had been "long and arduous."[13] His professional anxieties dovetailed with the gnawing awareness that he was no longer young. He had always been competitive, but insecurity over his age had sharpened that competitiveness to the point of aggression. The results weren't always pretty. On their annual Klosters holiday, Jewison took to the ice for a game of pick-up hockey, Canadians versus the Swiss. Perhaps he took the game too seriously. At one point, he was bashed to the ice and broke his arm. "I'm getting a little too old to take the puck down the ice, I'll tell you that," Jewison joked with reporters, after assuring them that Stallone hadn't broken the arm.[14]

Nothing brought out competition within the family like skiing. When they were first learning, Jewison remembered, Kevin, Michael and Jennifer used to waddle awkwardly down the slopes like chickens. "So I'll never forget the year my kids passed me." Kevin was seventeen, in the throes of his "first primitive push for power, because that's what it's all about. He passed me. The moment he did, he knew he would have to go. He knew I was going to chase him and I did. I chased the son of a bitch down the front slope of that mountain."

When Kevin fell, Norman blew past him without even stopping. "See, you're not ready for me yet," said his father, the same line that Edward G. Robinson, the superannuated card shark, delivered to McQueen at the end of *The Cincinnati Kid*. By that Easter, the kid had overtaken the man.

"And I never will catch him again for the rest of my life," Jewison said.[15]

* * *

. . . *And Justice for All* began with an original script by Valerie Curtin and Barry Levinson, who did extensive research by interviewing lawyers and observing trials. Some of the most outlandish, "Hollywood" moments in the script, such as when a judge played by Jack Warden produces a pistol from his robes and fired it at the ceiling to quell a riotous courtroom, came from first-hand accounts.[16]

The plot unfolds a series of case studies that reveal how the procedures of criminal law often produce immoral outcomes. Pacino's Kirkland knows that Judge Fleming is guilty, but professional conduct compelled him to defend a powerful man likely to rape again. *Justice* reflected a growing cultural anxiety around the unintended consequences of the

Warren Court's proceduralization of jurisprudence, which tended to shift legal energy away from a defendant's guilt or innocence and toward legal processes themselves.[17] The film's mood of towering moral outrage emerges from instances of procedural perversity, where professional legal norms (and "the rule of law" itself) seemed inimical to basic moral sense.

Columbia promoted the film as another entry in Hollywood's august series of courtroom dramas about exposing injustice (including *Mr. Smith Goes to Washington, Judgment at Nuremberg*, and *To Kill a Mockingbird*). But while the traditional courtroom drama often ends with tragedy (*Mockingbird's* Tom Robinson is convicted, after all), *Justice* reveals the real tragedy to be the legal institutions themselves. The system was a sham. That was the essence of Pacino's famous statement at the close of the film:

> Ladies and gentlemen of the jury, the prosecution is not going to get that man today. No! Because I'm going to get him! My client, the Honorable Henry T. Fleming, should go *right to fucking jail!* The son of a bitch is guilty! That man is guilty! That man is a slime! He is a slime! If he's allowed to go free, something really wrong is going on here!
>
> *You're* out of order! *You're* out of order! The *whole trial* is out of order!

Pacino's expectorating wrath was like a force of nature. The lines borrow heavily from Stallone's verbal eruption at the end of *F.I.S.T.* ("I hold you in contempt! I hold this hearing in contempt!" he barks at Rod Steiger), but Pacino's conviction sandblasts Stallone's monologue from memory. According to Jewison, the scene had initially struck Pacino as unrealistic: the actor went over the dialogue with an attorney and started to rewrite it. "I was just shocked," Jewison said. "The day before we were shooting,

Pacino came to me and said that he had made a few changes, and he had totally rewritten the scene. And of course it was boring! It didn't work."

He urged Pacino to embrace the theatricality of the moment. "The courtroom is a theatre," Jewison said, "and prosecutors and defense attorneys are always acting."[18] Pacino eventually agreed to shoot the original scene, and delivered what Michael Barker, the co-founder and co-president of Sony Pictures Classics, believes was "one of the best scenes pulled off by any actor in film history."

"Norman is really the key to that scene," Barker explains. It's in the technical decisions, like the editing rhythms and "where the camera is placed. It allows Al Pacino to do his thing in an operatic way, and the audience has such a release that a lawyer does this—it's so surprising and so crazy, it's a combination of screenplay, acting, and the camera movements, that make it so fantastic."[19]

* * *

By this time, it was clear that *Bethune* was not going to pan out. Jewison had envisioned an $8-million epic with Donald Sutherland in the lead role. Chinese officials, however, made it known that they preferred a narrated "docu-drama" approach—something more aesthetically aligned with the propaganda films consecrated by the party. Visiting with Chinese filmmakers, Jewison had the impression that "creative people have less interest in social and political systems, and more interest in exchanging ideas on style and technique."[20] But in China, no less than in Hollywood, creative people didn't have the power to greenlight films.

Jewison didn't immediately dismiss the idea of *Bethune* as a docudrama. With the right actors—Robert Redford and Jane Fonda both came up—it could have worked for art houses or as a television special, although Jewison concluded that it was "just not a commercial venture."[21]

* * *

The entire Jewison clan spent the 1978 holiday season at their Caledon farm. It was their first Christmas in Canada in nineteen years. "We were blessed with eight inches of fresh snow which made it possible to enjoy a snowshoe through our woods and enjoy the splendor of the Caledon hills," Jewison wrote a friend.[22] Come spring, the property, named "Putney Heath," after the region of their former UK home, would be alive with geese, ducks, wild deer, even the occasional wolf. The Jewisons had always kept animals, which now included a golden retriever named Byron, six-hundred head of Hereford cattle, horses, and the "Andrews Sisters," their three pigs. Jewison had intended to slaughter them for bacon; predictably enough, he'd grown to love the "marvelous" pigs, and decided to keep them on the pretense that they were good company for the dog.

In the months ahead, Jewison oversaw post-production and marketing efforts for *Justice*. Motion picture marketing had undergone its own revolution over the last few years and *Justice* was Jewison's first experience with an intensive, data-driven marketing strategy. A scholar from the Wharton Applied Research Centre led focus group sessions that helped determine the visual identity of the campaign. Follow-up testing by Columbia Pictures Marketing Research confirmed that the marketing strategy should be built around Pacino, rather than the film's logo or themes.[23]

Columbia's marketing efforts bore fruit. The film, released on September 15, 1979, eventually made $33 million against a budget of only $4 million.

Once again, critics were split. Roger Ebert praised the film as "an angry comedy crossed with an expose and held together by one of those high-voltage Al Pacino performances that's so sure of itself we hesitate to demur." Others would not only demur but were downright scathing. Vincent Canby called Pacino's character a "hyperventilating idiot." *Justice*, Canby ranted, "pretends to be about the shortcomings of our judicial system, but it's really an extended introduction in how to lose control, have a nervous breakdown, go crazy, commit suicide, and perform other antisocial acts." The *Washington Posts*'s Gary Arnold called *Justice* "a trigger happy, scatter-brained spectacle" and claimed that "no one has ever looked or acted or sounded less like a lawyer than Al Pacino in this insufferable travesty of a social comedy."

Canby and Arnold sounded more than a little defensive about Jewison's lack of piety toward the courtroom as a sacred cinematic space (compounded, perhaps, by a similar lack of regard for generic boundaries separating "comedy" from "drama.") Still, the director could not help taking the criticism to heart, and was always vulnerable to hometown critics. *Justice* had been chosen to close the 1979 Toronto International Film Festival (the "Festival of Festivals" as it was then called). In his *Globe and Mail* review, Jay Scott concluded that Jewison was "ready to inherit the gilded sackcloth and gem-set ashes of that other social-cause dilettante, Stanley Kramer. His heart's in the right place, but his head's nodding toward Babylon."

Jewison, shell-shocked, penned a series of apologetic letters to his colleagues at Columbia Pictures. He confessed to feeling "deeply depressed" about some critical reviews. "I'm sure you realize it has been difficult for me to accept the critical attack on the film from so many areas," he wrote in another letter. "It was just so unexpected and I'm afraid I became overconfident due to our successful sneak previews and early screenings for various opinion makers on both coasts."[24]

Charles Milhaupt, who worked alongside Jewison and Palmer as a producer in these years, was surprised by Jewison's vulnerability to criticism. "He is definitely interested in the opinions of critics, powerful movie executives—I mean, those people do affect his life, and as a realist he's not above that," said Milhaupt. "It's just that when you work with him as much as I did, there are times when you want to say to him, 'God, I wish you would just stop worrying about what other people think,' because he's so damn successful . . . There were times when I saw him inordinately affected by the opinions of others."[25]

Jewison knew the industry was gravitating away from his cinematic ideals. If *Star Wars* and *Jaws* implied a lesson, it was that big-budget treatment of B-movie content, along with a gleeful rejection of any kind of "message," was now the accepted template for box-office success. Jewison felt compelled to publicly repudiate "message pictures," a label that spelled doom at the box office. "I hope I am making social statements," he said at the time, "but you see I must never tell anybody or they won't go to see my films."

As Hal Ashby said of his former mentor, "Norman feels very strongly about having the social things in his pictures but not wanting to fail because he gets on a soap-box about it." Jewison had made peace with the fact that he was not a "pure" artist—which, to his mind, was an artist who "does not care whether anybody sees what he does because he is doing it for the sake of creating an artistic piece." He considered himself "too much a realist to spend two years creating an artful piece and be satisfied if nobody sees it."[26]

Still, for all of Jewison's consternation over "message" pictures, he nurtured a particular loathing for what he considered unartful entertainments. He hated *Smokey and the Bandit*, the 1977 Burt Reynolds-Sally Field car-chase comedy. "To me," he said to a reporter, "it's appalling that a picture like *Smokey and the Bandit* would be our second most successful film to an American audience in a whole year." Jewison pulled his baseball cap low over his eyes, and said in lazy, southern drawl, "Let's go see Burt Reynolds. Burt's a good ole' boy-ah."

"When I think of all the good films that've been made . . ." Jewison trailed off. "*Smokey* was not made for any other reason except entertainment. And I don't make those kinds of films."[27]

CHAPTER 17

Hollywood Redux

THE 53RD ACADEMY AWARDS WERE SCHEDULED to take place on Monday, March 30, 1981, at the Dorothy Chandler Pavilion. With his background in live television specials, Jewison was a natural fit to produce the Academy Awards. Besides, as he later joked, he was in the mood for "sheer terror."

The major issue of contention leading up to the show was how, or if, the Academy should honour Ronald Reagan, the former actor who had recently been elected president. Jewison was not fond of the idea. With their potential audience of three-hundred million people, the Oscars, Jewison felt, "should not be used as a vehicle for political propaganda." He also felt it would be a "great disservice" to the award winners if Reagan were to receive a special Oscar "not because of his artistic talent but because of his political position." In the end, the compromise was that Reagan would give pre-recorded welcome remarks at the opening of the ceremony. Then, hours before the festivities were set to begin, Reagan was shot by John Hinckley Jr. The would-be assassin dedicated the attempt to Jodie Foster, then a freshman at Yale, who had been nominated for an

Oscar for her work as a twelve-year-old in *Taxi Driver*. Strangers would later approach her in the street and say, "Ain't you the girl who shot the President?"[1]

Jewison recalls the "bizarre" feeling in the Pavilion upon hearing the news. "Dolly Parton was rehearsing on stage. I told her the president had been shot and she planted both hands on her hips and said, 'Well, Ah didn't do it!'" Jewison, perhaps recalling the Academy's reaction to the King assassination, insisted that the telecast be delayed by one day.

The highlight of the show, he later recalled, was the presentation of the Academy Honorary Award to Henry Fonda. Jewison remembers standing next to Fonda, "as his life literally flashed before his eyes. The clips came to an end. We were both on stage, behind the screen. I said, 'Make them wait, Henry, make them wait,' and I ran off stage. The entire audience got to its feet, and I got such goosebumps." Meaningful as the moment was, Jewison had no intention of returning to produce a second Oscars telecast.

"Trying to make that show work is like dragging a dinosaur across the stage," he said.[2]

* * *

The last time Jewison needed snow for a scene, in *Fiddler on the Roof*, an unseasonably warm winter in Yugoslavia wreaked havoc on his production schedule. So, in 1982, when Jewison once again found himself in need of a frozen wasteland, he decided on a sure bet. In an early scene from *Best Friends*, Burt Reynolds's breath is clearly visible as he steps off the train and immediately asks, "Haven't we been in Buffalo long enough?"

Screenwriting couple Richard Babson (Reynolds) and Paula McCullen (Goldie Hawn) are the eponymous best friends who work, talk, eat, and sleep together. Richard thinks they ought to get married, but Paula equates marriage with death. She soon relents, but their marriage won't survive the "meet the parents" honeymoon. Where the standard rom-com formula concocts a series of obstacles to keep the couple apart until marriage (or its promise) arrives at the end, *Best Friends* begins with the nuptials, using marriage itself as a wedge to pry the couple apart.

Jewison was not bullish on the project after reading a weak draft of the screenplay. However, Goldie Hawn had somehow obtained a copy and asked Jewison about his plans. Hawn, thirty-seven years old, was ready to pupate out of her "dumb blonde" persona and into a more serious version of herself. Jewison, she believed, was just the director to help her do so.

They discussed *Best Friends* over breakfast in Malibu. "She convinced me," Jewison remembered. "I had been impressed with her talent ever since *Sugarland Express*. I thought she was one of the most honest performers, so I said, 'If you'll do it, I'll do it.' We decided together on Burt. My instinct was that we should have star chemistry, like Cary Grant and Carole Lombard, or like I had on *The Thomas Crown Affair*."[3] Reynolds had lost out to Paul Burke for the role of the detective in *Crown*, but remembered that Jewison had let him down easily.

Best Friends was budgeted at $15 million, the most expensive picture Jewison had ever made. Compared with the epochal contests of ego that had defined the mood on his previous projects, however, the set of *Best Friends* was placid and professional. Hawn and Reynolds loved working together. Goldie was "essentially the most positive person you can have around," he said. [4] Jewison was hard-pressed to recall any tension on set. About the most scandalous thing he could remember was that he had to shush one of Hawn's children, who was sitting on his knee, during a take: "You be quiet, Mother's working."

For fifteen years, Jewison's films had been characterized by their ambitious social engagement and by the director's evolving interests in politics, race, religion, globalization, and the corruption of American institutions. *Best Friends* felt like a retreat from all that. It was also a turn inward, a Hollywood tale in form and content. ("I don't know how he got through *Best Friends*," was agent Larry Auerbach's frank assessment.[5]) "When I was a young man I wanted to change the world. I now know that there's very little possibility of me being able to deflect it one millimeter from its course," he said, summarizing his new mood.[6]

While *Best Friends* was not a film to "change the world," traces of the director are everywhere, from its gentle mockery of LA foodie culture to the poster of *Cincinnati Kid*'s Edward G. Robinson on one character's wall. For years, Jewison's films had featured various malevolent "executive" figures, and *Best Friends* features the most comically mendacious executive of all: Ron Silver plays a studio head who locks Richard and Paula in an office until they deliver the final pages of his film (Jewison insists the role was purely fictional). If, in its portrait of the stormy union of Hawn and Reynolds, *Best Friends* marriage as a suffocating, passion-killing trap, it also provided a sideways glance at Jewison's own turbulent marriage to the film industry.

* * *

On weekends during the Buffalo shoot, Jewison would return to Putney Heath. He had been moved when neighbouring farmers, from miles in every direction, had descended upon his property to greet the farm's firstborn foal, an old tradition in the area. Jewison, with his trendy jeans and aviator sunglasses, looked more Malibu than Caledon, but he felt accepted and legitimated by the community. Dixie, meanwhile, had started pickling vegetables. "He loves to grow things, and she loves to preserve things," Alan Bergman observed of the couple.[7]

The farm turned out to be a source of endless delight for Jewison. One business associate, attempting to reach him over the phone about *Best Friends*, was told to call back, because "Norm was out in the barn helping a cow give birth."[8] Some reporters of the period, eager for a few words about his latest motion picture, instead got an earful about Jewison's Hereford cow that had recently won the Grand Championship award at the Canadian National Exhibition. (He then sold the ten-month old cow for the record-breaking sum of $22,500.) Around the same time, he started producing maple syrup tapped from his own trees, selling it out of Fenton's Foods near his Gloucester St. office in downtown Toronto.[9] Even his bucolic passions turned a profit. If Jewison was going to make maple syrup, it seemed important that people would want to buy it.

* * *

Not long after wrapping up *Best Friends*, an anxious Norman Jewison was sitting opposite a psychic in Los Angeles, perturbed about a missing hat. The psychic took her time, engrossed in the theatre of clairvoyance. A vision was forming. Yes, she could see Jewison's hat. It was being worn by a young woman. She was sipping white wine.

Jewison had bought the blue baseball cap in Boston one day in the summer of 1967, while filming *The Thomas Crown Affair*. Steve McQueen had borrowed it for one of his scenes in *Crown*. Since then, Jewison had worn it while shooting all his films. It became weighted down with pins and buttons and other totems. "The hat became a thing with me," Jewison said. If something went awry on the set, one of the crew would inevitably yell "Get the hat!" Once, on location in the Israeli desert, production had to be halted for a large-scale search when the hat blew off his head.

In the spring of 1982, as production wound down on *Best Friends* in Los Angeles, the hat vanished. Jewison swore he'd left it hanging on a chair in the studio. Distraught, he posted a $1,000 reward for its safe return, but came up dry. That was when he'd visited the psychic. "It's silly and sad at the same time," Jewison said. "I'd give anything to get that hat back."[10]

Fortunately, the loss of the hat didn't foretell disaster for the film. *Best Friends*, which Jewison would always consider second-tier work, earned the director some of his most positive reviews in years. The *Washington Post*'s Gary Arnold, who had trashed . . . *And Justice for All*, called the film "exceptionally authentic and endearing—the most original and keenly observant romantic comedy to emerge from Hollywood" in years. The *New York Times*'s Janet Maslin praised Hawn and Reynolds as a "surprisingly appealing team" in a film that offered them greater-than-expected emotional amplitude. Roger Ebert said the film "overlooks the images of both performers and calls upon them as actors, asking them to interpret characters who were written as closely observed people." Hawn had wanted a more serious role, and the film had delivered. Jewison had also delivered another hit for the studios, albeit not a smash.

A curious pattern was developing. Since returning from the UK, Jewison had increasingly been called upon to help established stars (Stallone, Pacino, Hawn, and Reynolds) play against type. Paradoxically, his success in doing so may have worked against him at the box office: his films provided stars with opportunities to push themselves further than audiences were willing to go. The actors relished the experience: "I'd love to work with him again," Hawn said, while Reynolds called him "the nicest director, maybe, in the history of Hollywood."[11] The problem was that Jewison himself was becoming pigeonholed as the director stars turned to when they were in danger of becoming pigeonholed.

* * *

Professionally, Jewison was flailing in the early 1980s. As his friend William Goldman remembers, "Norman was charging from place to place and got his teeth kicked in fairly frequently." Jewison and Goldman had recently collaborated on a script for *Grand Hotel*, a remake of the 1932 film in which Greta Garbo and John Barrymore play conniving guests of a glamorous Berlin establishment. Jewison's version would take place in Las Vegas's MGM Grand. MGM turned out to be so protective of its "property" (in both senses) that it refused to give Jewison the final cut of the picture, so he walked.[12]

Goldman got a kick out of Jewison, whom he characterized as "very tough and abrasive." He "doesn't bullshit you," Goldman said. "I can hear Norman say, 'Do you expect me to shoot this? This awful scene? What is this, I thought you were a writer?' And you get into a fight with him, and out of that abrasiveness comes, very often, something positive."[13]

They tried again on an adaptation of Goldman's novel *The Princess Bride*, which Jewison adored. He imagined Robert Redford and Mel Brooks in lead roles. But he turned the project down because he feared the $20-million production would go $2 million over budget.

"A lot of people said to Norman, 'shoot the goddamn movie,' and go over by two million," Goldman said. "Two million over budget in these Spielberg-Lucas days is like being under budget. Norman wouldn't do it, which says a great deal for Norman."[14]

Around this time, Jewison's friend Charles "Chiz" Schultz, who had discovered *The Landlord* for him in the late sixties, insisted that Jewison see *A Soldier's Play*. A murder mystery set on a segregated military base in 1944, the play offered an unusually trenchant representation of Black-on-Black racism. After taking in the Negro Ensemble Company production, Jewison met playwright Charles Fuller for a late dinner near Central Park. The two men hit it off, and ended up brainstorming about a film version until 2 a.m. Fuller left convinced that Jewison could pull it off in a straightforward and unsentimental manner.[15]

An interviewer once asked Jewison if there was a moment when he realized that corporate thinking had finally come to dominate in Hollywood. Jewison didn't hesitate. "I noticed it the most in [trying to sell] *A Soldier's Story*," he said, "where there wasn't any interest whatsoever." The majority Black cast "was just an absolute turn-off" for executives. Industry consensus held that Black audiences wanted *Shaft*, *Superfly* and other exploitation fare, while white audiences wanted Eddie Murphy, "or Richard Pryor in a chicken suit," Jewison quipped.[16] Whites would watch *Roots* or *The Jeffersons* for free on TV, the thinking went, but they would not pay money to watch Black performers. A 1984 *Time* magazine article spoke of "one of the Black man's burdens: convincing a skeptical Hollywood Establishment that his experiences are worth putting on film and that they will attract an impressive number of moviegoers, Black and white." For Warner Bros., a serious period drama with a predominantly Black cast was a non-starter. MGM was next to turn Jewison down. Then Universal took a hard pass.

Finally, Jewison found himself doing his dance for Frank Price, president of Columbia Pictures. Jewison's usual arguments, that *A Soldier's Story* would earn money and become a prestigious film for the studio, fell upon deaf ears. Then Jewison tried something new: he offered to work for free. Price perked up. Jewison agreed to forego his salary in exchange for a small percentage of the gross (which Columbia was sure would be negligible).[17] In the end, the Directors Guild of America (DGA) rules stipulated that Jewison had to work for scale rather than for free. But his "tiny" piece of the gross after first dollar would quickly recuperate his usual salary of $1.5 million.[18]

* * *

Jewison began shooting *A Soldier's Story* on location in Clarendon, Arkansas, birthplace of Martin Luther King Jr., on September 12, 1983. Adolph Caesar and Denzel Washington (still best known for the NBC series *St. Elsewhere*), who had honed their characters over hundreds of live performances, resumed their roles in the film. From Clarendon, the production moved to Little Rock for two days of shooting a baseball scene. The Governor of Arkansas, a thirty-seven-year-old William Jefferson Clinton, visited the set. Clinton arrived having read the play and "seemed to be almost as excited about being on a movie set as our cast and crew were to meet him," Jewison said. He hoisted Clinton up on a crane and showed how they would make two hundred extras look like an immense crowd.[19] The rest was filmed on location at Ft. Chaffee, an unoccupied operational fort with barracks and mess halls which at one time had been used to warehouse Cuban refugees.[20]

Jewison hired as many Black crew members and production staff as possible. Patti LaBelle was given a couple of musical numbers in the film; Herbie Hancock did the score. "There was some rumbling from the liberal left and the Black community about, 'Jewison's doing his message picture again,' 'Jewison's doing his Black picture again,'" he recalls.[21] Friends joked that they were going to get him a T-shirt labelled "White Christian Methodist" to remind the director of who he was. His whiteness "could have been a problem," conceded Charles Milhaupt, the film's associate producer, but he was so enthusiastic and turned on by the material "that I don't think people questioned it."[22]

Columbia planned to position *A Soldier's Story* as a "Black picture" for Black audiences, with no intention of a wide release. A pair of successful previews for white suburban audiences in Northern California changed that view.[23] Sensing that some money might be made after all, Columbia opened the film gradually in markets around the country; it eventually made $22 million on a $6-million investment. Strong reviews probably helped. Rex Reed called it a "literate film that honours the almost defunct tradition of the well-constructed script."[24] It would earn three Academy Award nominations for Best Picture, Adapted Screenplay (Fuller), and Supporting Actor (Caesar). In the end, *Amadeus* beat out *A Soldier's Story* in every category on its way to winning eight Oscars. Still, *A Soldier's Story* was the third Norman Jewison film in three separate decades to be nominated for Best Picture. Even more significant, perhaps, was the film's modest success at the box office.

"If the film is a success," Charles Fuller said shortly after its release, "there just might be room for other stories acknowledging that America is a multiracial society. Because we are part of life in this country. We breathe. We buy Cottonelle. We go to the movies."[25]

* * *

Jewison's Los Angeles offices were housed in a Colonial Revival mansion on the Laird International Studios lot in Culver City. Built in 1918 by the silent cinema producer Thomas Ince, the studio had subsequently passed between a succession of high-profile owners including Joseph P. Kennedy Sr., David O. Selznick, and Howard Hughes.[26] The interior of Jewison's offices were lined with a career's worth of mementoes. Recent photographs from *Best Friends* shared wall space with pictures from *Russians* and *Crown*. A DGA award for *Heat* hung on the wall, as did an immense photograph of Judy Garland. Jewison's tooled-leather director's chair was in the corner. The office was, according to one visitor, a sanctuary of cinematic creativity. Yet all Jewison wanted to do was leave. "I've been here since mid-February," he said, "cutting, dubbing, looping, music, scoring. God, we're up to two and three in the morning. It's been a real concentrated period. I'm anxious to get home to the farm. I've got haying to do."[27]

The office's windows looked out on a twenty-eight-acre backlot on which many cinematic landmarks had been staged. This was the lot on which Orson Welles had made *Citizen Kane*, David O. Selznick had made *Gone with the Wind,* Hitchcock had made *Rebecca*. In some ways, Jewison felt a greater sense of connection with that history than he did with Hollywood's present. He was flabbergasted by the success of what he called "comic strip pictures," science fiction, and slasher fare like *Friday the 13th*. He wondered if their creators were "interested in making films that possibly they will be proud of having shown after they depart this world."[28] After a quarter-century in the business, after innumerable conflicts and compromises and disappointments, Jewison hadn't lost his idealistic belief in cinema's potential as public art, that "film was forever," as he often put it.

When Jewison returned to Hollywood from the UK, he'd made a deliberate attempt to rehabilitate his reputation among the industry elite and re-establish himself as a pillar of the film community. Larry Auerbach, Jewison's agent, believed the director had deliberately made amends after trash-talking the industry and America itself at every opportunity in the late sixties. Upon returning, Jewison had dedicated himself to professional service with the DGA. He'd demonstrated a willingness to play ball with the commercial frivolity on *Best Friends*. He'd even produced the Academy Awards. Yet no sooner had Jewison reconstituted himself in Hollywood than he realized he had no interest in making "Hollywood" films. Never were Jewison's artistic ambitions more at odds with the industry than 1984. The highest grossing films that year were effects-driven spectacles: *Ghostbusters, Indiana Jones and the Temple of Doom, Gremlins*. If it were possible to generate a concept with less box-office potential than a talky period piece with a predominantly Black cast, it was the project Jewison hoped to produce next: a talky excursus on faith in the modern world, set in a Quebec convent, starring an all-female cast.

Large photographs of various Quebec locations were mounted on Bristol boards around the office. Patrick Palmer was leading a search to find the perfect convent for *Agnes of God*. Columbia green lit the project after execs saw an early cut of *A Soldier's Story*, though *Agnes* wouldn't be scheduled for production until it had a director. Jewison was aboard strictly as a producer. Francis Ford Coppola was reportedly interested, although he came with a hefty price tag. "Basically, I'm tired," Jewison said about why he wouldn't direct. "I really just want to get back to Toronto and my life, and not have to start pre-production again."

"Whoever the director is," a journalist declared of *Agnes of God*, "it will not be Norman Jewison." [29]

CHAPTER 18

"Who Wants to Make a Film About a Nun?"

I N THE EARLY 1980s, an aspiring filmmaker named Bruce McDonald, then in his early 20s, rode his bike southbound on Yonge Street toward Jewison's Toronto office.

McDonald had idolized Jewison since seeing *Rollerball* at the Albion Mall in Rexdale, Ontario in the mid-1970s: he loved the violence, the camaraderie, the story of an individual "rebelling against the thing that made him," as he put it. In his final year of film studies at Ryerson University, McDonald had won the "Norman Jewison Award" for best student film. Now, out of film school and low on funds, McDonald wrote to his benefactor, who was back in the city, for some financial help to complete an unfinished film. McDonald needed $2,000, but thought a very specific figure would seem more professional, so he wrote Jewison a letter appealing for $2001. He didn't expect to hear back. They had never met. McDonald didn't know anyone who had met Norman Jewison.

Two weeks later, Bonnie Palef-Woolf, Jewison's assistant, called to set up a meeting.

The elevator in Jewison's building opened right onto the office, "like something out of James Bond," McDonald thought. There was a fireplace and a window overlooking the city, pictures of Steve McQueen on the wall. Jewison was seated behind his desk with what McDonald recalls as a look of "mischief" in his eye. "I'm starting to shake a little bit," says McDonald, recalling the feeling of unreality. "I was kind of thrown by his hospitality and the fact that he would take such an interest in a nobody student filmmaker." They talked about music—when McDonald name-dropped a professional musician he knew, Jewison asked, "Isn't that guy kind of square?"—and about McDonald's unfinished film, which involved tours of famous people's bedrooms. They shook hands and Jewison wished him luck.

The next day, McDonald was summoned back to the office, where Bonnie handed him an envelope. "Dear Bruce," said the note inside, "I wanted to give you the whole $2,001, but I spent a dollar on fish and chips." Enclosed was a cheque for $2,000.[1]

* * *

For years, Jewison had been speaking publicly about the absence of a viable film production culture in Canada. The infrastructure simply didn't exist. Even if Canadians could find their own funding sources, they still lacked professional facilities and experienced crews. But Jewison also suspected the dearth of Canadian films reflected a lack of nerve. "We haven't the confidence to make films from the heart and about ourselves," he said. "We've come to believe our [negative] media. Why do we have to shuffle in the corners of the rooms of the world?"[2]

By the 1980s, that was starting to change. Jewison was thinking about new forms of institutional support, about how a Canadian version of the American Film Institute could help catalyze the nascent industry. First, though, he decided to shoot a motion picture in Canada. After Coppola proved too expensive for *Agnes of God*, Jewison found that he had "succumbed" to the material.[3]

Agnes of God could have been set almost anywhere. "When we began working on the screenplay," playwright John Pielmeier remembers, "Jewison had the idea of setting most of our story in a convent in Quebec. It allowed us to create an environment that would be unfamiliar," as well as "to use two languages in the film."[4] The snow-covered Quebec locations inspired an austere, painterly visual aesthetic, more European than American. Jewison and cinematographer Sven Nykvist were especially inspired by the Dutch Baroque painter Vermeer. "I think of Vermeer's rich, dark tones and the way the light hits the faces and hands in the portraits," Jewison said. Several lingering shots of actor Meg Tilly's face would reference the painter's *Girl with the Pearl Earring*. The challenge of photographing the human face, Nykvist said, was "to try to find something of the soul in the human being."[5]

Around this time, Jewison's public image was undergoing yet another transformation. His latest persona, as one headline put it, was the "Thinking Man's Director." Jewison had never considered himself in those terms: "I'm not an intellectual filmmaker," he'd say a few years later, "I'm not a cerebral filmmaker."[6] His ambition was to make films in which "people actually talk to each other."[7] Mainstream American cinema in the mid-80s had moved decisively in the direction of numbing spectacle, such that films about adults speaking to one another seemed positively highbrow. Still, the Academy's Best Picture of 1985 had gone to a period drama about Wolfgang Amadeus Mozart, proving that a market remained for studio-financed "intellectual" films. *Agnes of God* was Jewison at his most self-consciously intellectual.

For Jewison, the main attraction to *Agnes* was the conflict between faith and logic in confrontational scenes between the psychologist (Jane Fonda) and Mother Superior (Anne Bancroft), "these battles where the two of them are slugging out their respective points of view."

The plot follows Fonda's psychologist, a lapsed Catholic, who is charged with ascertaining whether Agnes is mentally fit to stand trial for murdering her baby, who she believes was immaculately conceived. Bancroft's Mother Superior, meanwhile, wants to shield Agnes from the prying eyes of the law, believing that her psychological instability is evidence that she is "beautifully simple" and a "product of God's goodness." Pielmeier's script refused to settle the mystery of the baby's paternity, testing a contemporary film audience's capacity to believe in religious miracles.

While *Amadeus*, *Ghandi*, and *Terms of Endearment* proved there was still a market for adult fare, an all-female cast was a particularly hard sell. A newspaper item claimed that *Agnes* was "the only film in recent years to feature women in all the leading roles," concluding, euphemistically, that "this is considered a risk."[8]

By this time, the nearly all-Black *A Soldier's Story* had broken through critically and commercially, and an interviewer asked if that success had made it easier to sell the studio on *Agnes of God*. "And I said, no, it was like I was starting all over again," Jewison said. "Who wants to make a film about a nun?" he remembers executives asking. "Who wants to make a film about faith versus logic, a bunch of nuns sitting around with a psychiatrist talking about faith, I mean c'mon, Norman!" Columbia eventually conceded on the condition that Jewison secure Jane Fonda for a leading role and that he work for a third of his usual rate. Once again, he took a percentage of the gross from the first profitable dollar.[9]

Agnes of God would not have been green-lit without Jane Fonda, who was always Jewison's first choice for psychiatrist Martha Livingston. The character's fighting spirit and sharp opinions were qualities that Jewison associated with Fonda herself.[10] Bancroft, by contrast, had to convince Jewison that she was right for the role. He'd wanted to work with Bancroft for years, but still associated her with Mrs. Robinson from *The Graduate*. The last thing *Agnes of God* needed was a sexy nun: the film would become a farce. Only after he'd seen the fifty-four-year-old actress dressed in a wimple and veil, looking severe and a little weary, did he know he'd found his Mother Superior.[11]

Meg Tilly approached Jewison about the role of Agnes soon after the film was announced. Tilly, about twenty-two years old and "looking like a child," as Jewison said, was seven months pregnant at the time. The director immediately sensed a profound connection between Tilly and Agnes. "Her background really fit the character," he said. "She was a very private, quiet, sensitive girl who had grown up with a large family in a remote tiny village and had to milk the cow every day." Tilly was not Catholic but told the director she believed in God. More important, she said, "I believe in Agnes."

Jewison was taken aback when Tilly admitted she'd never seen the play. She had, however, read it. As they were discussing a second act scene between Agnes and Mother Miriam, Tilly "slid into dialogue and started to read the part, and all of a sudden it occurred to me she wasn't looking at the text—she had memorized the entire play. Now that doesn't happen very often when an actor comes to see a director."[12]

* * *

Jewison had his three lead actors in place. He had cinematographer Sven Nykvist, who had shot *Cries and Whispers* and other Ingmar Bergman masterpieces. He had Sir Ken Adam, production designer on *Dr. Strangelove* and other Kubrick masterpieces, who was in the process of transforming the Rockwood Academy for boys (near Guelph, Ontario) into *Les Petites Sœurs de Marie-Madeleine,* a Quebec convent. And, as his personal driver, he had one Bruce McDonald. Before getting the job, Dixie made McDonald drive her around Toronto, "to ensure I wasn't going to kill her husband," he remembers. When he started off too cautiously, she scolded, "Norman would have passed that guy."

Jewison was not a morning person. McDonald remembers that Bonnie Palef-Woolf, Jewison's assistant, gave him some sage advice: "Don't talk to him unless he talks to you." Have a *Globe and Mail* waiting in the back seat, and "just be available." Serving as Jewison's driver provided McDonald with an opportunity to witness the director at work. "I had no idea what a director really did or how they behaved or how they treated people," McDonald said. *Agnes of God* turned out to be a masterclass.

Two aspects of Jewison's directorial style would stay with McDonald for decades. The first was his near-telepathic connection with the actors. He seemed completely locked into the lines and emotional dynamics of the scene, but made the actors feel as though *they* were in control.

"He would say to me, 'I can't see through the camera, I'll have to stand over here, so you tell me—you are the only one who knows what's going on in here," Tilly remembers.[13]

The second was how distinctly Jewison would modulate his own performance as director depending upon who he was directing. Fonda, Bancroft, and Tilly were all powerful women, but Jewison provided a different style of direction for each.

With Bancroft, McDonald noted, "it was clearly a brother-sister relationship. Like they would crack jokes and tell stories and knew all the same people in New York; there was a real ease and sense of familiarity."

With Meg Tilly, it was a "father-daughter" thing. "He treated her very kindly and was very supportive." Tilly had won praise for her role in *The Big Chill*, but Agnes was "a very fragile role" and "a big thing" for Tilly. Jewison responded in kind.

With Fonda "it was like ex-girlfriend—like it was kind of sexual, but sort of more ex-boyfriend-girlfriend who are friends now. It just seemed really clear, and I don't know how he arrived at those assignments. But it just seemed like, oh—he's very different with each person. Not like he's faking it, but just that he knew that part of the director's job is knowing that you have to give these talented women your full support; you have to communicate and be as close to them as you can be. I was really impressed that he didn't seem to impose himself on them, but tried to adapt to them."[14]

Jewison's support may have been especially important in Tilly's case. Late in the film, after being hypnotized by Fonda's psychologist, Agnes reveals that she had been molested as a child. It wasn't until 2006 that Tilly herself came forward as a survivor of physical, sexual, and emotional abuse at the hands of her stepfather, "a pedophile with a sadistic streak."[15] It wasn't a shared spiritual journey that had caused Tilly to "believe in" Agnes, but a shared history of abuse. If that experience wasn't intense enough, Tilly found herself playing a child-murderer shortly after the birth of her first child.

Jewison, Tilly said, "made you feel loved so that you could do your best work."

"He had a crew that had that same kind of safe, protective quality, so you were able to bounce off the walls and really give it everything and let yourself really go, because people weren't judging," Tilly said. "You felt like you were safe."[16]

John Board, on the other hand, did not feel safe. As Jewison's assistant director on *Agnes of God*, Board's role was essentially logistical: to maintain shot lists, track progress, make sure the right people were on set at the right time. For reasons that are not entirely clear, Board came to fear his daily interactions with Jewison.

McDonald remembers Board scurrying around on set, saying, "He's going to shit on me! He's going to shit on me!" When asked to share his perspective on the making of *Agnes of God*, Board responded tersely, "No thanks!"

Jewison was curious and kind and supportive, but he could also be a "tough motherfucker," McDonald concedes. "He could be really tough on certain people," when he thought it necessary "to keep their game up."[17] While other male colleagues over the years (such as Joe Eszterhas and William Goldman) had thrived under what Goldman called Jewison's "abrasive" approach, the same treatment didn't work for John Board. Some observers were astounded by Jewison's empathy and ability to read people, yet he was also capable of alienating those who weren't up to his demands.

* * *

Agnes began shooting in and around Montreal (locations included la Bibliotheque Nationale and the Mary, Queen of the World Cathedral) in November 1984. By this time, all three of Jewison's children had joined his team. Kevin, twenty-nine, was first assistant cameraman; Michael, twenty-seven, served as location manager, and Jennifer, twenty-four, was an actress with bit parts in *Best Friends* and *Agnes*. "I tried to keep them out of the business," Jewison would tell reporters, "to turn them away from it because it has so much rejection, but I couldn't seem to do it. Movie families are like circus families. It's in the blood."[18]

The actors spent weeks researching their roles: Fonda shadowed forensic psychiatrists and witnessed hypnotisms. Bancroft got to know a Mother Superior at a Los Angeles convent. She and Tilly wore their nun's habits around in public, which took some getting used to. "We had to be very careful of what we said," Bancroft recalled with a laugh. On weekends during the latter part of the shoot, Fonda gave exercise classes at the Guelph town hall. Mel Brooks, Tom Hayden, and Tim Zinnemann arrived for Thanksgiving with their working wives.[19] Shooting continued apace, although nobody involved was confident about where they were headed.

"Up until the ending of the film I thought it was an absolutely exquisite piece, beautifully done by Norman," said Bancroft. "We all had big struggles with the ending."[20]

One problem was that nobody seemed to know the truth about Agnes's pregnancy. Tilly believed it was an immaculate conception. Jewison was operating on the theory that she had been seduced by a local farmhand, but believed it had been a religious experience. "John [Pielmeier] felt very strongly that I should cut to a young field hand in silhouette on the hill behind the convent," Jewison said. Pielmeier even wrote a new scene involving a mute young man from the village who drowned shortly after Agnes's pregnancy was exposed.

But Jewison didn't want any obvious red herrings. "I said you can't have it both ways, John," he recalled. "Let the audience make up their mind."[21] The courtroom scene, shot on location in Toronto's Old City Hall, established that Agnes was not criminally responsible for her baby's death and could return to the convent. (Three of Jewison's last five films had ended with someone going crazy in a courtroom.) Still, the film needed a final beat, a moment of resolution for its characters. Bancroft remembers shooting a teary scene with Fonda, with the nuns walking around the convent in the snow. "I'll never know why but we were walking in the snow," Bancroft recalls. "We were just trying to make an ending."[22]

Later, shooting a silent scene with Tilly in the belfry, a dove spontaneously alighted next to the actress. Jewison told her to try and reach out to it; the dove allowed Tilly to pick it up. Then, after a moment's caress, she released it.[23]

It wasn't satisfying in a narrative sense, but the sheer serendipity of the scene, the dove's angel-like wings beating against the sky, struck Jewison as a poetic note on which to end.

* * *

For his entire career, journalists had defined Jewison in terms of his youthful energy and appearance. The passage of years forced them to get more creative. The "pixie of Jarvis Street" was now "a silvery-haired man, neatly bearded and barbered. Dressed in shades of silver and pewter, with his lively brown eyes hidden by aviator glasses, he resembles a natty raccoon, at once alert and antic."[24] Jewison's choice of projects in this period reflected a growing awareness of his own mortality. He found himself musing on something Alfred Hitchcock had once told him: "Each of us has a certain number of films in us. So do not try everything."[25]

The film he planned to do next, a remake of the 1937 fantasy-comedy *The Man Who Could Work Miracles*, would return him to a magical moment of his childhood. "I saw it when I was ten-years-old in the east end of Toronto and I never forgot it for the rest of my life. And I cannot tell you why except, I guess . . . I guess it was one of those fantasies that grabbed me as a child."

The project received a major boost when Richard Pryor agreed to star as the ordinary shop clerk gifted omnipotent powers by the gods. Jewison was raring to go on *Miracles*. He considered Pryor to be "almost a genius," and the property itself couldn't have been more personal.[26] "It's always been a part of me," he said, "so when I say that I hope I will do it justice, I'm not just saying something nice."[27] Jewison had been collaborating on the rewrites of the original H.G. Wells screenplay over the past year, during the filming of *Agnes*. *Miracles*, which required the most extravagant special effects of Jewison's career, was budgeted for $19 million, and tentatively scheduled to begin shooting in Chicago the following spring.[28]

There was one final hurdle. Jewison's deal with Columbia called for final approval from the studio head, and that head had recently changed. In a surprise move, Columbia had replaced CEO Frank Price (under whom Jewison had negotiated his seven-picture deal with the studio) with forty-five-year-old David Puttnam, the first non-American to run a US film studio. According to the Hollywood trades, Puttnam's name (associated with prestige fare including *Chariots of Fire* and *The Killing Fields*) was "synonymous with quality" and represented the "triumph of a 'creative' over Hollywood suits."[29] If the chatter was to be believed, Puttnam's arrival should have been great news for Jewison. Yet, a week after submitting his *Miracles* script, he hadn't heard back. His agent prodded Puttnam. No answer was forthcoming.

About one month later, he finally received a letter from Puttnam explaining that Columbia would not move forward with *Miracles*.

"Just think," Jewison said later. "I'd spent a year of my life working on the H.G. Wells story. A year! I want to make the film. I want to do the picture with Richard Pryor, and Richard wants to do it—and all of a sudden I can't get to [Puttnam]."

According to author Andrew Yule, Jewison "phoned David, incensed that it had taken a month to be turned down. 'How do you keep me waiting!' he raged. 'Then you didn't even have the courtesy to call me personally!'" Puttnam later said he respected Jewison, although he'd found *Soldier's Story* and *Agnes of God* "dull." After the "abuse" Jewison had delivered over the phone, Puttnam decided that Jewison's contract would not be extended.[30]

Puttnam "didn't like the script," said David Picker, then president of Columbia under Puttnam. "It was as simple as that, and in fact he gave Jewison and the producer the opportunity to take it elsewhere. They couldn't set it up anywhere . . . but that's what happens in this business."[31]

He claimed to bear no grudges with Columbia, yet "after making money on [*Soldier's Story* and *Agnes*] you'd think the studio would say, 'well, if he feels the same way about H.G. Wells, why don't we take a chance on him?' And this is the same studio that turned me down." Even worse was the rejection that followed from every other studio in town.

"It's gonna be a big fucking defeat in a way because I've spent almost two years on it," Jewison said at the time. "I've given up so much to make it happen, and I guess because I've always been able to do it before . . ." Jewison trailed off, unable to complete the thought.[32] He used to think that once he'd sufficiently proved himself, once he'd delivered enough successful pictures, the dance would get easier. At sixty, Jewison was still facing rejection, still being told that his dreams wouldn't work, still fighting tooth-and-nail for every film.

Around this time, Jewison met with the director John Huston for what turned out to be the last time. Huston had started his legendary directing career in 1940 on *The Maltese Falcon*. Now, at seventy-eight, Huston was directing his thirty-ninth film, an adaptation of James Joyce's story "The Dead."

"Norman," Huston confided, his voice a raspy whisper, "it's just as tough now as it ever was."[33]

CHAPTER 19

Moonstruck

C HER INITIALLY PASSED ON *MOONSTRUCK*. Her schedule was packed: she was filming *The Witches of Eastwick*, the John Updike adaptation starring Jack Nicholson and Susan Sarandon, until November, then beginning Peter Yates's thriller *Suspect* into February. With Christmas break, she might have six working weeks between projects. She simply could not squeeze another starring role in that span. Plus, John Patrick Shanley's script didn't grab her. It wasn't big or flashy, and she wasn't sure there was much of an audience for it. In that assessment, she was far from alone.

In the mid-1980s, John Patrick Shanley was a moderately successful Bronx playwright who was "slowly starving to death." He recalls thinking "that if I was going to change my situation, I'd better write a movie."[1]

He wrote *The Bride and the Wolf*, a quirky, romantic fairytale of New York, specifically for Sally Field, but the actress couldn't get the project financed. When the screenplay turned up at Jewison's production company, Patrick Palmer quickly scanned it and made up his mind. "Palmer called [Shanley's agent] up and yelled at her for sending him such a bad screenplay," Shanley remembers. "Then Norman read it and called her up and said he wanted it."[2]

Jewison recollects how the coffee stains on the cover of *The Bride and the Wolf* told him that it had been making the rounds. Still, there was much in Shanley's script that spoke to him. It was theatrical, snappy, and (like almost all of Jewison's strongest work) situated within a specific ethnic and cultural milieu (Italian American, in this case; Jewison would dub Shanley "The Bard of the Bronx.") Best of all, he had written something that Norman felt was close to filmable. After Puttnam vetoed *The Man Who Could Work Miracles* following intensive development work, Jewison didn't have another year to develop something from scratch. He did, of course, have extensive notes, "almost always for cuts," Shanley remembers.

Shanley also remembers being impressed by Jewison's "adventurousness." "His career is really ballsy, really diverse," Shanley said at the time. He struck the writer as someone attracted to difficult situations. His desire to cast Cher, for example, was only heightened when he found out that her previous commitments made her unavailable. "As soon as he smelled the hunt," Shanley said, "his eyes lit up and he was happily into the fray."[3]

But before he could seriously pursue Cher or anyone else, Jewison needed a studio's commitment. He took the script, re-titled *Moonglow*—*The Bride and the Wolf* sounded like a horror movie, he thought—to Columbia's David Puttnam, who was unimpressed. The producer of *Midnight Express* and *The Mission* didn't see any prestige or money in it. It was a talky, low-key romance about an unglamorous, thirty-something widow who falls in love with her stodgy fiancé's wild younger brother. This time, Jewison wouldn't have long to wait for Puttnam's answer: Columbia would pass on *Moonglow*.

* * *

One day in November 1986, Jewison, Cher, Nicolas Cage, Olympia Dukakis, and other cast members were in New York rehearsing the film that was now called *Moonstruck*. Cher, hidden beneath an oversized black sweater and reflective aviator glasses, had exactly one day off between *The Witches of Eastwick* and this new project.[4] Jewison, dressed like a farmhand in blue jeans and cowboy boots, set down his Styrofoam coffee cup to grasp Olympia Dukakis by the hands, as though to physically transmit the emotion of the scene they were rehearsing. Filming would commence in days. According to Jewison, the screenplay had been with Alan Ladd Jr. at MGM/UA for all of two hours before an assistant phoned to convey their plans to proceed.[5]

The studio had plenty of ideas about who should star, including Liza Minnelli, Rosanna Arquette, Demi Moore, and Barbra Streisand. Jewison didn't seriously consider anyone but Cher for the role: she had a gritty street-wise quality that Jewison associated with Loretta Castorini. In their first meeting, Cher had looked Jewison straight in the eyes and said, "You know, I can be tough."[6] She told him she had more important things on the go than *Moonstruck*—two films and an album to finish in the next few months. If Jewison would wait a year, she would consider it.

"I told her that she'd be sorry," Jewison said, "that these things don't come along often. I said, 'Cher, I'm not gonna wait a year, I'll lose my passion.'"[7]

Jewison had followed Cher's career since the *Sonny & Cher Comedy Hour* in the early 1970s. "I thought she was wasted," he said of the show. "I thought she had a tremendous sense of humour. I said to her not long ago that I thought she would have been perfect for one of the daughters in *Fiddler on the Roof* and she said, 'Oh, Norman, no one took me seriously back then.'"[8]

Cher's career had foundered in the late 70s, until a turn in Robert Altman's off-Broadway *Come Back to the 5 and Dime, Jimmy Dean, Jimmy Dean* revived her fortunes as an actress. Even in 1986, while Cher was getting choice roles in Hollywood films, questions lingered about her star power in the medium, partly because nobody knew what "star power" really was.

Contemporary industry consensus held that there were three bankable female movie stars: Jane Fonda, Sally Field, and Meryl Streep (of whom Jewison was "not a fan"). "There is no clear evidence that Cher has pull," a 1987 *New York Times Magazine* story noted, and "some evidence that she doesn't." Surveys conducted by the private firm Marketing Evaluations / TV Q had found that Cher was well known, but not well liked. Her "Q" score, a supposedly objective measurement of brand appeal, was lower than the mean for actresses. "She's never been as popular as she was when she was on television in 1974," Steven Levitt, the company's president, said of Cher. "My prediction based on the data we have is that people are not going to go out of their way to see a movie she's in."[9] Had Jewison known about this research, it's unlikely that he would have cared. In his mind, Cher was Loretta Castorini.

Jewison was less committed when it came to the part of Ronny Cammareri. It seemed that almost every A-list actor in Hollywood (from Tom Cruise to Bill Murray) was put forward for consideration. Jewison scribbled "needs style," and "too young" next to Ray Liotta's name after his audition (the actor was ten years older than Nicolas Cage, who eventually won the role).[10] Ultimately, it was Cher who pushed for "Nicky." It was an unlikely choice: Cage was just twenty-three years old (seventeen years younger than his co-star) and missing two front teeth, which the Method actor had removed for his role in *Birdy* (1984). "He's not all that great looking," a *Cosmopolitan* writer claimed at the time. "Rather, it's his pouty, hangdog eyes, a look of vulnerability that's mindful of a lazy morning in bed . . . a brooding look that says, 'Baby, I can be very dangerous.'"[11]

Cage's Ronny was indeed more menacing than Jewison had anticipated. "Nicolas did have a darker interpretation of Ronny than I did," Jewison said, "but we both agreed that a poetic quality was central to the character. When Ronny is first introduced in the film he's in a basement slaving over hot ovens and he almost has the quality of a young Lord Byron."[12]

By all accounts, Cage, who was almost entirely nocturnal, brought a punk-like edge to the ensemble, which now included John Mahoney, Danny Aiello, Vincent Gardenia, and Feodor Chaliapin Jr. "My ideal living space," Cage mused at the time, "would have a study, a circular room, with my desk in the middle, and surrounding me completely would be an aquarium filled with saltwater and huge sharks, octopuses and creatures of the sea."

Cage owned two sharks, an exotic insect collection, and a jewel-encrusted tortoise. "I've always been fascinated by marine biology. I don't know why. It's sort of like my bible," Cage told *Playgirl*. "I have a picture of a fish in my wallet that is just going to knock your socks off."[13]

Cage was not the only eccentric member of the cast. Feodor Chaliapin Jr., who played Cher's grandfather (he ad-libbed interactions with his five dogs throughout the film), had great difficulty hearing the other actors. "He was so deaf," Jewison recalls, he got his cue by watching the lips of the actor with the lines ahead of him: when they stopped talking, he'd start. Before casting Chaliapin, Jewison phoned his old friend Sean Connery, who had worked with the actor on *In the Name of the Rose*. "Norman," Connery told him, "he canna see, he canna hear, and he'll steal every bloody scene in the film."[14]

* * *

It was the middle of the night, and there was more urgency than usual on the *Moonstruck* set. New York's Lincoln Center charged a flat $20,000 to film its facilities, and Jewison was determined to pick up the pace. Cher, Cage, Vincent Gardenia, Anita Gillette, and 107 extras were filming in the cloakroom of the Metropolitan Opera House. A bone-chilling December rain had kept the elaborately coiffed extras (adorned in leather, furs, and conspicuous jewels) inside the lobby for hours on end, and energy was beginning to flag: an assistant director periodically reminded them that they were supposed to be having fun. The rain had not deterred Cher's fans from congregating outside for a glimpse of what one scribe called an "elegantly tall woman" with "ebony hair corkscrewed into a cascade of curls, her lips the colour of sin on a Saturday night."[15] ("What a prop!" Pauline Kael declared of Cher's hair, which she described as a "huge dark mass of crinkly tendrils.")

Over the course of a long night they filmed fourteen takes of a crucial forty-five-second sequence in the film: Ronny has convinced Loretta to accompany him to Puccini's *La Bohème*, an occasion for her Pygmalion-like transformation, where Loretta (still engaged to Ronny's brother Johnny) spies her father with his mistress. She confronts him.

LORETTA: Pop? What are you doing here?

COSMO: What'd you do to your hair?

LORETTA: I got it done.

COSMO: What are you doing here?

LORETTA: What are you doing here?

COSMO: Who is this man? You're engaged!

LORETTA: You're married!

COSMO: Alright. I didn't see you here.

LORETTA: I don't know whether I saw you or not.

For many viewers, Shanley's words were the real star of *Moonstruck*. The screenplay was at once ethnically specific and universal, a cornball fairytale that was also knowing and worldly wise. After Ronny confesses his passionate love for Loretta, she slaps him across the face, appalled: "Snap out of it!" Pauline Kael described the "flipped-out" mood as "rose-tinted black comedy," a "giddy homage to our desire for grand passion."[16]

Jewison imagined Shanley's characters in operatic terms. "I see Loretta as the lyric soprano," he explained. "Her fiancé, Mr. Johnny, is the baritone; Mr. Johnny's younger brother, Ronny, is the tenor; and Loretta's father, Cosmo, is the bass."[17]

Where the typical three-act Hollywood screenplay scaffolds scenes according to a carefully controlled schema of narrative beats, *Moonstruck* luxuriated in long, character-building scenes that seemed superfluous from a narrative perspective. "*Moonstruck* is all kinds of stuff but really it hasn't got much of a spine," said William Goldman. "I'm a firm believer that the only thing that really matters in screenplays is the structure. Where do we start, let's get on with it, let's cut the narrative lines here and there, and that's our movie." For Goldman, *Moonstruck* was the rare example of a successful screenplay that broke all the rules. "The spine of the movie is really the family. For me the best scene in the movie is Olympia Dukakis and John Mahoney in the restaurant. Well, it is a glorious scene with two superb actors, but you can cut the whole scene, and nobody would say, 'What about the restaurant scene?' There's just stuff in the movie that falls off the spine, but that ultimately accumulates."

"If it hadn't have worked," Goldman added, "it would have been so awful, you would have been writhing in your seat, saying, 'What is this shit?' But the fact is it does work, and that's very audacious—a wonderful piece of work."[18]

* * *

In a case of life mirroring art, the cast of *Moonstruck* ended up replicating much of the love-hate dynamic between their characters. "We are all together in a very intense, close relationship," Jewison said, working within a frantic schedule that had been compressed to accommodate Cher.

The sexual *frisson* between Cage and Cher's characters stemmed at least partly from an ambivalence in their off-screen relationship. "I don't know if Nicky will ever be a huge mainstream actor," Cher said. "He takes unbelievable chances, and personally, I think he's crazy—sometimes he's a blast on set, other days I'd get real peeved at him." If anything, Cage was even less effusive about working with the singer he'd loved since he was ten years old. "I do think she needs a good director," Cage said of Cher. "Otherwise, she's in trouble."[19]

Cher's "toughness" revealed itself on set in various ways. One day, after an early-morning call and a number of lackluster takes, Jewison kept the cast and crew working until past noon. "It was about 1:30," Jewison remembers, "and I told her something authoritative like, 'We'll break when we get it right.' And Cher turned to everyone else and said, loud, so that they all heard, 'Did I just hear that? You're not going to let us have lunch?'" It was embarrassing, yet Jewison grudgingly appreciated that the star spoke her mind. "She'll tell you exactly what she thinks."[20]

Cher sometimes resisted direction, insisting she knew the character best. "There were certain things that Norman had a lot of trouble getting from her," said co-star Julie Bovasso, who also served as the film's dialect coach. "I think she has the blinders on a little bit."

Olympia Dukakis felt that Cher's "difficulty" had to be understood within the context of her career. "I think she's been through so much, and she's been very aware of people controlling her, so that she's really on guard," Dukakis said. "I think that's what working in this business taught her." Dukakis thought those close to Cher had told her not to do the film at all.[21]

The senior members of the cast appreciated Jewison's touch. They called him the "Canadian guru."[22]

"He never talked about acting," Olympia Dukakis said of Jewison. "For one scene, he came up to me and said, 'That one line in there . . . Can you just throw that away a little bit more?' And that was it. But he knew that if I was gonna do that, then the whole thing was going to change. And instead of talking about that change, he just figured out what was going to happen if I did it. That's pretty fabulous."[23]

Jewison's energy and physical presence remained a source of fascination for colleagues. "I was looking at him once on the set and I wondered how much of who he is came from his size, because he's a slight man," said Dukakis. "There's a power in him and a passion in him and a strength. I mean, I can remember going by his office and hearing him roaring in there, *roaring*."[24]

After two-and-a-half weeks in New York, *Moonstruck* moved to Toronto. The production facilities—a converted IBM factory in Scarborough— were a far cry from the old Culver City Selznick studios that housed Jewison's LA offices, but aside from some soundproofing issues, they did the job. Further locations were filmed in Toronto's Keg Mansion, Markham Theatre, and Little Trinity Church Park. Toronto's transformation over the last several decades continued to amaze Jewison. The Beaches, in particular, had gentrified from a tough, working-class neighbourhood into a chic borough with "everybody running around in jogging suits."[25]

* * *

Moonstruck didn't feel like a triumph to those who were acting in it. "We were all stupid and didn't understand what Norman Jewison was really doing," Dukakis remembers. "One day we were sitting around talking," she said, "and somebody asked Cher what she thought was going to happen, and she gave the thumbs-down. Nobody really expected too much out of it."[26]

Pent-up tension among the cast finally erupted in filming the climactic scene, in which each character congregates around the Castorini kitchen table for a final reckoning. It was a complicated sequence, and flubbed cues resulted in many failed takes. Actors started telling each other off; at one point, Danny Aiello clutched his testicles and bellowed at Cage, "you gotta give it to me from here!"

Jewison cleared the set to speak only with the actors. He vented his frank exasperation: normally, when he asks actors to try the scene a certain way, they listen. But this pigheaded group had stopped taking direction.[27] He urged them to pull it together and get the film across the finish line, but they launched right into another volley of failed takes. Cage became so consumed with rage that he hurled a chair at another actor, Jewison remembers.

Finally, Feodor Chaliapin Jr., rose to be heard. "Calma, calma, calma," he implored. He explained that they were working in the tradition of Feydeau farce, "and in a Feydeau farce we pull everything together in the last scene." Chaliapin's castmates may have been baffled by his reference to the nineteenth-century French playwright Georges Feydeau, but the elderly actor's intervention somehow de-escalated the situation.

"We did it again," Jewison remembers, "and everything fell into place."[28]

Moonstruck was about the deranging quality of romantic love, and of the family's ultimate capacity to contain that wild energy: a comic recasting of the "faith versus logic" conflict at the heart of *Agnes of God*. Where Fonda and Bancroft had debated the existence of miracles in the modern world, Cher and Cage dueled over the existence of passionate love as a palpable force in our lives.

Some critics decried what they perceived as the film's conservative sexual politics: writing in *Penthouse*, Marcia Pally argued that *Moonstruck* offered a comic version of *Fatal Attraction*'s "fuck-and-you-die" film morality. Doubtless, a traditional (some called it "puritanical") attitude toward sex prevailed behind the scenes, beginning with Cher: "I am not an easy lay," she said at the time. "I am monogamous; I have relationships, not lovers."[29] Cher even insisted on wearing a body suit during the film's (decorous) sex scene. Still, much of the film's manic energy comes from submission to the whims of unbridled, irrepressible, passionate love. Jewison revels in Cage's soaring monologue on the street outside his apartment: "We are not here to make things perfect," he yells at Loretta. "We are here to ruin ourselves and break our hearts and love the wrong people and die! . . . Now *get in my bed!*"

A comedy in the classical mode, *Moonstruck* ends with the promise of nuptials and the reconciliation of family. Along the way, the film deliriously embraces the mess and entanglements of love, sex, death, art, wine, music, and food. It was Jewison's most sensuous film: eggs and Italian peppers sizzling in the frying pan, strains of Puccini swelling over the soundtrack, the fizz of a sugar cube dropped in a flute of champagne. It was Cher in a black coat against the Manhattan skyline, kicking a tin can down the middle of the street in high heels, dreamy look on her face. *Moonstruck* was drunk with life.

It was also a love letter to Dixie. If Jewison had, over the years, privately invoked a version of Ronny's *carpe diem* philosophy to excuse his own sexual escapades, the ending of *Moonstruck* was like an *apologia*. When, in the film's closing moments, Rose Castorini insists that her husband break off an extra-marital affair, he slowly rises, smacks the table, and says "Okay." He blows her a kiss across the table, and, ever so subtly, Rose breathes it in. "Ti amo."

Like his characters, Norman knew something of the madness of passionate love, yet he was devoted to family and tradition. At a time when men of his profession routinely burned through three or four wives, Jewison and Dixie remained married for fifty-four years, parted by her death in 2004.

"To family," the Castorinis toast in the closing moments of *Moonstruck*, with Jewison's camera slowly retreating to linger on a framed photo of some ancient relatives, from whose passion it had all begun.

Above all, what the director brought to *Moonstruck*, what he activated within the material, was a capacity for joy. "The humour, the sheer lust of life, it's there in Norman," said Vincent Gardenia, who plays Cher's father in the film. "Most directors try to do that, create that atmosphere," he added, "but it's not real."[30]

As for Cher, she'd had a few "real tough" moments with her director— at one point she'd called him a "curmudgeon." Looking back, what she remembered was his obvious delight in the act of creation. "Norman laughs a lot," she said, "he even laughed during a take . . . I enjoy watching him enjoy it. I don't think I've ever worked with anybody who enjoys it so much."[31]

* * *

"Good evening, Hollywood phonies," was how host Chevy Chase kicked off the 60th Annual Academy Awards on April 11, 1988. *Moonstruck* was up for six Oscars, including Best Picture and Best Director. Asked about his picture's chances on the red carpet, Jewison responded: "Did you see the moon last night? Bella luna!"[32]

Olympia Dukakis remembers the moment when she realized that *Moonstruck* was more than a standard-issue rom-com. She was in the back of a car with Jewison, *en route* to a benefit screening in Toronto. "He said, 'You know, you're going to get an Academy Award for this,'" Dukakis remembers. "I looked at him like he was stark-raving mad. I thought, 'This little movie and that little Italian lady are gonna get an award?'" Dukakis suspected Jewison was just being nice because she'd made the trip to Toronto for the benefit.[33]

Soon enough, the Oscar buzz began in earnest. Jewison reached out to Cher and Dukakis with some specific advice. "He said, you're going to get the Academy Award for this, but you've got to do everything," Dukakis recalls. "Every interview. Every television appearance. You must do everything."

"You know, I did everything he told me," she added, "but it's interesting, because he knows what to do but he won't do it [himself]."

Rather than taking his own advice, Jewison spent the lead-up to the Oscars complaining in print that the Academy had snubbed the departed John Huston's accomplishment in *The Dead*.[34] Julie Bovasso, Dukasis's co-star, wondered if Jewison secretly didn't want to win. "When you don't win and everyone thinks you should have won—there's something more exclusive about that," Bovasso said.[35]

From his lower-bowl seat in the Shrine auditorium (the Oscars had moved from the Dorothy Chandler Pavilion to the 6000-seat venue to satisfy demand), Jewison saw John Patrick Shanley collect his original screenwriting Oscar (he thanked "everybody whoever punched or kissed me" and "the multi-media princess Cher.") He saw Dukakis win best supporting actor ("Okay, Michael, let's go!" she shouted in support of her cousin Michael Dukakis's 1988 run for the Democratic presidential nomination). He saw Cher, dressed in a sheer Bob Mackie negligee bodice, trip on her way up the stairs (blurting "Shit!") after winning Best Actress. Cher thanked "my hairdresser" and "the lady who taught me how to speak in this Brooklyn accent," but not Jewison. He saw one of his idols, Billy Wilder, accept the Irving G. Thalberg lifetime achievement Oscar. He vaguely saw Robin Williams present the award for Best Director— he'd removed his glasses, just in case, only to hear the rousing ovation Bernardo Bertolucci received for his achievement in *The Last Emperor*.[36]

The next presenter, Eddie Murphy, called for a round of applause "for the losers."

"You've got the tux on, you feel real stupid right now."

The Best Director loss was lacerating. But *Moonstruck* was an unexpected triumph. The wins for Cher and Dukakis further solidified Jewison's reputation as the pre-eminent actor's director; just as important, the film was a box-office smash, taking in $116 million against a budget of approximately $10 million.[37] *Moonstruck* had stunned the industry to become one of the highest earning films of the year, out-grossing blockbuster fare like *Lethal Weapon* and *The Untouchables*. *A Soldier's Story* and *Agnes of God* were successful on their own terms, but *Moonstruck* was successful on everyone's terms.

After so many years struggling to balance commercial and artistic imperatives, *Moonstruck* was an immense personal validation for Norman Jewison. When, decades later, his long-time assistant Elizabeth Broden was asked to name the highlight of his career, she didn't hesitate: *Moonstruck*.

While Jewison was rarely recognized or stopped on the streets, when he was, it was often with, "Hey, aren't you the director of *Moonstruck*?" On those rare occasions, he had his answer ready: "Snap out of it!"[38]

CHAPTER 20

The Wall

THE AUGUST HEAT WAS SUFFOCATING in Paducah, Kentucky's Walter C. Jetton Junior High School gymnasium. Jewison, perched next to a Panavision camera, was directing a scene with Bruce Willis and Judith Ivey. "You look like a Kentucky redbird," Willis mumbled, almost inaudible, as Ivey gently tugged him onto the dance floor. "Cut!" Jewison yelled. Not a bad take, but assistant director Gordon Boos soon corralled everyone back to their marks.

The school gym, decorated for a Vietnam veteran's dance, was draped in camouflage cloths and banners (one read: Chapter 337, Vietnam Veterans of America), and ringed with tables featuring photographs, medals, helmets, an M16. Much of the memorabilia was authentic, supplied by veterans who served as extras in the scene.[1]

Jewison was filming a scene for *In Country*, an adaptation of Bobbie Ann Mason's bestselling 1985 novel. *In Country* is the story of a seventeen-year-old named Sam who lives with her uncle Emmett (Willis), a Vietnam vet suffering from PTSD—at one point, he climbs a tree in a thunderstorm and challenges the lightening to "show me your face!"—and, perhaps, side

349

effects of agent orange. The summer after her high-school graduation, Sam discovers a trove of letters sent by her father, an American G.I. killed in Vietnam, to her pregnant mother, inciting a halting narrative of personal discovery and generational reconciliation. Sam's questions about her father and the experience of war mostly just annoy Emmett, though the ingénue (played with spunk by the seventeen-year-old British actress Emily Lloyd) gradually exerts a kind of therapeutic force on her uncle, forcing him to confront a past he'd prefer to ignore.

In Country, a film about how our public and private lives are shaped by history, was the product of Jewison's own history. He vividly remembered protesting the war and President Johnson outside the Century Plaza Hotel, where he and Hal Ashby had been beaten by mounted police. More vivid than any single memory was the mood of that period—the civil unrest, the sudden eruptions of violence, the assassinations that tore through public consciousness—compounded by a sickening sense of moral betrayal, a disillusionment, which fed into his decision to leave the US. "There were the endless lists of the dead," wrote the novelist James Salter, "the visible brutality, the many promises of victory that were never kept until the war seemed like some dissolute son who cannot ever be trusted or changed but must be taken in."[2]

"For a long while, I swore I'd never make a movie about that war. I'd turned down projects," Jewison said in 1989. A film about Vietnam, he felt, "is one subject I could not deal with emotionally, it is too close to my heart, it is too close to the bone."[3]

Jewison thought that Vietnam had been as important to twentieth-century America as the Civil War had been to the nineteenth, but that no film had captured its lingering significance.[4] Whatever Coppola thought he was saying about the war in *Apocalypse Now* had been dwarfed by the influence of Joseph Conrad, Jewison felt. As for *Deer Hunter*, "a film that made all the 'gooks' the heavies" and "where everyone stands around at the end and sings 'God Bless America,'" he considered it little more than right-wing propaganda.[5]

Platoon and *Full Metal Jacket* captured the spectacular violence of warfare, but didn't attempt to register the lingering psychological and social consequences. For Jewison, the beating heart of the story was the war's massive, often deforming, influence in the private lives of contemporary Americans, not just the veterans but also "their mothers and fathers and their grandparents and their daughters."[6]

In Country was enriched by the lived experience of actual veterans. Before filming, Jewison had attended a Vietnam memorabilia evening in Paducah, where he hoped to chat with a few vets. "We ended up staying for hours," he remembered, "poring over scrapbooks and the medals and everything, and we drank together, and talked together." Some vets appeared in the film as extras; others served as informal consultants. "I hear day in and day out in my office a lot of guys saying, what happened to me in Vietnam was difficult but tolerable, but what happened to me on getting back—that's where the intolerable came in," said one of these vets, now a psychologist. "Whatever happened in Vietnam, the worst treatment was when I came back," said another. "The American people spit at us and called us baby-killers. And after that I was ashamed to wear my uniform in public, because I didn't want the ridicule to come with it."[7]

"I have a feeling that [*In Country*] is my last film that is going to deal with an important social issue," Jewison said at the time, "because it's so hard, it was so hard to make this film."

In the Paducah gymnasium, Willis and Ivey were repeating their tentative trip to the dance floor for what felt like the umpteenth time. "You look like a Kentucky redbird," Willis said, as Ivey pulled him along. "Cut!" Jewison hollered. "That was great. Everybody go home."[8]

* * *

The meandering pace and reflective mood of *In Country* were far from what 1989 viewers expected from a "Vietnam picture." One critic described it as an "authentic American art film;" another noted that "nothing much happens in this picture; nothing, that is, except a series of very quiet, very controlled, very delicate scenes that gradually build to one overwhelming climax."[9]

Connecting those scenes were Sam's relationships with Emmett (who cannot move on) and Irene, her mother (who, she believes, moved on too fast.) The father with whom she tries to connect is beyond her comprehension. She thinks of him in terms of everything he missed: *E.T.,* or a Bruce Springsteen concert. (Springsteen's "I'm On Fire" serves as a musical leitmotif in the film, a blue-collar version of what Puccini did for *Moonstruck.*)

Casting the British Emily Lloyd as Sam was bound to raise a few eyebrows. "The American actresses I interviewed were seventeen going on thirty-five," Jewison explained.[10] Directing Lloyd was unlike anything Jewison had experienced with an actress since Judy Garland. Getting the nuances of her performances on film was like "catching quicksilver," he said. "She is extremely intelligent and very quick, but she has no technique to fall back on," he added.

In particularly tough moments, he would talk her through the scene and take his voice off the track in post. By fluke or by design, Lloyd's performance in the film was utterly transfixing.

While Jewison didn't know much about Willis—he hadn't seen *Moonlighting* or *Die Hard*—he knew the actor's rising star power would be an asset. Willis had also "agreed to read for it," Jewison said, "which for an actor of his stature is very rare." Jewison was struck by Willis's vulnerability, which he associated with Steve McQueen and Humphrey Bogart.[11] Willis put on weight and disappeared behind a Fu Manchu moustache for the role.

According to Willis, Jewison shot some scenes in different emotional registers. Nobody knew what would emerge from the editing room. In each case, according to Willis, Jewison used the most "dignified" take. "There's a very light touch to this film," Willis said. "I don't know if another [film] like this is going to come along in a long time."[12]

Over-acting was a particular hazard in the climactic confrontation between Willis and Lloyd. Sam has spent the night in a swamp—part vigil, part sensory re-creation of her father's wartime experience. Reading his pocket journal, she discovers that her father blew the "head clear off" of a Viet Cong soldier, only to find a picture of a baby in the dead soldier's pocket, a Vietnamese version of herself. When Emmett discovers Sam in the woods the next morning, she announces that she "doesn't like" her father anymore. For Emmett, Sam's reaction recapitulates America's reaction toward all Vietnam vets. Jewison wanted audiences to recognize the pain on both sides: American troops committed unspeakable atrocities in Vietnam. But America's failure to re-integrate its veterans and memorialize their experience had only compounded the tragedy.

Conscious memorialization was what Jewison hoped to accomplish at the Wall. In the director's mind, all their efforts so far had been about getting to the Vietnam Veteran's Memorial in Washington. The bombs, the marches and protests, the star-spangled coffins, the images of a generation—flower petals in a gun barrel, Vietnamese children crying in the streets—all of it led to the Wall.

"Because the Wall is where it all ends," Jewison said, "And I wanted to make a film about that Wall."[13]

* * *

The Vietnam Veterans Memorial consists of a pair of 250-foot-long polished granite walls, tapering from eight inches in height to over ten feet where they meet to form a V. Inscribed on it are the names of more than 55,000 American soldiers declared dead in Vietnam and Southeast Asia. The abstract design spurred controversy when it was unveiled in 1982: one veteran called it "the black gash of shame." Officials later authorized the addition of a bronze statue of three servicemen with guns in heroic pose.[14]

By 6:30 a.m. one morning in September 1988, members of the *In Country* production gathered on the National Mall between the Washington Monument and Lincoln Memorial. Jewison was tense. While he'd already photographed close-ups against a smoked-glass replica built in a farmer's pasture in Kentucky, he had just two days to work with the genuine artifact, and filming was highly regulated. By law, the Wall cannot be closed to the public, which meant that camera set-ups had to be 100-yards away. Since speeches and demonstrations were prohibited, film crews were barred from recording dialogue. Moreover, the *Washington Post* had ratcheted up the pressure by reporting that Bruce Willis would be filming at the Wall the next day, ensuring throngs of uncontrollable onlookers.

"I've got to get out of here today," Jewison said.[15]

Willis had wept upon first seeing the monument in person. He likened the experience to "being in a hallowed place."[16] As the sun came up, Jewison saw a humble assortment of offerings for the dead: medals, letters, ("We will miss you at our 25th reunion. Our prayers are with you, wherever you may be"), a can of Budweiser, a simple gold wedding band.

"The Wailing Wall of America is what it's become," Jewison said. "They don't want the medals, they leave them there. You saw the wedding ring. They're leaving their sadness behind."[17]

The climax of *In Country* drew emotional power from its simplicity: Sam finds her father's name, one among thousands, on the Wall. She requests a ladder to climb up and greet the name, pressing her lips against the engraved letters. As his characters leave the Wall, Jewison filmed their mirrored image on the obsidian surface, a place of literal and metaphorical reflection.

In his review of *In Country*, Roger Ebert likened the film to a "time bomb."

"You sit there," he wrote, "interested, absorbed, sometimes amused, sometimes moved, but wondering in the back of your mind what all of this is going to add up to. Then you find out."[18]

* * *

Following the commercial success of *Moonstruck*, Jewison had seriously considered directing *Dance Me Outside*, based on W. P. Kinsella short stories about angsty teenagers on the fictitious Kidabanesee Indian Reservation in Ontario. He commissioned a script by Larry McMurtry and Leslie Marmon Silko, a writer associated with the Native American Renaissance. Eventually, he decided to executive produce the project and assigned directing duties to Bruce McDonald, who brought a hard-rock sensibility to the material.

Given the choice between *Dance Me Outside* and *In Country*, Jewison felt a deeper connection to the American story. It wasn't just that Vietnam and its consequences had played a formative role in his own life. He also wanted the biggest possible stage for his cinema of ideas, and the grand theatricality of America and its stories was part of the allure. In Washington one night, he lingered alone near the Lincoln Memorial, reading the Gettysburg address, marvelling at the drama and theatricality of the scene. "I love this country," Jewison said of America. "Maybe I love it too much." On some level it bothered him that he'd never made a film about his own country.

Jewison's self-consciousness over never having told a Canadian story was part of what impelled him to found the Canadian Centre for Advanced Film Studies.

"When I left [Canada] in '58," he reflected, "there was no feature film industry in this country. Nothing." Even by the mid-1980s, Jewison felt that Canada still lacked the institutional infrastructure necessary for a national film culture. In 1986, he founded The Canadian Centre for Advanced Film Studies (re-Christened the Canadian Film Centre [CFC] in 1991) which he envisioned as Canada's answer to the American Film Institute: "Our mandate," he later explained in a letter to Ted Turner, "is to advance the artistic, technical, and business skills of our country's film, television, and new media communities. The young talents who pass through these doors represent our next generation of storytellers who will be defining Canada to Canadians." ("I hope the buffalo are procreating prolifically," he added in a personal aside to the rancher.)[19]

The CFC campus was to be situated on the Windfields Estate in Toronto, a picturesque eight-hectare property donated by the tycoon and horse breeder E. P. Taylor. Minutes from a 1987 board meeting reveal his directorial mind at work: "Norman suggested playing up the actual taking over of the property. Publicity pictures of Taylor handing the keys to [Toronto Mayor Mel] Lastman who then hands them to Norman."[20]

CFC directors Peter O'Brien (1988-91) and Wayne Clarkson (91-2005) oversaw development of the centre's signature initiatives: a resident program provided aspiring filmmakers with the opportunity to create their own short films; a feature film project was added in 1992. A sponsored lecture series allowed residents to network with established directors, actors, writers, and producers. Jewison worked a Rolodex that he had built up over a lifetime: lecturers came from the US (Martin Scorsese, Clint Eastwood), Britain (Roger Spottiswoode), Poland (Krzysztof Zanussi), and elsewhere. He drew heavily upon his collaborators: Rod Steiger, Beau Bridges, Margot Kidder, Sven Nykvist, and Danny DeVito all passed through the CFC to show films and speak with residents. Even David Puttnam, who had rejected *Agnes of God* and *Moonstruck* while the head of Columbia, visited the CFC for a shot-by-shot discussion of *The Killing Fields*.[21]

As founder, Jewison's involvements in the CFC were various, from attracting board members to outfitting the new institute with furniture (with Dixie's stamp of approval). Mostly, Jewison provided the centre with a public face, and some of his own boundless brio. "The arts are the only expression of a people that last," he said to a reporter at the time. "Long after the pulp and paper plants sink in the pools of their own pollution, long after the trees are cut down, it's the expression of a people that remains."

"At this point in time, we Canadians must start to nurture our talent and to express ourselves. Confidence is what people need. It's very important that we get down to it."[22]

Jewison "represented a kind of connection between an independent Canadian cinema and a successful long-term career in Hollywood," said filmmaker Don McKellar, a former resident. Jewison supported residents however he could, from viewing rough-cuts of films to helping residents secure US visas.

"Norman has been a kind of entire-career mentor for Clement [Virgo] and me," said producer Damon D'Oliveira. "He even found office space for our Conquering Lion Pictures and became our landlord for twenty years. He was always just a floor away." In 1995, with the assistance of the CFC,

Virgo and D'Oliveira released *Rude*, the first ever Canadian feature written, directed, and produced by people of colour.[23]

* * *

Jewison's own desire to bring Black stories to the screen had not diminished. Around this time, he was exploring at least three opportunities to do so: *Dreamgirls* was about how African American music could spur revolution (Whitney Houston was favoured to star). [24] *Lazarus and the Hurricane* told the story of Rubin "Hurricane" Carter, the boxer who had been wrongfully convicted of murder in 1963.[25] But the project that most excited Jewison's imagination was a film adaptation of *The Autobiography of Malcolm X*.

The idea came via Marvin Worth, who had purchased the rights to Malcolm X's *Autobiography* in 1967. Since then, Black and white filmmakers had united in failure to bring Malcolm to the screen. James Baldwin was the first to attempt a screenplay, although he worried about how the Nation of Islam would react (and Worth frankly thought he was distracted by personal problems). Calder Willingham (screenwriter of *The Graduate*), Sidney Lumet, David Mamet, and the novelist David Bradley had all struck out.[26] Richard Pryor and Eddie Murphy were both attached to the project at different points. After two decades of abortive attempts, *Malcolm X* was starting to seem like one of those legendary films that was destined to go unmade.

After Jewison inked a new deal with Warner Brothers (bringing the property and director under the same roof), several pieces quickly fell into place. Jewison commissioned *A Soldier's Story* screenwriter Charles Fuller to take a fresh crack at the screenplay. Denzel Washington, who played Malcolm in the Off-Broadway *When the Chickens Came Home to Roost*, was keen to reunite with Jewison. As for the director himself, one of the reasons he'd been so drawn to *Nat Turner* long ago was the clear echo between the historical revolutionary and Malcolm X: now he had the opportunity to bring Malcolm's story itself to the screen.

From Worth's perspective, things were finally looking up. After all, as Spike Lee had claimed in mid-1980s, everyone knew that "the best Hollywood films about Blacks were directed by Norman Jewison."[27]

The past couple of years, however, had given Lee cause to reassess. *Do the Right Thing*, released to rave reviews (and raging controversy) in 1989, heralded a sea change in African American cinema. By 1990, Lee was on *The Today Show* complaining that Warner Brothers had given the story of a Black nationalist and anti-white militant to a white director. "It's just never gonna be the same," Lee said. "You know, my hat is off to him but there's no way Norman Jewison—I mean, not to slight him, he's a great director—but there's no way he could do a better job on *The Autobiography of Malcolm X* than I can."[28]

Lee cranked up the volume of his campaign in a subsequent interview with the *New York Times*. "I have a big problem with Norman Jewison directing *The Autobiography of Malcolm X*," he fumed. "That disturbs me deeply, gravely. It's wrong with a capital 'W.' Blacks have to control these films."[29] Marvin Worth later claimed that, prior to contacting Jewison, he'd offered *Malcolm X* to Spike Lee in phone messages that went unreturned.[30]

Some African Americans took issue with Spike Lee claiming the racial megaphone on their behalf. "Spike said the director ought to be Black, which was Spike's way of saying it should be Spike," said James Earl Jones.

"Jones was a jerk to suggest I wanted to do it for selfish reasons," Lee countered. "I wouldn't trust a white to direct—to be honest—they just don't know what it feels like. There's stuff I go through every day . . . I don't care how many books they read, or if they grew up with a Black nanny, or what friends they had."[31]

Before long, letters protesting Jewison's involvement began pouring into the Gloucester St. office. His former assistant remembers them coming in by the bag. Many turned out to be carbon copies of letters sent to Warner Brothers CEO Terry Semel. By now, it seemed that Jewison's history on *Nat Turner* was repeating itself. But where the debate over *Turner* had focused on specific facets of Styron's recreation of the historical slave, the rhetorical fire this time focused on the director's race. No "European," as some letters described him, could "fully conceive [Malcolm's] pain."

While some of the protest letters argued that growing up or living in African American neighbourhoods was a prerequisite for understanding Malcolm, others fixated on racial biology. One writer explained that "white people think in linear and dichotomous left brain energy usages. Black people think in cyclical and diunital right brain energy usages."

Still others saw a more "diabolical" agenda: "We are fully aware of the doctrines of the Learned Elders of Zion," one protestor wrote, implying that Jewison—often mistaken for a Jew—was the agent of a nefarious Hollywood cabal.[32]

Publicly, Jewison said little in his own defense. He told a *New York Times* reporter that he thought it dangerous to assume that a director's race determined his sensibility, "because that's an apartheid idea, and I don't believe in apartheid."[33] Perhaps unrealistically, he believed his body of work spoke for itself. He'd made successful films about Jews suffering under pogroms, about nuns, about WWII-era Black soldiers, about housewives, about Jesus Christ. He did not believe that *Malcolm X* was beyond his imaginative scope.

Nor would it have occurred to Jewison that in bringing Malcolm X's story to the screen he was appropriating a story to which he had no right. The material appropriation had occurred decades earlier, when Betty Shabazz and Alex Haley sold the rights to Malcolm's *Autobiography* to

Marvin Worth. The question of Jewison's "right" was a legal matter, since Worth and Warner Brothers literally owned the rights to the *Autobiography*. Spike Lee didn't dispute that point: asked why he wasn't directing the picture on *The Today Show*, Lee answered, "Warner Bros. has a right, and you know, it's his [Jewison's] project."

Jewison's confidence was dampened, however, when Fuller's draft arrived. The director's frank assessment was that it did not "live up to the power and passion of this complex man." The screenplay was unfocussed, providing equal treatment to every area of its subject's life in the manner of a "docu-drama." Fuller's portrayal of Betty Shabazz as the "devoted, suffering" wife was cliché. Jewison loved Fuller's use of Malcolm's actual speeches, but worried about how to dramatize them on screen.[34]

In May 1990, Jewison and Worth had dinner with Spike Lee in New York. Nothing had officially changed by the end of the dinner, although Jewison noted Lee's "passion to do the film."

"We all decided to wait until we saw what the Charlie Fuller screenplay looked like," Marvin Worth reported. "That's where it sits."[35]

Fuller's second draft arrived about a month later. Jewison made a list of concerns on a sticky note as he read the revised screenplay: "Too long, too many flashbacks, too much detail in past, too heavy, too many events, too many people." As he wrote to Worth, "The most fascinating and entertaining portion of Malcolm's life" represented in Fuller's screenplay "seems to lie in the early years when he was on the streets, however, that's not where his greatness lies as a political revolutionary."[36] After nine months of work with Fuller, Malcolm X remained an enigma to Jewison. On August 27, he wrote to Denzel Washington.

It's not very often that I get discouraged with my dreams because all films are, in a way, dreams for filmmakers; sometimes out of focus, and other times crystal clear. Malcolm eludes me . . . I cannot somehow hold him in my grasp or truly understand where the important part of the story lies. I am torn between fact and fancy. Charles's script is based on fact and it reads like a docu-drama. It also doesn't have the flow and rhythm essential to a first-rate screenplay.

Maybe I am also affected by the resistance or push from a particular part of the Black community but, somehow, I feel that's not the real problem. When you have the opportunity to read Fuller's screenplay, let me have your opinion. Warner Brothers and Marvin Worth, at this point, have indicated they would rather give Spike Lee a shot. My advice is for you to sit tight until the right script comes along. You are an actor of immense talent and power. I will always be there for you . . .

Yours,

Norman[37]

CHAPTER 21

Old Ideas

J EWISON'S CAMERAS WERE ROLLING AT NO. 7 World Trade
Center on a crisp autumn morning in October 1990. Danny
DeVito, dressed in black topcoat and fedora, newspaper in hand,
marched through the cavernous lobby toward the elevator to his "securely
guarded temple of power," as Jewison called it. Between takes, Jewison
quizzed DeVito on specific details, nudging him to a more complete
understanding of his character, Larry the Liquidator.

"How many floors does Garfield investments have in this building?"

DeVito paused to think. "Three," he says.

"Is its trading floor here?" Jewison asked.

"Yes," came DeVito's reply. "And its executive offices too."[1]

At the 1988 Academy Awards, Jewison had watched Michael Douglas
win Best Actor for his portrayal of Gordon Gekko, the icon of 1980s
excess in Oliver Stone's *Wall Street*. Some critics accused Stone of neutering
his critique of corporate corruption by making Gekko guilty of insider
trading: the film was an indictment of an individual criminal, rather than
of the system itself. DeVito's Larry the Liquidator, by contrast, would

insist that greed could flourish within the ever-slackening laws governing behaviour on Wall Street. "All they can do is change the rules," Larry storms at one point. "They can never stop the game. I don't go away. I adapt."

Doubtless, the success of *Wall Street* paved the way for a more comic exploration of what Jewison called the "pig years" of the 1980s. Jewison believed that the supply-side dogmas of financial deregulation and lower taxes were changing not only America's economy but also its moral fabric. He bemoaned the fact that citizens were taught to "look out only for themselves." "Michael Milken, Ivan Boesky, Donald Trump, and other corporate takeover artists became our heroes," Jewison said.

"That's what pulled me toward this piece," he said. "The seduction of power, money and prestige."[2]

Jewison saw Jerry Sterner's off-Broadway play *Other People's Money* during its successful run in Greenwich in February 1989. A lukewarm review in the *New York Times* noted the manufactured and unconvincing nature of the romantic plot between the corporate raider and rival lawyer, and questioned actor Kevin Conway's portrayal of Lawrence Garfinkle in terms that "reinforced an ethnic stereotype."[3] Jewison, whose experience on *Jesus Christ Superstar* had provided enough accusations of anti-Semitism for one lifetime, changed the character's surname from Garfinkle to Garfield.

Other People's Money was no masterpiece of modern theatre, although it was voted the year's best off-Broadway production and contained some witty lines (peppered with corporate jargon of the day: "white knights," "shark repellents" and "poison pills"). The plot furnished Jewison with a broad allegory about the hollowing out of America's manufacturing sector and the self-cannibalizing nature of finance capitalism. "It's about

what is happening in America today—it's about lust and greed," Jewison
wrote to Michelle Pfeiffer, trying to entice her to play the female lead.[4]
Pfeiffer passed.

Most importantly, from the perspective of Warner Bros.—who would
foot the $400,000 bill for the play's rights—*OPM*'s successful theatrical
run (in New York, London, Chicago, and Los Angeles) confirmed proof
of concept. The play was particularly popular among the suspender-clad
Wall Street traders it supposedly parodied. Warner green lit the project
with a $30 million budget, the biggest of Jewison's career, $2 million of
which went to the director.[5]

What Jewison brought to the material was a sense of nostalgia, one
heightened by the presence of old friends. Haskell Wexler returned as
Jewison's cinematographer for the first time since *Thomas Crown Affair*,
imbuing the film with a rich, autumnal glow. For the president of New
England Wire and Cable, the mom and pop manufacturer Larry hopes
to liquidate, he turned to Gregory Peck. For Jewison, the actor behind
Atticus Finch harkened back to a departed era of cinematic dignity, and
Peck played the pipe-smoking, cardigan-wearing president as a living,
breathing Norman Rockwell portrait of American rectitude. Jewison was
capable of vast imaginative leaps in service of his material, but the wistful
yearning for American greatness that comes across in Peck's performance
(complete with dewy-eyed reminisces of meeting Harry S. Truman, set
against an American flag in the background) makes for an especially
jarring juxtaposition with the "ballot or the bullet" vision of American
history into which Jewison had apparently been prepared to throw himself
with *Malcolm X*. In truth, Jewison was less nostalgic for the actual America
of the 1960s (the riots, protests, and paranoia from which he had fled)
than for the cinema of the period, when films like *To Kill a Mockingbird*
meant something to some people.

* * *

Doughnut crumbs flecked Danny DeVito's Armani suit as the actor belched and mugged for the camera. "Cut! Oh Jesus, Danny ate a real doughnut," Jewison moaned, grimacing at the monitor. DeVito was supposed to consume the organic, fat-free, apple-juice-sweetened confections imported from California. With the cameras rolling, however, DeVito would snatch one of the real doughnuts, 400-calories a pop, getting himself "sorta jacked" on sugar.[6]

Jewison's first choice for the role had been Dustin Hoffman, but *Billy Bathgate* got in the way. DeVito, still widely known as Louie De Palma from *Taxi*, was branching into an intriguing directorial career of his own with *Throw Mama From the Train* and *War of the Roses*. The role of Kate Sullivan, the lawyer tasked with fending off Larry (financially and sexually) went to Penelope Ann Miller, the only actress Jewison tested who could hold her own against DeVito. Miller vamped through the part as the husky-voiced femme-fatale on the brink of self-parody, part Marilyn Monroe, part Jessica Rabbit.

The production moved from New York to a Connecticut factory in November, where they were plagued by an unusual amount of bad luck. There were car accidents, fires, crew members slipping off trucks, an assortment of freak injuries and hospitalizations. Julie Bloom, the second assistant director, was sent to hospital with copper flecks lodged in her eyes, scratching her cornea.[7] A protest scene produced still more injuries. Not since *Rollerball* had Jewison directed a film that was so accident prone.

Those on set may have wondered about the young man tailing Jewison virtually everywhere he went. David Wellington, an emerging director, was the official "director observer" on *Other People's Money*, and gained an intimate view on Jewison's work: indeed, Jewison told him to "stick to me like glue" during the shoot.

One of the things that struck Wellington was how Jewison devised camera set-ups in ways that played to his actors' strengths, rather than to suit his preconceived ideas about composition. He would arrive on set with a detailed list of the shots he wanted, then ignore it, preferring to work in the moment. "He showed me that meticulous preparation gives a director the freedom to be adventurous, to take chances, to fully explore the truth of each scene and ultimately, the truth of the film," Wellington said.[8]

In reality, Jewison was less than confident about "the truth of the film." Sterner's play ended with the triumph of Larry the Liquidator, who takes over New England Wire and Cable and marries Kate (named Bea in the play). While Jewison considered this ending too cynical for his audience, neither he nor veteran screenwriter Alvin Sargent could think of a more satisfying one. Sargent wrote at least five different endings for *OPM*, running the gamut of emotional registers. In one, Kate joins forces with Larry as his wife and business partner. Another provides Kate with a monologue in which she vows revenge against Larry. In still another, New England Wire and Cable is swallowed by the Mitsubishi Corporation. Eventually, they opted for a safe, happy ending in which the cable company is repurposed as an airbag manufacturer for a Japanese firm (saving the company's jobs). The romantic question is left hanging.[9]

Jewison's uncertainty about the ending reflected a larger uncertainty about its message. If the audience was supposed to be revolted by Larry and his brand of cutthroat capitalism, why had Jewison painted him as a lovable rapscallion who serenades Kate with a squawking violin rendition of "I'm in the Mood for Love"? (*Fiddler on the Roof* aficionados will note the signed photo of violinist Isaac Stern on Larry's piano). DeVito saw his character in sympathetic terms: to fixate upon Larry the Liquidator's "greed," DeVito said, "is like saying that Joe Montana is a very greedy quarterback because he throws a lot of touchdown passes or Willie Mays was a very greedy centrefielder because he caught a lot of fly balls."[10]

Asked about the film's message, Jewison said: "The lesson is, 'You'd better get back to work, you'd better start educating your youth and take education seriously, because knowledge will win.'"[11]

Little in the film supported the director's view of *Other People's Money* as a pro-education polemic. The truth was that neither Jewison nor DeVito had a clear sense of what their film was trying to say, which explains the director's unusual openness not only to alternate endings but also re-shoots and other tinkering in post-production intended to make the film more commercial. Critics seemed to sense that Jewison's heart wasn't in it. Janet Maslin noted DeVito's "deep-down wholesomeness" and predicted that the film would be "even more agreeable" to the Wall Street crowd than the play. So flaccid was *OPM*'s "satire" of finance capital that American Express sought a promotional deal with Warner that would incorporate the film's artwork into a mailer sent to 3.5 million cardholders.[12]

At the same time, the director's public statements about the power of film had become unusually soft, almost timid. "I like to think people think about movies after they leave the theatre and carry them for maybe years," he said in 1991, quickly adding, "maybe not. Maybe I'm totally wrong and movies don't mean anything except an hour-and-a-half of entertainment in the dark. I have no idea."[13]

Suffice to say, no one accused *Other People's Money* of being the work of a Canadian Pinko.

* * *

Despite their trouble cracking the ending of *OPM*, Jewison enjoyed working with screenwriter Alvin Sargent. They were both "a couple of old dogs," the director said, alike in age and sensibility. When Jewison decided to option the treatment that would become *Bogus*, about a boy forced into the care of his dissolute father after his mother dies, he turned to Sargent for help fleshing out the idea.

To accelerate the process, the director proposed a road trip. He met Sargent in Niagara Falls, and the pair took turns driving Jewison's new Jaguar convertible to Los Angeles over the next ten days.[14] They stopped at blues clubs, an NHL hockey game in St. Louis, the Cowboy Hall of Fame in Santa Fe, and the Hoover Dam. Whoever wasn't driving would read *New York Times* out loud. In the afternoons, they built up their story, about a boy and his imaginary friend, Bogus.[15] It would be a fanciful film, partially based upon Jewison's memories of his own imaginary friends in the early 1930s. The ones he remembered best were the Blah Blah Twins, who "didn't ever say anything, just 'blah blah blah.'"[16]

"We had the best time," Jewison said of their road trip. "By the time we reached San Bernardino, we were into the last moments of the story."[17]

Jewison pitched *Bogus* directly to the studio head at Warner Bros, rating his own salesmanship as "brilliant." And then, he said, "to my horror and disappointment, about a week and a half later I get this phone call from some kid vice president, some damned Brandeis graduate who's never written a word in his life, and it's like, 'Well, we've decided it's too dark.'"[18]

In the early 1990s, slapstick celebrations of rough-and-tumble boyhood were enjoying a mini-Renaissance. *Home Alone* (1990), *Problem Child* (1990), *Dennis the Menace* (1993), and *Little Rascals* (1994) were like Mark Twain remixed by the Marx Brothers, with double the violence and none of the irony. In this context, Jewison's story of a bereaved, hallucinating child struck executives as anemic. "Nobody wants to make a picture like this," he said of *Bogus*. "They're all doing roller-coaster rides and endless reels of mindless violence . . . it's unbelievable."[19]

Before Jewison had figured out his next move, fate intervened. In December 1992, Sony's TriStar Pictures paid $1 million in a pre-emptive purchase of *Him*, a spec-script by Diane Drake (original title: "Destino"). Studios including Columbia, Touchstone, Warner Bros., and Dino De Laurentiis Communications were all rumoured to be interested before TriStar made its pre-emptive strike. Drake's agent circulated the script to representatives of Julia Roberts, Demi Moore, Goldie Hawn, Meg Ryan, and Madonna. At some point, Hollywood trades started describing Drake's script as *Thelma and Louise* meets *Moonstruck*, which was how Jewison became involved.[20]

Drake's script for *Him* was whimsical enough to make *Moonstruck* look like something by Eugene O'Neill. One night, the eleven-year-old Faith and her younger brother learn from a Ouija board that her soulmate is named Damon Bradley. Fourteen years later, Faith abandons her fiancé to pursue Damon from Venice to Rome to Positano on the Amalfi coast. Twists include Faith's discovery that this "Damon Bradley" lied about his identity, and that the next "Damon Bradley" was a fake hired by the first fake Damon Bradley. Eventually, we learn that Faith's brother had manipulated the Ouija board to make up the whole thing in the first place.

Him was a frothy, high-concept confection, a spiritual descendent of the Universal romantic comedies from which Jewison had once fled. He would characterize the film as "an entertaining, accessible, feel-good film."[21]

In the 1960s, Jewison had been driven to create meaningful, socially engaged films like *Russians* and *Heat*. By the 1990s, he had made those films. The same fire wasn't there. The entire culture was drifting in a more complacent direction, lulled into a false sense of security and consensus. The White House was occupied by a Democrat who behaved like a Republican, building prisons and slashing regulations. Academics faffed about the "end of history." For Jewison, who was sixty-six-years-old, and who was used to filming in podunks like Paducah, Kentucky, or Fort Smith, Arkansas, ten weeks in Italy sounded nice.

Then there was the money. Because *Him* was sold as the next *Moonstruck*, Jewison's name would serve as an *imprimatur* of prestige for the whole endeavour. He hadn't invested a dime or a day of his life in developing the project, which allowed him to strike a "take-it-or-leave-it" pose in negotiation. In the end, he was paid $3,594,620 for his services.[22]

* * *

Elizabeth Broden, Jewison's assistant since *Moonstruck*, was responsible for his schedule, tracking his itineraries, and ensuring that his trailer and location headquarters were properly outfitted. On the film that became *Only You*, those necessities, including Cutty Sark Scotch, Red Rose tea, pistachios, Listerine, Aspirin, fruit (especially green seedless grapes), Sherman Natural Light "cigs," and light beer ("no Coors"), revealed a man of economical taste.[23] At the Toronto office on 18 Gloucester, Broden's duties were those of a "daytime wife."

"I used to say to Norman, 'I've got two husbands. I've got my daytime husband, you, and Connie at home.' He thought that was funny, but it was like that. I used to make his lunch. He liked spicy soup, and homemade sandwiches. Sometimes he asked me to go out and buy some veal for him to cook himself in the apartment." The top floor of the office was an apartment Jewison used if he wanted to spend the night in Toronto.

"I'd sew buttons on his shirts, buttons on his jackets," Broden recalled, although her employer was mostly oblivious when it came to fashion.

"Dixie used to say, 'Norman, you're *not* wearing that!'" Broden remembers.

The office itself, which had struck the young Bruce McDonald as glamorous, was showing its age. "The roof leaked," Broden remembers. "I don't know how many pots I put out. God almighty. And then I had to put a tarp over everything. I had a small computer that Michael Jewison didn't want anymore, and I had to put a tarp over that and the lamps before I left at night."[24] In *Only You*, Faith's brother is a roofer with a leaky roof, who keeps coffee cups positioned strategically around the office

Filming began at the end of August 1993, moving from Pittsburgh to Italy in early October. Jewison had always thought of the picture as an homage to William Wyler's *Roman Holiday*, and even recreated the moment in which Gregory Peck and Audrey Hepburn insert their hands into the "mouth of truth." He cast Robert Downey Jr. and Marisa Tomei in the leads primarily for the Old Hollywood vibe they brought to the picture. "There were moments in our first meeting when, as [Tomei] turned to me, I thought she was Audrey Hepburn," Jewison recalled. "I couldn't get her out of my head."[25]

Initially, Tomei, who had won an Oscar for *My Cousin Vinnie* in 1993, worried about the credibility of a character who would abandon her fiancé in hopes of finding a random individual whose name had come from a Ouija board. She had to play almost the entire film in a kind of romantic fugue state, from her chase through the Pittsburgh airport in her wedding dress in the first act, to her chase through the Rome airport in the finale.

"It's a simple story, nothing having to do with angst or deep psychology," Tomei later recognized. "I wanted a little more of that, actually, more psychologically driven humour, but Jewison kept saying 'No, no, it's plot driven, it's plot driven,' so I ran with it."[26]

After Downey's high-profile drug problems, TriStar could only get him insured with regular blood tests, though Jewison found him to be a consummate professional. One day, Jewison and Dixie took Downey to visit Gore Vidal and Howard Austin at Vidal's villa on the Amalfi coast. Norman and Gore maintained their friendship through the years. "We both enjoyed our last dinner with you and Dixie and the huge spectral presence of Mahatma K. Jeeves," Vidal later wrote, referencing a W.C. Fields *nom de plume* ("My hat and my cane, Jeeves"). "I hope you saw my nephew's *Igby Goes Down*—he is Jewisonian," Vidal declared, coining an adjective.[27]

* * *

After a number of studios passed, *Bogus* ended up at New Regency, who agreed to finance the film (to the tune of $25 million) on condition that it became a vehicle for Whoopi Goldberg.[28]

Overhauling *Bogus* was no straightforward task. "Alvin went off and wrote," Jewison said. "And then he was having trouble. And then he wanted to give up. This went on for a year and a half. Finally, I took him up to the farm, like I do with all writers—sort of trap them up there, like a screenwriter penal colony."[29]

To shoehorn Goldberg into the script, the role of "Harry," the bereaved boy's father, became "Harriet," his mother's estranged foster sister. Jewison inadvertently ended up with a gender-flipped version of *40 Pounds of Trouble*. In that film, a car accident left a seven-year-old girl in the care of Tony Curtis; in *Bogus*, a car accident would leave a seven-year-old boy in the care of Whoopi Goldberg.

The differences between *40 Pounds* and *Bogus* were an index of social change over the course of Jewison's career. The running gag in *40 Pounds* is that responsibility for a helpless child will cramp Tony Curtis's ability to seduce an endless succession of women. The equivalent running joke in *Bogus* is that the child will cramp Whoopi Goldberg's ability to focus on growing her small business. Where Curtis's character was defined by his libido, Harriet's heart is set aflutter by the prospect of purchasing discounted hotel and restaurant supplies.

Perhaps the most important element in *Bogus* was the child star at the centre of the action. "Without the kid, you don't have a film," Jewison said. "And when children act, they're not really acting. They simply are—they believe totally in the illusion of what you're doing."[30] Of the hundreds of children tested, Haley Joel Osment stood out for his charming chemistry with Gérard Depardieu, who had been cast as Bogus.[31]

Production began in the spring of 1995, shooting in Newark and Toronto. *Bogus* was a deeply personal endeavour for Jewison, in ways large and small. He endowed Osment's Albert with one of his favourite childhood activities: performing his own death. Throughout the film, Osment grasps his chest and collapses to the floor, feet rebounding comically upward. In his jean jacket and cowboy boots, Haley Joel Osment even looked like a miniature Jewison.

One scene in *Bogus* stands out for its biographical resonance. Midway through the film, while left alone in a restaurant supply warehouse, Albert hops on a bar stool and imagines ordering an extravagant banana split slathered with whipped cream and cherries, served up by his imaginary friend. The shot abruptly snaps back to Goldberg's "grown-up" POV, showing Osment, alone in the grey warehouse, lost in his reveries, muttering to himself. Goldberg looks at him as though he's crazy.

The scene amounts to a humourous recognition of the imagination gap separating adults from children. But it also reveals the personal anxiety of an artist who spent much of his time conjuring characters and stories that existed only in his own mind, and the corresponding insecurity he sometimes felt when trying to convey these fantasies to the "grown-ups" in the room, the executives who determined his artistic fate. *Bogus* was a window into the specific anxiety of a profession that required one to converse with things unseen.

* * *

Bogus was jarringly out of step with a children's market geared for *Home Alone*-style hijinks. There was not a single eye-gouge, crotch-kick, or violent moment of any kind, and Jewison's imaginative cues seemed to come from a different age: a final Fred Astaire-Ginger Rogers-style dance number with Goldberg and Depardieu was inspired by Fellini, while the overall aesthetic scheme (painted clowns, twirling parasols, card tricks) harkened back to the vaudeville of Jewison's youth. Its patient pace, its attentiveness to feeling and, perhaps, above all, the way it portrays sadness as permissible for children, all flew in the face of an industry committed to manic titillation as the default for children's entertainment. Jewison, who often said that his films were "personal statements," later called *Bogus* his "most personal film."[32]

Reviewers savaged the picture. "With Depardieu in the part, *Bogus* comes across more like some vagabond pervert" cackled Hal Hinson in the *Washington Post*. Joe Morgenstern of the *Wall Street Journal* argued that *Bogus* didn't work for 1990s kids who were "acclimated to massive doses of irony, cynicism, and McLuhanesque disjuncture," whatever that was. "In what amounts to consumer fraud, this movie tries to pass off shopworn whimsy as magic, sitcom twists for fantasy."

A *Newsday* critic made the obvious pun, arguing that "*Bogus*, alas, may also be the best way to describe the film's sentiment."[33]

Some critics seemed almost personally offended by the degree to which Jewison flouted the reigning Hollywood sensibility. The market reacted in kind: *Bogus* made back $4.4 million of its $25 million budget, Jewison's worst flop since *Gaily, Gaily* in 1969.

Perhaps, in the end, he made *Bogus* for himself, rather than for any particular audience. Surely, the film's parting words can be taken to stand for film directors as well as imaginary friends. "When they [kids, audiences] need us, we are there," Bogus says. "But when it's done: *poof.* We disappear. They never say goodbye. They never see us go. Sometimes they remember us later. Maybe not, but I cannot complain. It's my job."

CHAPTER 22

Closing Arguments

J EWISON WAS STARTLED BY THE DELICACY of Bob Dylan's handshake. It was October 29, 1998, and Dylan had just closed a double-billing with Joni Mitchell at Maple Leaf Gardens in Toronto. Joni wasn't used to playing in arenas, but Dylan revelled in the muddy acoustics. The future Nobel Prize winner threw his lyrics away in "garbled slurs," as one reviewer put it.[1]

For Jewison, the music was less important than the brief creative confluence it allowed. Denzel Washington, who had committed to play the part of Rubin "Hurricane" Carter, was in Toronto that night, as was Carter himself.[2] Here was a chance to bring the film's creators and subject together with Dylan, who had helped make Carter a cause célèbre with his song "Hurricane" in 1975. "All of Rubin's cards were marked in advance," Dylan sang, "The trial was a pig-circus, he never had a chance."

Backstage, Dylan embraced the former fighter. Jewison saw the tears in Carter's eyes, one of which was prosthetic thanks to a bungled prison surgery. Jewison would remember Dylan as "bent, pasty, and perspiring," clearly exhausted by the effort of the performance. Dylan admitted that he "didn't want to do the whole sixteen stanzas" of "Tangled Up in Blue," which had brought the audience to their feet.[3]

Jewison had hoped the meeting with Dylan would provide an emotional boost as they embarked upon an ambitious project. *Lazarus and the Hurricane* was now days away from shooting, but the pre-production had been rocky. Just one week before, he'd ended a letter to his executive producers with an ultimatum: accept his proposal on how to proceed with the script or he'd walk.

* * *

On June 17, 1966, two men walked into the Lafayette Bar and Grill in Paterson, N.J., and opened fire upon a bartender and three customers. Only one survived. Police characterized the incident as a violent robbery. In October, Rubin "Hurricane" Carter, a ranking contender for the middleweight championship, and a truck driver named John Artis were arrested for triple homicide. News reports at the time made prominent mention of Carter's "numerous scrapes with police" and published his home address.[4] Carter was sentenced to two consecutive life sentences for first degree murder with a minimum term of thirty years.

In a 1976 appeal, prosecutors presented a new motive for the murder: they now claimed it was racially motivated retribution for the slaying of a Black bartender hours before Carter's alleged crime.

Finally, in 1985, a federal judge cited "grave constitutional violations" and "an appeal to racism rather than reason" in his decision to overturn the conviction of Carter and Artis.[5] By then, Carter had spent nearly two decades in prison.

Jewison had been considering a movie about Carter's ordeal since 1991, when he'd been approached by John Ketcham, an aspiring producer who owned the rights to Carter's story. At the time, the director was preoccupied with *Malcolm X*, and the two parted ways.

Armyan Bernstein was responsible for resuscitating *The Hurricane*, as it was later known. Bernstein, a major Hollywood producer and founder of Beacon Pictures, had developed a close relationship with the Canadian activists who had fought for Carter's release. By 1997, Bernstein and co-screenwriter Dan Gordon had written a screenplay and were ready to engage a director.

If, in 1991, John Ketcham had needed Jewison, by 1998 Jewison needed *The Hurricane*. His post-*Moonstruck* films, while personally lucrative, had not generated the kind of impact he'd wanted. *Bogus* had flopped outright. At seventy-two, Jewison needed something ambitious, a career-capping statement. *The Hurricane* was an opportunity to return to America's unfinished struggle for civil rights, and would complete a loose trilogy with *In the Heat of the Night* and *A Soldier's Story*. It also provided an opportunity to tell a story in the vein of *Malcolm X*, with the very actor who had portrayed Malcolm in Spike Lee's film. Carter's powerful moments of self-reinvention in prison allowed the director to follow through with some of what he had envisioned for *Malcolm X*.

The Hurricane would mark a return to the socially conscious cinema of ideas that had always been Jewison's artistic forte. Still, Universal Pictures, who would distribute the film for Beacon Communications, was skeptical of his involvement. "Everyone said, 'Go young with this movie, find some MTV director, find some new young guy and bring a youthful, contemporary, stylish point of view to this story,'" said Armyan Bernstein. "I said, this is one of the youngest guys I've ever met. His fire hasn't gone out. In fact, it's blazing."[6]

While *The Hurricane* marked a return of sorts, Jewison's first independently financed film was also a departure for a director used to calling his own shots on studio-financed pictures. For most of his career, he had produced his own films, sometimes with one or two other producers. *The Hurricane* credits six executive producers, three producers, three co-producers, and one line producer. One of those producers, Bernstein, also happened to be one of the writers, friends with the film's subjects, and founder of the production company.

"Since I am accustomed to producing and directing my own projects, it is sometimes difficult for me to take advantage of all the help others can contribute," Jewison wrote to one executive producer with a touch of irony.[7]

"There were definitely big ego struggles in making this movie," Ketcham said.[8] Indeed, the complicated web of business arrangements necessary to bring Rubin Carter's story to the screen had set the stage for creative conflict, power plays, and infighting unlike anything Jewison had experienced in nearly four decades in the business.

* * *

"The relationship between producers and directors is essentially adversarial. That is what emerged today," Jewison seethed to Rudy Langlais, one of the film's executive producers, that August. It was the sort of thing he might have said to Hal Ashby in the 1960s; now he was saying it to the producers themselves. Jewison had become exasperated with endless dithering over the script, and with the contributions of his legion of producers. Months before, he decided to start over and commission a fresh script from writer Chris Cleveland ("history has proven that good scripts are rarely produced by a committee," as he said).[9]

Cleveland delivered a solid script, but now the producers had held him up with a month of "endless conference calls dealing with act one backstory and reiteration of what this film is really about," as he groused to Langlais. "I want to assure you, Rudy, I know what this story is about and I am confident I know how to tell it with passion, insight, and a sensitivity to racial issues that permeate practically every scene and affect every character's motivation."[10]

Behind the producers' questions about backstory was a lingering concern over the film's budget. *Lazarus and the Hurricane* was a sweeping epic with an extraordinarily complicated script: 220 scenes unfolding across 112 locations over forty years with 117 speaking parts. Jewison had promised to shoot the film in fifty days, a sprint, on a budget of just under $37 million, less than half of what comparable projects would receive at a major studio.[11] At least one producer believed it was impossible. What's more, the endless conference calls were resulting in additional scenes. Paper was the real estate by which producers measured the cost of film: "Scene 181 was originally $1/8$ page; it is now $1\,1/8$ pages," executive producer Bill Teitler noted at one point. "Scene 187 was $1\,1/8$ pages; this new scene is $2\,5/8$ pages. This will add approximately two days to the schedule, for a total of about $175,000."[12]

Jewison was keenly aware of the length problem: "Still too much story!" he wrote to Bernstein in September. As always when dealing with historical figures (in previous projects such as *Bethune* and *Malcolm X*), he believed that the life must be shaped according to the dramatic necessities of the story. "When we try to tell all the truth, all the true facts and incidents, it gets heavy and becomes a docu-drama," he added to Bernstein. "I suggest we cut down those areas which are confusing and non-dramatic and expand those scenes which hold dramatic promise."[13] The truth, for Jewison, was always dramatic truth. He wanted to zero in on the dramatic core of the narrative.

Jewison understood the financial stakes. At one point in negotiating his own services, he was given a choice between accepting a flat fee or a percentage of gross, to be negotiated with the studio. If the film was a hit, he could have earned far more than the $1.775-million fee that was on offer. But for a variety of reasons, including the fact that taking royalty payments would have meant that his first dollar was still eighteen months away, he took the more cautious approach.[14] A decade without a hit may have taken a toll on his confidence. Given how *The Hurricane* had been shaping up so far, he wasn't about to gamble at the box office.

* * *

Less than three weeks from the start of principal photography, Jewison received an updated script from Dan Gordon. (The Chris Cleveland script, subjected to severe cuts, was abandoned over the summer). The director had been under the impression that Gordon would concentrate specifically on strengthening "the Canadians" in a few key scenes; instead, Gordon turned in seventy pages of rewrites.

"This is an intolerable situation," Jewison wrote to his executive producers.

> We have not proceeded with casting and time has run out. The only thing I can suggest is that I put through any new changes which I feel encompass the strongest scenes discussed and that I agree to shoot.
>
> The other alternative is that I leave the film and you proceed with another director.[15]

For a time, Jewison believed he'd wrested back a degree of directorial autonomy. *Lazarus and the Hurricane* began shooting in November 1998, from a script by Gordon and Bernstein. Jewison completed a three-week stint in New Jersey and moved the company back to Toronto. By mid-December, he was forced to recognize that the length problem was acute. He wrote to the executive producers (cc'ing his lawyer) asking if their contract with Universal called for a specific running time of the final print. Having shot thirty-six pages of the script, he was on pace for a film that was 162-minutes and forty seconds. "My deepest fear is that I will be forced in the final edit to make so many drastic cuts that our film will become choppy and disjointed," he said.[16]

For Armyan Bernstein, length was only part of the problem. When he reviewed Jewison's footage he was disturbed by the way "the Canadians" were becoming "just middle-class white people" and "liberal do-gooders." He urged Jewison to abandon his conception of the Canadians as "everymen" and instead portray them as preternaturally "good people, living by a more selfless code than anyone we know." He wanted Jewison to shoot more scenes with them and offered to pay for the "extra material."[17]

Jewison was flabbergasted. "With a two-hour and forty-minute picture as it stands, we just cannot keep expanding scenes. It is totally self-defeating!" he responded to Bernstein.

Denzel Washington had meanwhile requested some "deeply complicated" fight choreography. He, too, was willing to pay for more boxing footage. "Please bear with me," Jewison wrote. "I am trying to keep the train moving. With two and a half feet of snow on the ground and frigid temperatures, it's not easy."[18]

Shortly after breaking for the holidays, tragedy struck. Dan Gordon's twenty-two-year-old son, Zaki, lost control of his Chevrolet Blazer while merging onto Ventura Freeway and fishtailed into a gasoline tanker. The truck rolled, spilled 9,000 gallons of gasoline, and exploded in a 100-foot fireball. Zaki's two younger brothers (aged eleven and fourteen) attempted to rescue him from the blaze, but the heat and flames were impenetrable.[19] On December 23, while Jewison was trying to recuperate his spirits in Europe, Gordon was burying his son. "Dan's eulogy to his boy was one of the most moving events I've ever seen," Langlais told Jewison on January 2. "He called him 'my sweet boy,' and 'Absalom, my son,' all the way through and cried uncontrollably."[20]

On January 12, less than three weeks after the funeral, Dan Gordon wrote to Bernstein, Langlais, Jewison, and Rubin Carter. "I feel, quite frankly, I no longer know what this movie is about," he said.

> In thirty-one years as a screenwriter, I have never run into a situation quite like this one, in which, in the middle of production, the director is fighting to make one movie, the producers another, the cast perhaps something else, and the writer yet another, and instead of one voice coming in to resolve the situation, there is an ongoing set of behind-the-scenes guerilla wars. Mike Landon always told me that on any given movie, someone had to know what the Hell the thing was about; one voice, one vision had to be there with everyone else signing on to it. I don't know what that vision is with regard to this film . . . As I told Rudy, this process has become too painful, in a period of time in which I have had about all the pain with which I can deal.[21]

Two days later, Jewison replied to Gordon.

> Your letter of Jan 12 was not unexpected. We are both old dogs! I have tried very hard to keep this train running on a solid set of tracks but every other day I receive script changes. I never really know who's writing these revisions. Army-Dan-Rudy-Rubin-Sam

384

. . . who knows?? In thirty-seven years, I too have never experienced a more chaotic process of working . . .

But I promise you one thing. I am devoted to Rubin's and Lesra's story and I will try my best to tell it in a way that will hopefully fulfill your intentions and passion.

I share your pain both as a writer and a father.[22]

* * *

At first, Jewison wasn't convinced that Denzel Washington could pull off the role of the Hurricane. The actor was forty-four-years-old and, before undertaking a gruelling training regimen, not in fighting form. (He lost thirty-five pounds for the role.) "I can't help you," Jewison told him. "You're going to be in the ring in a pair of shorts and boxing shoes. And have you still got any rage left in you? Can we press that button?"[23]

Washington found the rage, but it was his transcendence of rage, his stillness and gravitas, that lingered. He arrived with his own vision of the character, rejecting lines that he felt weren't right. Director and star were not always of one mind. "Perhaps you can convince him to try at least one take on it," Jewison suggested to Langlais in one such instance.[24]

Washington spent months training for boxing sequences that were shot in just three days. Jewison worked with cinematographer Roger Deakins to give each fight its own look. "Norman knows that he wants this angle to go with that angle," said Deakins. "It can be very elegant working in that way. It's very matter-of-fact . . . We didn't want to make big camera moves: it's a film that's best served by a low-key approach."[25]

Relationships continued to fray as filming picked up in the new year. On January 21, executive producer Bill Teitler wrote an urgent memo about a projected $1,225,678 in overages due to the constant addition and expansion of scenes.[26] Confusing timelines and apparent problems with narrative logic caused frustration among the actors, who sometimes couldn't understand where their characters were in the film. Bernstein continued to fret about the portrayal of the "Canadians." (Bernstein "really is in love with these people. They move him and speak to him," Langlais told Jewison.) While the film was running long, the director was still being bombarded with rewrites and additions. Eventually, Jewison started ignoring the new material, or making spontaneous revisions as he went, working from instinct.

Bernstein became incensed after Jewison cut one of the Canadians' scenes. "He feels that different scenes are being shot than the ones he knows about," Langlais reported to Jewison, "and that is driving him crazy . . . He feels that the collaboration has broken down when scenes he writes or approves are not shot, or are changed without his being given a chance to know why."

Langlais needed Jewison to appreciate the gravity of the situation: he described Bernstein feeling "crushed" and "cheated," as though "his interest in the movie was ignored." Bernstein had been crucial in getting the film off the ground, and Langlais now felt they were in real danger of losing him.

"Being part of the experience of making *Hurricane* is as important to him as financing the movie," Langlais explained. "It is part of how he wants to define his life and work. And it is killing him not to be. We make it worse for him by not giving him a chance to see the movie he wants to see or to know that he is not going to for a good reason."[27]

Jewison wasn't going to surrender his vision of the film, but he made a greater effort to keep Bernstein on board. The end was now within sight, and he was looking forward to reuniting with his old friend Rod Steiger: it seemed somehow appropriate that, in their third film together over three decades, the actor behind the bigoted sheriff from *In the Heat of the Night* would play the judge who freed Rubin Carter.

Jewison and Bernstein reconciled by the end of the shoot. "I know this process has been painful for you," Bernstein wrote, "but I feel that our struggle and our battles have been more than worth it."

My heart and your heart are buried very deep in this movie now, and this one will always be our child. You can be the dad if you want.

Best,

Army[28]

Little over one month later, forty-six million Americans watched Jewison dance on stage of the Dorothy Chandler Pavilion, where Nicolas Cage presented him with the Irving G. Thalberg Award. After three decades of nominations, after listening to hundreds of speeches at the Academy Awards, Jewison finally gave one of his own. "Forty years ago, I sat at William Wyler's feet and tried to learn how to make movies," he said, voice quivering on the edge of tears. "Willy Wyler was a god to me, and he won this award. And I think that's what's so meaningful to me: to join all those filmmakers who have gone before."

* * *

Jewison promised Piers Handling of the Toronto International Film Festival that *The Hurricane* would be ready for a 1999 gala screening, but that turned out to be wishful thinking. The frames weren't colour corrected; the score wasn't finished.[29] After some negotiation, Jewison agreed to show it as a "work in progress." Some questioned the wisdom of screening unfinished work, which could damage the film with bad word-of-mouth. But Jewison didn't want to disappoint. Racing against the clock to complete the title shots and closing credits before the screening, the director appeared "tired and irritable" at the Canadian Film Centre's annual TIFF barbeque within days of the screening.[30]

On stage at the Elgin Theatre, flanked by a dozen members of the cast and crew, Jewison briefly choked up while introducing the film. "The Canadians" were there, as was Washington, who brought Rubin Carter on stage to deliver a stirring oration about his road to freedom. By the time the just-completed credits rolled, someone could be heard yelling "Give them the Oscar now!" over the thunderous, minutes-long standing ovation.[31]

The ovations continued as the film opened across North America after Christmas. *The Hurricane*, the last major film release of the twentieth-century, appealed to an unusually wide swath of audiences. "Universal had never had a movie that drew ninety per cent approval from audiences both Black and white, both rural and urban," Jewison wrote.[32]

The sense of triumph would prove fleeting.

On December 28, 1999, the day before *The Hurricane*'s official release, the *New York Times* published a lengthy takedown of the film by Selwyn Raab, a crime reporter who had covered Carter's legal tribulations. According to Raab, Jewison had included "major fabrications" and "fairy tales" in a film that "falls into the category of history contorted by dramatic effect." Raab argued that Carter's criminal past had been deliberately omitted, that the role of the Canadians had been exaggerated and Carter's lawyers diminished, that separate trials had been conflated, and that John Artis (Carter's co-defendant) had been unjustly ignored. Most seriously, Raab argued, by pinning Carter's decades-long legal trouble on one malevolent cop, the film ignored the systemic racism endemic to American criminal justice, the "network of detectives, prosecutors, and judges" who injected "racial bias into the courtroom."[33]

Initially, Jewison believed that attacks on the film's historical accuracy would have little effect on its reception. Audiences loved it for what it was. But more accusers soon joined the chorus. In late January, Lewis Steel, one of Carter's lawyers, argued in the *Los Angeles Times* that *The Hurricane* crossed from "reasonable embellishment" into "pernicious distortion." Argued Steel: "By depriving the audience of the opportunity to see just how racist the criminal justice system can be, and to what extent prosecutors will go to obtain unjust convictions, the audience did not learn why so many Blacks feel they do not get a fair chance."[34]

"That's not the story I was telling," Jewison later said, "or even part of it. Maybe there's a whole other picture to be made, but it wouldn't be very exciting or uplifting." He'd struggled to streamline narrative elements and simplify the dramatic arc of the story. He specifically told his screenwriters to avoid representing "all the truth, all the facts," and instead focus on the story's dramatic core.

Jewison had shown scarcely more concern for historical accuracy in making *The Hurricane* than he had on *Jesus Christ Superstar*. His artistic aim had been to maximize the emotional payoff of Carter's wrongful imprisonment and eventual release. Countless scenes with lawyers, numerous trials, further attention to John Artis, greater focus on Rubin's past—all the baggage critics felt was missing from the story would have capsized the film. Carter himself insisted it was about "the miracle that occurred when ordinary people do something miraculous, not the bullshit that occurs when ordinary people are ordinary."[35]

Regardless of his dramatic intentions, or the ethics of his disregard for historical fact in pursuit of inspirational catharsis, Jewison believed

The Hurricane's reception had been hampered by those who expected Hollywood to teach history to the American public. *The Hurricane* succeeded at the box office, and was beloved by viewers, but the Academy snubbed it. Friends said that Jewison was heartbroken. He thought *The Hurricane* was "the best film I ever made."[36]

* * *

Jewison discovered that he was to be the director of *The Statement* when he read about it in the papers.

On September 9, 2001, *Variety* reported that Jewison had committed to direct an adaptation of Brian Moore's novel for the Toronto-based producer Robert Lantos, a story which soon percolated through the Canadian media. On September 10, Jewison wrote to agent Ken Kamins at ICM. "Isn't this a little premature? Didn't know we had a deal. Is this my next picture?"

To which Kamins responded: "Yes," "Don't quite yet," "Don't know, how's the Harwood draft?"[37]

Moore's *The Statement* was about the hunt for the elderly war criminal Pierre Brossard, who killed seven Jews while serving in the Milice, a French military force loyal to the Nazi occupiers in the Vichy government. Concealed for decades by right-wing elements within the Catholic Church, Brossard now finds himself caught between a French magistrate armed with a new "crimes against humanity" law and a cabal of Jewish assassins who want to leave a "statement" on his corpse marking him as a Nazi brought to justice. Lantos had decided to pursue a film adaptation before Moore had finished his manuscript.

Someone familiar with the project questioned its commercial appeal: "American audiences are too unfamiliar with the politics of the Vichy government to understand where the character of Brossard is coming from," while "French audiences probably don't want to be reminded of it at all."[38] Still, Lantos was determined. He considered Jewison, "a brilliant, visual storyteller with political awareness and a social conscience," perfect for the project.[39]

Despite the controversial reception of *The Hurricane*, Jewison had acquired a strange air of indestructibility in the media. "At an age when many of his contemporaries are no longer working," noted the *New York Times*, "Jewison is facing the odd prospect of a career resurgence in a business notorious for its obsession with youth."[40]

While seventy-five, Jewison appeared to be in formidable health and often said that he would continue making films until his legs gave out. The Canadian media called him "uncle Norm" and portrayed him as a permanent fixture of the national film scene, an affable craftsman who could be relied upon to excrete a new film every few years. If journalists wrote condescendingly of his "old school" films or dismissed many of them as "inoffensive entertainments," it hardly mattered, since a new movie would arrive soon enough.[41] Since *The Hurricane*, Jewison had already directed an intimate ninety-minute HBO movie called *Dinner with Friends* starring Greg Kinnear and Toni Collette, earning an Emmy nomination for best TV movie.

Jewison eventually did sign on to direct the new picture for Robert Lantos. No one, least of all the director, knew that it would be his last.

* * *

Jewison had reservations about the screenplay. The previous spring he spent time working with Ronald Harwood, a veteran Hollywood scribe who had recently won the Best Adapted Screenplay Oscar for his work on

Roman Polanski's *The Pianist*. They parted on a high note. "I so enjoyed our time together and now am trying to organize the material," wrote the sixty-nine-year-old screenwriter. "I'll start writing out cards next and then make a step outline and then—I'll probably light a cigarette and think about it some more! As you see, I ignore your advice about my tobacco intake. If I stopped smoking I wouldn't be able to write, and then where would you be?"[42]

Harwood's next draft was a disappointment. Jewison thought he'd failed to capture the sense of psychological interiority that "anchored" the Brian Moore novel, and wondered if they should use voice-over narration in scenes where Brossard was alone. He also worried that the story was "too simplistic." *The Statement* should not become a "chase movie" that was "all plot," Jewison wrote. The script needed to "reveal some of our own inner fears. Some of the conflicts that exist in human behaviour. Who is ultimately responsible for our own hypocritical tendencies, guilts, fears?"[43]

Jewison's first instinct was to offer the part of Brossard to Anthony Hopkins, who was available. Lantos urged him to consider Michael Caine. Hopkins had cornered the market on what Lantos called "likeable villains," whereas Caine, about to appear as Austin Powers's father in *Goldmember*, might prove the more unpredictable, attention-getting choice.

Jewison sent Caine the Brian Moore novel with a cover letter explaining that it was inspired by the true story of Paul Touvier, a fascist who had been pardoned by President Georges Pompidou in 1971 before being convicted for war-related crimes against humanity in 1994. (After the brouhaha over the historical veracity of *The Hurricane*, Jewison wasn't about to make a big deal of *The Statement*'s "real-life" inspiration in public). By the end of January 2002, agents had drawn up an offer for $1,250,000, plus a variety of bonuses, including an additional $150,000 should Caine win the Oscar for Best Actor.[44]

Jewison wanted Kristin Scott Thomas for the role of Annemarie Livi, the French magistrate obsessed with bringing Brossard to justice. When Thomas and Emma Thompson (his second choice) were unavailable, Tilda Swinton brought a severe, authoritative presence to the role. *The Statement,* said Swinton, "reminds me of those films in the 70s that I loved as a child where everybody is French but speaks with an English accent and wears a raincoat."[45]

Financing *The Statement* was, if anything, more complicated than financing *The Hurricane.* In the end, Lantos's Serendipity Point Films co-produced with Odessa Films and Company Pictures in association with Astral Media, Telefilm Canada, Corus Entertainment, Movision, and BBC Films. The all-important US distribution was through Michael Barker and Tom Bernard's Sony Pictures Classics. It felt to Jewison like "passing the hat around," but the major movie studios were less likely than ever to fund mid-budget, ideas-driven movies for adult audiences. He was candid about missing the "old days" of motion picture financing. "The decision to make *Moonstruck* was made between Alan Ladd Jr. and myself," Jewison recalled. "I gave him a price of what I thought I could do the film for, and told him I was going to go after Cher to play the lead. No other major stars. And he called me up and said, 'OK.' And I never saw him again, until I told him that the film was finished."

"That doesn't happen anymore," Jewison said.[46] "Most movies are for fourteen-year-olds." Indeed, by 2003, the American box office was completely dominated by children's films (*Finding Nemo*) or franchises (*Pirates of the Caribbean, The Matrix, Lord of the Rings*).

"In a sense, Norman was [always] a studio director," said Michael Barker. But the studios had committed to a blockbuster economy built on the success of tentpoles, with smaller companies like Sony Pictures

Classics or Fox Searchlight making and distributing low-budget, niche films. "Everything in between is almost impossible to get financed," Barker says. "Those were the movies that Norman Jewison and Hal Ashby and Robert Altman made. I think it's a *disaster* for film culture. Those great movies we know from the 1970s would not be made today . . . You could never see [Ashby's] *The Last Detail* again."

The studios once funded a "steady spate" of mid-budget, grown-up fare, but no more. "That's where [Norman] got stuck," said Barker. "Because he's making the kind of movies that studios, for all intents and purposes, don't do anymore."[47]

The Statement was a thorny morality play, inviting viewers to risk sympathizing with the elderly Brossard, while simultaneously condemning the French government and Catholic Church for their systemic efforts to shield the war criminal from justice. "Michael [Caine] had a theory—we're always on the side of the fugitive. We're always rooting for the hare, not the hounds," Jewison said.[48] But the director was anxious to prevent Brossard from becoming utterly despicable. Throughout the script revision process, he cut problematic lines, including one in which Brossard wonders if there "will be Jews in the afterlife," and another indicating that Brossard "personally supervised the deportation of French Jews to the gas chambers." Brossard's use of "yids" becomes "they" in later revisions, and a scene of Jews being shunted into cattle trucks was cut. The director presented Brossard as a character who persevered under the delusion that his actions had helped save France from the Communist "anti-Christs."[49]

Still, the director of *Fiddler on the Roof* was highly attuned to Jewish suffering. Most painful to direct was the scene in which the young Brossard participates in the murder of seven Jews, based on a historical photograph of corpses near a wall in in Rillieux-la-Pape. In casting the Jewish victims,

Jewison found himself having to separate Jewish from non-Jewish extras. (In the film, Brossard orders the victims to "get your pricks out" to ensure circumcision). Jewison was unnerved by this historical echo—the visual identification of Jews that, in this moment, united the director and his Nazi character.

"I almost started crying," Jewison recalled. "That, to me, was the most difficult moment in the film."[50]

* * *

The Statement turned out to be one of the fastest films he'd made in years. The production was scheduled for fifty-five shooting days in Europe (twenty-eight in Paris, twenty-seven in the South of France) starting in March 2003. By December, it was in theatres. Jewison later said he wished they hadn't rushed it out amidst a marketing push for Oscar consideration, allowing critics to satisfy their own vanity by "discovering" this hidden gem the following April.

Critics complained about the film's pace. Jewison intended it to be Hitchcockian; some reviewers found it sluggish. They complained about the absurdity of French characters speaking with English accents, despite the success of *The Pianist* and *Schindler's List*, which had featured much of the same. ("We'll get a lot of that," Jewison said of the accent complaint. "But when you hear a Frenchman speak English, you start to smile. Everybody's going to sound like Maurice Chevalier, and I'm going to be giggling all the time—there eez something funee about zee French accent.")[51]

Worse, critics alleged that the film didn't know what it was trying to say. "*The Statement* ultimately doesn't have the courage of whatever (presumably noble) convictions brought it into being," wrote the *New York Times*'s Stephen Holden.

"Jewison's films usually deliver a bold message," Brian D. Johnson observed, "but *The Statement* revels in moral ambiguity; it makes no statement."[52]

For some viewers, the meaning of *The Statement* was obvious. The following May, Jewison received a report indicating that censorship authorities at General Security in Beirut had formally banned the picture in Lebanon. The rationale was "repeated depiction of Jews as victims and as such considered promoting sympathy for the Jewish cause." Egypt was next to issue a formal banning certificate: "Contents constitute Jewish propaganda namely in their depiction as victims of persecution." *The Statement* was subsequently banned from much of the Middle East on DVD and all other media, including television.[53]

For those sensitive to sympathetic portrayal of Jewish persecution, the film's final shot was statement enough. A black-and-white photograph of Touvier's seven Jewish victims in Rillieux-la-Pape dissolves into a present-day image of the same scene, corpses replaced by a humble monument in front of an otherwise nondescript wall. ("The Wall is where it all ends," Jewison had said of the Vietnam Memorial, scene of the powerful closing moments of *In Country*). *The Statement* was dedicated to the 77,000 French Jews who died under the German occupation and the Vichy regime.

CODA

Dance Me Outside

NORMAN JEWISON RETURNED TO Victoria College in October 2019, on one of those glorious autumn days that feel left over from August, sun-filled leaves swaying in the breeze. Accompanied by his second wife, Lynne St. David Jewison, he made his way into a neo-gothic, cathedral-like classroom, where I would interview him before a packed audience of students and faculty.

Jennifer Jewison once said that her father dreaded falling out of touch, no longer being "hip."[1] He looked like the hippest nonagenarian I'd ever seen, wearing black jeans, a high-collared black sweater over a dress shirt, and a red and brown leather jacket from Roots. Only his shoes betrayed him. I found them strangely moving: black runners with thick Velcro ties, like the ones my son had worn as a toddler. They looked like the last pair of shoes a man could hope to wear.

Lynne St. David Jewison, with her slightly tousled bouffant and trademark oversized shades, embodies a throwback kind of glamour suggestive of Catherine Deneuve or Brigitte Bardot, tasteful-tailored yet vivacious. Lynne and Norman met in the early 1990s through their mutual friend, Jay Scott, the *Globe and Mail* film critic who was then working on a biography of the director. St. David, who attended studio junkets with Scott in these years, was a freelance writer for the *Globe* and other publications. In 1996, she interviewed Jewison alongside Kenneth Thomson and Hal Jackman, two of Canada's wealthiest people, for a *Report on Business* article called "The Penny-Pinching Ways of the Rich and Famous." (Norman's hot tip was to buy a coupon book of movie passes through the Canadian Film Centre.) Fourteen years later, beneath the Chuppah in their garden, St. David married her penny-pincher. Some of their happiest moments together have been aboard *The Sea Dream*, a ketch owned by Deer Valley ski friends, sailing around the Aeolian Islands and the Dalmatian coast. Lynne adores all of Norman's movies, but admits that *Bogus* holds a special place in her heart.[2]

By all accounts, the passage of years had been kind to Norman. Bruce McDonald described the last decade as "one giant victory lap" for Jewison. He has been constantly celebrated at film festivals, galas, and anniversary screenings of his films, including a fifteen-film retrospective at the Lincoln Center entitled "Norman Jewison: Relentless Renegade." In 2016, the Canadian Film Centre held a special ninetieth birthday celebration, where Jewison was honoured by friends and colleagues from throughout his career. Steven Spielberg and Martin Scorsese sent letters to be read at the occasion. Cher and Quincy Jones shared their recollections via a live video feed. Jewison sang for his guests, and danced into the night.[3]

He had never exactly retired. As recently as 2010, when he was eighty-four, he had spoken in concrete terms about filming a project called *High Alert* in Atlantic Canada. It was a comedy, *The Russians Are Coming* for the George W. Bush era, about Islamophobic paranoia. The funding would never materialize.[4]

Jewison was beloved in industry circles, but his broader legacy felt less certain. On the one hand (as Tevye might have said), some films remain as popular as ever. *Rollerball* has been remade once, while *The Thomas Crown Affair* is rumoured to have a second remake in the works. Homages to *Crown* pop up everywhere, from *The Queen's Gambit* to hip hop lyrics. The fiftieth anniversary of *In the Heat of the Night* confirmed its status as a cinematic landmark of the Civil Rights movement. In the depths of the COVID-19 lockdown, *Vulture* declared that "*Moonstruck* is the Morbid Spaghetti Rom-Com We All Need Right Now."

On the other hand, Jewison seemed to be vanishing from the critical conversation. His current overall importance to the field of film scholarship is suggested by the four-volume, 2,456-page *Wiley-Blackwell History of American Film*, in which Jewison's name does not so much as appear in the index.

Part of Jewison's critical problem, as Pauline Kael recognized in the mid-1980s, was his lack of "distinctive style." Kael saw him "in the tradition of old theatrical directors [who] go from subject to subject . . . you can't see anything really that links the movies together except his name on them." Asked how the world would remember Norman Jewison, Kael said: "As a man who made some lively movies. That's a pretty good way to remember somebody."[5]

In some ways, and despite Kael's mild condescension, "lively movies" is perfect for Jewison. The films remain as lively as their creator, who always struck observers as preternaturally full of life. Kael is also right to find a connection to the "old theatrical directors." Jewison came from the vaudeville tradition of the variety show, and seen from a certain angle, his filmography itself was a lifelong variety show.

But Kael was wrong about the lack of connective tissue between the films. Sidney Poitier once described that link as a "value frame," a coherent attitude toward the world, that you could sense beneath the surface of Jewison's comedies, dramas, and musicals.[6] Politics was part of it. But it was deeper than that—deeper, even, than the reoccurring thematic preoccupations with family, tradition, and betrayal. What linked the films, at bottom, was a conviction about film itself: a belief, forged at a time when people were not embarrassed to debate the "purpose" of cinema, that movies could change their audience in some small way. Maybe you could carry a film in your heart for the rest of your life, the medium of that transference being laughter and tears, the full range of human emotion evoked by images flickering on a screen. For a while, that seemed possible. It was the purpose of Norman Jewison's life.

* * *

Getting the director back to his old campus had been complicated. He was now ninety-three-years-old, tired quickly, and spent much of his time in Malibu. His assistant seemed hesitant to commit to anything, until it was suddenly decided that he could come for exactly one hour on a Friday afternoon in October.

Minutes before Jewison arrived, a bulb in the overhead digital projector failed, and the screen upon which we were to watch scenes from throughout his career went dark. Tension swept the room. At least, it swept through me. For months, I had imagined how I would introduce myself to Jewison. Now, like a complete schmuck, like the worst cliché of a befuddled university professor, I would have to explain to the legendary director that I couldn't get the movie to play.

He saved me by speaking first. "You know why movie directors always wear baseball hats?" he asked, doffing a cap adorned with his initials. "So they can look up at the sun when setting up a shot," he said. I felt like I should have known.

Jewison greeted some students, telling them about how, when he was Chancellor of Victoria, he used to host "Chats with the Chance" in the common room, where he would meet students for "a few beers" and conversation. The idea of a university chancellor fraternizing with students over beer sounded bizarre, until you remembered that this was Norman Jewison, and that was exactly the sort of thing he would have done.

Somehow, a replacement projector materialized, and we took our seats for the interview. One more time, for undergraduates who had been born around the time he was undertaking his final film, Jewison talked about screening *The Russians Are Coming* behind the Iron Curtain, about Rod Steiger using chewing gum to reveal his character's thinking in *In the Heat of the Night*, about Al Pacino's discovery that the courtroom was a theatre, about that time when Nicolas Cage got so frustrated on the set of *Moonstruck* that he hurled a chair across the set.

Toward the end, I asked Jewison how, deep into the presidency of Donald Trump, he managed to remain hopeful. Ever so gently, he rebuked the question.

"I don't make films because I think it's important we have hope," he answered, using the present tense. "Life is full of hope, and it's full of despair. There doesn't a day pass when I almost shed a tear about what's happening. There isn't a day that passes when I don't appreciate life, and I'm full of hope. The important thing is the search for truth. It's the meaning of all the arts. It's written on top of Victoria College: 'The Truth Shall Make You Free.' But you can't bore people with polemics, because that's propaganda, and I don't believe in that."

* * *

"When I think of my pictures, I see flashes of time, places," Jewison once said. "I measure my life by my films. Make something special, people will carry it around in their heart for the rest of their life."[7]

Many years ago, Jennifer Jewison was asked what her father feared most. "I think he's afraid of getting old," she said. Even back then he would do the "I'm the oldest man on earth" routine. "I've never seen him not doing something," she said. "I've never seen Dad just sit. When he's not reading, he's screwing in a doorknob that's loose. He's always doing something."

Jennifer recalls one morning in the garden. "One day we went out and we were planting in the spring, we were doing the tomatoes. We probably said four words to each other, and we were out there for about three hours. You just daydream, you know, and you think. I knew that, even though he was planting and weeding and making his garden all pretty, I know his mind was going a mile-a-minute. He just never stops."[8]

Notes

NORMAN JEWISON ONCE TOLD AN INTERVIEWER that "films are meant to be seen and not to be written about." Nevertheless, the creation of his films generated a staggering textual output, not only the scripts but the tens-of-thousands of pages of letters, memos, reports, and other behind-the-scenes documents, plus the thousands of articles and interviews in trade publications, national magazines, and the long-defunct local newspapers that trailed Jewison's film crews across middle America. While a fraction of this material is available online, this book draws primarily from physical archival holdings at the E. J. Pratt Library at Victoria College and at the Wisconsin Center for Film and Theatre Research. I am grateful for the important work of Tino Balio, Mark Harris, and other scholars and critics cited in the notes, as well as to the hundreds of journalists who have told parts of Norman Jewison's story over the past seven decades. I would especially like to recognize the work of Jay Scott, Canada's greatest film writer, who embarked upon a book about Jewison in the late 1980s. Tragically, Scott died of Aids-related complications at the age of 43. Some of Scott's legacy, especially portions of the interview transcripts housed in the E. J. Pratt archives, lives on in these pages.

ABBREVIATIONS USED IN THE NOTES:

NJSC = Norman Jewison Special Collection, E. J. Pratt Library, Victoria College in the University of Toronto

NJP = Norman Jewison Papers, Wisconsin Center for Film and Theatre Research, Wisconsin Historical Society

PREFACE

1 NJ interview, NJSC box 51, file 7.
2 The story of the 1968 Best Picture contest is superbly told by Mark Harris in *Pictures at a Revolution* (New York: Penguin, 2008).
3 Paul Rosenfield, "Magnificent Obsessions," *Los Angeles Times*, March 24, 1985.
4 Jay Scott, "Jewison Then and Now," *Globe and Mail*, October 30, 1987.
5 Transcript of interview with Larry Auerbach, NJSC box 53, file 27.
6 Transcript of interview with Jennifer Jewison, NJSC box 53, file 25.
7 Michael Barker, author interview, September 11, 2019.
8 Joe Eszterhas, author interview, August 2, 2019.
9 NJ interview, NJSC box 51, file 7.
10 NJ interview, NJSC box 51, file 5.
11 NJ interview, NJSC box 51, file 7.
12 NJ interview, NJSC box 51, file 7.
13 *Norman Jewison, Filmmaker*, dir. Doug Jackson (National Film Board of Canada, 1971).
14 NJ interview, NJSC box 51, file 7.

CHAPTER 1

1 Charis Cotter, *Toronto Between the Wars: Life in the City* 1919-1939 (Toronto: Firefly Books, 2004), p. 130.
2 Ibid., p. 13.
3 Jack Panozzo, "Norman Jewison: The Man and His Art," *Vic Report*, Vol X., no.2, (April, 1982), p. 11.
4 NJ interview, NJSC box 53, file 28.
5 Ibid.
6 George Horhota, "Jewison Shoots for the Truth," *Maclean's*, October 29, 1979.
7 Panozzo, op cit., pp. 10-11.
8 Ibid.

9 "Norman Jewison's Early Years," *CBC Digital Archives* (1997), https://www.cbc.ca/player/play/650095171549

10 Ibid.

11 Panozzo, op cit.

12 "Norman Jewison's Early Years."

13 NJ interview, NJSC box 53, file 28.

14 NJ interview, NJSC box 51, file 6.

15 Ibid.

16 Ibid.

17 "Shea's Hippodrome," *Urban Toronto*, July 19, 2010. https://urbantoronto.ca/news/2010/07/heritage-toronto-mondays-sheas-hippodrome.

18 Mike Filey, *Toronto Sketches: The Way We Were, Vol. 1* (Toronto: Dundern, 1992), pp. 108-109.

19 NJ interview, NJSC box 51, file 5.

20 "Norman Jewison's Early Years."

21 Peter Gzowski interview with NJ, *Morningside*, CBC Radio, April 17, 1997.

22 NJ interview, NJSC box 51, file 5.

23 Norman Jewison, *This Terrible Business Has Been Good to Me* (Toronto: Key Porter, 2004), p. 15.

24 "Hoodlum Street Gang Attacks Young Jew," *Toronto Star*, August 18, 1933.

25 "Draper Admits Receiving Riot Warning," *Toronto Star*, August 17, 1933.

26 "Hoodlum Street Gang Attacks Young Jew," op cit.

27 "Must Not Flaunt Swastika, Warning," *Toronto Star*, August 18, 1933.

28 Cotter, op cit., pp. 13 and 130.

29 NJ interview, NJSC box 53, file 28.

30 Ibid.

31 Bob Thomas, "Leading Director Likes Authenticity," *Progress-Bulletin*, September 9, 1968, NJP box 1, file 2.

32 Brian D. Johnson, "Eye of the Hurricane," *Maclean's*, December 6, 1999.

33 Keith Davey, *The Rainmaker: A Passion for Politics* (Toronto: Stoddart, 1986) p. 4.

34 Details and quotations in this paragraph draw from Vols. 72 (1947-48), 73 (1948-49) and 74 (1949-50) of *Acta Victoriana*, student literary journal of Victoria College.

35 Translation of "The Russians are Not Coming" (NJ interview) by Tankred Golenpolsky, NJSC box 7, file 9.

36 Northrop Frye, *The Educated Imagination* (Toronto: CBC Publications, 1963) pp. 5, 11.

37 Jewison, *This Terrible Business*, pp. 35-6.

38 Ibid., p. 37.

CHAPTER 2

1 Stephen Cole, *Here's Looking at Us: Celebrating 50 Years of CBC-TV* (Toronto: McClelland & Stewart, 2002), p. 17.

2   Peter Gzowski interview with NJ, *Morningside*, CBC Radio, April 17, 1997.

3   Norman Jewison, *This Terrible Business Has Been Good to Me* (Toronto: Key Porter, 2004), p. 39.

4   Peter Gzowski interview with NJ, op cit.

5   NJ notes, "T.V. Technical Philosophy," Jan 16, 1952, NJP box 1, file 8.

6   NJ's notes on TV production, Jan 15-29, 1952, NJP box 1, file 8.

7   Cole, op cit., p. 17.

8   Transcript of interview with Jennifer Jewison, NJSC box 53, file 25.

9   Blaine Allan, "Big Revue," *Directory of CBC Television Series*, 1952-1982, http://www.queensu.ca/filmandmedia/sites/webpublish.queensu.ca.fmwww/files/files/CBC Television Linked Listings.pdf

10 Cole, op cit. p. 16.

11 Ibid, p. 14.

12 George Horhota, "Jewison Shoots for the Truth," *Maclean's*, October 29, 1979.

13 "Some Advice from Norman Jewison," *Youth Special*, May 13, 1961, *CBC Digital Archives*, https://www.cbc.ca/player/play/1786963722

14 Transcript of interview with Mike Dann, NJSC box 53, file 14.

15 Ibid.

16 Judith Krantz, "Norman Jewison: The Star's Status Symbol," *Maclean's*, January 5, 1963 https://archive.macleans.ca/article/1963/1/5/norman-jewison-the-stars-status-symbol

17 Sheldon Kirshner, "Jewison, in *The Statement*, tackles French wartime racism," *Canadian Jewish News*, December 11, 2003.

18 Transcript of interview with Mike Dann, op cit.

19 Transcript of interview with Gary Smith, NJSC box 53, file 9.

20 Transcript of interview with Larry Auerbach, NJSC box 53, file 27.

21 Ibid.

22 Transcript of interview with Mike Dann, op cit.

23 NJ interview, NJSC box 51, file 6.

24 Transcript of interview with Larry Auerbach, op cit.

25 Transcript of interview with Mike Dann, op cit.

26 *Tonight with Belafonte*, dir. NJ, December 10, 1959, *YouTube* video, https://www.youtube.com/watch?v=otw0FtXjOKc

27 Transcript of interview with Gary Smith, op cit.

28 John P. Shanley, "'Tonight With Belafonte' Offered . . ." *New York Times*, December 11, 1959.

29 Jewison, *This Terrible Business*, p. 49.

30 A.S. (Doc) Young, "A Word for Belafonte: Magnificent," *Los Angeles Sentinel*, December 17, 1959.

31 "Some Advice from Norman Jewison," op cit.

32 Krantz, op cit.

33 "Norman Jewison's Early Years," *CBC Digital Archives* (1997), https://www.cbc.ca/player/play/650095171549

34 NJ interview, NJSC box 51, file 5.

35 Ibid.

36 Transcript of interview with Jennifer Jewison, op cit.

37 "Hollywood Housewife," *Toronto Star Weekly*, August 6, 1966, NJP box 1, file 3.

38 Krantz, op cit.

39 NJ interview, NJSC box 51, file 6.

40 "Some Advice from Norman Jewison," op cit.

41 Bernard Weinraub, "A Veteran Director Still Fights the Good Fight," *New York Times*, December 26, 1999.

42 Transcript of interview with Gary Smith, op cit.

43 Ibid.

44 Ibid.

45 Jack Gould, "Judy Garland's Hour," *New York Times*, February 26, 1962.

46 Horhota, op cit.

47 Treatments for "Focus" and "Words & Music: U.S.A.," NJP box 2, file 8.

48 NJ interview, NJSC box 51, file 6.

CHAPTER 3

1 NJ to Mike Merrick, April 23, 1962, NJP box 1, file 1.

2 NJ to Harry Belafonte, April 23, 1962, NJSC box 44, file 6.

3 NJ Interview, NJSC box 51, file 6.

4 NJ interview, NJSC box 51, file 7.

5 Norman Jewison, *This Terrible Business Has Been Good to Me* (Toronto: Key Porter, 2004), p. 64.

6 NJ to Belafonte, April 23, 1962, op cit.

7 Alex Barris, "Hollywood Scene Busy, Complicated," clipping, NJSC, box 57, file 1.

8 NJ to Wally Koster, May 11, 1962, NJSC, box 45 file 11.

9 Judith Krantz, "Norman Jewison: The Star's Status Symbol," *Maclean's*, January 5, 1963.

10 NJ to Belafonte, April 23, 1962, op cit.

11 NJ to Suzanne Pleshette, May 12, 1962, NJSC box 46, file 12.

12 Murray Schumach, "Disneyland Gets First Major Role," *New York Times*, April 18, 1962.

13 *40 Pounds of Trouble* Press Book, qtd. by Jim Korkis, "The Secret Story Behind *40 Pounds of Trouble* – Part Two," MousePlanet, August 5, 2015 https://www.mouseplanet. com/11111/The_Secret_Story_Behind_40_Pounds_of_Trouble__Part_Two

14 Thomas McDonald, "Film Men Glad Jewison Takes Directing Job," clipping, NJSC box 67, file 1.

15 Jewison, *This Terrible Business*, pp. 67-68.

16 Interview with Alice Lee "Boaty" Boatwright, August 22, 2018.

17 NJ to Alex Barris, July 25, 1962, NJSC box 44, file 6.

18 NJ to Allan Mannings, April 9, 1963, NJSC box 46, file 2.

19 NJ to Harry and Rosemary Butler, Jan 21, 1964, NJSC box 44, file 6.

20 NJ notes comparing film editing and television, NJSC, box 67, file 1; Murray Schumach, "Humour Pervades Set for Movie," *New York Times* clipping, NJSC box 67, file 1.

21 Itinerary, *40 Pounds* National Press Screening, NJSC, box 67, file 1.

22 Frank Rasky, "The Former Toronto Cabbie who Tells the Stars how to Act," *Toronto Star Weekly*, August 14, 1965, clipping, NJSC box 67, file 1.

23 Tamar Jeffers McDonald, *Doris Day Confidential* (London: Bloomsbury, 2013), pp. 8, 117; Al Capp, "The Day Dream," *Show*, December 1962, qtd. in McDonald, 113.

24 Krantz, op cit.

25 NJ to Boatwright, December 5, 1962, NJSC box 44, file 7.

26 Transcript of interview with Doris Day, NJSC box 53, file 12.

27 NJ Interview, NJSC box 51, file 7.

28 Ibid.

29 Krantz, op cit.

30 Interview with Bruce McDonald, July 4, 2018.

31 Betty Friedan, *The Feminine Mystique* (New York: W. W. Norton, 1963), p. 11.

32 NJ to Boatwright, December 5, 1962, NJSC box 44, file 7.

33 Boatwright to NJ [undated, probably late 1962], NJSC box 44, file 7.

34 NJ to Boatwright, December 5, 1962, op cit.

35 Boatwright to NJ, December 17, 1962, NJSC box 44, file 7.

36 NJ to Allan Mannings, April 9, 1963, NJSC box 46, file 2.

37 NJ to Harold Berkowitz, July 26, 1963, NJP box 3, file 1.

38 Ibid.

39 Beyard Berman to Robert Lasky, "Re: Jewison vs. The Stuart Company," November 5, 1963, NJP box 3, file 1.

40 NJ to Harold Berkowitz, op cit.

41 Craig Stevens to NJ, January 12, 1964, NJSC box 46, file 19.

42 Laurence "Larry" Naismith [dated "Friday"], NJP box 3, file 1.

CHAPTER 4

1 NJ to Ralph Sarson, April 8, 1963, NJSC box 46, file 19.

2 Tino Balio, *United Artists: The Company that Changed the Film Industry, Volume 2* (Madison: U of Wisconsin P, 1987), pp. 118, 125.

3 Stulberg qtd. in David Weddle, *If They Move . . . Kill 'Em! The Life and Times of Sam Peckinpah* (New York: Grove, 1994), pp. 234-25.

4 NJ to Jerry Leider, November 29, 1963, NJSC box 45, file 12.

5 NJ to Wally & Myra Koster, October 16, 1964, NJSC box 45, file 11.

6 Robert B. Frederick, "Conditions Currently Favor Films Having 'More Than Mere Escapism,'" clipping, NJSC box 67, file 1.

7   NJ to Stanley Margulies, September 16, 1964, NJSC box 46, file 2.

8   NJ to Wally & Myra Koster, op cit.

9   Frank Rasky, "The Former Toronto Cabbie Who Tells the Stars How to Act," *The Toronto Star Weekly*, August 14, 1965, NJSC box 67, file 1.

10 *New York Times*, Feb 5, 1963, clipping, NJSC box 67, file 1.

11 Rasky, op cit.

12 NJ to Jerry Leider, op cit.

13 Palmer qtd. in Balio, *United Artists*, p. 168.

14 Robert B. Frederick, op cit.

15 Balio, op cit., p. 166.

16 Ibid, p. 167.

17 Ibid, p. 165.

18 NJ to Boatwright, July 1, 1964, NJSC box 44, file 7.

19 Mirisch Corp. to NJ, July 8, 1964, NJSC box 46, file 3.

20 Mark Harris, *Pictures at a Revolution* (New York: Penguin, 2008), p. 187.

21 "The List: Norman Jewison, Part 1 of 3," *DP/30: The Oral History of Hollywood*. YouTube video, September 24, 2012. https://www.youtube.com/watch?v=oIn5KPdPS6M&t=1244s

22 William Rose to NJ (letter and telegram), January 28, 1964, NJSC box 46, file 17.

23 William Rose, "Notes for First Talks With Norman Jewison," April 2, 1964, NJSC box 46, file 17.

24 William Rose to NJ, April 2, 1964, NJSC box 46, file 17.

25 Ibid.

26 Ibid.

27 William Rose to NJ, May 20, 1964, NJSC box 46, file 17.

28 NJ to William Rose, June 1, 1964, NJSC box 46, file 17.

29 Boatwright to NJ, undated, NJSC box 44, file 7.

30 Boatwright to NJ, November 5, 1963, box 44, file 7.

31 Boatwright to NJ, November 25, 1963, NJSC box 44, file 7.

32 NJ to Boatwright, March 13, 1964, NJSC box 44, file 7.

33 NJ to William Rose, undated, NJSC box 46, file 17.

34 Stanley Margulies to NJ, July 15, 1964, NJSC box 46, file 2.

35 William Rose to NJ, June 3, 1964, NJSC box 46, file 17.

36 NJ to William Rose, June 9, 1964, NJSC box 46, file 17.

37 William Rose to NJ, June 7, 1964, NJSC box 46, file 17.

38 William Rose to NJ, July 5, 1964, NJSC box 46, file 17.

39 NJ to William Rose, July 2, 1964, NJSC box 46, file 17.

40 William Rose to NJ, August 4, 1965, NJSC box 44, file 7.

41 NJ to William Rose, September 1, 1964, NJSC box 44, file 7.

42 William Rose to NJ, September 15, 1964, NJSC box 44, file 7.

43 William Rose to NJ, November 18, 1964, NJSC box 44, file 7.

44 David Cobb, "Jewison Has a Way with Stars," *Toronto Star*, clipping, NJSC box 67 file 1.

45 Katie O'Sullavan, "Norman Jewison: Rebel From Canada," *Coronet*, August 1966.

46 Philip K. Scheuer, "An Interesting 'Kid' and an Unwanted 'Loved One,'" *Los Angeles Times*, November 7, 1965, NJSC box 67, file 1.

47 David Cobb, op cit.

48 "Director Ousted in Film Dispute," *New York Times*, December 8, 1964 https://www.nytimes.com/1964/12/08/archives/director-ousted-in-film-dispute-nude-scene-adds-to-woes-of-the.html.

49 "Jewison Takes 'Kid' From Sam Peckinpah," *Variety*, clipping, NJSC box 67 file 1.

50 "Director Ousted in Film Dispute," ibid.

51 Cobb, op cit.

52 Penina Spiegel, *McQueen: The Untold Story of a Bad Boy in Hollywood* (New York: Doubleday, 1986), p. 171.

53 Cobb, op cit.

54 Jewison, *This Terrible Business*, p. 96.

55 William Murray, "Sam Peckinpah: The Playboy Interview," *Playboy*, August 1972. https://scrapsfromtheloft.com/2017/08/17/sam-peckinpah-playboy-interview-1972/

56 Peter Bart, "'Russians' Is Here, Here," *New York Times*, June 5, 1966, NJP box 8, file 6.

57 William Rose to NJ, December 6, 1964, NJSC box 44, file 7.

58 NJ to Ray Kurtzman, April 14, 1965, NJSC box 44, file 7.

59 Jewison, *This Terrible Business*, p. 97.

60 Curtis Lee Hanson, "The Directors, Part One: Norman Jewison / 'The Cincinnati Kid,'" *Cinema Magazine*, NJSC box 67, file 1.

61 Ibid.

62 Ibid. The critic Michael Wilmington compared *The Cincinnati Kid* to *Lucky You* in his review of the latter.

63 Spiegel, *McQueen*, pp. 12, 13.

64 Ibid, 27.

65 "The List: Norman Jewison, Part 1 of 3," op cit.

66 Spiegel, *McQueen*, p. 172.

67 Christopher Sandford, *McQueen: The Biography* (London: HarperCollinsEntertainment, 2001), p. 172.

68 Ibid, p. 172. Cars named in Spiegel, p. 172.

69 Spiegel, p. 209

70 NJ to Martin Ransohoff, January 21, 1965, NJP box 4, file 4.

71 Sandford, *McQueen*, p. 173.

72 Nick Dawson, *Being Hal Ashby* (Lexington, Ky.: UP of Kentucky, 2009) p. 72.

73 NJ to Boatwright, February 17, 1965, NJSC box 44, file 7.

74 NJ, commentary track on *The Cincinnati Kid* (Warner Bros. Home Video, 2005).

75 See, for instance, Martin Harris, "Hand Histories: 50 Years of Debate Over the Last Hand of *The Cincinnati Kid*," *Poker News*, October 15, 2015. https://www.pokernews.com/strategy/hand-histories-50-years-of-debate-over-the-last-hand-of-the-23059.htm

76 Anthony Holden, *Big Deal: A Year as a Professional Poker Player* (New York: Abacus, 2002), p. 87.

77 Hanson, op cit.

78 Philip K. Scheuer, "Motion Pictures are Faster than Ever," clipping, NJSC box 67, file 1.

79 Ibid.

CHAPTER 5

1 NJ to Boatwright, February 17, 1965, NJSC box 44, file 7.

2 NJ to Alex Barris, July 20, 1965, NJSC box 44, file 6.

3 William Rose to NJ, February 25, 1965, NJSC box 46, file 17.

4 Peter Bart, "New Breed Scans New Horizons," *New York Times*, January 10, 1965, NJSC, box 67, file 1.

5 NJ to William Rose, March 3, 1965, NJSC box 46, file 17.

6 NJ to William Rose, April 30, 1965, NJSC box 46, file 17.

7 William Rose to NJ, June 26, 1964, NJSC box 46, file 17.

8 Jerry Rosen to *Daily Variety*, March 3, 1965, NJSC box 46, file 16.

9 Jerry Lieder to NJ, March 10, 1965, NJSC box 46, file 16.

10 William Morris Agency Inter-Office Correspondence from Leonard Hirshan, May 28, 1965, NJSC box 46, file 3.

11 NJ to Peter Ustinov, June 10, 1965, NJP box 6, file 7.

12 NJ to William Rose, undated, NJSC box 46, file 17.

13 NJ to William Rose, March 3, 1965, NJSC box 46, file 17.

14 William Rose to NJ, June 29, 1965, NJSC box 46, file 17.

15 NJ to Stanley Margulies, September 16, 1964, NJSC, box 46, file 2.

16 *Variety*, "The Art of Love," December 31, 1964, https://variety.com/1964/film/reviews/the-art-of-love-2-1200420776/

17 "Tasteless," "flogged to death," from *Time Out* review of *The Art of Love*. https://www.timeout.com/london/film/the-art-of-love; "Bloated with lunacy" from *TV Guide* review. https://www.tvguide.com/movies/the-art-of-love/review/124894/

18 Eugene Archer, "'Art of Love' Appears in Neighborhoods," *New York Times*, July 1, 1965 https://www.nytimes.com/1965/07/01/archives/art-of-love-appears-in-neighborhoods.html

19 "The List: Norman Jewison, Part 1 of 3," *DP/30: The Oral History of Hollywood*. YouTube video, September 24, 2012. https://www.youtube.com/watch?v=oIn5KPdPS6M&t=1244s

20 NJ to Alex Barris, July 20, 1965, NJSC box 44, file 6.

21 Robert C. Reed to NJ, August 27, 1965, NJSC box 46, file 16.

22 NJ to Robert C. Reed, August 31, 1965. NJSC box 46, file 16.

23 "Navy Torpedoes Its Sub Simulating Being 'Russian,'" *Daily Variety*, clipping, NJSC box 67, file 2.

24 "'Russian' Sub Launched at Noyo," clipping, NJSC box 67, file 2.

25 Stanley Eichelbaum, "Fort Bragg's Panic Scene," *Oakland Tribune*, clipping, NJSC box 67, file 2.

26 NJ to Howard and Lillian Broad, February 3, 1966, NJSC box 44, file 6.

27 Ibid.

28 Contract summaries in NJP box 6, file 6.

29 Katie O'Sullavan, "Norman Jewison: Rebel From Canada," *Coronet*, August 1966, NJSC, box 67, file 2.

30 Alan Arkin, *An Improvised Life: A Memoir* (Cambridge: Da Capo Press, 2011), p. 70.

31 O'Sullavan, op cit.

32 Ibid.

33 Herb Michelson, "The Sub Set," *Oakland Tribune*, October 6, 1965, NJSC box 67, file 2.

34 O'Sullavan, op cit.

35 Arkin, *An Improvised Life*, p. 70.

36 Eichelbaum, op cit.

37 George H. Jackson, "Gloom-Chasing Task for Jewison," *Los Angeles Herald Examiner*, June 4, 1966, NJSC box 67, file 2.

38 NJ to Stanley Margulies, October 16, 1965, NJSC box 46, file 2.

39 Tino Balio, *United Artists: The Company that Changed the Film Industry Volume 2: 1951-1978* (Madison: U Wisconsin P, 1987, 2009), p. 119.

40 Krim quoted in Balio, ibid, p. 166.

41 NJ to Stanley Margulies, October 16, op cit.

42 Jackson, op cit.

43 NJ to "Rosie" (last name not included), November 1, 1965, NJP box 4, file 4.

44 NJ to Brock and Didi Peters, November 30, 1965, NJSC box 46, file 12.

45 NJ to Stanley Margulies, October 16, op cit.

46 NJ to David Foster, September 25, 1965, NJSC box 45, file 4.

47 "'Cincinnati' Boff, 'King Rat' Fine, 'Ashes' Hot Along L.A. 1st-Run Films," "'Cincinnati' Huge 44G 1st Chi Lap, 'Nanny' Good 29G," clippings, NJSC box 67, file 1.

48 David Foster to NJ, November 2, 1965, NJSC box 45, file 4.

49 NJ to Brock and Didi Peters, November 30, 1965, NJSC box 46, file 12.

50 O'Sullavan, op cit.

51 NJ to Peter Bart, November 23, 1965, NJP box 5, file 4. Underline in original.

52 Kleiner to NJ, September 17 and October 12, 1965. NJP box 4, file 4; box 24, file 7, respectively.

53 *Judgment of Corey* script, October 1965, NJP box 24, file 8.

54 Harry Kleiner to NJ, October 22, 1965, NJP box 24, file 8.

55 Nadine Phinney to Hal Ashby, November 1, 1965, NJP box 5, file 4.

56 NJ to "Rosie," op cit.

57 NJ to Mike Rosenfeld, November 12, 1965, NJP box 5, file 4.

CHAPTER 6

1 NJ to Howard and Lillian Broad, February 3, 1966, NJSC box 44, file 6.

2 NJ to Mike Merrick, April 23, 1962, NJP box 1, file 1.

3 Jody Jacobs, "A Hell of a Movie Maker," *Women's Wear Daily*, June 11, 1968, NJP box 1, file 2.

4 Kevin Jewison to NJ, undated (probably mid-1960s), NJSC box 77, file 6.

5 Transcript of interview with Jennifer Jewison, NJSC box 53, file 25.

6 NJ to Boaty Boatwright, February 17, 1965, NJSC box 44, file 7.

7 Joan Didion, "Hollywood: Having Fun," *New York Review of Books*, March 22, 1973.

8 NJ to Boatwright, February 17, 1965, NJSC box 44, file 7.

9 Peter Bart, "'Russians' Is Here, Here," *New York Times*, June 5, 1966, NJP box 8, file 6.

10 NJ to Boatwright, May 11, 1966, NJSC box 44, file 7.

11 NJ to Addie Ries, February 17, 1966, NJSC box 46, file 16.

12 Hal Ashby, "Breaking Out of the Cutting Room," *Action!* September / October, 1970, NJSC box 38, file 9.

13 Transcript of Interview with Marvin Mirisch, NJSC box 53, file 11.

14 NJ to Herb Jaffe, March 17, 1966, NJP box 24, file 7.

15 Arnost Horlik Inter-Office Memo to Oscar Steinberg, March 23, 1966, NJP box 24, file 7.

16 NJ to Colonel Sherwood Mark, December 17, 1965, NJP box 5, file 4.

17 NJ to Colonel Sherwood Mark, March 16, 1966, NJP box 5, file 4.

18 Walter Mirisch, *I Thought We Were Making Movies, Not History* (Madison: University of Wisconsin P, 2008), p. 246.

19 Mirisch, pp. 246-47.

20 William Morris Inter-Office Memo from Leonard Hirshan, April 5, 1966, NJSC box 46, file 3.

21 Ibid.

22 Christopher Sandfield, *McQueen: The Biography* (New York: HarperCollinsEntertainment, 2001), p. 184.

23 Stuart Heaver, "When Steve McQueen was talk of the town in Hong Kong," *South China Morning Post*, April 13, 2016. https://www.scmp.com/magazines/post-magazine/film-tv/article/1935713/when-steve-mcqueen-was-talk-town-hong-kong

24 Pollack qtd. in Mark Harris's *Pictures at a Revolution*, p. 139.

25 Dialogue as recalled by Silliphant in "Dialogue on Film: Stirling Silliphant," *American Film*, March 1988, pp. 13-15.

26 Brian Kellow, *Can I Go Now? The Life of Sue Mengers, Hollywood's First Superagent* (New York: Viking, 2015), p. 55.

27 Boatwright to NJ, April 5, 1966, NJSC box 44, file 7.

28 NJ to Boatwright, May 11, 1966, NJSC box 44, file 7.

29 NJ to Al Fisher, May 25, 1966, NJP box 5, file 4.

30 Army Archard, *Variety*, clipping, NJSC box 67, file 2.

31 NJ to Al Fisher, op cit.

32 Ann Wood, "Evening Revives a Dress," *Washington Evening Star*, May 10, 1966, NJSC box 67, file 2.

33 Alvin Rosensweet, "Filming Russian 'Invasion' Tricky," *Pittsburgh Post-Gazette*, May 17, 1966, NJP box 8, file 6.

34 Peter Bart, "'Russians' Is Here, Here," *New York Times*, June 5, 1966, NJP box 8, file 6.

35 Congressional Record—Senate (Bound Edition), 11488, May 25, 1966. Available via *Catalog of U.S. Government Publications (CGP)*, https://catalog.gpo.gov/F

36 Nadine Phinney to "Addie" (last name not included), June 3, 1966, NJP box 5, file 5.

37 Robert Alden, "The Russians Are Coming: Broad Farce Arrives at Three Theatres," *New York Times*, May 26, 1966.

38 James Powers, "'Russians Coming' Brilliant Comedy Headed for Top Returns at Boxoffice," *The Hollywood Reporter*, May 26, 1966, NJSC box 67, file 2.

39 Marjory Adams, "Riotously Funny—Best of '66?" *Boston Globe*, June 23, 1966.

40 Alan Arkin, *An Improvised Life: A Memoir* (Cambridge, MA: Da Capo Press, 2011), p. 69.

41 John W. Davidson to NJ, February 5, 1967, NJP box 5, file 4.

42 Tony Shaw, "*The Russians Are Coming The Russians Are Coming* (1966): Reconsidering Hollywood's Cold War 'Turn' of the 1960s," *Film History: An International Journal*, vol. 22 no. 2, 2010, pp. 235-250.

43 Trade paper clippings, NJSC box 67, file 2.

44 Nadine Phinney letter to "Addie" (last name not included), June 3, 1966, NJP box 5, file 5.

45 Kirk Douglas to Marvin Mirisch, June 12, 1966, NJSC box 67, file 2.

46 NJ to Al Fisher, May 25, 1966, NJP box 5, file 4.

47 Rick Ingersoll to NJ, June 9, 1966, NJP box 5, file 4.

48 Jane Gaskell, "It just proves – you can make a Russian smile," *Daily Mail*, clipping, NJSC box 67, file 2.

49 NJ to Boatwright, July 19, 1966, NJSC box 44, file 7.

50 Berlin reviews of *Russians*, June 28, 1966, NJP box 5, file 4.

51 Gaskell, op cit.

52 "'Russians Are Coming' Gets Berlin Ovation," clipping, NJSC box 67, file 2.

53 Berlin reviews of *Russians*, ibid.

54 Gaskell, op cit.

55 "MP's Love 'Russians,'" clipping, NJSC box 67, file 2.

56 "Perfect Ealing Subject—from Hollywood," clipping, NJSC box 67, file 2.

57 NJ to Boatwright, July 19, 1966, NJSC box 44, file 7. London as NJ's "favourite city" in undated letter to Boatwright, NJSC box 44, file 7.

58 Untitled clipping, NJSC box 67, file 2.

59 Charles Champlin, "Russians Meet 'The Russians,'" *Los Angeles Times* Calendar, NJSC box 67, file 2.

60 NJ to Boatwright, July 19, op cit.

61 NJ to Ilya Lopert, August 2, 1966, NJP box 5, file 4.

62 NJ to David Chasman, July 19, 1966, NJP box 5, file 4.

63 John Flaxman to NJ, March 30, 1966, NJP box 12, file 5. Christie and Connery in leads: NJ letter to Boatwright, July 19, op cit.

64 Mirisch, *I Thought We Were Making Movies*, p. 250.

65 Mirisch, *I Thought We Were Making Movies*, p. 249.

66 NJ letter to Boatwright, July 19, op cit.

67 "Hollywood Movies Cash Crop for Small American Towns,"*Boston Globe*, August 6, 1967, NJP box 1, file 2. Allen M. Widem, "Coast to Coast," *Hartford Times*, December 15, 1966, NJP box 1, file 2. Dianne Keller, "Hollywood Bustles into 'Typically Southern' Sparta," *Southern Illinoisan*, October 9, 1966, NJP box 1, file 2.

68 NJ to Arnold Picker, August 2, 1966, NJP box 5, file 4.

69 Boatwright to NJ, August 1, 1966, NJSC box 44, file 7.

CHAPTER 7

1 NJ to Emma P. Carter, October 21, 1966, NJSC box 44, file 4.

2 Transcript of interview with David Picker, NJSC box 53, file 10.

3 NJ letter to Emma P. Carter, op cit.

4 Nick Dawson, *Being Hal Ashby* (Lexington: U of Kentucky P, 2009) p. 86

5 Transcript of interview with Sidney Poitier, NJSC box 53, file 7.

6 Katie Fiene, "We're in the movies! Film being shot here," *Sparta News-Plaindealer*, October 6, 1966, NJP box 11, file 4.

7 Ibid.

8 Ibid.

9 Haskell Wexler, commentary track on *In the Heat of the Night* (MGM Home Video, 2001).

10 Ibid.

11 Dianne Keller, "Hollywood Bustles into 'Typically Southern' Sparta," *Southern Illinoisan*, October 9, 1966, NJP box 11, file 4.

12 Mark Harris, *Pictures at a Revolution* (New York: Penguin, 2008), p. 218

13 NJ, commentary track on *In the Heat of the Night*.

14 Transcript of interview with Sidney Poitier, op cit.

15 NJ, commentary track on *In the Heat of the Night*.

16 Dickson Terry, "Slice of Movie Life in a Diner," *St Louis Post-Dispatch* Everyday Magazine, October 2, 1966, NJP box 11, file 4.

17 NJ, commentary track on *In the Heat of the Night*.

18 Joan Barthel, "He Doesn't Want to be Sexless Sidney," *New York Times*, August 6, 1967, NJP box 11, file 4.

19 "Poitier to play film detective," *New York Times*, June 19, 1965.

20 Barthel, op cit.

21 Ibid.

22 Transcript of interview with Rod Steiger, NJSC box 53, file 20.

23 Keller, op cit.

24 Dickson Terry, op cit.

25 Dawson, *Being Hal Ashby*, pp. 80-81

26 Walter Mirisch, *I Thought We Were Making Movies, Not History* (Madison: University of Wisconsin P, 2008), p. 251.

27 Wexler and NJ, commentary track on *In the Heat of the Night*. See also Harris, pp. 219-20.

28 Diane Keller, "Movie Life Requires Sacrifice," *Southern Illinoisan*, October 16, 1966, NJP box 11, file 4.

29 Transcript of interview with Rod Steiger, op cit.

30 Transcript of interview with Sidney Poitier, op cit.

31 NJ, commentary track on *In the Heat of the Night*.

32 NJ quoted in Harris, p. 225.

33 Transcript of interview with Rod Steiger, op cit.

34 Transcript of interview with Sidney Poitier, op cit.

35 Mirisch, *I Thought We Were Making Movies,* p. 251.

36 Ibid.

37 NJ, "Notes on Film as an Art Form, Entertainment and a Business," remarks delivered at Yale University, December 1966, NJP box 1, file 1.

38 John Dartigue to NJ, December 16, 1966, NJP, box 5, file 4.

39 Matthew Greenwald, review of Ray Charles's "In the Heat of the Night," Allmusic.com https://www.allmusic.com/song/in-the-heat-of-the-night-mt0012329680

40 Norman Jewison, Liner Notes for the *In the Heat of the Night* album, NJP box 10, file 8.

41 Martin Arnold, "To the Rich Who Ski by Day and Party at Night, Sun Valley's 'Neat' Again," *New York Times,* January 18, 1970.

42 "Bobby Kennedy's Son Fractures a Leg Skiing," *Chicago Tribune*, December 24, 1966.

43 Jewison, *This Terrible Business*, p. 136.

44 Transcript of interview with Rod Steiger, op cit.

CHAPTER 8

1 Telegram from Norman Jewison, undated, NJP box 5, file 4.

2 "Hollywood Housewife," *Toronto Star Weekly*, August 6, 1966, NJP box 1, file 3.

3 Transcript of interview with Jennifer Jewison, NJSC box 53, file 25.

4 Ibid.

5 Ibid.

6 Transcript of interview with Alan and Marilyn Bergman, NJSC box 53, file 3.

7 NJ to Steve McQueen, November 15, 1966, NJP box 12, file 5.

8 James Ruffin Webb to Walter Mirisch, August 26, 1966, NJP box 24, file 7.

9 David Picker to NJ, September 12, 1966, NJP box 24, file 7.

10 Richard Hatton to NJ, December 9, 1966, NJP box 14, file 5.

11 Boatwright and Terence Baker letter to NJ, December 29, 1966, NJP box 14, file 5.

12 Penina Spiegel, *McQueen: The Untold Story of a Bad Boy in Hollywood* (New York: Doubleday, 1986), p. 202.

13 Ibid.

14 Raymond Kurtzman to Joseph Schoenfeld, February 3, 1967, NJP box 14, file 4.

15 Morton H. Smithline to NJ, May 25, 1967, NJP box 14, file 4.

16 NJ to Steve McQueen, March 13, 1967, NJP box 12, file 5.

17 Nadine Phinney to NJ and Hal Ashby, March 3, 1967, NJP box 14, file 5.

18 Nadine Phinney to Alan Trustman, January 31 1967, NJP box 12, file 7.

19 Alan Trustman to NJ, January 15, 1967, NJP box 12, file 7.

20 "Notes from Trustman," March 4, 1967, NJP box 12, file 7.

21 Stanley Margulies to NJ, February 23, 1967, NJP box 5, file 4.

22 Tom Korman to NJ, February 7, 1967, NJP box 14, file 5.

23 NJ to Richard Gregson, March 21, 1967, NJP box 14, file 5.

24 Lynn Stalmaster to NJ, March 17, 1967, NJP box 14, file 5.

25 NJ to Alan Trustman, April 4, 1967, NJP box 12, file 7.

26 Nadine Phinney to Alan Trustman, April 19, 1967, NJP box 12, file 7.

27 Simone de Beauvoir, "The Lolita Syndrome," *Esquire*, August 1, 1959. https://classic.esquire.com/article/1959/8/1/brigitte-bardot-and-the-lolita-syndrome

28 "Nadia" (last name not included) to NJ, undated, NJP box 14, file 5.

29 NJ to Olga Horstig, undated, NJP box 14, file 5.

30 NJ to Olga Horstig, March 28, 1967, NJP box 12, file 5.

31 Nick Dawson, ed. *Hal Ashby Interviews* (Jackson: Mississippi UP, 2010), pp. 5-6.

32 NJ to Ilya Lopert, April 3, 1967, NJP box 14, file 5.

33 Ernest Callenbach, Albert Johnson, and Haskell Wexler, "'The Danger is Seduction': An Interview with Haskell Wexler," *Film Quarterly* Vol. 21, No. 3 (Spring, 1968), pp. 3-14.

34 Haskell Wexler, "The Name of the Game," NJP box 14, file 3.

35 Olga Horstig to NJ, April 3, 1967, NJP box 14, file 5.

36 NJ to Olga Horstig, April 6, 1967, NJP box 14, file 5.

37 Olga Horstig to NJ, April 10, 1967, NJP box 14, file 5.

38 Nadine Phinney to Raquel Welch, April 13, 1967, NJP box 14, file 5.

39 Nadine Phinney to NJ, May 5, 1967, NJP box 14, file 5.

40 Casting notes from Lynn Stalmaster to Marvin Mirisch and NJ, May 31, 1967, NJP box 14, file 4.

41 NJ to Irving Schecter, May 15, 1967, NJP box 14, file 5.

42 NJ, audio commentary track on *Thomas Crown Affair* (Metro-Goldwyn-Mayer, 1999).

43 Kaplan, Livingston, Goodwin, Berkowitz & Selvin to NJ, August 31, 1967, NJP box 14, file 5.

44 NJ, audio commentary track on *Thomas Crown Affair*.

45 John J. Gould to Jim Henderling, June 23, 1967, NJP box 12, file 5.

46 NJ, audio commentary track on *Thomas Crown Affair*

47 Harvey Pack, "Film 'Language of the Young," *The Wichita Eagle and Beacon Magazine*, June 23, 1968, NJP box 15, file 4.

48 NJ, audio commentary track on *Thomas Crown Affair*.

49 Christopher Sandfield, *McQueen: The Biography* (New York: HarperCollinsEntertainment, 2001), p. 198.

50 Spiegel, *McQueen*, p. 203.

51 NJ, audio commentary track on *Thomas Crown Affair*.

52 NJ interview in *Hal*, dir. Amy Scott, Oscilloscope, 2018.

53 Spiegel, *McQueen*, p. 208.

54 Ibid, p. 206.

55 Faye Dunaway, *Looking for Gatsby* (New York: Gallery Books, 1998) p. 168.

56 James Lipscomb, "Improvise! – Films are made of whimsy," *Life*, November 10, 1967, NJSC box 68, file 1.

57 Alex Barris, "Whoops, the image changes, now it's Steve McQueen, Superstar," Alex Barris, *The Toronto Telegram*, June 29, 1968, NJP box 15, file 4.

58 Ernest Callenbach, Albert Johnson, and Haskell Wexler, "'The Danger is Seduction': An Interview with Haskell Wexler,"op cit.

59 Allen Widem, "Steve McQueen Cites Value of N.E. Filming," *Hartford Times*, June 24, 1968, NJP box 15, file 4.

60 Spiegel, *McQueen*, pp. 206-207.

61 Faye Dunaway, *Looking for Gatsby*, p. 169.

62 Ibid, pp. 169-170.

63 Spiegel, *McQueen*, p. 207.

64 NJ, audio commentary track on *In the Heat of the Night*.

65 Charles Champlin, "Poitier and Steiger Star in 'In the Heat of the Night,'" *Los Angeles Times*, August 23, 1967.

66 Meredith Willson to NJ, January 10, 1968, NJP box 10, file 1.

67 Roger E. Ailes to NJ, September 21, 1967, NJP box 10, file 2.

68 Princess Grace to NJ, January 13, 1968, NJP box 10, file 1.

69 Sue Mengers to NJ, August 4, 1967, NJP box 10, file 1.

70 Dunaway, *Looking for Gatsby*, p. 166.

71 Lipscomb, op cit.

72 Dunaway, *Looking for Gatsby*, p. 159.

73 Lipscomb, op cit.

74 Dunaway, *Looking for Gatsby*, p. 166.

75 "Atque Vale," NJP box 12, file 7.

76 Lipscomb, op cit.

77 Nadine Phinney to John Gould, September 7, 1967, NJP box 12, file 5.

78 Lipscomb, op cit.

CHAPTER 9

1 DeNeen L. Brown, "'Sex kitten' vs. Lady Bird: The day Eartha Kitt attacked the Vietnam War at the White House," *Washington Post*, January 9, 2018. https://www.washingtonpost.

com/news/retropolis/wp/2018/01/19/sex-kitten-vs-first-lady-eartha-kitt-yells-at-lady-bird-johnson-about-vietnam/

2 Earl Wilson, "It Happened Last Night," *Pittsburgh Post-Gazette*, February 1, 1968.

3 NJ, *This Terrible Business*, p. 151.

4 NJ interview, NJSC box 52, file 2.

5 James Lipscomb, "Two-Headed Man: A Documentary with Real People Talking," NJP box 1, file 2.

6 James Lipscomb, "Improvise! – Films are made of whimsy," *Life*, November 10, 1967, NJSC box 68, file 1.

7 *Running Scared* Synopsis, NJP box 25, file 4.

8 Hal Ashby to NJ, May 16, 1967, NJP box 25, file 5.

9 Arthur Zeldin, "Norman Jewison: Don't Bug Him About Being A Hollywood Canadian," *Maclean's*, October 1, 1968. http://archive.macleans.ca/article/1968/10/1/jewison-jewison

10 Wayne Warga, "Civil Rights and a Producer's Dilemma," *Los Angeles Times* Calendar, April 14, 1968, NJP box 26, file 7.

11 James Lipscomb, "Improvise!—Films Are Made with Whimsy," op cit.

12 Jeff Livingston to NJ and Hal Ashby, May 27, 1968, NJP box 17, file 5.

13 Jewison, *This Terrible Business*, p. 172.

14 Transcript of interview with Patrick Palmer, NJSC box 53, file 18.

15 Ibid.

16 Steve McQueen to NJ, March 26, 1968, NJP box 12, file 5.

17 NJ to Steve McQueen, March 29, 1968, NJP box 12, file 5.

18 Hal Ashby to NJ, October 27, 1967, NJP box 17, file 3.

19 Sam Tanenhaus, "The Literary Battle for Nat Turner's Legacy," *Vanity Fair*, August 3, 2016. https://www.vanityfair.com/culture/2016/08/the-literary-battle-for-nat-turners-legacy

20 William Styron, "Author's Note," *The Confessions of Nat Turner* (New York: Random House, 1967). Gray's "Confession": https://digitalcommons.unl.edu/etas/15/

21 Philip Rahv, "Through the Midst of Jerusalem," *New York Review of Books*, October 26, 1967.

22 Lowell qtd. in Tanenhaus, op cit.

23 George Steiner, "The Fire Last Time," *New Yorker*, Nov. 25, 1967.

24 Roger Davis to Abe Lastfogel, NJP box 26, file 5.

25 "25 years": Deac Rossell, "Jewison excels among new breed of proficient, socially aware directors," *Boston After Dark*, NJP box 5, file 4. "Black Gideon": Ray Loynd, "Negroes Protest Turner Bio," *The Hollywood Reporter*, March 29, 1968, NJP box 26, file 7.

26 Henry Pelham Burn, "Norman Jewison moves into the Establishment . . . and survives," *PACE Magazine*, October 1968.

27 The Association to End the Defamation of Black People (Louise Meriweather, Chairman) to NJ and David Wolper, March 26, 1968, NJP box 26, file 1.

28 NJ to Brock Peters, February 26, 1968, NJSC box 46, file 12.

29 Dalton Trumbo to David Wolper, March 15, 1968, NJP box 26, file 1.

30 Lucy Kroll to Jerry Zeitman, March 13, 1968, NJP box 26, file 1.

31 NJ interview, NJSC box 51, file 8.

32 William Styron to NJ, March 26, 1968, NJP box 26, file 1.

33 The Association to End the Defamation of Black People (Louise Merriweather, Chairman) to NJ and David Wolper, op cit.

34 NJ to Anne Bancroft, February 14, 1968, NJP box 19, file 3.

35 Dalton Trumbo to NJ, March 12, 1968, NJP box 26, file 1.

36 Gregory Peck to Board of Governors of the Motion Picture Academy, April 5, 1968, NJSC box 46, file 12.

37 Nick Kotz, *Judgment Days: Lyndon Baines Johnson, Martin Luther King, Jr., and the laws that changed America* (Boston: Houghton Mifflin, 2005), p. 419.

38 Kevin Thomas, "Ceremony Took on Different Mood this Year," clipping, NJSC box 47, file 2.

39 "Hollywood: Forty is a Dangerous Age," *Time*, April 19, 1968, clipping, NJSC box 47, file 2.

40 Shirley Paul, "Stars on Parade: The Mark of Elegance," *Citizen-News / Valley Times*, April 11, 1968, NJP box 11, file 5.

41 Walter Mirisch, *I Thought We Were Making Movies, Not History*, p. 255.

42 Marilyn and Alan Bergman to NJ, April 11, 1968, NJP box 10, file 2.

43 Jennifer Wayne to NJ, April 15, 1968, NJP box 10, file 2.

44 NJ to Jennifer Wayne, May 15, 1968, NJP box 10, file 2.

45 Dick Kleiner, "'Nat Turner' is in for Trouble," *San Gabriel Valley Tribune*, June 16, 1968, NJP box 26, file 7.

46 NJ interview, NJSC box 51, file 8.

47 Warga, op cit.

48 Author interview with Alexandra Styron, February 5, 2020.

49 Army Archerd, "Just for Variety," *Variety*, May 27, 1968, NJP box 26, file 7.

50 Audio recording of the Davis-Styron debate, "James Baldwin Speaks! The Confessions of Nat Turner: with William Styron and Ossie Davis," YouTube video. https://www.youtube.com/watch?v=TCkpiRM0G4g&t=361s.

51 Wayne Warga, "The Issues: Ossie Davis vs. Nat Turner," *Los Angeles Times*, May 12, 1968, NJP box 26, file 7.

52 George Horhota, "Jewison Shoots for the Truth," *Maclean's*, October 29, 1979.

53 NJ, *This Terrible Business*, p. 172

CHAPTER 10

1 Ralph Wilcox to NJ, March 11, 1970, NJP box 30, file 7.

2 Thomas Rachal to NJ, October 11, 1969, NJSC box 46, file 16.

3 *Norman Jewison, Filmmaker* (dir. Doug Jackson, 1971).

4 NJ, commentary track on *Fiddler on the Roof* Special Edition (MGM Home Video, 2006), and *Norman Jewison, Filmmaker.*

5 *Boston Herald-Traveller*, "'Crown Affair' Premiere Wednesday at Music Hall," clipping, June 16, 1968, NJP box 15, file 4.

6 Ken Mayer, "'Crown' Premier to be Gala Affair," *Sunday Herald-Traveller*, May 26, 1968, NJP box 15, file 4; *Boston Herald-Traveller*, "'Crown Affair' Premiere Wednesday at Music Hall," op cit.; George McKinnon, "McQueen, 'Thomas Crown' draw huge premiere crowd," *Boston Globe*, June 20, 1968, NJP box 15 file 4.

7 *Hollywood Reporter*, June 26, 1968. https://www.hollywoodreporter.com/review/thomas-crown-affair-review-1968-movie-1016645

8 James W. Arnold, "'Crown Affair': Stylish but Vapid," *Milwaukee Journal*, clipping, NJP box 15, file 6.

9 Roger Ebert review of *Thomas Crown Affair*, August 27, 1968, RogerEbert.com, https://www.rogerebert.com/reviews/thomas-crown-affair-1968.

10 Clippings of French reviews, NJP box 15, file 6.

11 Henry Pelham Burn, "Norman Jewison moves into the Establishment . . . and survives," *PACE Magazine*, October 1968.

12 Arthur Zeldin, "Norman Jewison: Don't Bug Him About Being a Hollywood Canadian," *Maclean's*, October 1, 1968.

13 Roger Ebert, "'Gaily' Filming Hecht's Chicago," *Chicago Sun-Times*, June 22, 1968, NJP box 20, file 7.

14 Zeldin, op cit.

15 James Greenberg, "Did Hollywood sit on *Fences*?" *New York Times*, January 27, 1991.

16 Andrea Most, *Theatrical Liberalism: Jews and the Broadway Musical* (New York: NYU P, 2013), p. 153.

17 M. Kaufman Memorandum to Moshe Davis, Sept. 1, 1969, NJP box 30, file 15.

18 *Norman Jewison, Filmmaker.*

19 Lee Katz to Arnold and David Picker, "Some Eastern European Film Production Facilities," December 1, 1967, NJP box 30, file 12.

20 NJ, commentary track on *Fiddler on the Roof.*

21 *Norman Jewison, Filmmaker.*

22 NJ and Chaim Topol, commentary track on *Fiddler on the Roof.*

23 Ibid.

24 NJ to Anne Bancroft, December 19, 1969, NJP box 30, file 7.

25 "West German Government Condemns Arab Terrorist Attack on El Al Airline," February 12, 1970, Jewish Telegraphic Agency. https://www.jta.org/1970/02/12/archive/west-german-government-condemns-arab-terrorist-attack-on-el-al-airline

26 Theodore Bikel to NJ, July 10, 1969, NJSC box 44, file 6.

27 NJ to Theodore Bikel, July 17, 1969, NJSC box 44, file 6.

28 Zeldin, op cit.

29 Rex Reed, "Gaily, Gaily, romps along . . .," clipping, NJP box 20, file 7.

30 Vincent Canby, "Nostalgia Warms 'Gaily, Gaily,'" *New York Times*, December 17, 1969.

31 Transcript of interview with David Picker, NJSC box 53, file 10.

32 Transcript of interview with Marvin Mirisch, NJSC box 53, file 11.

33 *Norman Jewison, Filmmaker*

34 NJ interview, NJSC box 51, file 7.

35 Interview with Bruce McDonald, July 4, 2018.

36 NJ interview, NJSC box 51, file 7.

37 NJ, commentary track on *Fiddler on the Roof*

38 *Norman Jewison, Filmmaker*

39 "John Williams: Creating a Musical Tradition," featurette on *Fiddler on the Roof* Special Edition (MGM Home Video, 2006).

40 NJ interview, NJSC box 52, file 2.

41 "The Bergmans (Alan and Marilyn)," NJSC box 53, file 8.

42 David Picker interview, NJSC box 53, file 10.

43 NJ to Rupert Allan, July 9, 1970, NJSC box 45, file 4.

44 Saul Cooper to NJ, June 11, 1970, NJP box 30, file 8.

45 NJ to Walter Mirisch, June 16, 1970, NJP box 30, file 8.

46 Larry De Waay, "Insurance Claim Due to Norma Crane's Illness," July 21, 1971, NJP box 31, file 24.

47 Mirisch, op cit., 309.

48 Jewison, *This Terrible Business*, p. 180.

49 Mirisch, *I Thought We Were Making Movies*, p. 309.

50 Ibid, p. 286.

51 Transcript of interview with Marvin Mirisch, op cit.

52 *Norman Jewison, Filmmaker.*

53 Ibid.

54 NJ interview, NJSC box 51, file 7.

55 NJ, *This Terrible Business*, p. 176.

56 Mirisch, *I Thought We Were Making Movies*, p. 309.

CHAPTER 11

1 Transcript of interview with Gary Smith, NJSC box 53, file 9.

2 NJ to Chiz Schultz, August 6, 1971, NJSC box 46, file 19.

3 Transcript of interview with Henry Mancini, NJSC box 53, file 15.

4 NJ, typed notes on *Fiddler* and relocation to London, NJSC box 45, file 9.

5 NJ to Hal Ashby, March 3, 1971, NJSC, box 44, file 4.

6 Joe Broady, "Jewison Says 'Landlord' First Black Comedy Pic," *Variety*, Thursday, April 10, 1969, NJP box 23, file 11.

7 Boatwright to NJ, August 1, 1966, NJSC box 44, file 7.

8 Hal Ashby, "Breaking out of the Cutting Room," in *Hal Ashby Interviews* edited by Nick Dawson (Jackson: U Press of Mississippi, 2010), p. 6.

9 Ibid.
10 Ashby's letter to NJ qtd. in Dawson, *Being Hal Ashby* (Lexington, KY.: UP of Kentucky, 2009), p. 114.
11 Ibid, p. 113.
12 Ibid, p. 115.
13 NJ interview, NJSC box 51, File 7.
14 Hal Ashby to NJ, June 20, 1970, NJSC box 44, file 4.
15 Dawson, *Being Hal Ashby*, p. 110
16 Hal Ashby to NJ, July 8, 1970, NJSC box 44, file 4.
17 Ibid.
18 Hal Ashby to Irving Klein, March 29, 1971, NJSC box 44, file 4.
19 Transcript of interview with Patrick Palmer, NJSC box 53, file 18.
20 Irving Klein to Hal Ashby, April 1, 1971, NJSC box 44, file 4.
21 *Hal*, dir. Amy Scott, Oscilloscope, 2018.
22 Quinn Donoghue to Rick Ingersoll, December 15, 1970, NJSC box 45, file 4.
23 Rick Ingersoll to NJ, July 19, 1971, NJSC box 45, file 4.
24 NJ to Rick Ingersoll, July 7, 1971, NJSC box 45, file 4.
25 NJ to Rick Ingersoll, July 28, 1971, NJSC box 45, file 4.
26 "In the Heat of the Night Wins Best Picture: 1968 Oscars." YouTube video, https://www.youtube.com/watch?v=2XffOHjOywc&t=183s
27 Walter Mirisch to NJ, October 19, 1971, NJP box 32, file 14.
28 Marvin Mirisch interview, NJSC box 53, file 11.
29 NJ Telex to Marvin Mirisch, March 23, 1971, NJP box 32, file 15.
30 "Fiddler on the Roof" – Release Dates, July 5, 1971, NJP box 32, file 15.
31 NJ to Louis Chissick, July 9, 1971, NJP box 32, file 15.
32 NJ to Charles Berman, July 21, 1971, NJP box 32, file 15.
33 Betty (last name not included) to NJ, November 10, 1971, NJSC box 44, file 6.
34 Pauline Kael, "Fiddler on the Roof: A Bagel With a Bite Out of It," *For Keeps: 30 Years at the Movies* (New York: Dutton, 1994), pp. 395-400.
35 NJ to Gabe Sumner, December 9, 1971, NJP box 33, file 2.
36 NJ to Editor, *Toronto Daily Star*, Nov. 18, 1971, NJP box 33, file 2.
37 NJ to Editor, *The Globe and Mail*, Nov. 18, 1971, NJP box 33, file 2.
38 Gabe Sumner to NJ, January 6, 1972, NJP box 33, file 3.

CHAPTER 12

1 NJ to Chiz Schultz, August 6, 1971, NJSC box 46, file 19.
2 Kimberly Winston, "The Stormy, Surprising History of 'Jesus Christ Superstar'," *Religion News Service*, March 29, 2018. https://religionnews.com/2018/03/29/the-splainer-the-stormy-surprising-history-of-jesus-christ-superstar/
3 NJ interview with Vatican Press following *Superstar* screening, NJP box 53, file 13.

4 Andrew Lloyd Webber, *Unmasked: A Memoir* (New York: Harper, 2018), ch. 12 (Ebook).

5 NJ, interview for Shukan-Heibon (Japan), NJP box 35, file 13.

6 Andrew Lloyd Webber, op cit.

7 Tim Rice, *Oh What a Circus* (London: Hodder & Stoughton, 2000), ch. 21 (Ebook).

8 Patrick Palmer Interview Transcript, NJSC box 53, file 18.

9 Norman Jewison, "Film Making in Israel," December 15, 1972, NJP box 35, file 13.

10 NJ to Marlon Brando, March 20, 1972, NJP box 27, file 9.

11 NJ to Harold Berkowitz, June 8, 1972, NJSC box 1, file 12.

12 NJ on commentary track of *Jesus Christ Superstar* (Universal Studios DVD, 2004).

13 "Text for book of photographs – Jesus Christ Superstar," NJP box 33, file 15.

14 NJ to Jimmy Fraser, June 1, 1972, NJP, box 33, file 5.

15 NJ, handwritten casting notes on Beverly Hills Hotel stationary, NJP box 33, file 5.

16 "Quinn's Notes for Book – Jesus Christ Superstar," NJP box 33, box 15.

17 NJ interview with Vatican Press following *Superstar* screening, op cit.

18 "Quinn's Notes for Book – Jesus Christ Superstar," op cit.

19 Transcript of interview with Rob Iscove, NJSC box 53, file 17.

20 "Quinn's Notes for Book – Jesus Christ Superstar," op cit.

21 NJ on commentary track of *Jesus Christ Superstar*.

22 Norman Jewison, "Film Making in Israel," op cit.

23 Transcript of interview with Rob Iscove, op cit.

24 Atom Egoyan interview, June 20, 2018.

25 Transcript of interview with Rob Iscove, op cit.

26 Ted Neeley, audio commentary track of *Jesus Christ Superstar*.

27 Ibid.

28 Ibid.

29 Letter from NJ to Harold Berkowitz, May 10, 1972, NJSC box 1, file 12.

CHAPTER 13

1 NJ to Carl Reiner, December 7, 1971, NJP box 32, file 13.

2 Sheldon Kirshner, "Jewison, in *The Statement*, tackles French wartime racism," *Canadian Jewish News*, December 11, 2003.

3 Norman Jewison, *This Terrible Business Has Been Good To Me* (Toronto: Key Porter, 2004), p. 11.

4 Haim Bar-Lev to NJ, September 17, 1972, NJSC 45, file 6.

5 NJ to Nadine Phinney, May 10, 1973, NJSC box 46, file 12.

6 Rabbi Marc H. Tanenbaum, WINS Religion Commentary, October 10, 1971, NJP box 35, file 4.

7 Andrew Lloyd Webber to NJ, July 10, 1972, NJP box 35, file 4.

8 NJ to Allen Rivkin, May 10, 1972, NJP box 35, file 4.

9 Rolling pins: Sarah Laskin to NJ, undated, NJP box 31, file 17; clothespins: Ann Siegel to NJ, December 18, 1972, NJP box 31, file 17.

10 "'Superstar' Super-Demeaning," *B'nai B'rith Messenger*, July 6, 1973, NJP box 35, file 4.

11 Ibid.

12 Ze'ev Birger to NJ, August 7, 1973, NJP box 35, file 4.

13 NJ interview with Vatican press following screening of *Superstar*, NJP box 35, file 13.

14 Francois S. Ouzan, "Holocaust survivor Zev Birger's lasting imprint on Jerusalem," *The Jerusalem Post*, May 31, 2019. https://www.jpost.com/diaspora/zev-birgers-imprint-on-israel-and-its-capital-591200.

15 Ze'ev Birger to NJ, July 5, 1973, NJP box 35, file 4.

16 NJ to Haim Bar-Lev, July 9, 1973, NJP box 35, file 4.

17 Nat Shuster, "Norman Jewison: The Return of a Gifted and Successful Native Son," *Performing Arts in Canada Magazine*, Fall 1985, NJSC box 8, file 12.

18 Terrence Smith, "Israeli Government Moves to Dissociate Itself from 'Jesus Christ Superstar,'" *New York Times*, July 14, 1973, https://www.nytimes.com/1973/07/14/archives/article-1-no-title-other-steps-taken-assurances-given-exaggeration.html

19 Golda Meir to NJ, July 16, 1973, NJP box 35, file 4.

20 Roger Ebert review of *Jesus Christ Superstar*, August 15, 1973, RoberEbert.com, https://www.rogerebert.com/reviews/jesus-christ-superstar-1973

21 Howard Thompson, "Mod-Pop 'Superstar' Comes to Screen," *New York Times*, August 9, 1973. https://www.nytimes.com/1973/08/09/archives/modpop-superstar-comes-toscreen.html

22 Pauline Kael, "When the Saints Come Marching In," *The Age of Movies*, ed. Sanford Schwartz (Library of America, 2011), p. 432.

23 Bernard Gribble to NJ, June 4, 1973, NJP box 35, file 6.

24 Don Siegel to NJ, May 30, 1973, NJP box 35, file 6.

25 Roger Moore to NJ (undated), NJP box 35, file 6.

26 Susan Harrison to NJ (undated), NJP box 35, file 5.

27 Elizabeth Weiss to NJ (undated), NJP box 35, file 5.

28 NJ to Elizabeth Weiss, October 4, 1973, NJP box 35, file 5.

29 NJ to Yousuf Karsh, March 29, 1974, NJSC box 45, file 11.

30 Transcript of interview with Patrick Palmer, NJSC box 53, file 18.

31 Margot Kidder to NJ, March 1969, NJSC box 45, file 11.

32 NJ to Marshall Brickman, October 29, 1974, NJSC box 40, file 18.

33 Mordecai Richler to NJ, June 14, 1973, NJSC box 41, file 1.

CHAPTER 14

1 NJ to Lois Carruth, January 25, 1974, NJSC box 44, file 8.

2 Transcript of interview with Jennifer Jewison, NJSC box 53, file 25.

3 NJ to Lois Carruth, op cit.

4 Tom Schatz, "The Studio System and Conglomerate Hollywood," in *The Contemporary Hollywood Film Industry* edited by Paul McDonald and Janet Wasko (Malden, MA: Blackwell, 2008), pp. 18-19.

5 Richard Barnet and Robert Muller, *Global Reach: The Power of the Multinational Corporations* (New York: Simon & Schuster, 1974), p. 373.

6 NJ quoted in Andrew Nette, *Rollerball* (Leighton Buzzard: Auteur, 2018), p. 97.

7 Budget, NJSC box 1, file 20.

8 Roger Sherman to Larry de Waay, March 22, 1974, NJSC box 2, file 18.

9 Harrison qtd. in Nette, *Rollerball*, p. 32.

10 Dan Rissner to unnamed recipient, February 1, 1974, NJSC box 4, file 12.

11 Transcript of interview with Patrick Palmer, NJSC box 53, file 18.

12 Clint Eastwood interview, Jay Scott steno pads, NJSC box 51, file 1.

13 Roger Sherman to Bertram Fields, March 26th, 1974, NCSC, box 2, file 1.

14 Norman Jewison, audio commentary track on *Rollerball* (MGM DVD, 2004).

15 Transcript of interview with James Caan, NJSC box 53, file 23.

16 Bart Mills, "James Caan: Hollywood's Hottest Property and a Brute to Boot," *Cosmopolitan*, 1975 clipping, pp. 87-91, NJSC box 4, file 1.

17 NJ to James Caan, April 16, 1975, NJSC box 2, file 1.

18 NJ to Orson Welles, April 11, 1974, NJSC box 2, file 4.

19 Roger Sherman to Robert Raison, June 20, 1974, NJSC box 2, file 19.

20 Harrison qtd. in Nette, *Rollerball*, p. 39.

21 Transcript of interview with Patrick Palmer, op cit.

22 Rollerball Game Rules, NJSC box 2, file 13.

23 Injuries noted in *Rollerball* Progress Reports, NJSC box 3, file 11.

24 NJ quoted in *Films Illustrated*, September 1975 clipping, NJSC box 4, file 1.

25 Harrison qtd. in Nette, *Rollerball*, pp. 29-30.

26 Transcript of interview with Patrick Palmer, op cit.

27 Transcript of interview with James Caan, op cit.

28 Transcript of interview with Patrick Palmer, op cit.

29 Transcript of interview with James Caan, op cit.

30 Transcript of interview with Patrick Palmer, op cit.

31 Richard D. Hefner (CARA Chairman) to NJ, April 24, 1975, NJSC box 2, file 5.

32 NJ to Richard D. Hefner, May 5, 1975, NJSC box 2, file 5.

33 NJ, in "From Rome to Rollerball: The Full Circle," featurette, YouTube video, https://www.youtube.com/watch?v=Bd3HjKKX-RM

34 *Rollerball* publicity correspondence, NJSC box 3, file 13.

35 NJ to Rai Saunders, December 15, 1975, NJSC box 2, file 4.

36 Joseph Gelmis, "Rollerball is a Disquieting Spectacle," *Newsday*, June 29, 1975.

37 *The Listener*, September 18, 1975, clipping, NJSC box 4, file 1.

38 NJ to Ed Apfel, October 31, 1975, NJSC box 2, file 12.

39 NJ to William Harrison, November 5, 1975, NJSC box 2, file 17.

CHAPTER 15

1 NJ to Myra Koster, October 29, 1974, NJSC box 45, file 11.

2 NJ to Myra Koster, October 23, 1975, NJSC box 45, file 11.

3 Charles Foran, *Mordecai: The Life and Times* (Toronto: Alfred A. Knopf, 2010), p. 394.

4 NJ CBC-Radio interview with Ray Gallen, "Norman Jewison returns home," March 6, 1980. https://www.cbc.ca/archives/entry/jewison-returns-home

5 Tom Clark and Andrew Dilnot, "Long-term Trends in British Taxation and Spending," *Institute for Fiscal Studies* Briefing Note 25 (2002).

6 Transcript of interview with Larry Auerbach, NJSC box 53, file 27.

7 NJ to Jim Stacy, October 10, 1974, NJSC box 46, file 19.

8 Nat Shuster, "Norman Jewison: The Return of a Gifted and Successful Native Son," *Performing Arts in Canada Magazine*, Fall 1985, NJSC box 8, file 12.

9 Transcript of interview with Larry Auerbach, NJSC box 53, file 27.

10 "The Bergmans (Alan and Marilyn)," NJSC box 53, file 8.

11 Transcript of interview with Henry Mancini, NJSC box 53, file 15.

12 Transcript of interview with Larry Auerbach, op cit.

13 Joe Eszterhas, *Hollywood Animal: A Memoir* (New York: Knopf, 2004) p. 84.

14 Joe Eszterhas, author interview, August 2, 2019.

15 "Sylvester Stallone – Making of *F.I.S.T.*" 1977 featurette, YouTube video. https://www.youtube.com/watch?v=ICOY6Lm612U

16 TIFF archive, "Sylvester Stallone," File 2000-007-05.056

17 Scott Warren, "Sylvester Stallone opens up about his secret passion, and talent, for painting," *Daily Mail*, January 11, 2010. https://www.dailymail.co.uk/tvshowbiz/article-1242224/Sylvester-Stallone-opens-secret-passion-talent-painting.html.

18 Bob Thomas, "Stallone plays a Hoffa Type," Associated Press, clipping, NJSC box 56, file 1.

19 Loanout agreement between Huron Productions and Moonblood Productions, March 1, 1977, TIFF File 2000-007-05.056

20 *Dubuque Telegraph Herald*, "Focus on *F.I.S.T.*," April 26, 1978, NJSC box 56, file 1.

21 Ivor Davis, "It's Sly, 2 Hollywood, 0," *Los Angeles Magazine*, April 1978, NJSC box 56, file 1.

22 *Dubuque Telegraph Herald*, "Focus on *F.I.S.T.*," op cit.

23 Bob Lardine, "Did Success Spoil Sly Stallone?" *Sunday News Magazine*, April 23, 1978, NJSC box 56, file 1.

24 "Sylvester Stallone – Making of *F.I.S.T.*" (1977 featurette) YouTube video. https://www.youtube.com/watch?v=ICOY6Lm612U Accessed May 15, 2020.

25 Greg Kilday, "From 'F.I.S.T.' to 'Justice for All," *Los Angeles Times*, Nov. 20, 1979, NJSC box 56, file 1.

26 Ivor Davis, "Sly Stallone in "F.I.S.T.," *Today* magazine, clipping, NJSC box 56, file 1.

27 "Only Stallone says success hasn't changed him," *The Baltimore Sun*, May 22, 1978., clipping, NJSC box 56, file 1.

28 Kilday, op cit.

29 Jean Vallely, "Stallone's Latest Fight," *Esquire*, May 9, 1978, NJSC box 5, file 5.

30 Ibid.

31 Bruce Kirkland, "Norman Jewison Still Has That Same Old Drive," *Toronto Star*, clipping, NJSC box 56, file 1.

32 Vincent Canby, "F.I.S.T., Drama of Unionism," *New York Times*, April 26, 1978.

33 Ray Conlogue, "Jewison's $8-million punch is gripping to watch but ultimately misses the target," *Globe and Mail*, April 29, 1978.

34 Gregg Kilda, "After 'Rocky,' a raised 'F.I.S.T." *Washington Post*, July 17, 1977.

35 *Dubuque Telegraph Herald*, "Focus on F.I.S.T.," op cit.

36 Richard H. Sia, "For a 'nobody,' Jewison knows his cinema stuff," *Baltimore Sun*, December 19, 1978, NJSC box 56, file 1.

37 Interview with Sylvester Stallone, Jay Scott steno pads, NJSC box 51, file 1.

38 Joe Eszterhas, author interview, op cit.

CHAPTER 16

1 Mao Tse-tung, "In Memory of Jewison Bethune," December 21, 1939. https://www.marxists.org/reference/archive/mao/selected-works/volume-2/mswv2_25.htm

2 George Anthony, "See You in Court," clipping, NJSC box 56, file 1.

3 "Norman Jewison Directs . . . And Justice for All," *Millimeter, The Magazine of the Motion Picture and Television Production Industries*, October 1979, clipping, NJSC box 56, file 1.

4 Ibid.

5 Sid Adilman, "Another Coup for Jewison," *Toronto Star*, October 19, 1979.

6 Clarke Taylor, "'Lawyer' Pacino Carries a Brief for Comedy," *Los Angeles Times* Calendar, January 14, 1979, NJSC box 56, file 1.

7 NJ interview, NJSC box 53, file 28.

8 Lawrence Grobel, *Al Pacino* (New York: Simon and Schuster, 2006), p. 39.

9 Taylor, op cit.

10 Andrew Yule, *Life on the Wire: The Life and Art of Al Pacino* (D.I. Fine, 1991), p. 162.

11 Richard H. Sia, "For a 'nobody,' Jewison knows his cinema stuff," *Baltimore Sun*, December 19, 1978, NJSC box 56, file 1.

12 Transcript of interview with William Goldman, NJSC box 53, file 22.

13 NJ to Ely Landau, January 13, 1978, NJSC box 45, file 12.

14 Bruce Kirkland, "Norman Jewison Still Has That Same Old Drive," *Toronto Star*, clipping, NJSC box 56, file 1.

15 Ibid.

16 David Thompson, ed., *Levinson on Levinson* (London: Faber, 1993), pp. 32-36.

17 William J. Stuntz, *The Collapse of American Criminal Justice* (Cambridge, Mass: Belknap P, 2011), pp. 228-229.

18 Author interview with Norman Jewison, October 11, 2019.

19 Author Interview with Michael Barker, September 11, 2019.

20 NJ interview on China, NJSC box 45, file 5.

21 NJ to Michael Spencer, November 25, 1977, NJSC box 41, file 7.

22 NJ to Ron Barbaro, January 4, 1979, NJSC box 44, file 6.

23 Marketing and sneak preview results, NJSC box 5, file 14.

24 NJ letters to Brian Lindquist and Robert Cort, November 8, 1979, NJSC box 5, file 10.

25 Interview with Charles Milhaupt, NJSC box 52, file 9.

26 George Horhota, "Jewison Shoots for the Truth," *Maclean's*, October 29, 1979.

27 Sia, op cit.

CHAPTER 17

1 Jodie Foster, "Why Me?" *Esquire*, December 1, 1982. https://classic.esquire.com/article/1982/12/1/why-me-jodie-foster

2 Jay Scott, "A movie midwife's moments of terror," *The Globe and Mail*, December 24, 1982.

3 Ibid.

4 Ibid.

5 Transcript of interview with Larry Auerbach, NJSC box 53, file 27.

6 George Horhota, "Jewison Shoots for the Truth," *Maclean's*, October 29, 1979.

7 "The Bergmans (Alan and Marilyn)," NJSC box 53, file 8.

8 Scott, op cit.

9 Paul King, "Jewison taps syrup market," *Toronto Star*, October 26, 1982.

10 Albin Krebs and Robert McG, "Hats Off to Film-Maker—and That's the Problem," *New York Times*, April 19, 1982.

11 Jay Scott, "Jewison Then and Now," *Globe and Mail*, October 30, 1987.

12 NJ interview, NJSC box 51, file 7.

13 Transcript of interview with William Goldman, NJSC box 53, file 22.

14 Ibid.

15 NJ interview, NJSC box 51, file 8.

16 *Marquee* Magazine, September 1984, NJSC box 7, file 9.

17 NJ interview, NJSC box 51, file 5.

18 NJ interview, NJSC box 53, file 28. NJ's "usual" salary comes from Richard Corliss, "Blues for Black Actors," *Time*, October 1, 1984.

19 NJ, *This Terrible Business*, p. 222.

20 Todd Marmorstein, "Top Locations, Capital Rebates Lure Producers to the 'Land of Opportunity,'" *On Location: The Film and Videotape Production Magazine*, July 1984, NJSC box 7, file 9.

21 NJ interview, NJSC box 51, file 8.

22 Interview with Charles Milhaupt, NJSC box 52, file 9.

23 Michael London, "Jewison Puts Faith in Agnes," clipping, NJSC box 8, file 12.

24 Rex Reed, "Extraordinary *Soldier's Story* Splendidly Told in Black & White," *New York Post*, September 14, 1984.

25 Richard Corliss, "Blues for Black Actors," *Time*, October 1, 1984.

26 Jeff Burbank, "Dec. 15 Auction: Laird Studios, Historic Film Lot, Up for Sale," *Los Angeles Times*, October 29, 1986.

27 *Marquee* Magazine, op cit.

28 Ibid.

29 Ibid.

CHAPTER 18

1 Interview with Bruce McDonald, July 4, 2018.

2 Joanne Strong, "The Informal Norman Jewison," *Globe and Mail*, April 3, 1982.

3 Michael London, "Jewison puts faith in 'Agnes'" *Los Angeles Times*, November 30, 1984, NJSC box 8, file 12.

4 *Agnes of God* Columbia Pictures production information, NJSC box 8, file 11.

5 Ibid.

6 NJ interview, NJSC box 51, file 7.

7 Julia Cameron, "Jewison: Maverick . . . or the thinking Man's Director," *Chicago Tribune*, September 8, 1985.

8 Kirsten Warner, "Faith in God tested anew on set of movie," *New Zealand Herald*, March 5, 1986.

9 NJ interview, NJSC box 51, file 5.

10 NJ interview, NJSC box 53, file 28.

11 Douglass K. Daniel, *Anne Bancroft: A Life* (Lexington: U of Kentucky P, 2017).

12 NJ interview, NJSC box 53, file 28.

13 Transcript of interview with Meg Tilly, NJSC box 53, file 16.

14 Interview with Bruce McDonald, July 4, 2018.

15 Alexis Chiu, "Scars of Her Youth," *People*, September 11, 2006.

16 Transcript of interview with Meg Tilly, op cit.

17 Interview with Bruce McDonald, July 4, 2018.

18 Cameron, op cit.

19 London, op cit.

20 Interview with Anne Bancroft, NJSC box 52, file 8.

21 NJ interview, NJSC box 51, file 5.

22 Interview with Anne Bancfoft, op cit.

23 NJ, *This Terrible Business*, p. 248.

24 Cameron, op cit.

25 Golenpolsky, op cit.

26 NJ interview, NJSC box 51, file 8.

27 Philip Wuntch, "*Agnes of God* Director Pleases Critics and Crowd," *The Orlando Sentinel*, October 18, 1985.

28 Marilyn Beck, "Jewison Teams up with Pryor for *Miracles*," *Chicago Tribune*, September 23, 1985.

29 Kim Masters, "How the Notorious Firing of Columbia CEO David Puttnam Launched Her Own Career," *The Hollywood Reporter*, June 27, 2016.

30 Quotations from Andrew Yule's *Fast Fade* in Peter Goddard, "Only a few films left in me," *Toronto Star*, January 14, 1989.

31 Transcript of interview with David Picker, NJSC box 53, file 10.

32 NJ interview, NJSC box 51, file 5.

33 Peter Goddard, "Only a few films left in me," *Toronto Star*, January 14, 1989.

CHAPTER 19

1 John Patrick Shanley in *Moonstruck: At the Heart of an Italian Family* (*Moonstruck* DVD featurette, dir. J.M. Kenny, Sony Pictures Home Entertainment, 2006).

2 Ibid.

3 Jay Scott, "Shooting for the Moon," *Globe and Mail*, January 10, 1987.

4 Charles Leerhsen, Jennifer Foote, and Peter McKillop, "The Many Faces of Cher," *Newsweek*, November 30, 1987.

5 NJ in *Moonstruck: At the Heart of an Italian Family*.

6 Leerhsen, op cit.

7 Jay Scott, "Shooting for the Moon," op cit.

8 Ibid.

9 Bruce Weber, "Cher's Next Act," *New York Times Magazine*, October 18, 1987.

10 *Moonstruck* casting, NJSC box 10, file 7.

11 T. Klein, "Nicolas Cage: A Star is Struck," *Cosmopolitan*, October 1988.

12 Kristine McKenna, "A 'Moonstruck' Nicolas Cage Opens Up," *Los Angeles Times*, February 21, 1988.

13 K. W. Woods, "Nicolas Cage: Madman or Mystery?" *Playgirl*, January, 1988.

14 NJ in *Moonstruck: At the Heart of an Italian Family*.

15 Jay Scott, "Shooting for the Moon," op cit.

16 Pauline Kael, "*Moonstruck*: Loony Fugue," *For Keeps* (New York: Dutton, 1994), p. 1164.

17 *Moonstruck* production notes, NJSC box 12, file 13.

18 Transcript of interview with William Goldman, NJSC box 53, file 22.

19 Klein, op cit.

20 Weber, op cit.

21 Interview with Olympia Dukakis / Julie Bovasso, NJSC box 52, file 7.

22 Ibid.

23 Will Harris, "Olympia Dukakis on *A Little Game, Moonstruck, Tales of the City*, and *Death Wish*," *The A.V. Club*, February 11, 2015.

24 Interview with Olympia Dukakis / Julie Bovasso, op cit.

25 Nat Shuster, "Norman Jewison: The Return of a Gifted and Successful Native Son," *Performing Arts in Canada Magazine*, Fall 1985, NJSC box 8, file 12.

26 Harris, op cit.

27 Interview with Olympia Dukakis / Julie Bovasso, op cit.

28 Terrence Rafferty, "A Director of Ideas With Decades of Them," *New York Times*, May 20, 2011.

29 Leerhsen, op cit.

30 Vincent Gardenia in *Moonstruck: At the Heart of an Italian Family*.

31 Jay Scott, "Shooting for the Moon," op cit.

32 Judith Michaelson, "Old, New Stars Come Out for a Night at Shrine," *Los Angeles Times*, April 12, 1988.

33 Harris, op cit.

34 Jay Scott, "Oscar: Money, Art, and Playing the Game," *Globe and Mail*, April 8, 1988.

35 Interview with Olympia Dukakis / Julie Bovasso, op cit.

36 Clips of the 1988 Academy Awards all accessible on *YouTube*.

37 "Jewison signs deal with Warner," *Screen International*, February 11, 1989.

38 NJ in *Moonstruck: At the Heart of an Italian Family*.

CHAPTER 20

1 Mervyn Rothstein, "In Middle America, a Movie Finds its Milieu," *New York Times*, August 28, 1988.

2 James Salter, *All That Is* (New York: Knopf, 2013), p. 139.

3 NJ Interview, NJSC box 52, file 2.

4 Ibid.

5 Peter Goddard, "Only a few films left in me," *Toronto Star*, January 14, 1989.

6 Rothstein, op cit.

7 Ibid.

8 Ibid.

9 Rick Groen, "Insights of the round table: Willis and Jewison circulate with the story of *In Country*'s filming," *Globe and Mail*, September 9, 1989.

10 Jay Scott, "Jewison Looks at Vietnam's Legacy," *Globe and Mail*, October 7, 1988.

11 Ibid.

12 "Bruce Willis talks about acting in Norman Jewison's *In Country*," YouTube video, https://www.youtube.com/watch?v=I-5DtRBbF8I&t=385s

13 "The List: Norman Jewison, Part 3 of 3," *DP/30: The Oral History of Hollywood*. YouTube video, September 24, 2012. https://www.youtube.com/watch?v=D1Uc9izeMZ8

14 Paul Goldberger, "Vietnam Memorial: Questions of Architecture," *New York Times*, Oct. 7, 1982.

15 Jay Scott, "Jewison Looks at Vietnam's Legacy," ibid.

16 "Bobbie Wygant interviews Bruce Willis for In Country 1989," YouTube video, https://www.youtube.com/watch?v=EcWzK_n_cy8

17 Jay Scott, "Jewison Looks at Vietnam's Legacy," op cit.

18 Roger Ebert, "In Country," September 29, 1989, RogerEbert.com, https://www.rogerebert.com/reviews/in-country-1989

19 NJ to Ted Turner, March 11, 1999, NJSC box 48, file 12.

20 Canadian Centre for Advanced Film Studies Board, Meeting Minutes, October 22, 1987, NJSC box 48, file 10.

21 Judy Steed, "Canadian Film Prospers in Lean Times," *Toronto Star*, July 22, 1989.

22 Ibid.

23 Mary Dickie, "National Treasure," *Festival Style*, Fall 2019 http://s3.amazonaws.com/cfc.production/assets/assets/000/010/219/original/Festival_Style_Jewison_Jewison_CFC_Feature_Autumn_2019.pdf?1568739293

24 *Dreamgirls* project notes, NJSC box 41, file 11.

25 Hall, N. "Fighting words from the Hurricane," *The Vancouver Sun* May 4, 1991.

26 Terry Pristin, "By All Necessary Means," *Los Angeles Times*, November 15, 1992.

27 Jay Scott, "'You have to be where you aren't' when you're an artist," *Globe and Mail*, August 13, 1990.

28 Transcript of Spike Lee interview on *The Today Show*, January 19, 1990, NJSC box 41, file 13.

29 James Greenberg, "The Controversy over Malcolm X," *New York Times*, January 27, 1991.

30 Jim Slotek, "Did Spike Lee Do the Right Thing?" clipping, NJSC box 41, file 17.

31 Anne Thompson, "Malcolm X Movie: Film Project Controversial as His Life," *Mother Jones*, July 21, 1991.

32 Letters from Miranda Ransom, Susan Coleman, and Kimba (Secretary, UBAN), January-February 1990, NJSC box 41, file 13.

33 James Greenberg, "Did Hollywood sit on *Fences*?" *New York Times*, January 27, 1991.

34 NJ to Charles Fuller, June 7, 1990, NJSC box 41, file 15.

35 "Lee May Direct Malcolm X Biopic," *Variety*, May 21, 1990.

36 NJ to Marvin Worth, June 27, 1990, NJSC box 41, file 15.

37 NJ to Denzel Washington, August 27, 1990, NJSC box 41, file 14.

CHAPTER 21

1 Mervyn Rothstein, "Getting a Tale of 80's Avarice on Screen," *New York Times*, October 31, 1990.

2 *Other People's Money* production notes, NJSC box 15, file 8.

3 Mel Gussow, "Straightforward Corporate Raider," *New York Times*, February 17, 1989.

4 NJ to Michelle Pfeiffer, December 22, 1989, NJSC box 14, file 22.

5 NJ salary in *OPM* cost reports, NJSC box 14, file 12.

6 Hilary de Vries, "On Location: Trashing the Pig Years in Norman Jewison's film of the play 'Other People's Money,'" *Los Angeles Times*, January 13, 1991.

7 *OPM* daily production reports, NJSC box 14, file 14.

8 David Wellington to the Academy of Canadian Cinema, March 15, 1991, NJSC box 14, file 6.

9 Alternate endings in NJSC box 15, file 8.

10 Rothstein, op cit.

11 "Jewison, DeVito agree on Film's Message," *Baltimore Sun*, October 18, 1991.

12 Mary Murphy to Kelly Baker, June 23, 1991, NJSC box 17, file 4.

13 Bob Thomas, "Norman Jewison talks about 'Other People's Money' and other people," *Las Vegas Review*, October 26, 1991.

14 Rob Salem, "Canadians Kick it Off: Norman Jewison Comes Home for Gala Showing of Long-Term Project Bogus," *Toronto Star*, September 6, 1996.

15 NJ, *This Terrible Business*, p. 18.

16 Marc Horton, "'Real' Pals Behind Jewison's Bogus," *Montreal Gazette*, September 8, 1996.

17 John Evan Frook, "Par Makes 'Bogus' Deal," *Daily Variety*, May 10, 1993.

18 Salem, op cit..

19 Ibid.

20 Claudia Eller and John Evan Frook, "TriStar Ponies Up $1 mil for 'Him,'" *Daily Variety*, December 11, 1992.

21 NJ to Marc Platt, September 1, 1994, NJSC box 17, file 11.

22 *Him* budget, September 2, 1993 NJSC box 17, file 12.

23 "Items for Jewison's Trailer," NJSC box 17, file 11.

24 Author interview with Elizabeth Broden, July 20, 2018.

25 Jeff Silverman, "Marisa the Magnificent," *Cosmopolitan*, August 1994.

26 John Anderson, "Looking for a Perfect Match," *Newsday*, October 2, 1994.

27 Gore Vidal to NJ, undated, NJSC box 77, file 5.

28 Salem, op cit.

29 Ibid.

30 Horton, op cit.

31 Salem, op cit.

32 Ben Kaplan, "Flashes of Time," *National Post* December 12, 2009.

33 Hal Hinson, "'Bogus'? You Got That Right," *Washington Post*, September 6, 1996; Joe Morgenstern, "Kids Flick: The Tried and the True," *Wall Street Journal*, September 6, 1996; Jack Mathews, "A Lonely Boy Conjures Up an Imaginary Pal," *Newsday*, September 6, 1996.

CHAPTER 22

1 Alan Niester, "Dylan, Mitchell Play on their Own Terms," *Globe and Mail*, October 30, 1998.

2 NJ to Jeff Rosen, October 19, 1998, NJSC box 32, file 6.

3 NJ notes for autobiography, NJSC box 55, file 17.

4 "Hurricane Carter, Trucker are Held in Triple Murder," *Newsday*, October 17, 1966.

5 Selwyn Raab, "Reversal is Won by Rubin Carter in Murder Case," *New York Times*, November 8, 1985.

6 Bernard Weinraub, "A Veteran Director Still Fights the Good Fight," *New York Times*, December 26, 1999.

7 NJ to Rudy Langlais, August 4, 1998, NJSC box 32, file 8.

8 Brian D. Johnson, "Eye of the Hurricane," *Maclean's*, December 6, 1999.

9 NJ to Armyan Bernstein, September 9, 1998, NJSC box 33, file 12.

10 NJ to Rudy Langlais, August 4, 1998, NJSC box 32, file 8.

11 Bill Teitler to Tom Bliss, Rudy Langlais, Nancy Rae Stone, and NJ, August 10, 1998, NJSC32, file 8.

12 Bill Teitler to Tom Bliss, January 21, 1999, NJSC box 33, file 13.

13 NJ to Armyan Bernstein, September 9, 1998, NJSC box 33, file 12.

14 International Creative Management to NJ, July 21, 1998, NJSC box 32, file 6.

15 NJ to Bernstein, Rudy Langlais, Suzann Ellis, Tom Bliss, Bill Teitler, October 21 1998, NJSC box 33, file 12.

16 NJ to Armyan Bernstein, Tom Bliss, et al., December 14, 1998, NJSC box 32, file 5.

17 Armyan Bernstein to NJ, January 1, 1999, NJSC box 32, file 6.

18 NJ to Armyan Bernstein, January 4, 1999, NJSC box 32, file 6.

19 Sue Fox and Holly Wolcott, "Crash Kills 1, Snarls Freeway Traffic," *Los Angeles Times*, December 20, 1998.

20 Rudy Langlais to NJ, January 2, 1999, NJSC box 32, file 6.

21 Dan Gordon to Armyan Bernstein, Rudy Langlais, NJ, Rubin Carter, January 12, 1999, NJSC box 32, file 6.

22 NJ to Dan Gordon, January 14, 1999, NJSC box 32, file 6.

23 Johnson, op cit.

24 Letter from Bernstein to NJ (and Jewison's handwritten response), February 8, 1999, NJSC box 32, file 6.

25 *The Hurricane* press info, NJSC box 32, file 13.

26 Bill Teitler to Tom Bliss, January 21, 1999, NJSC box 33, file 13.

27 Rudy Langlais to NJ, January 4, 1999, NJSC box 32, file 6.

28 Armyan Bernstein to NJ, February 11, 1999, NJSC box 32, file 6.

29 Maryam Sanati, "Norman Jewison's Obsession," *National Post*, December 27, 1999.

30 Doug Saunders, "World Premiere a 'work in Progress'," *Globe and Mail*, September 16, 1999.

31 Sanati, op cit.

32 NJ, *This Terrible Business*, p. 228.

33 Selwyn Raab, "Separating Truth from Fiction in *The Hurricane*," *New York Times*, December 28, 1999.

34 Lewis Steel, "History's on the Ropes in *Hurricane*," *Los Angeles Times*, January 24, 2000.

35 Johnson, op cit.

36 Sarah Hampson, "A Statement of Ambition," *Globe and Mail*, December 6, 2003.

37 NJ to Ken Kamins (and Kamins's response), September 10, 2001, NJSC box 34, file 1.

38 Notes on Moore novel, NJSC box 34, file 1.

39 Robert Lantos comments in press materials, NJSC box 34, file 5.

40 Bernard Weinraub, "A Veteran Director Still Fights the Good Fight," *New York Times*, December 26, 1999.

41 "inoffensive entertainments," is from Geoff Pevere and Greig Dymond's *Mondo Canuck*, qtd. in Sanati, op cit.

42 Ronald Harwood to NJ, May 11, 2001, NJSC box 34, file 1.

43 NJ to Ronald Harwood, September 18, 2001, NJSC box 34, file 1.

44 Michael Caine offer, January 25, 2002, NJSC box 34, file 1.

45 *The Statement* press kit, NJSC box 34, file 5.

46 Weinraub, op cit.

47 Michael Barker, author interview, September 11, 2019.

48 Brian D. Johnson, "Our Lion in Winter," *Maclean's*, December 2003.

49 *The Statement* Draft 2 polish, February 26, 2002, NJSC box 35, file 3.

50 Sheldon Kirshner, "Jewison, in *The Statement*, tackles French wartime racism," *Canadian Jewish News*, December 11, 2003.

51 Johnson, "Our Lion in Winter," op cit.

52 Stephen Holden, "A Frenchman on the Run from His Vichy Past," *The New York Times*, December 12, 2003; Brian D. Johnson, op cit.

53 Correspondence re: banning of *The Statement* in Lebanon and Egypt, NJSC (2008.06) box 1, file 4.

CODA

1 Transcript of interview with Jennifer Jewison, NJSC box 53, file 25.

2 Lynne St. David Jewison email to author, January 19, 2021.

3 Author interview with Bruce McDonald, July 4, 2018.

4 David Jablin, "The Norman Jewison Satire Hollywood Wouldn't Make," *Medium*, February 8, 2019.

5 Interview with Pauline Kael, NJSC box 53, file 24.

6 Transcript of interview with Sidney Poitier, NJSC box 53, file 7.

7 Ben Kaplan, "Flashes of Time," *National Post* December 12, 2009.

8 Transcript of interview with Jennifer Jewison, op cit.

Acknowledgments

This book was made possible by the archival resources, librarians, and spirit of fellowship and generosity at Victoria College in the University of Toronto. My deepest thanks to the supportive staff of the E. J. Pratt Library, as well as to the Jackman Humanities Institute and the Scholars-in-Residence program, to the knowledgeable archivists at the Wisconsin Historical Society, and to each of the individuals who enriched these pages (and the life of their author) over the last three years:

Ryan Akler-Bishop

Judith Arnold

Nathalie Atkinson

Amelia Bailey

Tino Balio

Carol Beattie

Agatha Barc

Michael Barker

Randy Boyagoda

Elizabeth Broden

Matthew Bucemi

Kelley Castle

Khadija Coxon

Robert Davidson

Nick Dawson

Christopher De Barros

Colin Deinhardt

John Duncan

Atom Egoyan

Angela Esterhammer

Joe Eszterhas

Jeff Glickman

Joel Goldbach

Paul Gooch

Mary Heinmaa

Mary Huelsbeck

John Hutchison

Sally Hutchison

Jessica Johnson

Roma Kail

Charlie Keil

Alison Keith

Mark Kingwell

Halyna Kozar

Paul Kutasi

Murray Leeder

Andrea Lenczner

Ron Ma

Bruce McDonald

Diane Michaud

Devonnia Miller

Lisa Newman

Kasia Peruzzi

Anna Porter

Jamie Quadros

Sarah Ratzlaff

William Robins

Lisa Sherlock

Beck Siegal

Carmine Starnino

Lynne St. David Jewison

Alexandra Styron

Larry Tye

Eddy Wang

Douglas Wells

Gillian Wells

Grace Wells

Samuel Wells

Kenneth Whyte

David Yaffe

Kimberly Yates

Louise Yearwood

Above all, thanks to Norman Jewison for everything he has done for the next generation and those to come, and for the movies.

Index